Computational Science, Engineering and Technology Series: 34

Patterns for
Parallel Programming
on GPUs

Computational Science, Engineering and Technology Series

Substructuring Techniques and Domain Decomposition Methods
Edited by: F. Magoulès

Soft Computing in Civil and Structural Engineering
Edited by: B.H.V. Topping and Y. Tsompanakis

Trends in Civil and Structural Engineering Computing
Edited by: B.H.V. Topping, L.F. Costa Neves and R.C. Barros

Parallel, Distributed and Grid Computing for Engineering
Edited by: B.H.V. Topping and P. Iványi

Trends in Engineering Computational Technology
Edited by: M. Papadrakakis and B.H.V. Topping

Trends in Computational Structures Technology
Edited by: B.H.V. Topping and M. Papadrakakis

Computational Methods for Acoustics Problems
Edited by: F. Magoulès

Mesh Partitioning Techniques and Domain Decomposition Methods
Edited by: F. Magoulès

Computational Mechanics using High Performance Computing
Edited by: B.H.V. Topping

High Performance Computing for Computational Mechanics
Edited by: B.H.V. Topping, L. Lämmer

Parallel and Distributed Processing for Computational Mechanics: Systems and Tools
Edited by: B.H.V. Topping

Saxe-Coburg Publications:

Programming Distributed Finite Element Analysis: An Object Oriented Approach
R.I. Mackie

Object Oriented Methods and Finite Element Analysis
R.I. Mackie

Domain Decomposition Methods for Distributed Computing
J. Kruis

Computer Aided Design of Cable-Membrane Structures
B.H.V. Topping and P. Iványi

Patterns for
Parallel Programming
on GPUs

Edited by
F. Magoulès

SAXE-COBURG
PUBLICATIONS

© Saxe-Coburg Publications, Kippen, Stirling, Scotland

published 2014 by
Saxe-Coburg Publications
Civil-Comp Ltd, Dun Eaglais, Station Brae
Kippen, Stirlingshire, FK8 3DY, Scotland

Saxe-Coburg Publications is an imprint of Civil-Comp Ltd

Computational Science, Engineering and Technology Series: 34
ISSN 1759-3158
ISBN 978-1-874672-57-9

British Library Cataloguing in Publication Data
A catalogue record for this book is available from the British Library

Publisher's production & editorial team: Steven Miller, Jane Tabor, Rosemary Brodie
Printed in Great Britain by Bell & Bain Ltd, Glasgow

Contents

3 High Level GPGPU Programming with Parallel Skeletons   57

M. Bourgoin, E. Chailloux and J.-L. Lamotte

4 Programming GPUs from High Level Data Flow Models   **73**

M. Barreteau, R. Barrère and E. Lenormand

5 Optimization methodology for Parallel Programming of Homogeneous or Hybrid Clusters

111

S. Vialle and S. Contassot-Vivier

8 OpenCL: A Suitable Solution to Simplify and Unify High Performance Computing Developments

J. Passerat-Palmbach and D.R.C. Hill

9 Parallel Preconditioned Conjugate Gradient Algorithm on GPU

F. Andzembe and J. Koko

Foreword

Our modern society is increasingly relying on computers. They are ubiquitous in our daily life even if they are hidden in most cases (in appliances, cars, telephones, USB keys, *etc.*). Digital television (TV) would not be the unique broadcasting system today without important compute resources at the recording end and in the display. TV sets nowadays use advanced graphics processing units (GPU) to upscale digital Versatile Disc (DVD) images (not to mention BluRays®) or pan and zoom your favorite show. The anti-lock braking system (ABS) of your car is controlled by a computer. The latest three-dimensional scan of a baby would not be possible without computers and powerful GPUs. This list would be too tedious to make exhaustive.

In the scientific and technical world, computers also play an ever growing role, frequently replacing experiments. Numerical simulation has an increasing economical weight in various domains ranging from car crashes to the evaluation of the biological effects of a new pharmaceutical molecule. Simulations have replaced experiments in many cases either because they reduce costs by allowing many variations of experimental conditions (in destructive experiments such as car crashes) or simply because experiments are not feasible (*e.g.* seeing a protein unfolding in which case *in vitro* experimentation has been replaced by *"in silico"* analysis).

In all cases, using simulations help the scientists to understand complex phenomena. Yet this understanding is closely related to the size of the simulation: the finer the simulation, the greater the insight can be. A finer simulation is for example to predict the weather for areas of $10km^2$ instead of $100km^2$. As a consequence the larger a simulation is, the more compute capability is required. For example, dividing the size of a cubic simulation by two in each dimension of space increases the number of elements to process by 8 (which means that the processing time also has increased by a factor of 8 or more, depending on the type of simulation). Users (or customers) are not always ready to pay for such an increase in simulation time and they dream of speedier computers solving larger problems in a constant time. Since computers are powered by electricity, deploying more compute power leads to more electrical consumption. This cannot be an endless process for the price of electricity will eventually limit the growth of the supercomputers. Current petaflop machines are in the range of 5MW. With a simple extrapolation, an exaflop machine could be in the order of 100MW or more without a technology change.

To overcome this practical (infrastructure size) and economic limit (*i.e.* the budget to run the installation in the long run), a true disruptive technology is required and is in fact already emerging. The evolution of supercomputers processing elements is parallel to the one of commodity hardware (*e.g.* smartphones): the number of processing units per chip is increasing to deliver greater performances within a constrained energy budget (limit the number of megawatts for the former, longer battery life for the latter). This is especially true of the usage of graphical processing units for general purpose computations (GPGPU).

Envisioned at CEA as early as 2007, the use of GPU computing is becoming widespread (medicine, avionics, HPC) if not mainstream (Apple is harnessing the GPU power through OpenCL and its OS X, your smartphone relies of its GPU to playback videos and so on). GPUs solve part of the equation for a number of applications: they are of an order of magnitude more efficient than regular processors for the same electrical needs, on some algorithms. An increasing number of success stories demonstrates that GPUs are here to stay for a long time in high performance computing (either embedded or not). In that respect, the Titane and Curie machines hosted at CEA (see `http://www-hpc.cea.fr`) are good examples of advanced architectures which have found a community of users for their ability to produce results for the hardest problems yet in a limited time.

The introduction of new hardware compute technologies forces evolutions in the software stack used by programmers. Operating systems, compiler chains as well as libraries are not immune to the nature of the underlying hardware. But the development of a comprehensive software stack takes a significant amount of time. It is therefore very important to start the developments as soon as possible to make sure that the code developers have all the necessary tools for their daily job, when the given technology will spread to the masses. It means also that those developers will have to change their programming habits and adapt themselves to the new technologies.

GPU computing is still a vast field of research which encompasses various domains such as programming languages, compiler technologies, parallelization techniques or linear algebra methods. Such research is fundamental in every field of computer science. They aim to increase the productivity of the developers, yield a better maintainability of the code and reach the best possible performances. The impact of the results achieved is enhanced if the underlying technologies rely on open specifications and are themselves made available open to the whole community of developers and users. Along this line, OpenCL is emerging as the only viable low level technology to drive many forms of compute units, yet in a portable manner.

OpenGPU, a project of the systematic cluster of competitiveness, is clearly at the crossroads of all these needs (such as high performance or portability) and techniques (use of a GPU, CUDA or OpenCL programming). OpenGPU has proved to be a good platform to go forward in the understanding of the pros and cons of GPUs and, at the same time, to promote GPUs' diffusion through the development of a viable ecosystem. This book, entitled *Patterns for Parallel Programming on GPU* edited by Frédéric Magoulès, summarizes some of the achievements of the OpenGPU project. It is an invitation for the reader to deep dive into the fascinating world of GPU programming and usage.

Guillaume Colin de Verdière
CEA, France

Preface

At present, multi-core and many-core platforms lead the computer industry, forcing software developers to adopt new programming paradigms, in order to fully exploit their computing capabilities. Graphics Processing Units (GPUs) are one representative of many-core architectures, and certainly the most widespread.

GPU-based application development requires a great effort from application programmers. On one hand, they must take advantage of the massively parallel platform in the problem modeling. On the other, the applications have to make an efficient use of the heterogeneous memory system, managing several levels that are software or hardware controlled. Generally the programmers' methodology consists in evaluating several mapping alternatives, guided by their experience and intuition, which becomes inefficient for software development and maintenance.

In order to help the programmers to make the good choices, this book presents in thirteen chapters some methodologies and design patterns for parallel programing on GPUs. Each chapter, written by different authors, presents a state-of-the-art of some innovative methods, techniques or algorithms, useful for GPU computing. A bibliography is included at the end of each chapter for the reader who wishes to go further.

This book starts at Chapter 1 with an evaluation of state-of-the-art parallelizing compilers generating CUDA code for heterogeneous computing. This chapter evaluates and compares tool frameworks that automatically generate code for GPUs, saving time and effort to programmers. These frameworks take advantage of polyhedral model techniques to exploit parallelism and to satisfy the specific GPU constraints. The authors show the key features of some of these source-to-source compilers and analyze the codes generated. Finally, the authors discuss the importance of some key aspects such as data mapping and code quality.

In Chapter 2, the authors present an unusual strategy to perform dynamic code generation for GPUs. Usual compiler relies on assumption that are not always true, which can lead to sub-optimal code due to a lack of information available to the compiler. By using a code generator called deGoal that can produce a code in a pseudo-assembly code representation for GPUs, the authors show how to dynamically generate code usable by the GPU. This chapter illustrates the tool usage by the matrix multiplication on various configurations. This example show that it allows to develop an application and get near optimal results faster than developing a specialized version.

Chapter 3 shows how to achieve on GPUs great performance with applications commonly handled by CPU only. This hybrid system leads to complex programming designs combining multiple paradigms to manage each hardware architecture. The authors present how parallel skeletons can help tackle this challenge by abstracting some of these programming designs while automating optimizations. Through a simple example using the OCaml programming language to develop and compose skeletons, this chapter demonstrates how simple modifications in using parallel skeletons can ease GPU programming while offering good performance speed-ups.

Chapter 4 shows how data flow applications can be efficiently programmed on GPUs from a unique high level capture. The authors rely on a tooling approach, through the SPEAR design environment, to point out the underlying productivity gain with regard to performance. For efficient code generation purposes, several optimisations at different levels are detailed, followed by some numerical experiments performed on a representative radar application.

Chapter 5 proposes a study of the optimization process of parallel applications run on modern hybrid architectures. Different optimization schemes are proposed for overlapping computations with communications; and for computation kernels. Development methodologies are introduced to obtain different optimization degrees and specific criteria are defined to help developers to find the most suited degree of optimization according to the application and parallel system considered. Both the performance and code complexity increase are analyzed.This last point is an important issue, as it directly impacts on development and maintenance costs. Experiments are performed to evaluate the different variants of a benchmark application that consists in a dense matrix product.

Porting and maintaining multiple versions of a code base require different skills; and the efforts required in the process, as well as the increased complexity in debugging and testing, are time consuming. Some solutions based on compilers emerge. They are based either on directives added to C in openhmpp or openacc or on automatic solutions like pocc, Pluto, ppcg, or par4all. However compilers cannot retarget in an efficient way any program written in a low-level language such as unconstrained C. Programmers should follow good practices when writing code so that compilers have more room to perform the transformations required for efficient execution on heterogeneous targets.

Chapter 6 explores the impact of different patterns used by programmers, and defines a set of good practices allowing a compiler to generate efficient code.

Chapter 7 introduces the Melt framework and domain-specific language to extend the Gcc compiler. It explains the major internal representations (Gimple, Tree-s, *etc.*) and the overall organization of Gcc. It shows the major features of Melt and illustrates why extending and customizing the Gcc compiler using Melt is useful; for instance, to use GPUs through OpenCL. It gives some concrete advice and guidelines for the development of such extensions with Melt.

In Chapter 8, the authors study the opportunities that OpenCL offers to high performance computing applications to provide a solution to unify new developments. In order to overcome the lack of native OpenCL support for some architectures, the authors survey the third-party research work that propose a source-to-source approach to transform OpenCL into other parallel programming languages. For instance, FPGAs are considered as a case study, because of their dramatic OpenCL support compared to GPUs. These transformation approaches could also lead to potential works in the model driven engineering (MDE) field as conceptualized in this chapter. Moreover, OpenCL's standard API is quite rough. Thus, the authors introduce several APIs from the simple high-level binder to the source code generator to ease and boost the development process of any OpenCL application.

In Chapter 9, the authors propose a parallel implementation of the preconditioned conjugate gradient algorithm on a GPU platform. The preconditioning matrix is a first order approximate inverse derived from the SSOR preconditioner. Used through sparse matrix-vector multiplication, the preconditioner proposed by the authors is well-suited to massively parallel architecture like GPUs. As compared to CPU implementation of the conjugate gradient algorithm, the GPU preconditioned conjugate gradient implementation is between eight and sixteen times faster.

In Chapter 10, the authors present the implementation on GPUs of two classical methods for solving sparse linear systems. Those methods are the conjugate gradient method which is usually used for solving symmetric linear systems, and the generalized minimal residual method (GMRES), which is commonly used for solving unsymmetric linear systems. For each method, the authors describe how they have adapted the sequential version for the GPU with the CUDA programming environment. The performances of these parallel algorithms are tested and analyzed on GPU and on CPU clusters.

Non-coding ribonucleic acid (RNA) are functional RNAs that are not translated into proteins. Computational studies of non-coding RNAs have recently become an important challenge in bioinformatics, including their identification and structure prediction. In Chapter 11, the authors present several algorithms for these applications. With the development of next-generation sequencing technologies, huge amounts of genomic and RNA sequences data have been produced, and a parallelization of such tools is required to overcome the long execution time. In this chapter, miRNAFold, an algorithm developed by the authors for the search for microRNAs in genomic sequences, is described together with its implementation in CUDA on GPUs.

Chapter 12 aims to provide both a feedback and a methodological approach on how to port a legacy application to GPU clusters for quantitative metagenomic data, i.e., studying many organisms with whole deoxyribonucleic acid (DNA) information, without getting access to the single and pure species information. The proposed approach is based on the clustering principles that rely on a large correlation matrix computation on polled data. To allow fast computation and get the best of the GPU, many optimizations to cover several optimization strategies are investigated by the authors. This chapter explores dynamic and static optimizations and presents benchmarks on supercomputers and small clusters of GPUs.

Testing random numbers relies on a heavy battery of statistical tests that can take hours of computations or small samplings of numbers. In Chapter 13, the authors demystify this slow checking process by showing the parallel nature of two representative tests and how to implement them on GPU with OpenCL. The authors illustrates these concepts with two examples of test codes translated from C to OpenCL. In addition, an original algorithm, made in the context of testing the quality of the true random number generator is illustrated, and provides a totally new and safe way of dealing with random number generator.

Naturally, the present book cannot provide a complete record of the many approaches, applications, features and schemes related to GPUs. However, it does provide a useful synopsis of the recent methodologies used in academic circles and in industry to handle efficiently hybrid architectures. This book will be of interest to engineers, computer scientists and applied mathematicians. The editor wishes to thank the authors for their willingness to contribute to this book dedicated to patterns for parallel programming on GPUs.

Frédéric Magoulès
Ecole Centrale Paris, France

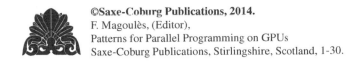

©Saxe-Coburg Publications, 2014.
F. Magoulès, (Editor),
Patterns for Parallel Programming on GPUs
Saxe-Coburg Publications, Stirlingshire, Scotland, 1-30.

Chapter 1

Evaluation of State-of-the-Art Parallelizing Compilers Generating CUDA Code for Heterogeneous CPU/GPU Computing

J.C. Juega[1], S. Verdoolaege[2], A. Cohen[2], J.I. Gómez[1]
C. Tenllado[1] and F. Catthoor[3]

[1] *Universidad Complutense de Madrid, Spain*
[2] *INRIA and École Normale Supérieure, Cachan, France*
[3] *IMEC, Leuven, Belgium*

Abstract

At present, multi-core and many-core platforms lead the computer industry, forcing software developers to adopt new programming paradigms, in order fully to exploit their computing capabilities. Nowadays, Graphics Processing Units (GPUs) are one representative of many-core architectures, and certainly the most widespread.

GPU application development requires a great effort from application programmers. On one hand, they must take advantage of the massively parallel platform in the problem modeling. On the other hand, the applications have to make an efficient use of the heterogeneous memory system, managing several levels that are software or hardware controlled. Generally the programmers' methodology consists of evaluating several mapping alternatives, guided by their experience and intuition, which becomes inefficient for software development and maintenance.

This chapter evaluates and compares tool frameworks that automatically generate code for GPUs, saving time and effort for programmers. These frameworks take advantage of Polyhedral Model techniques to exploit parallelism and to satisfy the specific GPU constraints. The chapter shows the key features of some of these source-to-source compilers and analyzes the code that they generate. Finally we discuss the importance of some key aspects such as data mapping and code quality.

Keywords: polyhedral model, GPU, CUDA, code generation, compilers, loop transformations, C-to-CUDA, Par4All, PPCG.

1.1   Introduction

GPU devices are extremely difficult to program; it is not only crucial to extract parallelism but it has to be mapped carefully to the GPU to maximize performance. Many hardware details are exposed to the programmer, who must tune them effectively while meeting platform restrictions regarding the memory hierarchy, thread synchronization and resource management.

Thus a clear need exists for tool support assisting the programmer in this difficult task. Both auto-tuning and *ad-hoc* parallelizing compiler techniques have been proposed to this end. An ideal tool flow would take sequential code with loops and arrays and produce efficient code to be run on a system with (several) CPUs and GPUs. This process would entail parallelism extraction, defining GPU kernels and finally efficiently mapping them onto the GPU.

Recently, several frameworks have been trying, at least partially, to fulfill this ambitious task. We are particularly interested in those frameworks based on polyhedral compilation techniques, which have been shown to be very effective in more traditional parallel environments. Most of them are source-to-source tools that generate CUDA code out of sequential C code, then relying on *nvcc* to perform the final compilation steps.

For this work, we have selected three representative tools within this context: Par4All, C-to-CUDA and PPCG. We describe their common underlying approaches to generate code for GPU platforms. We will show that they all follow common steps during the mapping process, but that they differ significantly in terms of program representation and transformation heuristics to explain large performance differences.

We have evaluated these three tools on the entire *PolyBench* suite [35] version 3.1, targeting two different families of NVIDIA GPUs.

This comparison illustrates once more that GPU code is very sensitive to mapping decisions. Although it remains very difficult to automate, the three tools make significant progress in tackling the well known trade-off between parallelism and locality. Huge performance improvements can be obtained, fully automatically, and involving both the CPU and GPU sides of the heterogeneous execution. The comparison also shows that some benchmarks yield impressive performance differences depending on how the tools tackle the parallelism/locality trade-off.

When the memory architecture becomes more hardware controlled, simpler strategies (like the one from Par4All) that do not explicitly manage data transfers, become more competitive. Results show that two of the tools (Par4All and PPCG) are quite mature and robust, producing valid parallel code for most of the input benchmarks. However, automatic code generation for real larger applications is still too ambitious.

1.2 Related Work

GPGPU programming languages such as CUDA and OpenCL present application developers with a relatively abstract model of a SIMD, multithreaded, manycore architecture. However, platform-specific details remain largely exposed: it is critical to utilize the hardware resources efficiently in order to achieve high performance. So far, the practice of GPU programming has remained dominated by heroic porting and tuning efforts, resulting in a large number of application-specific studies.

1.2.1 Performance Modeling and Tuning

Porting applications are complicated by the heterogeneity of GPU-accelerated platforms with distributed memory, and the restrictions of the GPGPU programming models. Ryoo *et al.* have shown that the optimization space for CUDA programs can be highly non-linear, and highly challenging for model-based heuristics, performance modeling, or feedback-directed methods [41, 42]. G-ADAPT is a compiler framework to search and predict the best configuration for different input sizes for GPGPU programs [51]; it starts from already optimized code and aims to adapt the code to different input sizes.

The previous methods are not fully automatic or integrated into a GPGPU compiler. Progress towards fully automatic performance tuning has been achieved by the Crest [48] and CHiLL [16] projects.

Rather than targeting a low-level programming model like OpenCL or CUDA, Apricot [39] focuses on the automatic insertion of offload constructs, targeting LEO. It circumvents some of the performance tuning difficulties by performing selective offloading at runtime. As the hardware and tool flow mature, we believe the performance tuning aspects will become more and more important and challenging.

1.2.2 Programming Models

CUDA-lite [47] started a trend to achieve better performance portability on CUDA programs. The user provides basic annotations about parallelism exploitation and deals with the offloading of live-in and live-out data. Based on these, the compiler performs loop tiling and unrolling to exploit temporal locality, local (shared) memory management, and attempts to help memory coalescing. In the same spirit, the PGI Accelerator language and framework [36] focusing on abstracting the performance details of the target and automating much of the tuning, aims for the high-performance computing domain. In parallel, the Cetus compiler framework was used to translate OpenMP to CUDA [26]; it can handle dynamic, data-dependent control flow. This trend led to the design of OpenACC [33], merging with independent efforts to port OpenMP to heterogeneous architectures [20] and with the more pragmatic and explicit HMPP approach by CAPS [24].

Short vector SIMD architectures have also been the subject of active programming model research and development. Offload [17] is a set of high-level C++ extensions,

a compiler and a runtime system to accelerate kernels on the Cell BE. Intel designed
the very similar, and contemporary, LEO programming model (Language Extensions
for Offload), targeting its x86-based GPU architecture [43]. Microsoft's AMP is also
very similar [4].

GPGPU compilers, programming models, and active libraries have also been proposed for managed or dynamic languages, such as Matlab [37] and Python (NumPy)
[21]. These approaches facilitate the automatic (largely dynamic) extraction of offloaded kernels, with their live-in and live-out data. Loop and array-oriented transformations are still needed to reduce the abstraction penalty and eliminate spurious
synchronizations and communications. On the other hand, the objectives of these
approaches are to take advantage of GPU accelerators but not to compete with the
efficiency of lower level programming models.

1.2.3   Polyhedral Compilation

The polyhedral model has been the basis for major advances in automatic optimization and parallelization of programs [13, 15, 18, 19, 28]. Many efforts have been invested to developing source-to-source compilers such as PoCC [34], PLUTO [14]
and CHiLL [16], which use a polyhedral framework to perform loop transformations.
Nowadays traditional compilers such as GCC, LLVM [22] and IBM XL make use of
polyhedral frameworks to compile for multicore architectures. Progress is also under-
way to extend the applicability of polyhedral techniques to dynamic, data dependent
control flow [9].

With the emergence of GPUs, the polyhedral model has been applied to develop
efficient source-to-source compilers for them. Baskaran's C-to-CUDA [6] is the first
end-to-end, automatic source-to-source polyhedral compiler for GPU targets. It is
based on PLUTO's algorithms and explicitly manages the software controllable part
of the memory system. However, it remains a prototype and handles only a small set
of benchmarks. Building on Baskaran's experience, Reservoir Labs developed its own
compiler based on R-Stream [27], which introduces a more avanced algorithm to exploit the memory hierarchy. However, the paper does not describe all the details, and
no source code is available. Gpuloc is a variation of the approach proposed by Baghdadi *et al.* [5], which is also based on PLUTO. It uses a ranking based technique [23] to
transfer data to and from shared memory, which results in inefficient accesses to memory that limit the overall performance. Attempts to mitigate this tends to waste shared
memory and limits the GPU computation power. In addition, it is not in development
anymore. Par4All [3, 38] is an open source initiative developed by HPC Project to
unify efforts concerning compilers for parallel architectures. It supports the automatic
integrated compilation of applications for hybrid architectures including GPUs. The
compiler is not based on the polyhedral model, but uses abstract interpretation for
array regions which also involve polyhedra; this allows Par4All to perform powerful interprocedural analysis on the input code. CHiLL developers also extended their
compiler to generate GPU code, they introduced CUDA-CHiLL [40] during 2011.
The framework does not perform an automatic parallelization and mapping to CUDA

but instead offers high-level constructs that allow a user or search engine to perform such a transformation. PPCG (Polyhedral Parallel Code Generator) is a relatively new tool developed by Verdoolaege [52]. PPCG tries to overcome previous limitations and efficiently manages the memory system and exhibits a very robust behavior.

The tools mentioned above were compared with both hand-tuned GPU implementations and CPU implementations when they were introduced. However they have never been compared to each other. We selected C-to-CUDA, Par4All and PPCG because they were publicly available. Unfortunately we were unable to obtain a copy of R-Stream or CUDA-CHILL for such a comparison. We also considered comparison with the approach of Baghdadi *et al.* [5], but our preliminary implementation showed the technique for memory management on the GPU to be inappropriate. For this reason and because it is no longer in development, we did not include Gpuloc.

The PolyBench suite [35] puts Par4All, PPCG and C-to-CUDA on an equal footing in terms of fitness of the source code to the precise static analysis of array references. These aspects are common to any automatic parallelization method for loop nests. Nevertheless, it should be noted that Par4All distinguishes itself by being able to process a larger class of programs than the current versions of PPCG and C-to-CUDA and that it can automatically offload kernels from larger programs than the latter two thanks to advanced interprocedural analyses.

1.2.4 Automatic Vectorization

Fine-grained data level parallelism is one of the most effective ways of achieving scalable performance of numerical computations. It is pervasive in graphical accelerators, although some GPUs use different schemes to expose vector computations: current NVIDIA GPUs use multiple levels of fine-grain threads, while others use explicit short-vector instructions, and AMD have been using a combination of both. It is thus interesting to compare code generation for GPUs with traditional short-vector vectorization techniques.

Automatic vectorization for modern short-SIMD instructions has been a popular topic, with target-specific as well as retargetable compilers, for the ARM Neon, Intel AVX and SSE, IBM Altivec and Cell SPU. All of these had a successful impact on production compilers [10,30,31,54]. Exploiting subword parallelism in modern SIMD architectures, however, suffers from several limitations and overheads involving alignment, redundant loads and stores, support for reductions and more. These overheads complicate the optimization dramatically. Automatic vectorization was also extended to handle more sophisticated control-flow restructuring including if-conversion [45] and outer-loop vectorization [31]. Classical techniques of loop distribution and loop interchange [1,46,53] can have a dramatic impact on the profitability of vectorization.

Leading optimizing compilers recognize the importance of devising a cost model for vectorization, but have so far provided only partial solutions [10,54]. On the other hand, opportunities may be missed due to overly conservative heuristics. These state-of-the-art vectorizing compilers incorporate a cost model to decide whether vectorization is expected to be profitable. These models however typically apply to a single loop or basic-block, and do not consider alternatives combined with other transformations at the loop-nest level.

Combined loop-nest auto-vectorization and loop-interchange have been addressed in the context of vector supercomputers [1, 2, 53]. Overheads related to short-SIMD architectures (such as alignment and fine-grained reuse) or GPUs were not considered until recently. Realignment and data-reuse were considered together with loop-unrolling [44] in the context of straight-line code vectorization. A cost model for vectorization of accesses with non-unit strides was proposed in [30], but it does not consider other overheads or loop transformations. The most advanced cost model for loop transformations-enabled vectorization was proposed by Trifunovic *et al.* [46]. It is based on polyhedral compilation, capturing the main factors contributing to the profitability of vectorization in the polyhedral representation itself.

1.3   CUDA Programming Model

The three tools evaluated generate code for NVIDIA GPUs using the CUDA programming model [32]. This model represents the GPU as a coprocessor that can run data-parallel kernels and provides extensions to the C language to (1) allocate data on the GPU, (2) transfer data between the GPU and the CPU and (3) launch kernels.

A CUDA kernel executes a piece of sequential code on a large number of threads in parallel. These threads are organized into a grid of *CUDA Blocks*. Threads within a block can cooperate with each other by (1) efficiently sharing data through a shared low latency local memory and (2) synchronizing their execution via barriers. The scheduling unit is not the individual thread but a group of threads called a *warp*. During every cycle, the scheduler in each multiprocessor chooses the next warp to execute. If threads in a warp execute different code paths, only threads on the same path can be executed simultaneously and a penalty is incurred.

All the details above must be exposed to the compiler in order efficiently to generate CUDA code. However, some other aspects, such as fine grained multithreading or *threadblock* to multiprocessor mapping, are hidden. In short the GPU can be seen as an arbitrary large number of (virtual) SIMD-like processors which could be present, each with its own register file and private scratchpad memory, all sharing a common DRAM based main memory. In addition, some constraints are defined when accessing these different memory levels. Unlike the execution model, where the execution unit is the warp, the memory access unit is the *half-warp*. When threads within the same half-warp access global memory, the threads must access consecutive memory positions, or more than one request is launched; this is commonly called *uncoalesced access*. On the other hand, the shared memory is a banked memory; so threads within the same half-warp that access different elements in the same bank will incur *bank conflicts*. The violation of these restrictions usually result in slowdowns.

Given the paramount importance of the memory system, the compiler must be aware of the coalescing requirements, so it must explicitly take into account the difference between a *warp* and a *block* of threads even if they are executed on the same virtual SIMD processor.

1.4   Polyhedral Model Overview

The polyhedral model is a high-level mathematical representation of a program. It uses polyhedra and related mathematical abstractions to represent all dynamic instances of the statements surrounded by loops, and all dependences between any pair of dynamic instances of any pair of statements. It is applicable to the so called Static Control Parts (SCoP) of the program [8], which are formed by loops with affine manifest boundaries and bodies with statements accessing arrays with subscript expressions affine in the surrounding loop iterators and the problem parameters.

The polyhedral model assigns to each statement an *iteration vector*, with one dimension per loop surrounding the statement. The first dimension represents the outermost loop, the next dimension the following loop, and so forth. Each valid *iteration vector* for a statement represents one of the dynamic executions of the statement, corresponding to a valid combination of values for the loop iterators in the loops surrounding the statement. Each of these dynamic executions of a statement is called an *operation*. The set of all valid *iteration vectors* for a statement is called the statement *domain*.

In addition, the polyhedral model provides a compact representation of all the data dependences between all pairs of operations. For a given pair of statements S_1 and S_2, all the dependences from any operation of S_1 to any operation of S_2 form a relation between the domains of S_1 and S_2. This relation is called the *dependence relation* between S_1 and S_2.

A SCoP is then represented in the polyhedral model by a directed graph. Each node represents a statement, and is tagged with its domain. An edge going from S_1 to S_2 represents all the dependences from any operation of S_1 to any operation of S_2, and is tagged with the Dependence Relation from S_1 to S_2.

This representation has been shown to be very useful in finding correct transformations of the original SCoP exhibiting some interesting properties, such as exposed parallelism [12, 18, 19] or improved locality [3, 12, 27]. The usual way to handle code transformation in the polyhedral model is by the construction of a *schedule* for each statement. A *schedule* is an affine function that assigns to each point in the original domain of the statement a point in a target space. The target space is common for all statements, but several points of the original domains can be mapped to the same point in the target space. Usually this target space is seen as a *date* space, in which the first dimension is more important than the second dimension and so forth (like hours, minutes, ...). In this way the schedule fixes a relative and partial ordering for all the operations. The transformed code is obtained by generating code that scans all the statement domains respecting the partial ordering specified by the schedule [7, 49]. However, it is also possible to build schedules in which some dimensions have different interpretations, for instance mapping to computing units (processors) instead of time units (*dates*). In addition, a non injective schedule can be extended to an injective schedule by adding new dimensions that are in essence parallel.

The process to build the schedule depends on the goal, whether it is parallelism, locality, *etc.* Feautrier proposed an algorithm to find the set of all valid affine schedules for a given SCoP [18, 19]. The algorithm exploits the affine form of the Farkas Lemma, expressing the constraints on the schedule for a statement as an affine combination of the inequalities in the dependence relation. It basically consists of building a system of equations on the coefficients of the affine combination, expressing the causality condition: if there is a data dependence from one operation to another operation, the latter must be executed at a later date than the former. The valid solutions can be obtained by solving this system of equations with any ILP solver. The set of all valid solutions forms a convex $\mathcal{Z}$-polyhedron in the parameter space. To select among all valid schedules, usually the ILP problem is re-formulated as a minimization problem. Selecting a good minimization criterion to achieve a given goal is not trivial [18].

1.5   Tools for GPU Code Generation

We can split the methodologies followed by the tools selected for the evaluation, C-to-CUDA [6], Par4All [38] and PPCG, in four main stages:[1]

- *Exposing parallelism.* Both C-to-CUDA and PPCG use the polyhedral model for this stage. Basically they select the schedules for each statement that produce as many parallel dimensions as possible in the target space. On the other hand, Par4All only uses loop distribution to expose parallelism.

- *Mapping to the CUDA model.* The parallel dimensions are mapped to CUDA's *thread block* and *thread* identifiers.

- *Data mapping.* Basically, the tools decide where, in the memory hierarchy, to place all data that is being accessed. If some array is to be placed in the shared memory, specific code is added to take care of the transfers from global memory to shared memory.

- *Code generation.* For both the host and the kernels.

The first stage is similar for the three tools. However, some differences exist that affect performance. Par4All treats each original loop nest independently, generating a specific kernel for each one. On the other hand, C-to-CUDA and PPCG work on SCoPs as large as possible and apply some locality optimization criteria to generate the *schedule*. As a result, the different loop nests can be fused, at least partially. The generation of the *schedule* in both C-to-CUDA and PPCG is based on the algorithm proposed in PLUTO [11, 14], although currently they evolve independently. Par4All uses the schedule provided in the input source.

In the second stage, the three tools look for a *parallel band* in their respective *schedules*. In this context, a *parallel band* is a set of one or more consecutive parallel dimensions (loops). If more than one *parallel band* exists all three tools select the outermost band. The selected parallel band is then mapped onto CUDA's *thread block*

---

[1]We used the implementation of C-to-CUDA included in pluto 0.6.2, Par4All 1.3 and version 3bf74858 from PPCG's git repository.

and *thread* identifiers. Some important differences exist between the three tools in how this mapping is performed.

In Par4All at most two parallel dimensions are selected from the *parallel band*, which are then tiled. Tiling two dimensions translates into strip-mining each dimension and permuting the two loops in the middle (out of four). Strip-mining divides the dimension into stripes, and replacing the original dimension by a set of two new dimensions, the first identifying the stripe and the second one identifying the point inside the stripe. Combined with interchange, these stripes form multidimensional tiles. The outer dimensions on stripes are called *tile dimensions* and the inner ones on points inside tiles is called *point dimensions*. The rest of the *schedule*'s dimensions are not modified. The *tile dimensions* are then mapped onto *thread block* identifiers. The *point dimensions* are mapped onto *thread* identifiers. Furthermore, Par4All always chooses between the same two tile sizes, 16×16 for two dimensional parallelism or 1×512 for one dimensional parallelism, *i.e.*, it always uses 16×16 or 1×512 *thread blocks* independently of the algorithm being mapped. This leads to suboptimal solutions in many cases.

On the other hand, both C-to-CUDA and PPCG also tile the dimensions following the first two parallel ones. In some cases, the additional sequential *tile dimensions* (that translate to loops in the kernel code) before the parallel *point loops*, may increase the chances of exploiting data reuse in the shared memory at the expense of introducing some thread synchronizations. However, we should highlight that no analysis is performed to evaluate the effect on performance of these extra tilings and reorderings, for the code being mapped.

In addition, both C-to-CUDA and PPCG take the tile sizes, *thread block* sizes and *grid* sizes as user parameters. This translates into the necessity of applying extra tilings on the parallel *tile* and *point* dimensions, to wrap those dimensions on the actual *thread block* and *grid* sizes selected by the user. This has its advantages and drawbacks. On one hand, the user can fine tune these parameters for a given algorithm. However, a non expert user, without knowledge on how the tool works, would probably need an exhaustive search to find those optimal parameters. On the other hand, an extra degree of complexity is introduced for the final code generation stage, as the *schedule* dimensions increase with these extra levels of tiling, making it sometimes inefficient. In our opinion, the tool should select the values for these parameters, after an analysis of the code being compiled: for the designer that decision is indeed too tedious and complex to make. Using default values independently of the code being compiled, like Par4All does, is also suboptimal.

The tools also differ in the *data mapping* stage. Par4All does not consider the exploitation of reuse in the shared memory or the register file. All accesses are performed directly on the global memory. For the most advanced Fermi architectures, it configures the memory hierarchy to use as much hardware cache as possible, relying on it to exploit data reuse.

C-to-CUDA takes a different systematic approach, every array is mapped to the shared memory. Thanks to the hierarchical tiling within a parallel band, this is frequently possible. However, as no analysis was performed on the code to perform these tilings, it can lead to invalid codes that use too much shared memory. In addition, mapping an array to shared memory when it does not exhibit inter-thread data reuse reduces performance, as we have the extra accesses to the shared memory without any compensation. We will see that this translates into a poor performance in many cases.

PPCG is, in this aspect, the most advanced tool. It performs the following analysis to decide if a given array is to be accessed directly from the global memory or if it is to be mapped on the shared memory or the registers file:

- If the data can be put in registers and there is reuse, then put it in registers.

- Otherwise, if the data can be put in shared memory and either there is reuse or the access is non-coalesced, then put it in shared memory.

- Otherwise, put it in global memory.

The tools also differ in the *code generation* stage. Only Par4All and PPCG generate both host and kernel codes, including all code to manage CPU-GPU transfers. In addition, while all three tools are capable of generating parametric code, Par4All is much better at detecting that a seemingly parametric input program is in fact not parametric thanks to its powerful interprocedural analysis. This has the advantage of generating simpler kernel codes, significantly reducing the number of dynamic instructions executed by the kernel. On the other hand, as mentioned before, the extra tilings introduced leave the user with control over the tiling parameters, and may lead to very complex kernel codes, frequently inefficient. This could be solved through more sophisticated code generation algorithms in the *Mapping to the CUDA model* stage.

Finally, Par4All is the only tool to support retargettable code generation, supporting scalar and SIMD instructions on CPUs, CUDA and OpenCL. This is achieved through a two-step code generation approach. The first step follows a generic CUDA/OpenCL hierarchical data parallelization, but relies on generic Par4All macros. These are specialized for one or more different targets in a second step.

1.6   Experimental Results

In this section, we present experimental results to assess the effectiveness of the CUDA code generated by the tools introduced in Section 1.5. Whenever possible we compare the performance of the codes generated by each tool.

The experiments were performed on a host with two 2.4 GHz Intel Xeon E5530 chips, each with four cores and HyperThreading, resulting in 16 virtual cores. On the device side, we used two different generations of GPUs:

- NVIDIA Tesla C1060 based on the *Tesla* architecture. The device has 4096 MB of DRAM and includes 30 multiprocessors at 1.3 GHz. Each multiprocessor has 8 processor cores which share 16384 registers and 16KB of software-controlled shared memory.

- NVIDIA Tesla M2070 based on the *Fermi* architecture. The device has 6144 MB of DRAM and includes 14 multiprocessors @ 1.15 GHz. Each multiprocessor has 32 processor cores which share 32768 registers and 64KB L1 memory. The L1 memory was configured to provide 16KB of software-controlled shared memory and 48KB of cache memory for the Par4All experiments and 48KB of software-controlled shared memory and 16KB of cache memory for PPCG and C-to-CUDA ones.

The CUDA code was compiled using the NVIDIA CUDA Compiler (NVCC) 4.0, while the CPU code was compiled using GCC 4.5 with option `-O3`. As the test bed we used the PolyBench 3.1 suite plus the matrix transpose algorithm. The PolyBench suite includes many common kernels from fields such as linear algebra, data mining and image processing, areas where GPUs has been intensively used over the last few years. We configured PolyBench to use single precision for all our comparisons. Finally, all results presented here are the average of 100 executions and the time measurements include GPU initialization, data transfers and kernel execution time.

Both Par4All and PPCG provide several input options to guide their operation. An exhaustive comparison of all possible values for these knobs would become unaffordably large and clearly out of the scope of this text. Thus, we chose, for each of the tools, the command line options that behave the best on average for all benchmarks. More precisely, we compiled all benchmarks under Par4All using the `--cuda` and `--com-optimization` options. PPCG was used with the flag `--isl-schedule -maximize-band-depth` and manually setting kernel parameters (namely block and tile size).

This analysis is structured into two sections. The first one is dedicated to matrix multiplication (also part of PolyBench), probably the most studied benchmark in the GPGPU field but still under revision at every new platform [29, 50]. We used this benchmark to provide an in-depth analysis of the internals of the three tools. In the second section of this analysis we provide the comparison of the rest of the benchmarks. Three of them are further analyzed through a CUDA profile because of their peculiar behavior.

1.6.1 Matrix Multiply (gemm)

We have picked out the platform-specific CUBLAS implementation of matrix multiply (*gemm*) as an ideal reference for the automatically generated code.

Figure 1.1 describes the scheme followed by C-to-CUDA and PPCG to perform the computations. We also rely on pseudo-code to assist the description (Listing 1.1 and Listing 1.2). Both tools apply tiling to each dimension so they are later able to exploit data reuse on shared memory and registers. Both map A and B to shared memory, but only PPCG promotes accesses to C to register.

C-to-CUDA decides to map C to shared memory instead. Furthermore C-to-CUDA's schedule is slightly different: it misses the exploitation of some data reuse on shared memory because it computes an entire partial value of C before it starts with the oth-

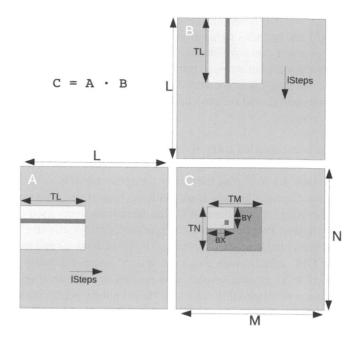

Figure 1.1: Mapping matrix multiplication to CUDA (C-to-CUDA and PPCG)

ers. These decisions make the difference between PPCG and C-to-CUDA and their effects are reflected in performance results.

Each threadblock has $BX * BY$ threads that compute a tile of C of size $TN * TM$. Based on the ratios TN/BY and TM/BX, each thread can compute more than one element of C. In our experiments, each thread computes 8 elements.[2] This means some parallelism is sacrificed in order to improve exploitation of data reuse on shared memory.

On the other hand Par4All generates simpler code putting parallelism before locality: each thread computes a single element of the result matrix. This way, it is only able to exploit reuse on C, whereas A and B are always read from global memory. Listing 1.3 shows the computation order found by Par4All.

Figure 1.2 and Figure 1.3 compare the performance of the generated code for *gemm* by the different parallelizing compilers and CUBLAS for both GPU architectures: Tesla and Fermi respectively.

CUDA defines the occupancy as the ratio between the *number of active warps* and the *maximum number of active warps*, which is different on Tesla and Fermi. On Tesla the maximum number of active warps is 32 while on Fermi it is 48, so actually an occupancy of 1 on Tesla C1060 is comparable with 0.667 on Tesla M2070.

---

[2]Parameters are manually fixed according to the optimal values found in our previous work [25].

```
__global__ void ctocudamxmkernel(...){
  int b0 = blockIdx.y, b1 = blockIdx.x;
  int t0 = threadIdx.y, t1 = threadIdx.x;


  __shared__ float C_loc_0[32][64];
  __shared__ float A_loc_0[32][16];
  __shared__ float B_loc_0[16][64];


  for(pi=0; pi<32; pi+=16)
    for(pj=0; pj<64; pj+=16)
      write_shared_C(pi+t0, pj+t1, 0.0);

  for(tl=0; tl<L; tl+=16){
    for(pi=0; pi<32; pi+=16)
      read_shared_A((b0*32+pi+t0)*L + (tl+t1));

    for(pj=0; pj<64; pj+=16)
      read_shared_B((tl+t0)*M + (b1*64+pj+t1));

    __syncthreads();
    for(pi=0; pi<32; pi+=16)
      for(pj=0; pj<64; pj+=16)
        for(pl=0; pl<16; pl++)
          compute_C(b0+pi+t0, b1+pj+t1, tl+pl);

    __syncthreads();
  }

  for(pi=0; pi<32; pi+=16)
    for(pj=0; pj<64; pj+=16)
      write_C(b0+pi+t0, b1+pj+t1);
}
```

Listing 1.1: pseudo code generated by C-to-CUDA

The Tesla architecture provides a software-managed L1 memory layer, favoring tools with a more elaborate *Data Mapping* strategy (PPCG and C-to-CUDA in the present experiments). As soon as the problem size becomes relevant this intuition is confirmed as shown in Figure 1.2. Maximizing the use of shared memory makes the platform occupancy drop to 50% for PPCG and 25% for C-to-CUDA. Nevertheless, they both outperform Par4All stressing the paramount importance of data locality exploitation. PPCG clearly outperforms C-to-CUDA due to the more efficient compilation of the accesses to the C matrix, which allows for higher occupancies and prevents unneeded writes to the shared memory.

```
__global__ void ppcgmxmkernel(...){
  int b0 = blockIdx.y, b1 = blockIdx.x;
  int t0 = threadIdx.y, t1 = threadIdx.x;
  __shared__ float shared_A[32][16];
  __shared__ float shared_B[16][64];
  float private_C[2][4];

  write_register_C(0, 0, 0.0);
  ...
  write_register_C(1, 3, 0.0);

  for(tl=0; tl<L; tl+=16){
    for(pi=0; pi<32; pi+=16)
      read_shared_A((b0*32+pi+t0)*L + (tl+t1));

    for(pj=0; pj<64; pj+=16)
      read_shared_B((tl+t0)*M + (b1*64+pj+t1));


    __syncthreads();
    for(pl=0; pl<16; pl++){
      compute_C(0, 0);
      ...
      compute_C(1, 3);
    }

    __syncthreads();
  }

  write_C((b0*32+t0) + (b1*64+t1));
  ...
  write_C(b0*32+16+t0) + (b1*64+48+t1));
}
```

Listing 1.2: MxM pseudo code generated by PPCG

Indeed, PPCG gets very close to the hand-tuned CUBLAS implementation. However, when the problem size is not a multiple of the tile size a minor issue in the code generation phase results in less efficient code, which explains the unexpected slow-down for large and extra-large problem sizes. Solving this issue would allow PPCG not to overcome CUBLAS but at least to keep the gap with it.

When moving to the newer Fermi architecture (Tesla M2070), Par4All is the most favored. It takes a huge advantage of the newly introduced L1 cache memory and

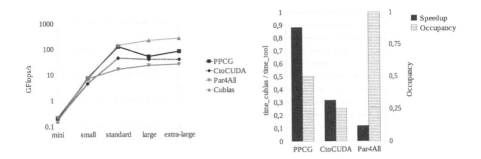

Figure 1.2: Gemm comparison on Tesla C1060. Left: performance for the five problem sizes defined in PolyBench: mini=32, small=128, standard=1024,
large=2000, and extra-large=4000 (including CPU, GPU, and transfer
times). Right: tools performance relative to CUBLAS and occupancy
(standard problem size)

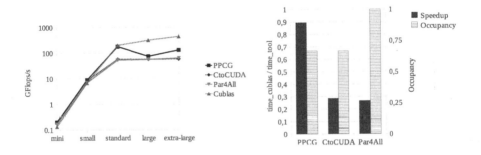

Figure 1.3: Gemm comparison on Tesla M2070. Left: performance for the five problem sizes defined in PolyBench: mini=32, small=128, standard=1024,
large=2000, and extra-large=4000 (CPU, GPU and transfer times). Right:
performance relative to CUBLAS and occupancy (standard size)

achieves an improvement of 2.5x on average against the previous generation, equaling
the performance of C-to-CUDA.

1.6.2 Other Benchmarks

We now conduct an overall analysis of the remaining benchmarks, and for three of
them, *bicg*, *mvt* and *jacobi-2d*, we provide a more detailed analysis using hardware
counters and profiling.

Unlike the Matrix Multiply case, we do not have a hand-tuned implementation
for each benchmark, so we show the speedup against the sequential execution on
CPU. In addition, we include comparisons with the parallel CPU code generated by

```
__global__ void par4allmxm(...) {
    int i = blockIdx.y * blockDim.y + threadIdx.y;
    int j = blockIdx.x * blockDim.x + threadIdx.x;
    int k;
    float C_0;

    if (i <= N-1 && j <= M-1) {
        C_0 = 0;
        for(k = 0; k <= L-1; k += 1)
            C_0 += A[i][k] * B[k][j];
    }
    C[i][j] = C_0;
}
```

Listing 1.3: MxM pseudo code generated by Par4All

PLUTO [14] (v0.7), which relies on OpenMP directives.

Unfortunately the three tools are not robust enough to deal with all benchmarks. PPCG generates code for 30 out of 31 polybenchs. We use only 20 benchmarks with Par4All because the other 11 benchmarks do not result in the extraction of a CUDA kernel. Finally, C-to-CUDA generates code for 11, but only 4 of 11 benchmarks compiled with C-to-CUDA were correctly executed. So, in order to show a wide range of results, we first show in Figure 1.4 and Figure 1.5 the comparison of the three tools, and then we will analyze the codes generated by Par4All and PPCG for all the benchmarks.

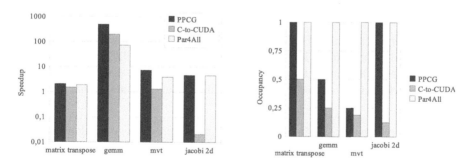

Figure 1.4: Comparison between the three tools on Tesla C1060. Left: speedup, CPU sequential version as baseline. Right: occupancy of the generated code

PPCG shows the best performance for all the benchmarks running on the Tesla C1060 as is shown in Figure 1.4.[3] With the exception of *gemm*, differences in performance are small among all the tools, which is easily explained by the poor data reuse

---

[3]C-to-CUDA did not generate correct code for *jacobi-2d*.

exposed by the benchmarks. Both C-to-CUDA and PPCG sometimes fail to achieve high occupancy values because of the shared memory requirements. Although the effect of shared memory is noticeable, it is less remarkable due to the poor data reuse. On the other hand Par4All shows the highest concurrent resources utilization since it does not use shared memory.

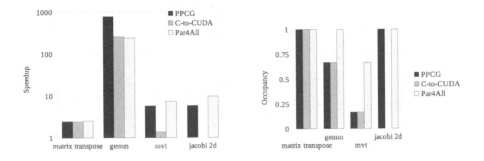

Figure 1.5: Comparison between the three tools on Tesla M2070. Left: speedup, CPU sequential version as baseline. Right: occupancy of the generated code

The results on the Tesla M2070 are slightly different as is shown in Figure 1.5. The effect of the cache memory speeds up to a greater extent the codes compiled with Par4All than the other ones. So Par4All becomes the fastest for those benchmarks in which the difference in performance was small on the Tesla C1060. The main benefit for C-to-CUDA and PPCG is the increase of the occupancy due to the extra memory and a larger register file provided by the Fermi architecture. A more detailed analysis of *mvt* and *jacobi-2d* is provided in Section 1.6.2.3 and Section 1.6.2.2 respectively.

Figure 1.6 shows a global comparison for default problem sizes on Tesla C1060. The results do not include C-to-CUDA as it fails to produce any code for most of the benchmarks. However we include CPU parallel code generated by PLUTO (OpenMP). We removed some benchmarks from the figure because nine of them perform worse than their sequential CPU version. These are all algorithms where the tools fail to expose enough parallelism. Some of them could be handled after some preliminary transformations, like scalar expansion (privatization). Unfortunately neither PPCG nor Par4All implement this transformation automatically. We leave *gramschmidt* in as a representative of this group.[4] It is likely that better performances could be achieved by tuning the tile sizes, especially for the stencil benchmarks, but this is beyond the scope of this work.

The figure shows that the algorithms that do not exhibit enough parallelism are better mapped to OpenMP by PLUTO. PPCG performs better than Par4All in the remaining 10 benchmarks, where the software-controlled shared memory is used by PPCG to exploit data reuse. The exploitation of the shared memory sometimes incurs a loss of effective parallelism as is reflected in the occupancy in Figure 1.7. The figure shows

---

[4]Missing bars for *gramschmidt* and *jacobi-1d-imper* correspond to slowdowns greater than 10.

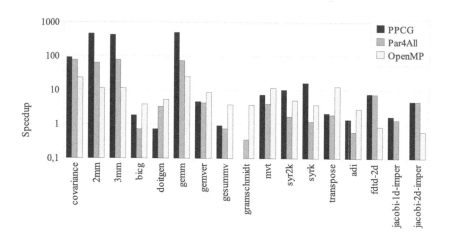

Figure 1.6: PPCG and Par4All speedup on Tesla C1060 and PLUTO (OpenMP) speedup on CPU (baseline sequential CPU)

that Par4All exploits all the computational resources in almost all cases, while PPCG often sacrifices computational potential to reuse the large amount of data in shared memory.

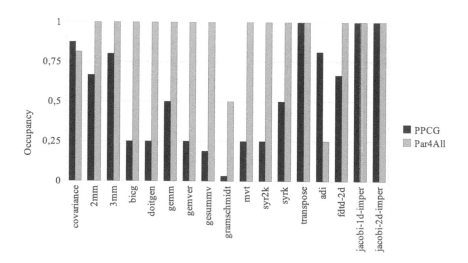

Figure 1.7: PPCG and Par4All occupancy on Tesla C1060

We also ran the code generated by Par4All and PPCG on the Tesla M2070 (Fermi).

Both improve performance, as seen in Figures 1.8 and 1.9.[5] Par4All appears to be the most favored by the effects of cache memory, which allows Par4All to reuse data avoiding the possible loss of computational potential. It was better in three of the 10

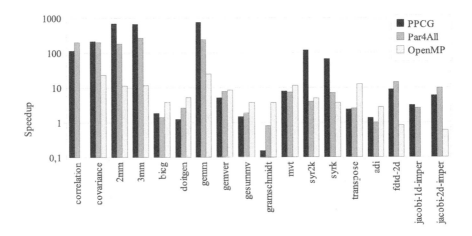

Figure 1.8: PPCG and Par4All speedup on Tesla M2070 and PLUTO (OpenMP) speedup on CPU (baseline sequential CPU)

remaining cases, while PPCG performs better than Par4All in the other seven cases, where the hardware cache is not performing as good as the software-controlled shared memory exploited by PPCG.

Although most benchmarks analyzed so far are relatively simple, the codes generated by the tools present important differences. Both PPCG and C-to-CUDA must include the code to manage the software-controlled shared memory which may involve a bigger control code. In addition the control code generated by C-to-CUDA usually uses a lot of registers. On the other hand Par4All always tries to generate the simplest kernel code, even if the host code may then incur thousands of invocations of the kernel, which may lead to slowdowns.

On more complex benchmarks like *covariance*, *2mm*, *3mm* and *doitgen*. PPCG finds different schedules based on the fusion strategy. The more ambitious ones, `maximal fusion` and `maximize band depth`, try to bring data closer to its consumption; and sometimes, these strategies incur a loss of parallelism and excessive resource requirements. C-to-CUDA also provides options to change the scheduling strategy, however it is not able to deal with these complex benchmarks. On the other hand, Par4All tries to extract parallelism within the input schedule, so if the source is clear enough, Par4All will generate the simplest code; so it is easier for Par4All to deal with more complex algorithms.

---

[5]Missing bars correspond to slowdowns greater than 10.

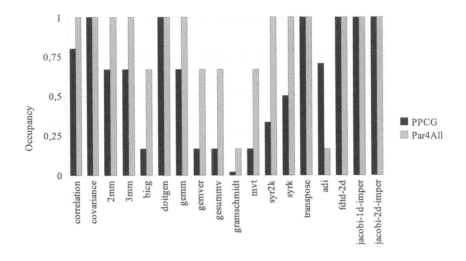

Figure 1.9: PPCG and Par4All occupancy on Tesla M2070

The following subsections analyze three benchmarks in detail. However we will not discuss how each tool is mapping the algorithms but we will analyze the empirical results obtained by the CUDA profiler. Unfortunately the hardware counters differ from one GPU generation to the other, so we cannot compare Tesla against Fermi. We will see that although the tools find similar schedules, the code generation stage is different, which prompts big differences in the total instructions executed. Furthermore we will evaluate the accesses to the different memory levels. To make this analysis more comprehensible, we provide the source codes as they are included in PolyBench in Listing 1.4, Listing 1.5 and Listing 1.6.

1.6.2.1   bicg

The *bicg* kernel only exhibits one parallel dimension and high data reuse, however the data layout has two dimensions. This type of algorithm leads to low occupancy due to the amount of shared memory needed to exploit the data reuse.

Figure 1.10 shows the relevant hardware counters for *bicg* on the Tesla C1060. PPCG generates much more dynamic instructions because of the shared memory management, however the benefits of shared memory make up for the extra instructions. The effect of shared memory can be seen in the memory counters *gld_coherent* and *gst_coherent*, which are the loads from and stores to global memory respectively. However the difference in the stores is not only due to the lack of shared memory accesses in Par4All, but also to the fact that Par4All launches more than 4000 kernels; it uses global memory to communicate data across them. On the other hand, PPCG only launches one kernel. The *warp_serialize* counter exposes a minor issue in the code generation which prompts conflicts when accessing to the shared memory. It

```
for (i = 0; i < ny; i++)
  s[i] = 0;

for (i = 0; i < nx; i++){
  q[i] = 0;
  for (j = 0; j < ny; j++){
    s[j] = s[j] + r[i] * A[i][j];
    q[i] = q[i] + A[i][j] * p[j];
  }
}
```

Listing 1.4: bicg original code

would be easily solved by applying padding which would lead to 1.3× speedup, but PPCG does not apply this optimization automatically.

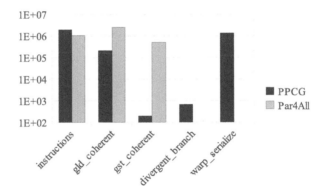

Figure 1.10: Hardware counters for bicg on Tesla C1060: number of *instructions* executed, number of loads (*gld_coherent*) and stores (*gst_coherent*) executed, number of branches (*divergent_branch*) that result in serial execution and number of serializations (*warp_serialize*) produced by bank conflicts in shared memory

Finally, Figure 1.11 shows the hardware counters on the Tesla M2070. This architecture provides counters to measure the accesses to shared memory, so we can estimate the reuse at that memory level. In the case of *bicg* this ratio (*shared_load/shared_store*) is 2.8, which does not demonstrate a high level of reuse, but still indicates a reduction in the total number of accesses global memory. Although Par4All is still performing the same accesses to global memory, these accesses are almost all cached and only 43% of the loads finally access the global memory. PPCG's case is different; it already uses shared memory to bring data closer to the multiprocessor, accessing the global memory as little as possible. PPCG usually accesses global memory once and

```
for (t = 0; t < tsteps; t++){
  for (i = 1; i < n - 1; i++)
    for (j = 1; j < n - 1; j++)
      B[i][j] = 0.2 * (A[i][j] + A[i][j-1] +
             A[i][1+j] + A[1+i][j] + A[i-1][j]);

  for (i = 1; i < n-1; i++)
    for (j = 1; j < n-1; j++)
      A[i][j] = B[i][j];
}
```

Listing 1.5: jacobi original code

moves the data to the shared memory, which populates the L1 cache with useless data. In addition it uses only 16KB of L1 cache. As a result the miss rate (92%) is much higher, but on a much lower total number of accesses. To validate this analysis, we manually switched off the L1 cache using `nvcc`'s options `-Xptxas -dlcm=cg`; the performance did not vary significantly because the code generated by PPCG for *bicg* is dominated by accesses to global memory.

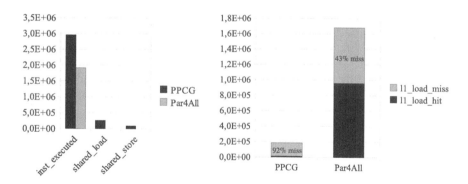

Figure 1.11: Hardware counters for bicg on Tesla M2070. Left: general counters. Right: accesses to global memory and miss rate

1.6.2.2   jacobi-2d

The *jacobi-2d* kernel exhibits much more parallelism than *bicg* but a poorer data reuse, which makes the use of shared memory less interesting. This can be seen in Figure 1.12 and Figure 1.13. The figures show that the accesses to global memory are similar under both PPCG and Par4All. On the Tesla M2070 the data reuse ratio on shared memory for PPCG is now 1.47, which is an especially low reuse ratio. Moreover the smaller size of the cache memory on PPCG produces a higher miss rate. Contrary to *bicg*, PPCG generates code for *jacobi-2d* that only accesses to global memory to move data closer to the multiprocessor. In this situation, switching off the L1 cache at compile time, leads to speedups of $1.32\times$.

On the other hand, the standard problem size defined on PolyBench for *jacobi-2d* is not a multiple of the tile sizes defined by PPCG, C-to-CUDA nor Par4All. We have already seen in Figure 1.2 and Figure 1.3 that this fact prompts large slowdowns in PPCG. The Figure 1.12 and Figure 1.13 show this issue also affects C-to-CUDA, however Par4All does not expose this problem. The schedules found by both C-to-CUDA and PPCG, incur many *divergent_branches* within the border threadblocks. Although C-to-CUDA incurs a higher rate of divergent branches due to its worse code generation stage.

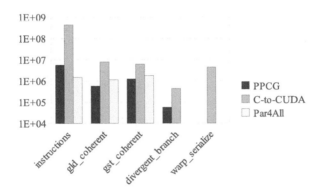

Figure 1.12: Hardware counters for jacobi-2d-imper on Tesla C1060

Regarding C-to-CUDA, it is not able to generate competitive code for *jacobi-2d*. For this algorithm, the code generation stage of C-to-CUDA performs especially badly. It generates dozens of complex conditions which (1) increase hugely the number of registers required by each thread, (2) scales up the number of instructions executed and (3) induces many divergent branches which serialize the execution. Moreover, the code generated by C-to-CUDA does not work under Fermi: apparently it uses the C-to-CUDA threadblock synchronization mechanism, which assumes some constraints that are not true on Fermi anymore.

1.6.2.3 mvt

The *mvt* kernel is very similar to *bicg*. It also exposes one-dimensional-limited parallelism, but exhibits data reuse in a two-dimensional layout, which again leads to low occupancy. However, for this kernel we are able to provide results for C-to-CUDA. Figure 1.14 shows the counter results for Tesla architecture. Apparently C-to-CUDA incurs many more accesses to global memory, which indeed happens, but the difference is not as big as it is shown in the figure since the schedule found by C-to-CUDA

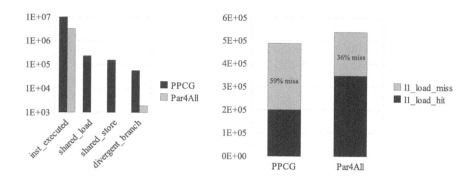

Figure 1.13: Hardware counters for jacobi-2d-imper on Tesla M2070. Left: general
counters. Right: accesses to global memory and miss rate

```
for (i = 0; i < n; i++)
  for (j = 0; j < n; j++)
    x1[i] = x1[i] + A[i][j] * y_1[j];

for (i = 0; i < n; i++)
  for (j = 0; j < n; j++)
    x2[i] = x2[i] + A[j][i] * y_2[j];
```

Listing 1.6: mvt original code

assigns 16 times more work to each block. As for *bicg*, Par4All generates thousands
of kernel calls which explains the high number of stores to global memory. Both
C-to-CUDA and PPCG produce conflicts when accessing shared memory (reflected
by *warp_serialize* counter). If these tools applied padding, they would improve their
performance up to $1.32\times$.

Figure 1.15 shows the counters for Fermi. Although both PPCG and C-to-CUDA
use shared memory, PPCG is exploiting better the shared memory efficiency since it
obtains a data reuse in shared memory of 2.7, while C-to-CUDA gets 1. So C-to-
CUDA actually does not reuse anything in the shared memory.

1.7   Lessons Learned

With the increasing use of GPUs for general purpose development, automatic or semi-
automatic tools take on an ever greater importance to assist programmers in their daily
work.

In this chapter we have evaluated the current state of the art of the polyhedral model
based tools for automatic code generation for GPUs, giving a detailed functional de-

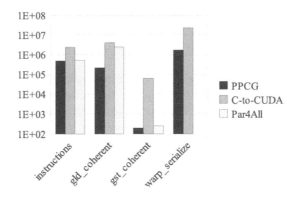

Figure 1.14: Hardware counters for mvt on Tesla C1060

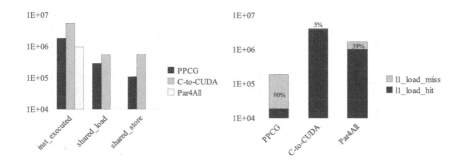

Figure 1.15: Hardware counters for mvt on Tesla M2070. Left: general counters. Right: accesses to global memory and miss rate

scription of three of them: PPCG, Par4All, C-to-CUDA. The results show that such tools are already mature enough to deal with most of the numerical kernels in the PolyBench 3.1 suite.

To gain some perspective on the quality of the code generated by these tools, we selected some of the benchmarks to compare with hand-tuned versions for GPUs, with automatically generated parallel versions for regular SMPs and with sequential versions executed on high performance CPUs. The performance achieved by the automatically generated GPU code is, in some cases close the best known manual implementation. We have not found any case in which the code generated by the tools outperformed the hand-tuned counterpart.

For almost all the algorithms in the PolyBench, the combined CPU/GPU code that the tools generate outperforms the CPU sequential versions. However, a few exceptions have been found. For these algorithms, the parallelization on regular SMP platforms, which exploit much less data level parallelism than the GPUs, is the best option.

Following these results, it seems reasonable to think that including some strategy to decide whether a potential kernel is appropriate for its execution on the GPU, or if on the contrary it would be better to execute it on the CPU, parallelized or not, would help to improve these tools.

Regarding the comparison of the three tools under study, we found that the efficiency in the exploitation of the memory hierarchy largely determines the performance of the code generated. On GPUs that only incorporate software controlled shared memories, PPCG has generally shown the best performance. This tool incorporates the most complex memory mapping strategy among the three, and in some cases sacrifices some parallelism to enable a better exploitation of the memory hierarchy. However, on the Fermi architecture that also incorporates hardware managed caches, the differences in performance are significantly reduced. Par4All fully relies on the efficiency of the hardware caches, and this allows it to generates a very simple code. When locality is efficiently captured by the cache this strategy performs better than the one followed by PPCG, that exploits all the locality through the shared memory. The reason is that the simple code has fewer instructions and warp divergence, and sometimes also translates to a larger occupancy. Moreover, the results for PPCG show that it is even better to disable the hardware cache when all the locality is exploited through the shared memory.

None of the tools incorporate a memory mapping strategy adapted to a hierarchy that includes both software managed shared memories and hardware managed caches. These results show that the best performance is achieved only when both are conveniently used, pointing out another direction for improvement in these tools.

Acknowledgements

This work was partly funded by the European FP7 project CARP id. 287767. We are extremely grateful to Louis-Noël Pouchet for his detailed feedback on an earlier version of this chapter. This work would not have been possible without the support from the Par4All developers, and from Mehdi Amini in particular.

References

[1] R. Allen, K. Kennedy, "Optimizing Compilers for Modern Architectures", Morgan Kaufmann Publishers, 2001.

[2] R. Allen, K. Kennedy, "Automatic translation of fortran programs to vector form", ACM Tr. on Programming Languages and Systems, v9, n4, 491–542, 1987.

[3] M. Amini, F. Coelho, F. Irigoin, R. Keryell, "Static compilation analysis for host-accelerator communication optimization", in *Workshop on Languages and Compilers for Parallel Computing (LCPC'11)*, LNCS, Springer-Verlag, Oct. 2011.

[4] "C++ accelerated massive parallelism". http://msdn.microsoft.com/en-us/library/hh265137

[5] S. Baghdadi, A. Grösslinger, A. Cohen, "Putting automatic polyhedral compilation for gpgpu to work", *Proc. Compilers for Parallel Computer (CPC)*, 2010.

[6] M. Baskaran, J. Ramanujam, P. Sadayappan, "Automatic C-to-CUDA code generation for affine programs", *Compiler Construction, 19th International Conference, CC 2010*, Held as Part of the Joint European Conferences on Theory and Practice of Software, ETAPS 2010, Paphos, Cyprus, March 20-28, 2010, Proceedings, Volume 6011 of Lecture Notes in Computer Science, 244-263, Springer, 2010.

[7] C. Bastoul, "Code Generation in the Polyhedral Model Is Easier Than You Think", in *PACT'13 IEEE International Conference on Parallel Architecture and Compilation Techniques*, 7–16, Juan-les-Pins, France, September 2004.

[8] C. Bastoul, A. Cohen, S. Girbal, S. Sharma, O. Temam, "Putting Polyhedral Loop Transformations to Work", in *Workshop on Languages and Compilers for Parallel Computing (LCPC'03)*, LNCS, 23–30, Springer-Verlag, College Station, Texas, Oct. 2003.

[9] M.W. Benabderrahmane, L.N. Pouchet, A. Cohen, C. Bastoul, "The Polyhedral Model Is More Widely Applicable Than You Think", in *Proceedings of the International Conference on Compiler Construction (CC'10)*, LNCS, 6011, Springer-Verlag, Paphos, Cyprus, Mar. 2010.

[10] A.J.C. Bik, "The Software Vectorization Handbook. Applying Multimedia Extensions for Maximum Performance", Intel Press, 2004.

[11] U. Bondhugula, "PLuTo: An automatic parallelizer and locality optimizer for multicores". http://pluto-compiler.sourceforge.net/

[12] U. Bondhugula, M. Baskaran, S. Krishnamoorthy, J. Ramanujam, A. Rountev, P. Sadayappan, "Automatic transformations for communication-minimized parallelization and locality optimization in the polyhedral model", *LNCS*, 132–146, 2008.

[13] U. Bondhugula, A. Hartono, J. Ramanujam, P. Sadayappan, "A practical automatic polyhedral parallelizer and locality optimizer", *SIGPLAN Not.*, 43:101–113, June 2008. doi:10.1145/1379022.1375595

[14] U. Bondhugula, J. Ramanujam, *et al.*, "PLuTo: A practical and fully automatic polyhedral program optimization system", in *Proceedings of the ACM SIGPLAN 2008 Conference on Programming Language Design and Implementation (PLDI) 08*, 2008.

[15] P. Boulet, A. Darte, G.A. Silber, F. Vivien, "Loop parallelization algorithms: from parallelism extraction to code generation", *Parallel Comput.*, 24:421–444, May 1998. doi:10.1016/S0167-8191(98)00020-9

[16] C. Chen, J. Chame, M. Hall, "A framework for composing high-level loop transformations", Technical report, USC Computer Science, 2008.

[17] P. Cooper, U. Dolinsky, A.F. Donaldson, A. Richards, C. Riley, G. Russell, "Offload - Automating Code Migration to Heterogeneous Multicore Systems", in *HiPEAC*, 337–352, 2010.

[18] P. Feautrier, "Some efficient solutions to the affine scheduling problem. Part I. One-dimensional time", *International Journal of Parallel Programming*, 21:

313–347, 1992. doi:10.1007/BF01407835.

[19] P. Feautrier, "Some efficient solutions to the affine scheduling problem. Part II. Multidimensional time", *International Journal of Parallel Programming*, 21: 389–420, 1992. doi:10.1007/BF01379404.

[20] R. Ferrer, V. Beltran, M. González, X. Martorell, E. Ayguadé, "Analysis of Task Offloading for Accelerators", in *HiPEAC*, 322–336, 2010.

[21] R. Garg, J.N. Amaral, "Compiling Python to a hybrid execution environment", in *Proc. of the 3rd Workshop on General-Purpose Computation on Graphics Processing Units (GPGPU'10)*, 2010.

[22] T. Grosser, H. Zheng, A. Raghesh, A. Simbürger, A. Grösslinger, L.N. Pouchet, "Polly: Polyhedral optimization in LLVM", in *First International Workshop on Polyhedral Compilation Techniques (IMPACT'11)*, Chamonix, France, Apr. 2011.

[23] A. Grösslinger, "Precise management of scratchpad memories for localising array accesses in scientific codes", *Proceedings of the 18th International Conference on Compiler Construction: Held as Part of the Joint European Conferences on Theory and Practice of Software, ETAPS 2009*, 2009.

[24] "HMPP workbench: a directive-based multi-language and multi-target hybrid programming model". http://www.caps-entreprise.com/hmpp.html

[25] J.C. Juega, "GPU performance study", Master's thesis, Complutense University of Madrid, Spain, 2010.

[26] S. Lee, S.J. Min, , R. Eigenmann, "OpenMP to GPGPU: A compiler framework for automatic translation and optimization", in *Proc. Symp. on Principles and Practice of Parallel Programming*, 2009.

[27] A. Leung, N. Vasilache, B. Meister, M. Baskaran, D. Wohlford, C. Bastoul, R. Lethin, "A mapping path for multi-GPGPU accelerated computers from a portable high level programming abstraction", in *Proceedings of the 3rd Workshop on General-Purpose Computation on Graphics Processing Units*, GPGPU '10, 51–61, ACM, New York, NY, USA, 2010. doi:10.1145/1735688.1735698

[28] A. Lim, "Improving Parallelism and Data Locality with Affine Partitioning", Master's thesis, Stanford University, 2001.

[29] R. Nath, S. Tomov, J. Dongarra, "An Improved MAGMA GEMM for Fermi GPUs", 2010.

[30] D. Nuzman, I. Rosen, A. Zaks, "Auto-Vectorization of Interleaved Data for SIMD", Proc. Conf. on Programming Language Design and Implementation (PLDI'06), 2006.

[31] D. Nuzman, A. Zaks, "Outer-Loop Vectorization - Revisited for Short SIMD Architectures", Intl. Conf. on Parallel Architecture and Compilation Techniques (PACT'08), October, 2008.

[32] NVIDIA Corporation, *NVIDIA CUDA Programming guide 4.0*, 2011.

[33] "OpenACC: Directives for accelerators". http://www.openacc-standard.org

[34] "PoCC: the Polyhedral Compiler Collection". http://www.cse.

ohio-state.edu/~pouchet/software/pocc

[35] "PolyBench: the Polyhedral Benchmark suite". http://www.cse. ohio-state.edu/~pouchet/software/polybench

[36] The Portland Group, *PGI Accelerator Programming Model for Fortran & C*, v1.3 edition, Nov. 2010.

[37] A. Prasad, J. Anantpur, R. Govindarajan, "Automatic Compilation of MATLAB Programs for Synergistic Execution on Heterogeneous Processors", in *Proc. Conf. on Programming Language Design and Implementation (PLDI'11)*, June 2011.

[38] HPC Project, "Par4All automatic parallelization". http://www.par4all. org

[39] N. Ravi, Y. Yang, T. Bao, S. Chakradhar, "Apricot: An Optimizing Compiler and Productivity Tool for x86-compatible Many-core Coprocessors", in *Intl. Conf. on Supercomputing (ICS'12)*, June 2012.

[40] G. Rudy, M.M. Khan, M. Hall, C. Chen, C. Jacqueline, "A programming language interface to describe transformations and code generation", in *Proceedings of the 23rd international conference on Languages and compilers for parallel computing*, LCPC'10, 136–150, Springer-Verlag, Berlin, Heidelberg, 2011. http://dl.acm.org/citation.cfm?id=1964536.1964546

[41] S. Ryoo, C.I. Rodrigues, S.S. Baghsorkhi, S.S. Stone, D.B. Kirk, W.M. Hwu, "Optimization principles and application perform- ance evaluation of a multithreaded GPU using CUDA", in *Proc. Symp. on Principles and Practice of Parallel Programming (PPoPP'08)*, Jan. 2008.

[42] S. Ryoo, C.I. Rodrigues, S.S. Stone, S.S. Baghsorkhi, S. Ueng, J.A. Stratton, W.M. Hwu, "Optimization space pruning for a multithreaded GPU", in *Proc. Intl. Symp. on Code Generation and Optimization (CGO'08)*, Oct. 2008.

[43] L. Seiler, D. Carmean, et al., "Larrabee: a many-core x86 architecture for visual computing", in *ACM SIGGRAPH*, 18:1–18:15, 2008.

[44] J. Shin, J. Chame, M.W. Hall, "Compiler-Controlled Caching in Superword Register Files for Multimedia Extension Architectures", Intl. Conf. on Parallel Architecture and Compilation Techniques (PACT'02), September, 2002.

[45] J. Shin, M. Hall, J. Chame, "Superword-Level Parallelism in the Presence of Control Flow", Proc. Intl. Symp. on Code Generation and Optimization (CGO'05), March, 2005.

[46] K. Trifunović, D. Nuzman, A. Cohen, A. Zaks, I. Rosen, "Polyhedral-Model Guided Loop-Nest Auto-Vectorization", Intl. Conf. on Parallel Architecture and Compilation Techniques (PACT'09), Raleigh, North Carolina, September, 2009.

[47] S. Ueng, M. Lathara, S.S. Baghsorkhi, W.M. Hwu, "CUDA-lite: Reducing GPU programming Complexity", in *Proc. Workshop on Languages and Compilers for Parallel Computing (LCPC'08)*, Oct. 2008.

[48] S. Unkule, C. Shaltz, A. Qasem, "Automatic Restructuring of GPU Kernels for Exploiting Inter-thread Data Locality", in *International Conference on Compiler Construction (CC'12)*, LNCS, 7210, Springer-Verlag, 2012.

[49] N. Vasilache, C. Bastoul, A. Cohen, "Polyhedral Code Generation in the Real

World", in *Proceedings of the International Conference on Compiler Construc-tion (ETAPS CC'06)*, LNCS, 3923, 185–201, Springer-Verlag, Vienna, Austria, Mar. 2006.

[50] V. Volkov, J.W. Demmel, "Benchmarking GPUs to tune dense linear algebra", *ACM/IEEE Conference on Supercomputing (SC08)*, 2008.

[51] Y. Liu, E.Z. Zhang, X. Shen, "A Cross-Input Adaptive Framework for GPU Programs Optimization", in *Proc. IEEE International Parallel & Distributed Processing Symp.*, 2009.

[52] S. Verdoolaege, J.C. Juega, A. Cohen, J.I. Gómez, C. Tenllado, F. Catthoor, "Polyhedral parallel code generation for CUDA", ACM Trans. Archit. Code Optim, v9, n4, 54:1–54:23, 2013.

[53] M. Wolfe, "High Performance Compilers for Parallel Computing", Addison Wesley, 1996.

[54] P. Wu, A.E. Eichenberger, A. Wang, P. Zhao, "An Integrated Simdization Frame-work Using Virtual Vectors", Intl. Conf. on Supercomputing (ICS'05), 2005.

©Saxe-Coburg Publications, 2014.
F. Magoulès, (Editor),
Patterns for Parallel Programming on GPUs
Saxe-Coburg Publications, Stirlingshire, Scotland, 31-55.

Chapter 2

Data Size and Data Type Dynamic GPU Code Generation

H.-P. Charles and V. Lomüller

CEA-LIST, Gif-sur-Yvette, France

Abstract

In this chapter, we present an unusual strategy to perform dynamic code generation for NVIDIA GPUs. The usual compiler relies on assumptions that are not always true, which can lead to sub-optimal code resulting from a lack of information available to the compiler. By using a code generator `deGoal` that can produce a code in a pseudo-assembly code representation for NVIDIA GPUs, we will show how to dynamically generate code usable by the GPU. `deGoal` uses a low level intermediate representation to produce, at run-time, code that benefits from run-time information to produce more optimal and/or flexible GPU routines. This approach removes the need to statically specialize the code for a wide variety of configurations and still produces good performances. We illustrate our tool usage by the matrix multiplication on various configurations. This example shows that it allows us to develop an application and get near optimal results faster than developing a specialized version.

Keywords: dynamic code generation, compiler, GPU programming.

2.1 Introduction

In this chapter we present unusual tools for code generation, the "dynamic code generation". The usual compilation tools such as NVIDIA compiler [12] or HMPP code restructuring [6] relies on two assumptions that are not always true :

1. **Programming languages are smart enough to describe complex applications for complex hardware.**

When a new application domain arises (red box 1 on the left of Figure 2.1), two or three years later the processor architects build a new hardware answer to solve the computing problems of the new domain (red box 2 on the right). The answer can be a new hardware operator and/or a new instruction set able to drive this operator.

In the past integer arithmetic for algorithmic description was the main focus of compiler optimization, then we had floating point vector operations for linear algebra (MMX and SSE).

New examples are multimedia instructions set with very specialized instruction such as sum of absolute differences (SAD) for video compression, *etc.*

Unfortunately the main programming languages (green box 3) were fixed in the 80s. As an example, the C language reference was submitted on October, 31 1988 to the ANSI[1]. This type of compiled language contains only operators for basic data types (integer and floating point) and all useful construction such as vector, matrix, RGB pixels, pixels blocks should be constructed using arrays and structures and there is no support at all for unusual arithmetic such as fixed point numbers, saturated arithmetic or pixels operations.

Compilers (orange box 4 in 1) are always in last in this race because they are the last to be build in this chain. They try to reconstruct missing information such as low level parallelism (ILP), data dependencies, parallel constructions. But they often failed to produce efficient codes because programmers have too many ways to write the same semantically equivalent codes.

2. **Native compilers will always produce an optimal code**.

   Native compilers are based on complex analysis of source code, but we have seen in the previous item that programming language can be a poor vehicle for complex algorithm description and *static compilation time* may not be a good "time" for code production.

   On modern processors important information for efficient execution is only known dynamically: loop count, memory alignments, data size and more generally data values are only known at run-time and vary from one execution to an other. This is because many new algorithms are data dependent.

Based on the idea that these two assumptions are false, we have developed an infrastructure to build *high level optimizations* depicted in green in Figure 2.1.

We call these optimizations *compilettes*. They can be defined as small code generators embedded into the application. They can generate code :

1. using specific instructions that a classic compiler cannot generate even by using special libraries or *intrinsic*[2]

---

[1]Even if new norms were submitted (C99 and C11), no real hardware adapations emerged.

[2]**Intrinsic** is a way to insert a specific assembly instruction inside the classical flow of instructions.

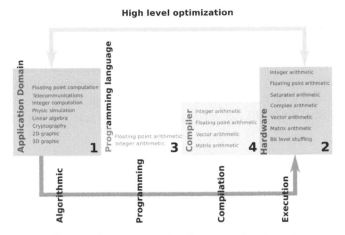

Figure 2.1: Programming language bottleneck

2. by using user data information at run-time. Compilettes are fast enough to re-generate code as needed for each new set of data.

In this chapter we present our activity in code optimization. In the following sub-section we present the context in which we are actually working. The ITEA2 project H4H allows us to implement this type of optimization in the `Scilab` interpretor.

2.1.1   H4H ITEA2 Project

Our work is funded by the ITEA2 H4H European project.

The full description of the ITEA2 H4H project can be found at the following URL `http://www.h4h-itea2.org/`:

> "The objective of H4H is to provide compute-intensive application devel-opers with a highly efficient hybrid programming environment for het-erogeneous computing clusters composed of a mix of classical processors and hardware accelerators."

In this context we are implementing a *compilette* inside the `Scilab` interpretor. At the time of writing, we are at the middle of the project and we have begun to have results on our work.

2.1.2   `Scilab` Interpretor

`Scilab http://www.scilab.org` is a free open source software for numer-ical computation. Many implementations exist for many operating systems (Linux, FreeBSD, MaxOSX, Windows, ...) for 32 or 64 bits processors.

Scilab is an interpreted programming language which is based mainly on dense linear algebra even if many other objects can be used (sparse matrix, polynomials functions, *etc.*). Each formula is parsed, evaluated and the result computed.

The internal representation of values in Scilab are matrices and for any computation between values, Scilab uses accelerated matrix computation libraries available such as refblas-netlib, ATLAS [16] or a more complex routine like LAPACK. Work is actually done using the CUBLAS version where Nvidia Cuda is available.

2.2   Code Generation for Accelerators

An heterogeneous computer contains processors with different programming paradigms. An example of such a computer is the BullX system which mixes Intel Xeon CISC processors and Nvidia GPU accelerators.

The challenge in using this type of system is to port code smoothly on these processors with incompatible programming models (CISC and massively parallel)

In this section we list the multiple options available to program GPU accelerators.

2.2.1   CUDA Programming Language

CUDA is a programming language used to program NVIDIA GPU. These processors are defined as a set of SIMD multiprocessors with on-chip shared memory [3].

The main characteristics of these processors are :

- a very high parallelism level, for example 448 thread processors on a C2050 Nvidia card

- a very complex memory hierarchy : main memory, GPU memory, shared memory, texture memory, local memory, and registers that are explicit in the programming model.

In the NVIDIA programming model implemented in CUDA, programmers have to explicitly write memory transfers from CPU to GPU, handle memory hierarchy with different timing : texture, constant, global, local, shared, register.

The compilation flow has to segregate the code which will run on the GPU from the code which will run on the CPU. Figure 2.2 shows a simplified scheme of the CUDA compilation flow. The cuda source code is split into two parts, one which will run on the CPU, and one which will run on the GPU. The GPU code is loaded on the GPU target by the CPU code either by embedding the GPU assembly code in the CPU binary code or by loading the files (using the PTX assembly format).

In this case, the programming language is only for NVIDIA GPU.

2.2.2   CUDA and PTX

Several distinguished scheme are proposed by Nvidia to build and run CUDA code. Source code are CU files, those files are the CUDA "C like" with special semantic

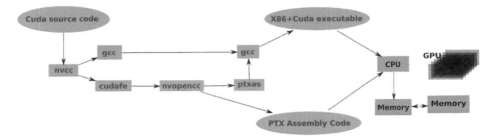

Figure 2.2: CUDA programming flow

files, which are statically compiled into one of the next files :

- CUBIN files, those files are graphic cards with a specific binary code. The main advantage of using such files is that they do not require any compilation at run-time to launch the kernels, but they suffer from a lack of forward support for graphic card evolution. They can be manually loaded at run-time or embedded in the application (as shown on Figure 2.2)

- PTX virtual assembly files (PTX for Parallel Thread EXecution), those files are text files loaded and compiled at run-time.

  This configuration allows the PTX compiler to optimize and specialize the code for the graphic card actually being used and offer forward support for newer graphic cards, but a part of the compilation has to be paid at run-time (just like the *compilette* system).

Nvidia GPUs are released in different generations. Each generation adds a major improvement in functionality and/or in hardware architecture. Those improvements may lead to binary incompatibility [4], due to a different ISA, encoding ... For now two generations coexist: TESLA (sm_10 to sm_13) and FERMI (sm_20). A binary compiled for an architecture sm_10 will run on any TESLA GPUs but may not on FERMI GPUs.

To ensure portability across generations, Nvidia provide a just in time (JIT) infrastructure. Instead of compiling your application into a binary format that would only be executable with a subset CUDA compatible GPU, the CUDA code can be compiled into the PTX format. The PTX describes the minimum compute capability (C.C.) required to run the application, but can still be used across newer generations. For instance, if your application is compiled into a PTX file for sm_12 GPU cards, on the one hand the application will be able to run on the existing sm_12, sm_13 and sm_20 GPUs, and on the other hand future GPU version that are still not released will also be supported.

Nvidia supports another system for portability via static code specialization and device code repository. Different code versions can be statically compiled to support a large variety of GPUs. At run-time, when the user asks for the function, the CUDA driver will search for the device code repository and select the right implementation for the card being used. Obviously, the compilation cost does not have to be paid at run-time, but forward support is very limited.

In conclusion, the use of PTX files proposes a flexible solution for deploying CUDA code: 1) the code is optimized for the graphic card actually used (and not the one used to develop or chosen for deployment) 2) perfectly run across graphic cards generation. Also, the run-time PTX compiler (PTXAS) has an acceptable compilation time that can be easily amortized. But in both cases it is a hardware adaptation, it is impossible to take a dataset adaptation.

2.2.3 OpenCL

> "OpenCL is the first open, royalty-free standard for cross-platform, parallel programming of modern processors found in personal computers, servers and handheld/embedded devices". [10]

OpenCL targets a much wider architectural spectrum where the CPU and the accelerator can share the same memory or not. Depending on the hardware vendor, the accelerator can have different capabilities which implies that the code can not be portable from one architecture to another.

In this case, the programming language is standardized and for any hardware accelerator which support OpenCL.

2.2.4 Using Libraries

Another possibility for using hardware accelerators is to program in a classical programming language and use a specialized library (standardized if possible).

In this situation program portability relies on the existence of this library on the target platform.

We give some existing examples in the following sections :

2.2.4.1 Linear Algebra Domain

BLAS (Basic Linear Algebra Subprograms) is a classical example. It defines an interface for vector-vector operations (BLAS level 1 operations), vector-matrix operations (BLAS level 2 operations) and matrix-matrix operations (BLAS level 3 operations). This is a *de facto* application programming interface (API).

Each operation is defined for single and double precision numbers, and for real and complex numbers.

Multiple versions exist :

- The reference version is an old FORTRAN implementation [7] which has been used to fix the API. The reference article explains how the code was distributed (by email service; it was before the invention of the www).

- ATLAS [16] is an implementation of this linear algebra library. Its main functionality is its ability to automatically tune itself by detecting at installation time, the machine specific parameters that are essential to obtain good performances.

- NVIDIA CUBLAS : tuned to run on NVIDIA GPU [13]. We do not have information about the implementation of this library.

- INTEL MKL: tuned to run on Intel's x86 processors. It relies heavily on MMX/SSE instructions, and on OpenMP for thread management. No code generation is performed at run-time, but code specialization is used instead and the best implementation is selected at the function call.

- IBM BLAS included in the ISSL library [3]

A program relying on this type of library can be sure to have functionality by using the reference version, and may perform using a specialized version optimized by a hardware constructor. This is the approach used by SCILAB in their interpretor.

It is important to note that BLAS in only a *de facto* standard, and it took time to fix the API of the first version in the 80's and when new hardware came, it took time to develop a full implementation which used the possible performance to the full. NVIDIA's implementation has developed support for double precision recently, the Intel MKL has still room for improvement [17].

2.2.4.2 Message Passing Domain

MPI is an other example of a *de facto* standard in a message passing library used in parallel computing on distributed memory computers [8]. This library is extensively used on massively parallel computers. The basic primitive allows one to *send* and *receive* data from other processors.

The MPI effort began in 1991, and the 1.0 version was released in 1994.

At this time many different libraries were in competition. We can cite PVM [9] and PPCM [2] but MPI has emerged as the standard.

A parallel hardware vendor should provide an optimized version of MPI on his machine using hardware specificities: no copy on shared memory processors, routing optimization on network topologies, *etc.*

2.2.4.3 Graphical Libraries

In a graphical library domain, multiple libraries exist. We give only one example on the OpenGL graphical library. This is a library used to do graphical rendering from mobile phones up to supercomputers.

Like MPI OpenGL is defined as an API used to program a rendering pipeline for graphical application.

---

[3]http://publib.boulder.ibm.com/clresctr/windows/public/esslbooks.html

- MESA3D is a portable OpenGL implementation [4]. This implementation is included in most free Linux distribution as three-dimensional image rendering.

- Each graphical card hardware vendor provides an accelerated implementation such as NVIDIA [5] or AMD.

2.2.4.4   Other Domains

As shown in Figure 2.1, the first block "application domain" has evolved a lot. Let us show two new application domains where libraries and implementations are not as stable as the previous domain:

Communication 4G (3GPP LTE)   In telecommunication, the 4G is the fourth generation of cellular wireless standards. This set of protocols needs a lot of computing power in various optimization modes.

If the terminal should be optimized with power consumption in mind, the base station should be optimized with bandwidth capabilities in mind.

Image Multimedia

- OpenCV[6], an open source toolbox for image processing. The library includes a wide range of algorithms from histogram to machine learning.

- GpuCV[7] is a port of OpenCV for GPU to accelerate some algorithms and is retro-compatible with OpenCV.

It is hard to predict how many times these kinds of libraries will need

1. to converge to a common API

2. to be ported on a new platform

3. and to have peak performances on this new platform

These last two points are very difficult to track because they need to integrate hardware specificities deeply into an application. It could be as complex as modifying a compiler or worse to modifying the computation model (from sequential to parallel or from shared memory to common, ...).

These observations lead to the necessity to build tools which allow use of all hardware specificity, without diving into the "semantical bottleneck" of a programming language.

Our goal is not to compete and replace native compilers but to improve possibilities in run-time adaptation, using hardware instruction set specificities.

---

[4] http://www.mesa3d.org
[5] http://developer.nvidia.com/opengl-driver
[6] http://opencvlibrary.sourceforge.net/
[7] http://picoforge.int-evry.fr/projects/gpucv

2.3 `deGoal` Code Generator Generator

Based on the previously described observations, we propose a new tool called `deGoal` which helps to build *compilettes* code generators. A *compilette* is a small code generator included in applications which allows generation at run time of efficient code based on run-time information.

The global scheme is shown in Figure 2.3. This figure shows the classical flow from an idea to an algorithm which implements this idea, then a program in a specific language and the classical compilation flow up to the runnable code.

A classic strategy called iterative compilation [1] is shown at the bottom of Figure 2.3. Based on the profile information gathered on one dataset, the compiler optimizes the code on this profile. This is a very efficient process but it cannot be used at run-time because it needs a full compiler which is either too slow and difficult to use in some contexts such as in embedded systems. This is why iterative compilation is not used.

In the lower part of the figure is described a *compilette* which acts at run time based on information given by the user. It needs an inspection of the algorithm to select which optimization is the most efficient to implement at run-time. But when in use, the code generation is fast enough to allow code generation just before a function call. The iterative loop on the right is short enough to be run during application execution.

Of course, writing this kind of code generator is complicated without support and unfortunately there are not many tools allowing generation of binary code at run-time.

In the following sections we will describe the main characteristics of the `deGoal` tool which was actually developed in order to ease the development of such a code generator and to aid experimentation in code generation and optimization.

2.3.1 Neutral but Rich Instruction Set

Like LLVM, `deGoal` uses a neutral RISC instruction set which allows one to write applications at assembly level but without being specific to only one architecture. Our goal is to go further than LLVM with a richer instruction set focused on a vectorial and multimedia instruction set and allow the specialization of code with data set characteristics.

Our instruction set contains the following characteristics :

classical arithmetic instructions (`add`, `sub`, `mul`, `div`) but also instructions specific to a multimedia domain such as `sad` (sum of absolute differences), `mma` (matrix multiply and add) and FFT butterfly.

These instructions work on a register of variable length.

load and store with stride description which permits one to describe `load` and `store` operations for complex memory access patterns.

variable length register set the instruction set uses a virtual vectorial register with variable width and variable number of elements, *i.e.* the programmer could use

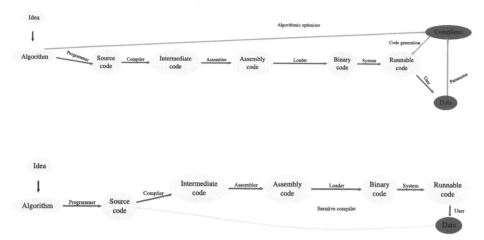

Figure 2.3: Dynamic compilation (on top) versus iterative optimization (below)

`VectorType f float 64 8` which allows them to use any `f` register as a vector of 8 elements of 64 bits floating point values.

Supported data types are integer, floating point and complex numbers. Supported arithmetics are signed, unsigned, saturated.

Thanks to this high level instruction set `deGoal` can generate corresponding instructions for processors which have native support or generate optimized code for processors without support. In both cases code generation is fast and produces efficient code.

This allows one to write multimedia kernels easily at assembly level but with the feature of a mix of run-time data information (values, alignments, data size, *etc.*) and assembly code.

2.3.2   Assembly and Expressions Interleaving

Thanks to the run-time code generation scheme, `deGoal` can easily take advantage of run-time data information to produce efficient code.

1. An expression or a C variable included in the instruction flow will be included in the binary generated code and become a constant. For example in the following instruction declaration:

   ```
   mul in0, in0, #(multiplyValue)
   ```

   `multiplyValue` is a variable of the embedded program, its value is only known at run-time.

2. This scheme can also be used to drive register usage. The following instruction:

```
        case '*': --Top;
#[ mul a(Top), a(Top), a(Top+1) ]# break;
```

uses the a virtual register file as a stack. The C variable Top contains a value containing the number of the first available register.

2.3.3 Small Example

The following small example will explain some of the main capabilities of deGoal. Let us imagine that we want to specialize a running code which does a multiplication between two numbers. This function could be written as:

```
int multiplyFunc_classical(int a, int b)
{
   return a*b;
}
```

A classical code optimization is called *code specialization*. It is often implemented by removing a function argument and replacing this argument by a constant value.

We can do *code specialization* on the previous function by replacing the integer argument b by the constant value 42 :

```
int multiplyFunc_static(int i)
{
   return i*42;
}
```

This type of optimization is a classical optimization usually done in the embedded domain where a lot of "constant" values have to be embedded in an application.

The expected effect of this optimization is to give a simpler code to the compiler, and expect that it will generate a better code. This optimization is unable to take into account a run-time value.

The following code is a minimalist *compilette* example. This function will produce a code buffer containing an executable specialized function. The "constant" value is only known at run-time and can even change during the execution of the program.

```
 1  #include <stdio.h> /* -*- c -*- */
 2
 3  typedef int (*pifi)(int);
 4
 5  pifi multiplyCompile(int multiplyValue)
 6  {
 7     cdgInsnT *code= CDGALLOC(1024);
 8     printf("Code gen. for value %d code at %p\n",
 9             multiplyValue, code);
10     #[
```

```
11      Begin code Prelude
12      VectorType in int 32 1
13      RegAlloc in 1
14      Arg in0
15      mul in0, in0, #(multiplyValue)
16      rtn
17      End
18    ]#;
19    return (pifi)code;
20 }
```

The description of this *compilette* uses our deGoal programming language. The explanation of the lines are :

10 and 18 are the markers which delimit the code to be produced. All included lines will be generated for a further execution, all excluded line will be executed as a normal C code.

11 is the Begin of the generated code. code is the name of the memory buffer, and Prelude indicates that a full function has to be generated (take care of the context, calling parameters, *etc.*).

12 VectorType defines in as a "register type" using integer arithmetic, 32 bits width and only 1 register element. All subsequent operations on an in register will use the predefined semantics.

13 Allocate 1 in register

15 is the operation that will be dynamically generated. in0 contains the input parameter and will be multiplied by a "constant" value contained in the multiply-Value variable.

Again this example is just a tutorial sample, we do not expect to optimize so simple an example.

2.3.4 Instructions Meta Information and Fast Code Generation

Previous work in this domain with code generators such as ccg [14] or HPBCG [15] was difficult because a lot of effort required to be done to extract information from databooks.

For example the ARM instruction set contains four distinct ISA (8 bits jazelle, thumb 16 bits, ARM 32bits and NEON extension). Each of them contains encoding variants (4 for the THUMB, 3 for ARM, *etc.*).

deGoal has automated instruction set architecture (ISA) extraction from PDF databooks. Each databook has an ISA extractor which extracts the instruction encoding and classifies the instruction into a category.

The following encoding is automatically extracted from the ISA ARM databook :

```
0010100 i1_22-22 r2_4 r1_4 i1_11-0 | i_1_32 add r1,r2,i1
```

The left part contains the binary instruction encoding, the right part the assembly description and a description of the data type used (`i_1_32`) which mean "Integer, 1x32 bits value".

From this compact description an automated tool can automatically generate macro instructions allowing us to produce binary code very efficiently (around 30 clock cycles per instruction).

2.3.5 Current Status

At the time of writing `deGoal` is able to generate binary code for multiple targets :

ARM we support all instruction set variants of the ARM platform (Thumb, ARM32, NEON, ...)

xp70 which is an embedded processor included in the ST P2012 platform

NVIDIA accelerator is supported. Unfortunately the programming model of this platform obliges us to generate only textual assembly code which is dynamically translated to binary code by the NVIDIA driver.

This programming model kills the code generation performances because we have to generate a textual representation of the PTX code which is tranlated by the driver. However, as will be shown in the following section, we are able to reach good code performance and add more flexibility in data type management.

We have ongoing work to port `deGoal` to more architectures, mainly on embedded processors, but also on processors used in HPC domain.

2.4 Experimentations

In this section we explain the experimentations we carried out on the NVIDIA GPU.

2.4.1 Experimental Compilette

In this section, we will show the result of the specialization of a matrix-matrix multiplication algorithm for GPU : through code specialization, it is possible to: 1) get an increase in performance, and 2) gain in flexibility.

This part assumes that the reader is already familiar with the CUDA programming model [3].

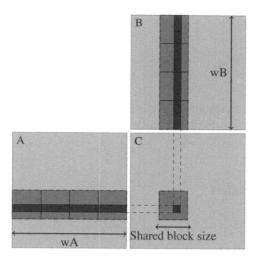

Figure 2.4: Matrix multiplication using shared memory. To run the algorithm, we map
each element in C to a thread, each thread will work with a shared memory
of n elements (shared block size × shared block size) in cooperation with
n threads. Each thread in a group loads one element from A and B into the
shared memory, uses the required elements in the shared memory (orange
areas), and repeats the operation on a new block until all requirements are
processed

2.4.1.1   Reference Implementation

The reference implementation taken is the matrix-matrix multiplication that can be
found as an example at the Nvidia website [8]. This implementation is not the most
optimized version that can be found, but the purpose here is to show how an algorithm can benefit from run-time code generation to increase its flexibility in data type
management and performances.

The matrix multiplication is done in this way:

1. The matrix is divided into blocks of 16×16 or 32×32 elements (those sizes
   correspond to hardware constraints). This size corresponds to the amount of
   shared memory that will be used.

2. For each relevant block, each thread will load one element from A and one from
   B (yellow blocks in Figure 2.4) and move it into the shared memory.

3. The matrix multiplication is performed using elements in the shared memory
   and the results are stored into an accumulator (one register per thread).

4. The operation is repeated until all blocks are processed.

---

[8]http://developer.nvidia.com/cuda-cc-sdk-code-samples

5. The result is stored into the main memory.

Figure 2.4 illustrates the different steps.
As you might have observed:

- The algorithm relies on shared memory for which the size is statically fixed at compile time (matrix of 16×16 or 32×32 elements per sub-matrix). The reference implementation puts a #pragma to explicitly force the compiler to unroll the loop that iterates over the element of stored in the shared matrix.

- The matrix size is not known at compile time but only at run-time.

- The data type is fixed at compile time, so the algorithm has to be statically specialized for each data types.

2.4.1.2 deGoal Implementation

First of all, the *compilette* implementation that was made is strictly equivalent to the reference implementation in the sense that the *compilette* does not do any optimization that is doable in the reference implementation in the CUDA C code. But this does not include any opportunity that might have been missed by the NVCC compiler.

From Run-Time Value to Constant: when generating the code at run-time, the matrix size and the matrix values are known, as well as the device and the environment on which the algorithm is run. That information allows us to turn run-time values into constants such as offset computation, number of loops to perform.

The knowledge of the run-time environment during the compilation also allows some fine tuning for the algorithm. For instance, the size of the shared memory to be used can be efficiently chosen at this moment: older devices like the GeForce 8400M G (C.C. 1.1) do not have any shared memory on the chip. The shared memory can be used as the device has a 1.1 C.C. but this memory is mapped to the main memory, and so the use of this memory will slow down the application.

In our implementation, we propagate every value that became constant (such as matrix size dependent values, used shared data size, the number of iteration to perform ...). Also our implementation supports all CUDA supported data types, in other words, the data type is one parameter of the code generator functions. To summarize, our *compilette* is doing the following optimization:

- Constant propagation: many registers used in the static version became constants with the *compilette*. Constants are propagated so they can be used as immediate values, it also marginally reduces the number of required operations.

- Since the matrix size is known when the code is being generated, the number of outer loop iterations is also known (matrix side size divided by the shared matrix side size). A simple optimization is to add a counter that is increased by one at each turn and compare the counter to the number of loops to perform (that is an immediate value)

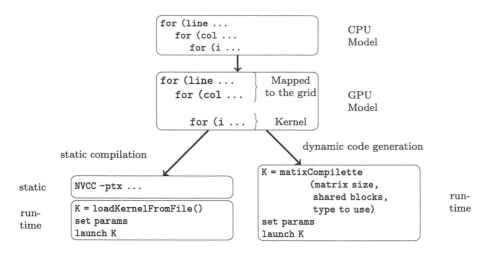

Figure 2.5: Illustration of the slight difference between the design of an algorithm for GPU in the classic way (involving static compilation) and the dynamic way (involving a *compilette* for dynamic code generation)

- The inner loop (the one that iterates over the element of the shared memory) is unrolled, like the static version and like classical optimization done by compilers.

Usage: Figure 2.5 illustrates the slight difference between the design of an algorithm for GPU. We start from the basic CPU design and rearrange it to map the CUDA model. The classic way involves a static compiler to produce a static file that will be loaded at run-time. The dynamic way involves a *compilette* that will dynamically generate the code at run-time using run-time information.

For example the following listing gives an extract example of the generated code (double precision version):

```
1   ../..
2   mov.u16 %loopNB0,0;
3   mov.f64 %DI0,0.;
4  loopStart:
5   add.u16 %loopNB0,%loopNB0,1;
6   ld.global.f64 %DI1,[%loc0];
7   st.shared.f64 [%loc7+0],%DI1;
8   ld.global.f64 %DI2,[%loc1];
9   st.shared.f64 [%loc8+0],%DI2;
10  bar.sync 0;
11  setp.lt.u16 %p,%loopNB0,32;
12  add.u64 %loc0,%loc0,128;
13  add.u64 %loc1,%loc1,65536;
```

```
14 | ld.shared.f64 %DI3,[%loc3+0];
15 | ld.shared.f64 %DI4,[%loc4+0];
16 | ld.shared.f64 %DI5,[%loc3+8];
17 | ld.shared.f64 %DI6,[%loc4+128];
18 | mad.rn.f64 %DI0,%DI3,%DI4,%DI0;
19 | ../..
```

line 5 and 11 show an example of loop "constant" inlining. Since we known the size of the matrix and the size of the shared memory used we are able determine in advance the value of the loop count.

line 11 we compare the counter to the immediate value

line 14 to 17 start the inner loop body (unrolled)

line 18 start to use multiply and add

2.4.1.3   Hardware and Software Setup

The experiments were done on two parallel bullx HPC systems from BULL.

In both cases, the HPC system is based on an Intel Xeon E5640 running at 2.67 Ghz and 2 Nvidia GPU cards described below.

The environment is the same for both HPC machines. Both machines are running a 2.6.18 Linux kernel, with the CUDA toolkit 4.0.17 and the Nvidia drivers 270.41.19.

Configuration 1 The HPC machine got two Nvidia M2050 GPU (Compute capability 2.0). The GPU count is 448 CUDA cores running at 1.15 Ghz and a memory bandwidth of 148 Gbits/s.

Configuration 2 The HPC machine got two Nvidia M2075 GPU (Compute capability 2.0). The GPU count is 448 CUDA cores running at 1.15 Ghz and a memory bandwidth of 150 Gbits/s

The applications were built with `gcc` 4.1.2 using the `-O3` option. The reference implementation was built using `nvcc` with the `-arch=sm_20` option and targeting PTX output.

The time measurements are expressed in clock cycle view from the CPU. More exactly, it is the time stamp counter, which is incremented at a constant rate of 2.6 GHz (20×133.33MHz to be precise) for both configurations.

2.4.1.4   Results

Experiment Procedure: Figures 2.6 and 2.7 show the speed up when using the *compilette* for signed 32 bits integer numbers and simple and double precision floating point numbers using the configuration 1. Figures 2.8 and 2.9 show the results when

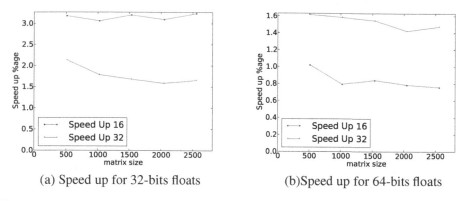

(a) Speed up for 32-bits floats   (b)Speed up for 64-bits floats

Figure 2.6: Matrix-Matrix multiplication execution results for simple and double precision floating point numbers for various matrix sizes (the size is the size of the matrix side, in number of elements) for Configuration 1. For simple precision number, the *compilette* achieves 188.3 GFlops when using 32×32 shared elements and 184.9 GFlops when using 16×16 shared elements. The static version achieves 185.3 and 179.1 GFlops respectively. For double precision, the *compilette* achieves 98.2 GFlops when using 32×32 shared elements and 96.4 GFlops when using 16×16 shared elements. The static version achieves 96.8 and 95.6 GFlops respectively

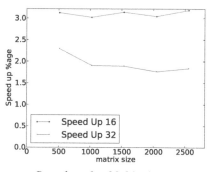

Speed up for 32-bits integers

Figure 2.7: Matrix-Matrix multiplication execution results for signed 32-bits integer numbers for various matrix sizes (the size is the size of the matrix side, in number of elements) for Configuration 1

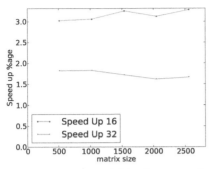 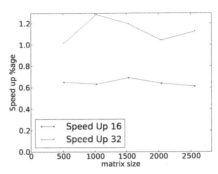

(a) Speed up for 32-bits floats number   (b) Speed up for 64-bits floats number

Figure 2.8: Matrix-Matrix multiplication execution results for simple and double precision floating point numbers for various matrix sizes (the size is the size of the matrix side, in number of elements) for Configuration 2. For simple precision number, the *compilette* achieves 188.3 GFlops when using 32×32 shared elements and 185 GFlops when using 16×16 shared elements. The static version achieves 185.3 and 179 GFlops respectively. For double precision, the *compilette* achieves 98 GFlops when using 32×32 shared elements and 96.1 GFlops when using 16×16 shared elements. The static version achieves 97 and 95.8 GFlops respectively

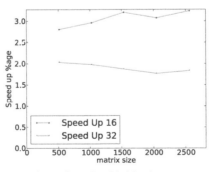

Speed up for 32-bits integers

Figure 2.9: Matrix-Matrix multiplication execution results for signed 32-bits integer numbers for various matrix sizes (the size is the size of the matrix side, in number of elements) for Configuration 2

using configuration 2. The abscissa represents the matrix side size and the ordinate the percentage of speed up.

Configuration 1:   the execution results are shown in Figures 2.6 and 2.7. The peak speed up is achieved for signed integer and single precision numbers with 3% of speed up, the worst speed up is at almost 0.7% for double precision numbers. Below are listed some timing results (in ms):

When using 16×16 shared memory:

Matrix size	int		float		double	
	static	*compilette*	static	*compilette*	static	*compilette*
512×512	1.54	1.49	1.54	1.49	2.86	2.83
1536×1536	40.51	39.28	40.50	39.25	75.90	75.27
2560×2560	187.36	181.57	187.33	181.45	351.54	348.91

When using 32×32 shared memory:

Matrix size	int		float		double	
	static	*compilette*	static	*compilette*	static	*compilette*
512×512	1.49	1.45	1.48	1.45	2.90	2.85
1536×1536	39.36	38.63	39.21	38.56	75.45	74.30
2560×2560	181.85	178.58	181.18	178.23	349.03	343.96

Configuration 2:   the execution results are shown in Figures 2.8 and 2.9. The peak speed up here is also achieved for signed integer and single precision numbers with a 3% of speed up, and a worst at almost 0.6% for double precision numbers. Below are listed some timing results (in ms):

When using 16×16 shared memory:

Matrix size	int		float		double	
	static	*compilette*	static	*compilette*	static	*compilette*
512×512	1.57	1.53	1.57	1.52	2.88	2.86
1536×1536	40.55	39.29	40.53	39.25	75.82	75.30
2560×2560	187.46	181.58	187.37	181.42	351.04	348.91

It is, indeed, not that high and may seem irrelevant at some points. The main reason for that is the lack of optimization opportunity that we have in these examples. But on the other hand, we gain in flexibility. Through the same function, we are able to produce GPU for different data types, different amounts of shared memory. Handling the different data types via static specialization can be done without too much effort (the

When using 32×32 shared memory:

Matrix size	int		float		double	
	static	*compilette*	static	*compilette*	static	*compilette*
512×512	1.51	1.48	1.50	1.48	2.92	2.89
1536×1536	39.37	38.65	39.23	38.57	75.40	74.51
2560×2560	181.90	178.62	181.25	178.28	347.97	344.10

reference version provided by Nvidia uses a template function that is statically specialized for the different data types). But handling efficiently different shared memory can be much more difficult since some tuning may be required of the data size (that is only known at run-time). It is also easier for the *compilette* to adapt to the current situation and for future devices. A cooperative thread block is limited to 512 threads for 1.x C.C. GPUs and 1024 thread for 2.0 C.C GPUs. But in the future, a block size may increase, a situation that easily can be handled with a *compilette*.

The execution time is the essentially the same between the two configurations. It is not surprising since the two cards have the same computation power. They differ from each other by the bandwidth size and the total available RAM (3 GB for the M2050 and 6 GB for the M2075). Differences are not very great, and the unoptimized configuration presented here does not allow the algorithm to use the full bandwidth of the bus.

2.4.2   Scilab Integration

SCILAB does not do computations by itself, but is based on a linear algebra library such as Netlib BLAS, ATLAS or CUBLAS.

Our goal in the H4H project is to replace the basic call to the matrix and vector basic operator by the call to a *compilette* generated version.

As the *compilette* has generated the code for one given matrix size, the specialized code could be reused for any matrix operation on argument of the same size, which occur frequently in matrix computation.

2.5   Related Works

Some tools are related to our work but with different approaches.

2.5.1   HMPP

HMPP is a tool developed by Caps Enterprise http://www.caps-entreprise.com/. This tool allow a programmer to port his code on GPU accelerators by inserting pragmas in his code.

HMPP is then in charge to

- separate code to be compiled on the CPU and the code for the GPU

- generate the "glue" code which will handle data transfers between CPU and GPU memories

This powerful tool is able to handle coarse grain parallelism level and work at static compile time. It also allows the programmer to stay with the same CPU programming paradigm.

Our approach is able to handle fine grain parallelism, instruction level parallelism, SIMD and multimedia instruction set, data specialization at run-time.

2.5.2   Scilab

SCILAB is an open source, cross-platform numerical computational package and a high-level, numerically oriented programming language. It is developed by SCILAB Consortium.

This is a high level programming language which is based on low level libraries like BLAS. It knows how to use the most efficient library version on a given platform.

We are working with them in the H4H project context.

2.5.3   LLVM

LLVM (Low Level Virtual Machine)[9] is compilation framework that can target lots of architecture, including X86, ARM or PTX. One of its advantages is the unified internal representation (LLVM IR) that encodes a virtual low level instruction with some high level information embedded on it. Various tools were build on top of it, starting with Clang which is the C/C++/Objective-C compiler.

Another great advantage of this library is its infrastructure, entirely written in C++ and well engineered which makes it a good research and industrial tool for building compilers.

Many industrial projects are now based on this technology such as the following projects.

2.5.3.1   GCD Grand Central Dispatch

Grand central dispatch (GCD) is a way to dispatch tasks in multi-core applications. It implements task parallelism based on thread pool pattern. It is developed by Apple and has been integrated into other operating systems like FreeBSD.

It is not directly related to our technology, except by the fact that tasks are dynamically affected to thread, based upon the availability of a thread in the pool.

2.5.3.2   Nvidia Compiler

With the release of the CUDA toolkit 4.1, Nvidia open sourced a part of its static compiler (NVCC). The new compiler based on LLVM can only target PTX code, but

---

[9]http://llvm.org/

by this method, applications get better performance (better code generation) compared to the older version of NVCC. Also domain specific language can more easily support code generation for Nvidia GPUs.

2.5.4 Ocelot

Ocelot[10] is a project that aims to use PTX code and run it on various heterogeneous targets without having to rebuild the code [5]. The Ocelot can run PTX code on Nvidia GPUs of course but also on AMD GPUs, and on x86 (using the LLVM tool chain) by dynamically compiling the PTX code for the targeted architecture. It also includes an emulation module for PTX debugging.

It does code translation from PTX but does not implement any kernel computation.

2.5.5 Scipy

Scipy[11] is an open source library for Python. The aim is to provide high performance tools for scientific applications in Python. Scipy is close to Scilab and Matlab in the sense that it tries to aim as closely as they behave but in Python.

The library relies on BLAS operations to get high performances (the BLAS library version to use can be choosen). And like Scilab, the right function to call is selected at run-time.

2.6 Conclusion

In this chapter we have shown that some programming situations cannot be correctly handled by classical static compilers.

Our *compilette* technology has shown to be both efficient in performance and more flexible than the classical code :

Performance: we are able to generate code for a matrix multiplication as fast as a classical compiler implementation. It is not a faster implementation, but neither is it so naive.

We did not pretend in this experimentation to compete with highly optimized versions such as ATLAS or CUBLAS [11] which achieve near optimal performance.

In this chapter we have focussed on the matrix multiplication algorithm, but this is only an example of a library that is easily generated and adapted to the run-time context using our `deGoal` tool.

Flexibility: our implementation is able to adapt itself at run-time to different data parameter (matrix size and matrix data type) and to harwdare parameters.

---

[10]`http://code.google.com/p/gpuocelot/`
[11]`http://www.scipy.org/`

We are able to quickly generate a multitude of code variants depending on data type (integer, floating point) and data size, which is not possible to do with a classical compilation chain.

Our `deGoal` infrastructure can be used in the context of high performance computing (HPC) where performance and flexibility is the only metric and in the context of embedded systems where performances and flexibility are important as well as memory footprint and power consumption.

This infrastructure will be available soon on the web site `http://degoal.org`[12].

We are working on the integration of our first *compilette* version in SCILAB and compute the speedups with this integration, then we will continue to implement more optimization in order to compete with reference implementations such as `cuBlas`.

References

[1] M. Barreteau, F. Bodin, Z. Chamski, H.P. Charles, C. Eisenbeis, J.R. Gurd, J. Hoogerbrugge, P. Hu, W. Jalby, T. Kisuki, P.M.W. Knijnenburg, P. van der Mark, A. Nisbet, M.F.P. O'Boyle, E. Rohou, A. Seznec, E. Stohr, M. Treffers, H.A.G. Wijshoff, "OCEANS - Optimising Compilers for Embedded Applications", in *European Conference on Parallel Processing*, pages 1171–1175, 1999. `citeseer.ist.psu.edu/article/barreteau98oceans.html`

[2] H.P. Charles, O. Baby, A. Fouilloux, S. Miguet, L. Perroton, Y. Robert, S. Ubeda, "PPCM: A Portable Parallel Communication Module", Rapport Technique 92-04, Laboratoire de l'Informatique du Paralllisme, June 1992.

[3] *Cuda programmin guide*, NVIDIA Corporation, 2007.

[4] *The CUDA Compiler Driver NVCC*, Ver 4.1, NVIDIA Corporation, Oct. 2011,

[5] G.F. Diamos, A.R. Kerr, S. Yalamanchili, N. Clark, "Ocelot: a dynamic optimization framework for bulk-synchronous applications in heterogeneous systems", in *Proceedings of the 19th international conference on Parallel architectures and compilation techniques*, PACT '10, 353–364, ACM, New York, NY, USA, 2010. doi:10.1145/1854273.1854318

[6] R. Dolbeau, S. Bihan, F. Bodin, "HMPP: A hybrid multi-core parallel programming environment", in *Workshop on General Purpose Processing on Graphics Processing Units (GPGPU 2007)*, 2007.

[7] J.J. Dongarra, E. Grosse, "Distribution of mathematical software via electronic mail", *Commun. ACM*, 30: 403–407, May 1987. doi:10.1145/22899.22904

[8] E. Gabriel, G.E. Fagg, G. Bosilca, T. Angskun, J.J. Dongarra, J.M. Squyres, V. Sahay, P. Kambadur, B. Barrett, A. Lumsdaine, R.H. Castain, D.J. Daniel, R.L. Graham, T.S. Woodall, "Open MPI: Goals, Concept, and Design of a Next Generation MPI Implementation", in *Proceedings, 11th European PVM/MPI Users' Group Meeting*, 97–104, Budapest, Hungary, September 2004.

---

[12]This infrastructure contains the tools and code samples, but not the more complex matrix multiply implementation.

[9] A. Geist, *PVM: Parallel virtual machine: a users' guide and tutorial for networked parallel computing*, The MIT Press, 1994.

[10] Khronos OpenCL Working Group and others, "The opencl specification", *A. Munshi, Ed*, 2008. `http://www.khronos.org/opencl`

[11] J. Kurzak, S. Tomov, "Autotunning GEMMs for Fermi", *IEEE transation on parallel and distributed Systems*, 2011.

[12] *Parallel Thread Execution Isa Version 3.0*, NVIDIA Corporation, 2011.

[13] *CUBLAS Library*, NVIDIA Corporation, 2008.

[14] I. Piumarta, F. Ogel, B. Folliot, "Ynvm: dynamic compilation in support of software evolution", 2001. `citeseer.ist.psu.edu/piumarta01ynvm.html`

[15] K. Sajjad, *Porting Different Compilation phases to Runtime*, PhD thesis, Université de Versailles Saint-Quentin-en-Yvelines, 2011.

[16] R.C. Whaley, J. Dongarra, "Automatically Tuned Linear Algebra Software", in *SuperComputing 1998: High Performance Networking and Computing*, 1998. `http://www.cs.utsa.edu/~whaley/papers/atlas_sc98.ps`

[17] S. Zuckerman, M. Pérache, W. Jalby, "Fine Tuning Matrix Multiplications on Multicore", in P. Sadayappan, M. Parashar, R. Badrinath, V. Prasanna (Editors), *High Performance Computing - HiPC 2008*, LNCS, 5374, 30–41, Springer, Berlin / Heidelberg, 2008. doi:10.1007/978-3-540-89894-8_7

©Saxe-Coburg Publications, 2014.
F. Magoulès, (Editor),
Patterns for Parallel Programming on GPUs
Saxe-Coburg Publications, Stirlingshire, Scotland, 57-71.

Chapter 3

High Level GPGPU Programming with Parallel Skeletons

M. Bourgoin, E. Chailloux and J.-L. Lamotte

Laboratoire d'Informatique de Paris 6 (LIP6 - UMR 7606)
Université Pierre et Marie Curie (UPMC - Paris 6)
Sorbonne Universités
Paris, France

Abstract

General purpose GPU programming implies associating highly parallel graphical computing units with classic CPUs to achieve great performance on applications commonly handled by CPU only. This hybrid system leads to complex programming designs combining multiple paradigms to manage each hardware architecture (CPU and GPGPU devices). In this chapter, we present how parallel skeletons can help tackle this challenge by abstracting some of these programming designs while automatizing optimizations. Through a simple example using the OCaml programming language to develop and compose skeletons, we will present how simple modifications to use parallel skeletons can ease GPGPU programming while offering performance speedups.

Keywords: GPGPU, parallel skeletons, OCaml, parallel abstractions, design patterns.

3.1 Introduction

General purpose GPU (GPGPU) programming is a highly parallel programming field. In the past decades, many programmers have handled previous parallel architectures with programming recipes known as design patterns as well as with abstract programming constructs known as parallel skeletons. GPGPU programmers are currently mainly using low-level tools and frameworks to harness the numerous cores of their hardware. We used a high level programming language to develop parallel skeletons providing high-level abstractions to help harness GPGPU programming. While offering abstraction over current low-level APIs we also focused on providing a highly efficient solution. This leads us to use a library binding external kernels with the managing program. It allows us to develop highly optimized external kernels while benefitting from the high-level abstractions to simplify programming as well as improving software safety (particularly type and memory safety).

Our programming language will be OCaml. We developed the SPOC library to manage GPGPU devices and memory transfers as described in Section 3.2. We will present some parallel skeletons developed for GPGPU programming in Section 3.3. Then, we will show in Section 3.4 how we can compose those skeletons to achieve better abstraction while allowing automatic optimizations. The modifications (from OCaml programs already using the SPOC library) needed to use parallel skeletons, and compositions, will be presented through a simple example throughout this chapter as well as performance results obtained with those modifications. We then present other approaches around skeletons for GPGPU programming in Section 3.5 before concluding remarks on our approach and presenting our future work in Section 3.6.

3.2   OCaml and SPOC

Our main motivation is to offer high level abstractions to help harnessing GPGPU programming. Parallel programming, and GPGPU programming in particular, is very complex and it is now common to use high level programming languages to compose optimized parallel (or GPGPU) computations. This allows the use of high expressivity of high level languages to describe a complex algorithm while benefitting from those language features to reduce complex hardware and system management. For our work, we looked for a language with specific criteria:

- being able to manage GPGPU programming though Cuda and OpenCL C/C++ libraries,

- providing an automatic memory manager with a garbage collector to reduce complex and error-prone explicit memory management,

- featuring multiple programming paradigms such as the imperative paradigm to describe the linear structure used for CPU/GPGPU communications easily and also the functional paradigm to increase expressivity and simplify composition,

- increasing type safety and productivity through strong and static type checking,

- easily extensible through macros or preprocessor customization to allow the introduction of specific extensions dedicated to GPGPU programming.

We chose the OCaml language, with the SPOC library to manage GPGPU programming. OCaml (and the ML language family) has already been used for various experiments in parallel programming such as BSML [1] for data-parallelism or OCamlP3L

[2] for parallel programming skeletons. Functional programming languages, such as OCaml [3] or Microsoft's F# [4] (highly based on OCaml), can help describe and implement numerical computations [5].

3.2.1   OCaml

OCaml [6] is a general purpose high-level programming language developed at Inria. It has been designed with safety, reliability and expressivity in mind. It is a multiparadigm language supporting functional, imperative, modular and object oriented programming styles. It is strongly and statically typed. It offers automatic memory management with a fast incremental garbage collector (GC). This garbage collector is multigenerational and consists of a fast Stop&Copy algorithm associated with an incremental Mark&Sweep&Compact algorithm ensuring memory safety (memory leaks, dangling/wild pointers) while automatically limiting memory occupancy. Inria's OCaml distribution proposes two kinds of compilers. Ones that compile OCaml code to portable bytecode (compatible OCaml virtual machines exist for many architectures) while others compile to efficient native code for many architectures. OCaml also features a foreign function interface (FFI) which allows easy interoperability with C code.

SPOC is an OCaml library managing GPGPU devices and memory that allows developers to run GPGPU computations. It benefits particularly from several features of OCaml. First, being a library binding OCaml with C APIs from the Cuda and OpenCL frameworks, it relies heavily on OCaml FFI. SPOC focuses on GPGPU, as well as on high performance, making mandatory the use of an efficient programming language for sequential computations. The OCaml native compilers offer such high sequential performance for the OCaml language. Besides, SPOC aims at simplifying GPGPU programming while increasing software reliability and productivity. OCaml type-safety associated with its memory manager improve reliability by detecting common programming errors at compile time. We will present in Section 3.2.3 how SPOC benefits directly from the OCaml memory manager for GPGPU programming. Lastly, OCaml multiple paradigms offer a great basis to experiment on high level abstractions for GPGPU programming, allowing SPOC to be a starting point for further abstractions as we will present in Section 3.3.

3.2.2   GPGPU Programming

GPGPU programming consists of managing specific devices (GPGPU devices) to handle general computations. Mainly two frameworks are used: Cuda and OpenCL. Both provide languages (mainly C/C++ extensions) to write programs (called kernels) which will run on GPGPU devices. They also feature low-level APIs to manage kernels and data-transfers between CPUs and GPGPU devices.

Frameworks   Cuda and OpenCL are very similar but incompatible. Data transferred via OpenCL APIs cannot be used by Cuda kernels, and *vice versa*. Furthermore, some devices might be incompatible with one of the two frameworks. With Cuda being proprietary, only NVIDIA devices can directly use it (some third party tools (Swan [7], CU2CL [8], ...) automatically translate Cuda code to C or OpenCL). However, many tools and a library have been developed for Cuda, which can greatly improve productivity. Most hardware vendors currently provide an OpenCL implementation for their GPGPU devices which makes it a better choice for portability although providing efficient programs for multiple GPGPU architectures can imply many modifications for each architecture. Having two incompatible frameworks makes achieving high performance with great portability very difficult.

Kernels   To write kernels, both frameworks provide C/C++ extensions. However, GPGPU are highly parallel architectures which demand specific programming models. Both frameworks are based on the Stream Processing paradigm which defines GPGPU devices as multiprocessors, each consisting of many computation units. It then simplifies the parallelism description by restricting computations to the application of a given kernel to each element of a data set (the stream). Actually, each hardware computation unit will compute the kernel on one element of the data stream in parallel. Both frameworks demand describing computations as a grid containing blocks of computation units which will compute the kernel. When launching a kernel they map this description to the GPGPU multiprocessors, automatically optimizing block mapping to enhance multiprocessor occupancy and maximize parallelism. Mapping kernels on grids with more blocks than actual GPGPU multiprocessors induces some multiprocessors to run the kernel multiple times. By contrast, mapping fewer blocks reduces occupancy and so limits performance.

Transfers   Combining heterogeneous architectures (CPU and GPGPU devices) implies transferring data from the CPU memory to GPGPU's. GPGPU devices are commonly seen as discrete guests with dedicated memory linked to their CPU host through a PCI-E interface. This interface provides a limited bandwidth compared to the GPGPU memory bandwidth (see Table 3.1). This implies slow transfers which thus become as important as kernel optimization to achieve high performance.

	Bandwidth(GB/s)	speedup/PCI-E 2.0	speedup/PCI-E 3.0
PCI-E (one way)2.0	8	1	0.5
PCI-E (one way)3.0	16	2	1
CPU Intel i7-3930K	51.2	6.4	3.2
CPU AMD FX-8150	21	2.6	1.3
GPU NVIDIA GTX-580	192.4	24	12
GPU Radeon HD 7970	264	33	16.5

Table 3.1: Theoretical memory bandwidth

3.2.3 SPOC

SPOC [9] is an OCaml library allowing GPGPU programming with the OCaml language. It consists of an OCaml extension with a runtime library. The extension allows the declaration of external GPGPU kernels usable within an OCaml program, while the library offers functions to manage those kernels as well as the data needed to run them. External kernels must be written in Cuda assembly (ptx) or in OpenCL C99 programming language (of course it is possible to generate Cuda assembly from Cuda C/C++ with Cuda compilers).

SPOC offers some abstraction over both Cuda and OpenCL frameworks by unifying those frameworks into one library. This eases portability and simplifies the use of very heterogeneous architectures. SPOC also allows the use of multiple GPGPU devices (from both frameworks) in parallel.

Furthermore, SPOC abstracts memory transfers with special data sets (vectors) which are automatically transferred where they are needed.

Frameworks As multiple frameworks exist for GPGPU programming, it can be difficult to achieve portability as well as efficiency. SPOC looks for any device compatible with the Cuda or OpenCL framework during initialization and makes them usable by the OCaml program. It also unifies both frameworks specifying its behavior during runtime depending on the device being used and the framework corresponding to this device. This allows SPOC programs to run on multiple GPGPU architectures and to use multiple GPGPU devices managed conjointly by both incompatible frameworks.

Kernels SPOC allows the use of external kernels written in Cuda assembly (ptx) or C for OpenCL. It offers an OCaml extension to declare those external kernels in a similar way to an OCaml external C functions declaration. This extension enables type-checking of kernel arguments at compile-time reducing risks of any hard-to-debug error during runtime. Figure 3.1 shows a simple OpenCL kernel and how to use it through SPOC. The OpenCL kernel, *vec_add*, takes three vectors (*__global float **) stored in the GPGPU global memory as parameters, as well as an integer representing the size of the vectors to add. With this kernel, each computations unit (id is obtained through *get_global_id(0)*) will compute the addition over one element of each vector. The OCaml code allows one to use such an external kernel within an OCaml program. It consists of the declaration of the name of the kernel (as it will be used later by the OCaml program) followed by its type and two strings. The type of a kernel consists of the types of its parameters and its return type (GPGPU kernels work through a side effect so the return type should always be the OCaml *unit* type)). The two strings are the name of the file containing the kernel (without extension to allow SPOC to search automatically for a Cuda or OpenCL file depending on the device used to run the kernel) associated with the name of the function corresponding to the kernel. Here we can see that the parameter types must be translated, to be compatible with SPOC and OCaml, from *__global float** to *Spoc.Vector.float32*.

Transfers As presented in Section 3.2.2, GPGPU programming implies memory transfers between a CPU host and GPGPU guests. Both GPGPU frameworks offer explicit transfers through low-level APIs. Besides, to achieve high performance for complex programs, it is mandatory to optimize transfer scheduling. Two main optimizations exist: the simplest one is to reduce transfers to limit the overhead they induce, the second one is to overlap transfers with computation using asynchronous transfers. SPOC uses OCaml memory manager to reduce the number of transfers by transferring data only when it is needed. To do so, SPOC introduces a type of data-set called *vectors*. At runtime, when accessing a vector (by the CPU or during a kernel launch), SPOC checks the vector current location and moves it if needed. Vectors are managed by the OCaml memory manager. It offers automatic allocation and deallocation on the CPU, as well as on GPU memory banks. This relieves programmers from memory transfers managment which is a complex part of GPGPU programming with low-level APIs.

3.2.4   A Small Example

Using the kernel declared in Section 3.2.3, it is now possible to use it directly from OCaml. The example in Figure 3.2 presents a complete program adding two vectors using this kernel. This figure shows how vectors are automatically transferred between host and guest.

SPOC must first be initialized to enable access to all the devices compatible with Cuda or OpenCL on the system (line 4). Then, it is possible to declare vectors which are automatically allocated on CPU memory by the OCaml memory manager (lines 6-8). Those vectors remain on CPU memory while they are not used by a GPGPU kernel. To launch a kernel it is necessary to describe blocks and grid mapping which will be used to map the kernel to the GPGPU multiprocessors (lines 13-18). Here the grid

```
1   __kernel void vec_add(__global const float * a,
2                         __global const float * b,
3                         __global float * c, int vector_size)
4   {
5       int nIndex = get_global_id(0);
6       if (nIndex < N)
7           c[nIndex] = a[nIndex] + b[nIndex];
8   }
```

OpenCL code

```
1   kernel vector_add :
2   Spoc.Vector.vfloat32 -> Spoc.Vector.vfloat32 -> Spoc.Vector.vfloat32 ->
3   int -> unit = "kernel_file" "vec_add"
```

SPOC kernel declaration

Figure 3.1: SPOC kernel extension

		Vector location		
		a	**b**	**c**
1	`let example () =`			
2	`(* SPOC Initialization *)`			
3	`(* returns an array containing every compatible devices *)`	CPU		
4	`let devs = Spoc.Devices.init () in`			
5	`(* vectors declaration *)`			
6	`let a = Spoc.Vector.create Spoc.Vector.float32 1024`			
7	`and b = Spoc.Vector.create Spoc.Vector.float32 1024`	CPU	CPU	
8	`and c = Spoc.Vector.create Spoc.Vector.float32 1024`			
9	`in`			
10	`(* vectors are filled with random values *)`	CPU	CPU	CPU
11	`fill_vectors [a; b; c];`			
12	`(* block and grid mapping description *)`			
13	`let blk = {Spoc.Kernel.blockX = 256;`			
14	`Spoc.Kernel.blockY = 1;`			
15	`Spoc.Kernel.blockZ = 1;}`	CPU	CPU	CPU
16	`and grd = {Spoc.Kernel.gridX = 4;`			
17	`Spoc.Kernel.gridY = 1;`			
18	`Spoc.Kernel.gridZ = 1;}`			
19	`in`			
20	`(* the kernel is run the first device*)`	**GPU**	**GPU**	**GPU**
21	`Spoc.Kernel.run devs.(0)(blk,grd) vector_add (a, b, c, 1024);`			
22	`(* results are printed*)`			
23	`for i = 0 to 1023 do`	**GPU**	**GPU**	CPU
24	`Printf.printf "%g\n" (c.[<i>])`			
25	`done ;;`			

Figure 3.2: Simple example with dynamic transfers

and blocks are declared in order to dedicate one thread for each element to compute, using 256 threads for each block. When a kernel is launched (line 21), every vector needed by this kernel is automatically transferred to the device running the kernel. When a vector is reused by the CPU (here to print the result of the computation) (lines 23 to 25), it is automatically transferred back to CPU memory. Other vectors stay on guest memory to minimize transfers in case of future kernel computations. Thus, SPOC limits transfers by transferring vectors only when needed. Keeping vectors on guest memory can reduce its capacity. Being handled by the OCaml memory manager allows the OCaml garbage collector to free unused vectors on guest memory when possible.

Using OCaml and SPOC as a basis it is now feasible to offer more abstractions and automatic optimizations (such as automatic kernel mapping or memory transfers overlapping) to developers.

3.3   Design Patterns and Skeletons

To achieve great performance and productivity it is common to apply specific design patterns during development. Design patterns are programming recipes which present software designs answering specific design problems. They are parametrized and adapted for each software using them. Some specific parallel design patterns can be generalized to algorithmic constructs. Those constructs take advantage of common patterns to abstract the complexity of corresponding applications. Commonly used for distributed and parallel programming those pre-programmed parallel design patterns are called *skeletons* ([10], [11], [12]).

Using high-level features of OCaml, we propose using SPOC to build GPGPU skeletons simplifying software designs and offering automatic optimization of those skeletons. As presented in Section 3.2.3, SPOC only allows the use of external kernels; while allowing GPGPU programming from OCaml, this is not sufficient to express skeletons. The major issue comes from the fact that external kernels take parameters and modify those parameters through side effects. External kernel parameters do not explicitly exhibit input and output for each kernel computation. Input and output are mandatory to specify skeletons manipulating kernels and data automatically.

To solve this problem we introduced an *application* data structure associating:

- an externel kernel

- an execution environment (consisting of the kernel parameters)

- an input (included in the execution environment)

- an output (included in the execution environment)

Input and output have to be SPOC vectors which automatically can be transferred to and from GPGPU devices. We started by defining the two mostly used skeletons `Map` and `Reduce`.

- `Map` is a skeleton taking an application and a vector as parameters. It returns a vector. Each element of the returned vector is the application's kernel applied to the corresponding element of the input vector.

- `Reduce` also takes an application and a vector as parameters. Our `Reduce` returns a vector containing only one value. This value is computed by recursively combining elements of the input vector using the application's kernel to do the combination. Reduction is complex to parellelize, needing much synchronization between threads, and cannot benefit fully from all the computation units of GPGPU devices.

Those skeletons are programming constructs which have to be run on a target GPGPU device. To run those skeletons we provide two functions:

- *run* which runs the skeleton on one device

- *par_run* which tries to divide computation by running the skeleton on a list of target devices

3.3.1 Example

Figure 3.3 presents three versions (which will be detailed later) of a more complex example than in 3.2.4: the iteration loop of a power iteration algorithm (computing the largest eigen value of a given matrix). This algorithm is described by the iteration

$$b_{k+1} = \frac{A \times b_k}{||A \times b_k||}$$

At every iteration, the vector b_k is multiplied by the matrix A and normalized. These examples use three very simple kernels :

- *kernel_init* which computes the matrix-vector multiply

- *kernel_divide* which simply divides one data set by another

- *kernel_norm* which computes the norm of an input vector

Figure 3.4 presents the time spent for 10,000 iterations on different devices and the speedup compared to an OCaml program (using an external C program for sequential computation) for each version of the program. Version (a) uses only SPOC to manage kernels and data transfers. Here, it also computes the maximum of a vector sum using classic OCaml iterators. SPOC provides asynchronous kernel launch with both frameworks but only OpenCL transfers are asynchronous. Thus, the Tesla C2070 (using Cuda) provides lower performance than the AMD Radeon 6950 (using OpenCL) while they both offer the same level of theoretical performance. Using OpenCL with the NVIDIA Tesla provides lower performance than with Cuda which might be induced by specific optimizations coming from the Cuda compiler absent from the NVIDIA OpenCL compiler.

Using the two skeletons just presented it is now possible to rewrite this example. Version (b) (in Figure 3.3) presents this modification. Each kernel run is translated to a map skeleton run and each maximum computation to a Reduce skeleton. A major difference comes from the automatic description of blocks and grid mapping. The use of a Reduce skeleton also helps by limiting transfers. Using CPU iterators previously forced SPOC to transfer vectors back while the Reduce skeleton directly computes on the GPU.

Figure 3.4 (b) presents the time spent for 10,000 iterations on different devices and the speedups compared to an OCaml sequential computation as well as to previous results.

3.3.2 Benefits

Skeletons offer many benefits. Through them, developers can express their algorithm more easily as they explicitly describe relations between kernels and data. Furthermore, with those skeletons, SPOC can automatically optimize kernel mapping on GPGPU devices managing GPGPU thread blocks and grids to dynamically achieve the best results on the running hardware.

```
1   (**** OCaml program using the SPOC library ****)
2   open Kernel
3   ...
4
5   let block = {blockX = 256; blockY = 1; blockZ = 1;}
6   and grid = {gridX = (Vector.length vn) / 256; gridY = 1; gridZ = 1;}
7
8   while (!norm > eps && !iter < max_iter) do
9     incr iter;
10    maximum.[<0>] <- 0.;
11    run dev (block,grid) kernel_init (vn, v, a, n);
12      (* Tools.fold_left max 0. v recursively computes the *)
13      (* maximum of the vector v  (computes on CPU) *)
14    maximum.[<0>] <- Tools.fold_left max 0. vn;
15
16    run dev (block, grid) kernel_divide (vn, maximum, n);
17    run dev (block, grid) kernel_norm (vn, v, v_norm, n);
18
19    norm := Tools.fold_left max 0. v_norm;
20  done;
```

(a) Power Iteration

```
1   (**** Modifications to use skeletons ****)
2   open Compose
3   ...
4   while (!norm > eps && !iter < max_iter) do
5     incr iter;
6     maximum.[<0>] <- 0.;
7     vn := (run
8            (map kernel_init vn (vn, v, a, n )) dev vn);
9     maximum := (run
10            (reduce spoc_max maximum (vn, maximum,n)) dev vn);
11
12    vn := (run
13            (map kernel_divide vn (vn, maximum, n)) dev vn);
14    v_norm := (run
```

(b) Power Iteration with skeletons

```
1   (**** Modifications to use skeleton composition ****)
2   open Compose
3   ...
4   while (!norme > eps && !iter < max_iter) do
5     incr iter;
6     max := (run (pipe
7            (map k_init vn (vn, v, a, n ))
8            (reduce spoc_max max (vn, max,n))) dev vn);
9
10    norm := (run (pipe
11            (pipe
12              (map k_divide vn (vn, max, n))
13              (map k_norm v_norm (vn, v, v_norm, n)))
14            (reduce spoc_max max2 (v_norm!, max2, n))) dev vn ).[<0>];
15  done;
```

(c) Power Iteration with skeleton compositons

Figure 3.3: *Power Iteration* examples

From a Map skeleton, it is possible to generate this mapping knowing the size of the input vector as well as the multiprocessor configuration of the target GPGPU device.

SPOC	Theoretical	Framework	Time (s)	Speedup
Device	GFLOPS(DP)			
Core-i7 960	12.8 (1 core)	OCaml+C (1 Thread)	**805**	×1
Tesla C2070	515	Cuda	**150**	×5.36
		OpenCL	**271**	×2.97
Radeon HD 6950	562.5	OpenCL	**101**	×7.97

(a) Results with SPOC

Skeletons	Framework	Time (s)	Speedups	
Devices			OCaml+C	SPOC (a)
Core-i7 960	OCaml+C	805	-	-
Tesla C2070	Cuda	**135**	×5.96	×1.11
	OpenCL	**119**	×6.76	×2.28
Radeon HD 6950	OpenCL	**81**	×9.94	×1.25

(b) Results with skeletons

Composition	Framework	Time (s)	Speedups		
Devices			Ocaml+C	SPOC (a)	Skeletons (b)
Core-i7 960	OCaml+C	805	-	-	-
Tesla C2070	Cuda	**133**	×6.05	×1.13	×1.02
	OpenCL	**116**	×14.02	×6.94	×1.03
Radeon HD 6950	OpenCL	**74**	×10.88	×1.36	×1.09

(c) Results with skeleton composition

Figure 3.4: *Power Iteration* results

Using *par_run*, it is also possible to divide a Map skeleton into several sub-maps each running on different devices dividing the input vector into sub-vectors and merging resulting outputs into a single output vector. Reduce skeletons are more difficult to parallelize. We currently limited the parallelism to the use of one block, which limits performance. However, using a reduction skeleton also improves performances by avoiding unnecessary transfers.

3.4 Skeletons Composition

Having introduced common skeletons, it is now possible to provide composition constructs over skeletons. We propose two skeleton compositions : Pipe and Par.

- Pipe takes two skeletons and returns a skeleton computing both skeletons sequentially using the first skeleton output as the input of the second one.

- Par takes two skeletons and returns a skeleton which will run both in parallel (on one or multiple devices using *run* or *par_run* functions) if the hardware allows it.

3.4.1   Back to the Example

As we can see in Section 3.3.1, in our example, many computed results are reused as input for the next skeleton computation. Using the `Pipe` composition it is now possible to simplify this example. Version (c) (Figure 3.3) shows that it first reduces the number of skeleton runs. Besides, for each run, SPOC tries to optimize kernel launch and data transfers scheduling. Each *pipe* allows SPOC to overlap data transfers for the second skeleton by the computation of the first one. Figure 3.4 (c) presents the time spent for 10,000 iterations on different devices and the speedups compared to an OCaml sequential computation as well as to previous results. In this example, only few data need to be retransferred at each iteration which explains why enabling transfers overlapping with `Pipe` skeletons improves performance only slightly.

3.4.2   Benefits

Composing skeletons allows the explicit dependency description between kernels and data used by those kernels. Besides, this also allows SPOC to provide optimizations over data transfers, for each `Pipe` composition. The data needed by the second skeleton will be transferred during the computation of the first skeleton, allowing some transfers overlapping by computation, reducing the performance loss induced by costly transfers. Furthermore, each run implies data computation from SPOC. Limiting runs by composing skeletons also improves performances over simple skeleton usage.

3.5   Related Works

Skeletons have been widely used for parallel programming. This approach has also been used recently to tackle GPGPU programming. The development of skeletons based on SPOC and OCaml is closely related to other works in this domain.

C/C++ based approaches   NVIDIA [13] offers the Thrust library with its Cuda distribution which provides specific iterators (similar to skeletons) over host and device vectors automatizing GPGPU computations.

SkePU [14] and SkelCL [15] provide similar constructs over arrays. SkePU offers a backend targeting Cuda as well as OpenCL, OpenMP and sequential C code providing more portability.

CUDPP [16] provides a set of data-parallel algorithm primitives such as parallel sort and reduction which can be translated to Cuda code.

The main diference between those approaches and ours comes from the language used as a basis for GPGPU programming. Using OCaml allows us to benefit from its static type-checking as well as from its memory manager. SPOC is managing data and memory transfers through the OCaml memory manager which allows efficiency while ensuring memory safety. However, using C/C++ eases OpenCL and Cuda kernels generation or binding while retaining efficiency.

Other approaches Accelerate [17] is a Haskell embedded language targeting computations over multidimensional arrays. It provides a skeleton-based dynamic Cuda-code generator.

ScalaCL [18] provides a Scala library of collections. It offers an OpenCL implementation for computations such as `Map` or `Filter` over those collections using a compiler plugin converting Sacla code into OpenCL kernels.

Jacket [19] is a Matlab extension introducing new matrix data types allocated in the device memory. It then overloads operations over those matrices to replace computations over those data types to GPU kernels.

The main difference with our approach comes from the use of external kernels over generated ones. This provides less automatization but allows more hand-coded optimization and ensures performance is retained.

3.6   Conclusion & Future Work

3.6.1   Conclusion

We introduced a skeleton library based on the SPOC[1] library to achieve further abstractions and optimize GPGPU programming with OCaml. This library uses external kernels and vectors data-type managed by SPOC to provide parallel skeletons for GPGPU programming. We showed that using skeletons helps to simplify GPGPU programming by enabling automatic management of many low-level hardware-related optimizations such as the mapping of kernels computations to a GPGPU device. Our library also offers some composition over skeletons allowing us to explicitly describe relations between kernels, and vectors associated with them. This allows higher optimizations based on these relations. We presented, through an example, the simple modifications from a SPOC program needed to profit from skeletons and the associated speedups.

3.6.2   Future Work

Models and Extensions Our library currently offers few skeletons and obvious future work is to implement more of them with SPOC. CamlP3L is a compiler based on OCaml providing parallel skeletons. We intend to port those skeletons to GPGPU programming extending our library as well as providing an easy way to translate current CamlP3L code to profit from GPGPU high performance.

As presented in Section 3.5, most other approaches are generating kernel code instead of using predefined external kernels. OCaml provides tools such as the CamlP4

---

[1]`http://www.algo-prog.info/spoc`

preprocessor to develop language extensions. SPOC already uses such extensions and a DSL embedded into OCaml could be proposed to describe kernels and skeletons.

Real World Use Case   In order to test SPOC as well as skeletons we intend to translate a numerical software from FORTRAN+Cuda into (OCaml+SPOC)+Cuda. This software (PROP) is part of the 2DRMP suite [20]. It computes energy propagations during proton-electron interactions. An effort has already been made to translate its matrix computations to Cuda kernels [21] and we intend to translate the managing host program to OCaml reusing those kernels with the SPOC library. It targets many parallel architectures (multicore processors, GPGPU computers, computer grids, GPGPU grids) and skeletons could help handle those by modifying and optimizing their behavior depending on running architectures.

Acknowledgments

The work presented in this paper is a part of the "OpenGPU" project. This project is partially funded by the SYSTEMATIC PARIS-REGION Cluster in the System Design and Development Tools thematic group (http://opengpu.net/).

References

[1] J. Tesson, F. Loulergue, *et al.*, "A Verified Bulk Synchronous Parallel ML Heat Diffusion Simulation", Procedia Computer Science, 4, 36–45, 2011.

[2] R.D. Cosmo, Z. Li, S. Pelagatti, P. Weis, "Skeletal Parallel Programming with OCamlP3l 2.0", Parallel Processing Letters, 18(1), 149–164, 2008.

[3] J. Harrop, "OCaml for Scientists", Flying Frog Consultancy, 2005.

[4] J. Harrop, "F# for Scientists", Wiley Online Library, 2008.

[5] K. Hinsen, "The promises of functional programming", Computing in Science & Engineering, 11(4), 86–90, 2009.

[6] X. Leroy, "The Objective Caml system release 3.12 : Documentation and user's manual", Technical report, Inria, 2011. http://caml.inria.fr

[7] M. Harvey, G. De Fabritiis, "Swan: A tool for porting CUDA programs to OpenCL", Computer Physics Communications, 2011.

[8] G. Martinez, M. Gardner, W. Feng, "CU2CL: A CUDA-to-OpenCL Translator for Multi-and Many-core Architectures", in 2011 IEEE 17th International Conference on Parallel and Distributed Systems (ICPADS), 300–307, IEEE, 2011.

[9] M. Bourgoin, E. Chailloux, J.L. Lamotte, "SPOC: GPGPU Programming through Stream Processing with OCaml", in Intl. Workshop on High-level Programming for Heterogeneous and Hierarchical Parallel Systems (HLPGPU), HiPEAC, Jan 2012.

[10] M. Aldinucci, L. Anardu, M. Danelutto, M. Torquati, P. Kilpatrick, "Parallel patterns+ Macro Data Flow for multi-core programming", in 2012 20th Euromicro

International Conference on Parallel, Distributed and Network-Based Processing (PDP), 27–36, IEEE, 2012.

[11] M. Cole, "Bringing skeletons out of the closet: a pragmatic manifesto for skeletal parallel programming", Parallel computing, 30(3), 389–406, 2004.

[12] H. Kuchen, "A skeleton library", Euro-Par 2002 Parallel Processing, 85–124, 2002.

[13] J. Hoberock, N. Bell, "Thrust: C++ Template Library for CUDA", 2009. http://code.google.com/p/thrust/

[14] J. Enmyren, C.W. Kessler, "SkePU: a multi-backend skeleton programming library for multi-GPU systems", in Proceedings of the fourth international workshop on High-level parallel programming and applications, HLPP '10, 5–14, ACM, 2010.

[15] M. Steuwer, P. Kegel, S. Gorlatch, "SkelCL-A Portable Skeleton Library for High-Level GPU Programming", in 2011 IEEE International Symposium on Parallel and Distributed Processing Workshops and Phd Forum (IPDPSW), 1176–1182, IEEE, 2011.

[16] M. Harris, J. Owens, S. Sengupta, Y. Zhang, A. Davidson, "CUDPP: CUDA data parallel primitives library", 2007. http://code.google.com/p/cudpp/

[17] M. Chakravarty, G. Keller, S. Lee, T. McDonell, V. Grover, "Accelerating Haskell array codes with multicore GPUs", in Proceedings of the sixth workshop on Declarative aspects of multicore programming, 3–14, ACM, 2011.

[18] R. Beck, H. Larsen, T. Jensen, B. Thomsen, "Extending Scala with General Purpose GPU Programming", Technical report, Adlborg University, Department of Computer Science, 2011.

[19] G. Pryor, B. Lucey, S. Maddipatla, C. McClanahan, J. Melonakos, V. Venugopalakrishnan, K. Patel, P. Yalamanchili, J. Malcolm, "High-level GPU computing with jacket for MATLAB and C/C++", in Proceedings of International Society for Optical Engineering, 8060, Society of Photo-Optical Instrumentation Engineers, 2011.

[20] N. Scott, M. Scott, P. Burke, T. Stitt, V. Faro-Maza, C. Denis, A. Maniopoulou, "2DRMP: A suite of two-dimensional R-matrix propagation codes", Computer Physics Communications, 180(12), 2424–2449, 2009.

[21] P. Fortin, R. Habel, F. Jezequel, J.L. Lamotte, N. Scott, "Deployment on GPUs of an application in computational atomic physics", in 2011 IEEE International Symposium on Parallel and Distributed Processing Workshops and Phd Forum (IPDPSW), 1359–1366, IEEE, 2011.

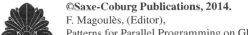

©Saxe-Coburg Publications, 2014.
F. Magoulès, (Editor),
Patterns for Parallel Programming on GPUs
Saxe-Coburg Publications, Stirlingshire, Scotland, 73-109.

Chapter 4

Programming GPUs from High Level Data Flow Models

M. Barreteau, R. Barrère and E. Lenormand

Thales Research & Technology, Palaiseau, France

Abstract

This chapter shows how data flow applications can be programmed efficiently on GPUs from a unique high level capture. We will rely on a tooling approach (through the SPEAR Design Environment) to point out the underlying productivity gain with respect to performance. For efficient code generation purpose, several optimisations at different levels will be detailed. A representative Radar application will illustrate our results.

Keywords: GPU, OPENCL , high level programming, design tool, data flow applications, efficient code generation.

4.1 Introduction

Graphics processing units (GPUs) currently are a major actor in high performance computing after having been driven by the market of games. If we look at the Top500 Supercomputers [1], we can observe that the first ones often include GPUs. Although power consumption can be seen as a drawback for such execution platforms, GPUs remain a potential target for many embedded systems. That is why we decided to explore the capabilities of GPUs to implement high performance embedded applications.

As we intended to develop a tooling approach that joins durability and yields good (not necessarily optimal) performances, we decided to rely here on the OPENCL standard: it enables the production of an OPENCL code that can work on multiple execution platforms (*e.g.* Core-i7 CPU, NVIDIA / AMD GPU, Fusion / SandyBridge APU,

Cell, . . .) even though best performance on a given platform in general necessitates a specific tuning of the code. Nevertheless our approach can easily be adapted to CUDA (since CUDA is simpler to generate).

To begin with, we will characterise an OPENCL program. It consists of two parts: a part run by the CPU which plays the role of manager, and a part run by the accelerating device, as for example a graphics card. The code run by the CPU is called the *host* code. It enables the management of the communications in the computer memory towards the embedded memory of the accelerator, to compile and launch computations on this accelerator, then to move back results towards the computer memory. Any action on the accelerator requires this part of the code. The code run on GPU (or any other OPENCL device) consists of several different tasks which are mostly called sequentially, to perform a function of specific computation (*e.g.* FFT, matrix-vector or matrix-matrix multiplication). These functions of remote computation are called *kernels*. These notions will help the understanding of the following.

This chapter is organised as follows: the next section introduces the problem of generating an efficient OPENCL code; the next one (Section 4.3) describes our data flow application. Then Section 4.4 presents the tool design flow. The code generation step is detailed both at *host* (Section 4.5) and *kernel* (Section 4.6) levels. Optimisations are discussed in (see Section 4.7). Finally results are shown in Section 4.8.

4.2 Problem and Related Work

GPU programmers have to face multiple difficulties when aiming to reach good performance:

- GPUs show an increasing and heterogeneous (*e.g.* vector, scalar, cache) complexity: it requires a thorough knowledge of this hardware from a programmer point of view.

- OPENCL is significantly verbose (in terms of the number of lines) in comparison with CUDA.

- The glue code (on the *host*) is very tedious to write; nevertheless it has a key impact on performance.

- No legacy code is well-written for GPU targets: it means that rewriting such a code is unavoidable anyway.

There are three ways of porting a C code (in OPENCL) on a GPU:

1. manually: the GPU programmer rewrites it in OPENCL from scratch; this demands a significant knowledge of both the target hardware and the OPENCL language. Although this approach potentially reaches the best performances (it is usually used for game developers with hard coding), it may require a long development process (several months). Moreover this probably needs major rework when targeting a new GPU.

2. automatically: the user can rely on a parallelising compiler to automatically generate the underlying OPENCL code: he must add some compilation directives in the whole (Fortran or C) legacy code to guide the parallelising tool. Usually (the first time at least) he is helped by the tool provider for such a service. To this end, the user must:

   - adapt the whole code to the tool coding rules
   - add tool-specific pragmas
   - iteratively tune the code according to performances of the code generated by the parallelising compiler

   This process allows the user hardware-agnostic but requires a thorough knowledge of the compilation pragmas to insert them in order to produce an efficient code (for performance purpose). It usually takes weeks to months depending on the application complexity.

3. semi-automatically: the application provider captures the data flow application from a high level modeling, graphically parallelises it and allows the tool generating the OPENCL optimised code from seconds to a few minutes. Hence the major effort is focused on the modeling step and the kernels library. The goal is to abandon tedious tasks to gain in productivity while reaching performances as close as possible to optimal ones (manual coding) .

The first approach is chosen by most developments because usually the goal is to obtain the best performances and the application does not change (*e.g.* exploring various parallelisation schemes is not required).

Several tools are based on the second approach: both PAR4ALL [2] (open source tool) and HMPP [3] (product) recently offered an OPENCL code generation; the PGCL [4] product targets ARM. HMPP absolutely requires proprietary pragmas (linked with the OPENACC initiative [5]) to guide its compilation, whereas PAR4ALL does not (even if it could rely on the same kind of directives to improve the efficiency of its underlying code generation). Both tools are supposed to address legacy (Fortran or C) codes.

Note that our tool is able to generate the coding rules and the compilation directives required by these parallelising compilers.

GEDAE [6], a much less recent tool, is rather oriented to the last approach (that is programming from high level models) but does not address OPENCL to our knowledge. Ours (the third approach too) will be further detailed through both the SPEAR Design Environment (SPEARDE for short) tool [7, 8] and the following Radar application.

4.3 The Adaptive Beam Forming Application

The adaptive beam forming application (ABF for short) is a typical signal processing application from the radar domain. It is an example of the so-called burst processing function performed on the streams of digitized echoes received by the radar, and is usually the most computation-intensive part of the radar processing. Based on nests of loops, it lends itself easily to parallel implementations such as with GPUs.

4.3.1   Adaptive Beamforming Basic Description

An active radar basically emits sequences which each consist of repeating periodically a *pulse* signal a given number of times. Such a sequence is called a *burst*. Each reflecting object (target) found on the electromagnetic path of the signal at a given distance and radial speed relative to the radar sends back an echo of the burst. Besides noise and other perturbations, an echo is mainly a replica of the burst with a delay proportional to the distance of the target and a phase shift from pulse to pulse proportional to its radial speed. Consequently, burst processing includes a matched filtering of the received signal to put in evidence the delayed pulses, and a bench of filters each based on a given phase shift between pulses. The former step, which provides estimations of distance, quantified in so-called *range gates*, is called pulse compression (CI box in the graph), while the second which provides estimations of radial speed is called Doppler filtering (DOP box).

In addition, receiving echoes on several physical receivers of the antenna gives the possibility of discriminating between the directions of arrival. Applying a set of weighting factors to the signals received on the different receivers at the same time permits favoring the echoes received within a cone which is sharper than the natural width of the electromagnetic beam sent by the radar. Applying several fixed sets of weighting coefficients permits the creation of several such synthetic beams. This operation is called beamforming. The algorithm presented here is a refinement of this technique, where weighting coefficients are no longer constant but re-calculated at each burst in order to attenuate at best the effects of strong unwanted external (*i.e.* not due to the radar) signals. The adaptive beamforming consists then of calculating for each direction (beam) the filter to apply that maximizes the signal to noise ratio for this direction. The algorithm (from least mean square techniques) is based on an estimation of the second order statistical properties of the signal received on receivers, expressed as a *covariance matrix*. A vector of weights noted W for a beam is obtained by solving a system of linear equations of the form $Cov * W = S$, where Cov is the covariance matrix and S a fixed vector (called *steering vector*) specific to the beam. It is generally more efficient to invert the matrix Cov once and compute the Ws' as matrix-vector products. Once the W have been computed, they can be applied to the signal in the same way as a classical beamforming.

The covariance matrix is computed by averaging cross products between couples of receiver samples over some parts of the received signal. The fact that the samples used in the averaging are taken at moments where the useful signals are not present has a strong impact on performance, as in the contrary case the calculated filter would have the counter productive effect of cancelling the useful signal itself in the same way as a jammer. The role of box SEL is to select the portions of signal eligible to participate in the averaging process, while CORR and ADD_CORR is the averaging itself, INV the covariance matrix inversion, CTR the matrix-vector products that create the weighting vectors W, and finally DBF the application of the weights to create the beams.

The processing above manipulates multi-dimensional arrays of data, as the samples of signals coming from different receivers of the antenna can be classified using the numbers of the receiver, the range gate, *etc.* to which they correspond. In addition, it consists mostly of nested parallel loops that read and write patterns in those arrays at indices which are affine functions of the loop counters. This category of operations is particularly favourable for data parallelism. Computations use complex float and single precision numbers.

The following further details the different steps of the algorithm. Dimensions in the array are each referenced by appropriate names, in particular:

- *rg* as the range gate number

- *pul* as the pulse number

- *ant* as the number of the antenna receiver

- *beam* as the number of the synthetic beam

Care must be taken to avoid identifying the order in which dimensions appear at this step in an array (*e.g.* $C(rg, pul, ant)$) and the order in which data are written in physical memories. For example, *ant* being the last dimension of C does not imply that data of C with the same indices *rg* and *pul* are written at contiguous addresses in the memory. $C(rg, pul, ant)$ is a purely functional notation, and the way it lies in the memory is left open for a later decision that is relevant to implementation on a particular target.

4.3.2 Description of the ABF Functions

This section includes a more precise description of the different stages of the application, in order to facilitate the understanding of the algorithm and the various possibilities of parallelisation. The production order of data uses the C formalism.

The radar chain is depicted in Figure 4.1.

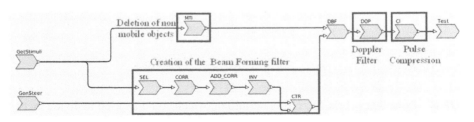

Figure 4.1: ABF application

Test Support Functions   Those functions are not part of the actual radar processing, and are not candidates for parallelisation. `GetStimuli` is in charge of emulating the echoes of targets on a burst by computing the values of the samples expected at the input of the radar digital processing and produces the array $C(rg, pul, ant)$. Such values might be alternatively read from a file. Note that the size of the C array is 2000 range gates, 19 pulses and 64 antennas. Function `GenSteer` generates a fixed array $S(ant2, beam)$ used by function `CTR`. Function `Test` compares obtained results with the expected ones to make sure that they are correct.

MTI   Its objective is to cancel the echoes from fixed (not moving) objects, which have no phase shift between successive pulses of the burst (see Equation (4.1)).

$$MTI(rg, pul, ant) = \begin{cases} C(rg, pul, ant) & if \{0 \le pul < 3\} \\ C(rg, pul, ant) - C(rg, pul - 1, ant) & if \{3 \le pul < P\} \end{cases}$$
$$(4.1)$$

SEL   In the current simplified example, it selects three separate slices of the three-dimensional array C corresponding to three segments of consecutive range gates (see Figure 4.2), and merges them into a unique three-dimensional array $SEL(rg, pul, ant)$.

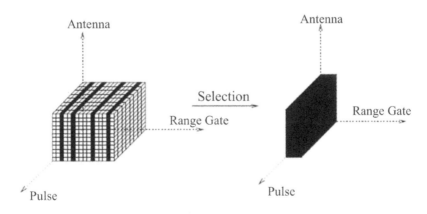

Figure 4.2: SEL function

CORR   Note that matrix $CORR$ is hermitian, which could be used to divide by two the number of computations, although this is not exploited here. In Equation (4.2), $*$ means a complex conjugate.

$$CORR(ant1, ant2, rg, pul) = SEL(rg, pul, ant1) * SEL(rg, pul, ant2)^* \quad (4.2)$$

ADD_CORR ADD_CORR is the averaging of $CORR$ on all its pulses and range gates (see Equation (4.3)).

$$ADD\_CORR(ant1, ant2) = \sum_{rg} \sum_{pul} CORR(ant1, ant2, rg, pul) \qquad (4.3)$$

INV $INV(ant1, ant2)$ is the inverse of matrix $ADD\_CORR(ant1, ant2)$.

CTR A two-dimensional array of steering vectors $S(ant, beam)$ is provided, where the vector taken at a given index b in S is the steering vector used to compute the vector of weights to be applied later in order to create the beam number b (Equation (4.4)).

$$CTR(ant, beam) = \sum_{ant2} INV(ant, ant2) * S(ant2, beam) \qquad (4.4)$$

DBF Beamforming is expressed in Equation (4.5).

$$DBF(rg, pul, beam) = \sum_{ant} CTR(ant, beam) * MTI(rg, pul, ant) \qquad (4.5)$$

DOP In this example Doppler filtering is done with a fast Fourier transform (FFT) on the pulse dimension (pul). To this end, the DBF array must be padded with zeroes up to the next power of two that is convenient for the FFT as shown in Equation (4.6). The Doppler gate (dg) dimension is introduced for speed.

$$DOP(rg, dg, beam) = FFT_{pul}(zero\_padded\_DBF(rg, pul, beam)) \qquad (4.6)$$

CI This function applies a sliding filter F with an impulse response of length LF matched to the pulse on the signal from DOP (see Equation (4.7)).

$$CI(rg, dg, beam) = \sum_{i=0}^{LF-1} [F(i) * DOP(rg + 1, dg, beam)] \qquad (4.7)$$

4.3.3 Corner-Turns

This ABF example reflects one of the typical characteristics of (in particular) radar signal processing, which is that successive processing steps often operate on different dimensions of the arrays. Each processing step is a nest of loops that iterates a particular kernel. This kernel is generally designed to be reusable in different applications, and it is based on a generic, application-independent, assumption of how the data it manipulates are physically distributed in the memory. Then, an application where a processing step requires the kernel to operate on data read from, say, the second or third dimension of an array, *i.e.* not written contiguously in memory, will need to re-write this data in a different order before application of the kernel. This type of operation is sometimes called *corner-turn*.

The resulting graph of the functional (runnable on a processor) ABF application is shown in Figure 4.3.

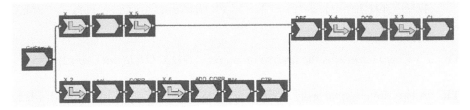

Figure 4.3: Sequential ABF application

4.4   Tool Design Flow

SPEARDE obeys the design flow depicted in Figure 4.4. After a modeling phase of both the application and the execution platform, the parallelisation takes the benefit of this high level modeling to improve the mapping on the target. The optimisation step allowed this work to generate an efficient code. Note that the performance simulation step will not be described for GPU targets.

4.4.1   Modeling

Both application and execution platforms are modelled using a GUI that enables one to import or drag and drop icons in order to quickly build the related system.

4.4.1.1   Application Capture

The application is graphically captured (or imported) as a non cyclic graph of tasks that handle arrays (the suited data structure for data flow applications). The SPEARDE formalism is derived from Array-OL [9], which characterises tasks as perfect nested loops with affine accesses to arrays. It exhibits all the parallelism potentially available for mapping. The cores (can be compared to *kernels* in the OPENCL vocabulary) of loops are anticipated to be available from processor specific libraries of functions, with each function having possibly several optimised implementations for different target processors.

The ABF application model has been shown in Figure 4.1.

4.4.1.2   Execution Platform Capture

The execution platform model can be seen as an abstract view of both hardware and software which provides computation and communication services plus the machine topology (*e.g.* hierarchical levels of memory); it is composed by importing or dragging

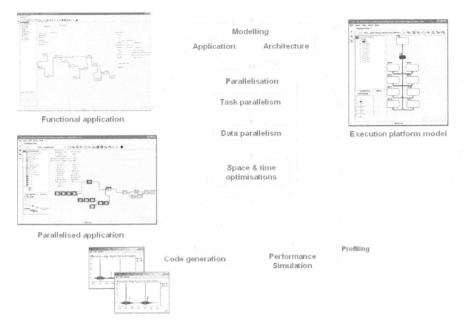

Figure 4.4: SPEARDE design flow

and dropping of hierarchical models from a library of abstract hardware or firmware blocks. Hence the communication services offered by the execution platform are part of the execution platform model (see top right side of Figure 4.4). For mapping purposes, they are described as functions operating on distributions of data (arrays). Models of hardware blocks and communications are also used for performance simulation, where they characterise the real-time behaviour of resources.

Figure 4.5 shows how to hierarchically capture a (GPU) execution platform. A few simple objects are dragged and dropped: computing resources in light blue, memory ones in dark blue and communication resources in red (Orange `Initiator` objects are used for performance simulation; which is out of the scope of this chapter).

4.4.2 Parallelisation

The design environment gives the user the means to manage parallelism both at task and data levels. The first level builds a multi-SPMD (Single Programme Multiple Data) programming model; that is it creates coarse grain clusters of application tasks, that will communicate through FIFOs (Kahn process networks). The second one focuses on data parallelism, which incurs partitioning and distributing loops and arrays. Then some space and time optimisations are applied to improve the efficiency of code

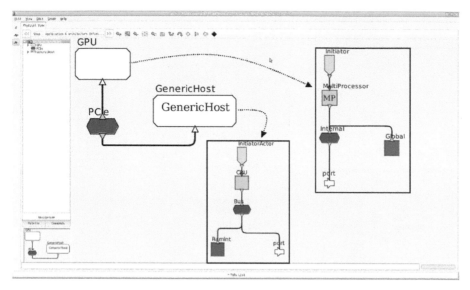

Figure 4.5: Hierarchical capture of a GPU execution platform

generation.

Any graphical parallelisation action matches a command. Macro-commands can be implemented by assembling basic commands depending on the user habits (design decisions). Sequences of commands are recorded to be automatically replayed in order to make the design process faster. These parameterised commands cover the following steps.

4.4.2.1   Task Parallelism

At task level (coarse grain allocation), groups of processing tasks (similar to Kahn processes) are identified and allocated to groups of hardware resources (also called processing elements or PE for short) that are defined accordingly. Each resulting *segment* is currently supposed to work on a single program multiple data (SPMD) basis, so that a fine grain partitioning of the tasks can be done. While the hardware used in different segments may be of a different nature, each SPMD segment of the architecture is supposedly homogeneous, *i.e.* it offers a structure (in fact a multi-dimensional array) of identical PE.

Each SPMD segment is depicted by a colour. This segment gathers all the selected computing tasks (funtions) that will simultaneously run on the selected group of hardware resources.

When hardware resources are GPU accelerators, we can question whether this step is useful because greedy functions (in terms of performances) will be run by the GPU anyway. Hence it can be automated depending on the profiling. Nevertheless this step is still relevant when considering several GPUs (few tools are able to manage several

GPUs) as shown in Figure 4.6.

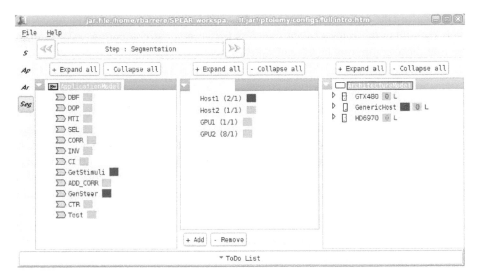

Figure 4.6: Multi-GPU allocation

4.4.2.2 Data Parallelism

A nest of loops is characterised by a multidimensional space of iterations, each referenced by its counter at each level of the nest: this is called the *iteration space*. Loop
parallelism consists of partitioning this space and allocating parts to PEs, which results
in each PE having to execute a part of the iterations with the known affine relations
between iterations and the position of the data that they access in the arrays. This
results in partitioning data also, that is data parallelism.

Fine grain partitioning within a segment is done by splitting the iteration space
(loops) of tasks (visible in the Array-OL description) and distributing the different
parts on the multi-dimensional array of PE. When the array is an input, the minimum
distribution required for each PE to do its work is indicated, while it is the actual distribution when the array is an output. Partitioning the iteration space of a given task
then results in known subarrays of data needed at the inputs and produced at the outputs of the task. The tool displays these distributions. On this basis, when the user
decides how to split the iteration space, the tool controls the background array distributions and whether tasks find all the data they need in their memories (unless a flag
is set to red) and whether data are written in memory in the right order (unless a flag
is orange).

4.4.2.3 Space and Time Optimisations

As partially seen above, communications have to be inserted into the application graph before starting the optimisation process. They enable the completion of the functional graph by adding the relevant data transfers between some computing tasks to make sure that these computing tasks read suited arrays.

Communications   Once loop iterations have been allocated to hardware resources, the mapping must define how data will be produced into or transferred to the appropriate memories. The architecture of the execution platform shows a hierarchical organisation of memories and PEs connected to memories. The general case is a mixture of shared and distributed memories. An impact of the latter is that data need sometimes to be moved between different memories; this is done by defining communications, which were not originally part of the functional graph of the application. Many strategies might be applied to decide automatically, from mere considerations on the size of arrays up to more elaborate ones, but so far none of them can claim to be sufficiently general to cover the diversity of current needs. While the tool can determine from the computation tasks themselves which data need to be moved from source to destination memories, the choice of making the transfer and of the communication service is thus left to the user (nevertheless this step of communication insertion can be automated if requested). The tool checks whether the selected communication service, as described in the execution platform model, is capable of conveying data to their destinations.

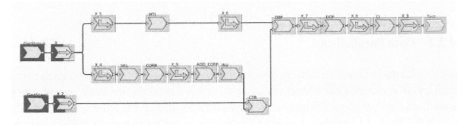

Figure 4.7: ABF mapped application

The final (mapped) ABF graph is shown in Figure 4.7. Tasks that begins with an X_- are communications tasks (they include a green arrow inside the related icon). A green curved arrow represents a corner-turn; that is a communication task that only permutes some dimensions of an array (see 4.3.3 for more details). A green straight arrow is a communication task that transfers an array from a memory to another (it relies on the memory hierarchy).

Task Fusion and Scheduling   Implicitly the natural way to schedule a sequence of tasks in a segment is to execute each of them completely, one after the other. *Fusion* consists of creating a composite parent task which consists, at each iteration, of executing sequentially its children tasks, each with a reduced iteration space. Fusion is in particular used for software pipelining and permits simultaneous execution of activities like communications and computations, and/or handling smaller amounts of data to reduce memory needs. It may further improve performance figures as latency or memory occupancy. Tasks to be fused are selected by the designer; then the tool automatically computes the appropriate tiling for each of them.

4.4.3 Code Generation

The output of the parallelisation phase is held in an XML file (without any graphics entries such as the position of icons), that can be further processed by XSLT sheets (*e.g.* one per target or method of programming) to produce the code (OPENCL here) for the processors. This step is specifically described in the following section (first at *host* level then at *kernel* one) because it is crucial for GPU targets.

4.5 Host Code Generation

When an OPENCL application is run, the following execution order is respected:

- [**Host**]: allocation of resources on the GPU,

- [**Host**]: compilation of kernels,

- [**Host**]: data transfer from the main memory towards the GPU memory,

- [**Host**]: call of one or several kernels with the right arguments (input / output arrays, parameters, *etc.*),

- [**GPU**]: run of the called kernels on the parallel processors,

- [**Host**]: transfer from the GPU memory towards the main memory,

- [**Host**]: release of the resources used by the GPU.

Before running a computation on a GPU, this whole process is necessary, and remains incompressible whatever the number of kernels is. Furthermore, every call to a kernel comes along with a number of lines at least equal to the number of arguments of this kernel, several lines to distribute the computation on the parallel processors of the GPU, plus one line for the call to the kernel itself.

The execution order above determines what code is to be generated. Some parts are execution platform-independent (see 4.5.1), others are not (see 4.5.2).

4.5.1   Execution Platform-Independent Code

The OPENCL language is relatively verbose since it allows the use of a large number of parallel architectures sometimes with very different characteristics. Hence the writing of a *host* OPENCL code contains a large number of lines, significantly more than a C code. For example, regarding our ABF application, the `main()` function includes 50 lines in C but 280 lines in OPENCL ; the call to a function of a unique C line is from 7 to 15 lines in OPENCL (see Listing 4.1 for instance).

As previously described, the use of an OPENCL device requires declarations, allocations, the collection of the kernels code and their compilation, as well as all the mechanisms to implement computations on the GPU. Even if this code is often repetitive, it becomes tedious to have to write it by hand (in particular for large applications).

Furthermore, one should not neglect the fact that a well written *host* code is crucial to obtain good performance on the GPU. Writing this part of code is laborious and can waste a lot of time for a developer, but it requires careful work.

The SPEARDE tool is able to automatically generate this *host* code and hence increase the productivity. But the first step consists of implementing an OPENCL code that simply runs and computes the right results without considering performance: this is the *functional* code.

4.5.1.1   Functional Code

This part of the code (automatically generated by SPEARDE) does not present any particular difficulty. Any developer who programs in OPENCL necessarily must write what follows to be able to run the code on a GPU:

- Declaration of working contexts, devices used,

- Declarations of at least one *command queue* so that the host can manage the GPU,

- Declaration of the programs to be compiled for the GPU,

- Declarations of the kernels which are going to be run on the GPU,

- Declaration of arrays used on the GPU,

- Collection of the information declared (contexts, devices, queues, program, kernels),

- Allocation of arrays.

At the end of the application, one has to cleanly free all the resources used by the program. This (non-exhaustive) list shows how cumbersome the implementation is through the OPENCL language; this implementation is nevertheless necessary before any run of a computation on a GPU. SPEARDE makes this demand transparent for the developer who can focus on other more interesting work. Considering the *asynchronous* paradigm would improve the functional code.

```
// Set kernel arguments

// Init kernels
numKernel = 0;
CHECK_STATUS(clSetKernelArg(ocl_SEL_GPU_kernel, numKernel++, sizeof(cl_mem),
   (void *) &d_ApplicationModel_X_4_out_GPU));
int tab_size = 5;
CHECK_STATUS(clSetKernelArg(ocl_SEL_GPU_kernel, numKernel++, sizeof(int),
   &tab_size));
CHECK_STATUS(clSetKernelArg(ocl_SEL_GPU_kernel, numKernel++, sizeof(cl_mem),
   &d_tab_index_GPU));
int nb_per_slot = 40;
CHECK_STATUS(clSetKernelArg(ocl_SEL_GPU_kernel, numKernel++, sizeof(int),
   &nb_per_slot));
CHECK_STATUS(clSetKernelArg(ocl_SEL_GPU_kernel, numKernel++, sizeof(cl_mem),
   (void *) &d_ApplicationModel_SEL_out_GPU));
int rg = 2000;
CHECK_STATUS(clSetKernelArg(ocl_SEL_GPU_kernel, numKernel++, sizeof(int),
   &rg));

// Event list to wait for
event_list[0]= event_ApplicationModel_X_4_GPU;
event_list[1]= event_tab_index_GPU;

// Gridification
global_work_size[0]= 64;
global_work_size[1]= 19;

local_work_size[0]= 64;
local_work_size[1]= 1;

// Kernel call
CHECK_STATUS(clEnqueueNDRangeKernel(computation_queue_GPU,
   ocl_SEL_GPU_kernel, 2, NULL, global_work_size, local_work_size, 2,
   event_list, ));
clFlush(computation_queue_GPU);
```

Listing 4.1: Call to an OPENCL kernel

4.5.1.2 Asynchronous Code

A way of coding a program on GPU is to program it in a *synchronous* way: statements are sequentially run; it means that one has to wait for the end of an instruction to be able to run the following one (implicit synchronisation). This way of scheduling is the most obvious for a programmer, because it strongly resembles like any sequential language and it is an efficient way of making sure that the causal order is respected.

However this method presents some disadvantages: the running time on the GPU is not optimal and the CPU cannot perform other tasks while the GPU works. Indeed, every action on the GPU has to wait for the previous one to end before being sent, which adds an overhead every time. Furthermore, the synchronisation barriers are expensive in the number of cycles.

A solution to improve these points is to write an *asynchronous* code. That is the work to be run on the GPU (communications and computations) is prepared in advance, on the CPU, in a *command queue* (OPENCL vocabulary); then this command queue is sent to the GPU which is going to be able to work in a offline way. The CPU then remains free to make computations from its side. Only the moment when the CPU is going to want to use results produced by the GPU requires a synchronisation barrier.

In asynchronous mode, it is necessary to make sure that the causal order is respected so that the code is correct. OPENCL supplies *events* to synchronise the various tasks between them. These events are transferred in arguments of the various calls that are put in the command queue, to make sure that every task (computation or communication) begins only when the previous task (computation or communication) has ended and that the necessary data are really in memory.

SPEARDE generates asynchronous code by default, what means that:

- Both communications and computations are placed in a command queue in a non blocking way,

- Events are set to ensure that the scheduling is correct,

- The synchronisation barriers are inserted appropriately to synchronise both the CPU and the GPU,

- The CPU is not blocked while the GPU works (under the condition that the CPU does not need any results produced by the GPU).

Figure 4.8 shows the difference between synchronous and asynchronous programming.

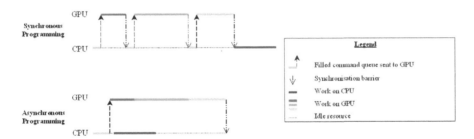

Figure 4.8: Synchronous and asynchronous programming

Another reason for using asynchronous code is that the OPENCL language allows, according to its specifications, processing in an *out of order* mode. Obviously, this processing remains dependent on the implementation inherent to every execution platform. However, when this feature is implemented, potentially it enables a gain of time during the run.

The principle is the following one: a task T_n is put in a command queue, then a task T_{n+1} follows. If the way of processing *out of order* is not active, T_n will always run before T_{n+1}. On the othe hand, if the causal conditions of T_n are not fulfilled, but those of T_{n+1} are, the latter will begin before T_n, despite being put after T_n in the command queue. This way of processing requires one to work in a asynchronous way, but also imposes a causal order of every task so that the scheduling is correct.

The code generated by SPEARDE uses events in such a way that the mode *out of order* can be used while making sure, by forcing the causal orders, that the application produces the good results.

4.5.1.3 Data Transfer Optimisation

Regarding our ABF application (but also true for many real-time data flow applications), a significant part of the running time of an application on a GPU matches communications; that is the data transfer from the computer memory towards the GPU memory (called global memory) or the transfer in the opposite direction.

These transfers can be optimised by directly using the memory controller of the computer, rather than the CPU itself. This transfer is a direct memory access (DMA). This direct access to the memory allows direct transfer from the computer memory to the global memory of the GPU, without loading the CPU with this work. For this optimisation, the memory used to store the data in computer memory has to be directly addressed in the physical memory (that is not protected by the operating system, not paginable, *etc.*).

This memory is called *pinned memory*. Exploiting this memory during transfers of the computer memory towards the global memory of the GPU (via the PCI Express bus) has a direct impact on the bandwidth that can be reached during transfers. On the other hand its use in the other cases has no interest.

Figure 4.9 (experimental measurements on a NVIDIA GPU) shows the bandwidth reached according to the transfer size (abscissa) and the use or not of the pinned memory:

To summarise, it is better to have transfers of large size (> 1 MB), and especially use the pinned memory to avoid a limitation of 3 GB/s instead of the 6 possible GB/s (8 theoretical GB/s on a bus PCIe 2.0 16x).

On the other hand, since it is not paginable by the operating system, the excess use of the pinned memory in a program can lead to instability of the system, or to the impossibility of the memory allocation and thus to the run of a program. Hence it is not appropriate to map all the data arrays that are in the computer memory by using the pinned memory; there are no underlying performance gains except for the CPU-GPU transfers.

SPEARDE knows, from the application graph mapped onto the execution platform, the arrays which are going to be used to transfer data to/from the GPU. Allocations in pinned memory are automatically performed for (and only for) these arrays. The pinned memory is used where straight green arrows are in the graph when referring to Figure 4.7: X_ and X_2 to transfer data from the CPU to the GPU and X_3 to transfer data from the GPU to the CPU.

4.5.1.4 Multiple Command Queues

A DMA controller is a programmable resource, as any other processor, with the difference that it is specialised in data transfer. The OPENCL language allows program-

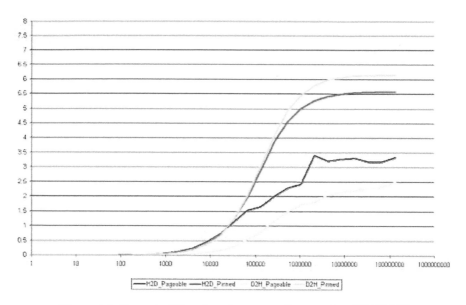

Figure 4.9: Impact of the pinned memory for transfers (GTX 480)

ming of this DMA controller clearly from the GPU. To this end, one must use another command queue that is different from the one used to launch the computations.

So communication tasks (data transfer) will use a command queue, while the computation tasks will use the other one. In Figure 4.7, the two-colored tasks X_, X_2 and X_3 (communication tasks) will thus occupy a different command queue in comparison with the other orange tasks (computation tasks on GPU). In this example, the communication X_ is apparently necessary before any other task on the GPU due to data dependences. On the other hand X_2 can be run at the same time as a part of the computation tasks on the GPU because the data transferred by X_2 will be used only by CTR. At the same time as X_2, nine other tasks can be run and the communication is completely hidden at the temporal level.

The risk of using several command queues is the same as when the mode *out of order* is active: one has to ensure that the communication is completed before starting a computation task which depends on it, or vice versa. The use of OPENCL events is thus necessary.

The example of the Figure 4.10 watches that the use of a unique command queue imposes the sequential run of every task; the total running time is equal at least to the sum of the running time of every task. Here the running time is greater than or equal to T1+T2+T3.

Using another command queue raises this constraint. On the other hand, using several queues imposes local synchronisations (events) to preserve the scheduling and thus keep a functional code (the blue task has to wait until the green one is ended before beginning). The second communication has apparently no consequence at the

level of the global running time, and thus the running time is greater than or equal to
T1+T3 only.

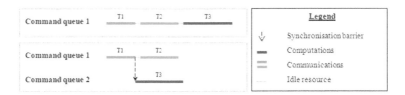

Figure 4.10: Use of several command queues

Certain professional boards of the NVIDIA trademark (Tesla, Quadro) allow the use
of the characteristics of the PCI Express bus (not checked for the Fermi architecture);
indeed it enables work in full duplex (even if it is more correct to say that consumer
boards are clamped in a software way at the drivers level by NVIDIA). Then one has
to use three command queues: one for computations, one for communications in a
direction and the last one for communications in the other direction (since three tasks
can be run in parallel with these boards).

SPEARDE automatically assigns the various (computations, communications) tasks
to related command queues, so as to be able to execute some of them in parallel (if the
causal order permits it).

4.5.2 Execution Platform-Dependent Optimisations

SPEARDE allows the selection of the target architecture from the execution platform
(*e.g.* AMD board) and from the type of device used (*e.g.* CPU, GPU). This selection
is made through the execution platform modelled under SPEARDE , and during the
deployment phase of the application on the computations resources (see 4.4.2.1).

During the selection of the execution platform used, the user has several possible
choices:

- he selects the execution platform (AMD, NVIDIA, Intel, ...) but lets the program determine the most powerful resource of computation that is available on
  this execution platform at run time to perform computations. The program is
  more portable, but performances can vary greatly according to the installed devices.

- he selects the execution platform and forces the device to be used by specifying
  its name in the execution platform model. If the indicated device is not present,
  the program cannot run (an error will be raised).

4.5.2.1   Execution Platform-Specific Code Generation

Once the execution platform model has been indicated to run the application, SPEARDE can generate the OPENCL code. However, some primitives or optimisations are more efficient than others according to the board providers, the type of resource (*e.g.* GPU, CPU, accelerator). According to the chosen resource, the generated code can be more or less different, the objective being to have the most efficient code (in terms of performance) for the chosen target.

According to the OPENCL implementations and resources used, these optimisations can evolve from time to time. Using a tool such as SPEARDE allows the user to generate the optimal code for the chosen execution platform without having a good understanding of the underlying hardware.

4.5.2.2   Multiple Devices Code Generation

One of the difficulties related to the OPENCL language is the use of several devices, to perform task and/or data parallelism on several GPUs (when possible). Figure 4.11 shows an execution platform model with two different GPU boards that can be run in parallel.

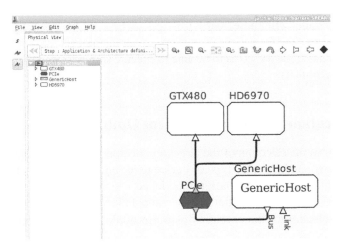

Figure 4.11: Multi-GPUs execution platform model

SPEARDE is a tool initially devoted to facilitate the use of task / data parallelism on parallel architectures that include several computing resources. The fact that these resources are in fact GPUs with hundreds of elementary processors does not change the first feature of SPEARDE . It is thus natural to be able to use several GPUs in parallel, of which each will run some thousands of operations also in parallel. Data partitioning and distributing only require some mouse clicks, whether GPUs are identical or not, and belong to the same platform or another.

Nevertheless there is still a hard point: it seems to be impossible to use the *pinned memory* for several devices at the same time, which can decrease communications speed. However, exploiting several GPUs is useful in the case of computation intensive applications, where communications represent a low percentage of the total running time. This limitation should not have a big impact. Till now few tools are able to manage several GPUs.

4.5.2.3 Gridification

An important problem working with a GPU is to deploy an application with hundreds / thousands of processors (many-cores). This is the problem we focus on here. A quick definition of *gridification* could be: how to split thousands of threads into optimal groupings to distribute among hundreds of processors.

The following definitions are needed to understand OPENCL programming:

Most of the time, an application that will be deployed to a GPU is composed of nested loops that are executed sequentially to achieve the whole processing. The process of gridification consists of converting these different nested loops into a grid of threads (a thread can process a single iteration or more), that will be deployed and computed by the GPU processors. Each thread that will be executed on an elementary processor is called a *work-item* (similar to a CUDA thread). The whole set of work-items represents the same work that the nested loop would be, and is called the *NDRange*.

Another concept used in OPENCL is called *work-group*. This concept is strongly linked to the hardware architecture. Indeed, a quick definition of a work-group is a subset of work-items that will be computed by one compute unit, which very much depends on the architecture: a core on a multi-core CPU, a scalar or streaming multiprocessor (called *SM*) on a GPU. So a work-group is processed by only one compute unit, although a compute unit can handle several work-groups concurrently (one working at a time while the others are waiting).

These concepts are necessary to tune an OPENCL application in terms of performance. In order to obtain good performance, some rules would be followed about work-groups :

- The number of work-groups has to be greater than the number of compute units (otherwise some compute units will remain idle)

- If possible, a compute unit would have a large number of work-groups to have a better scaling, the goal is to have elementary processor load (occupancy) close to 100%.

So the way work-items are split into work-groups has a big impact, as it is important to have the best load balancing on the different compute units of the architecture to achieve a good performance.

Another consequence of the gridification is memory access. Indeed, any access to the device global memory is very expensive in terms of latency (400 to 600 cycles).

Depending on the way the NDRange is split into work-groups, access to global memory can be coalesced into a single operation (or just a few) or not: in this case, non-coalesced access to global memory can have a huge impact on performance. In some cases, a better grid in terms of load balancing will bring worse performance because of non-coalesced access to memory.

The final point is shared memory. On a GPU, a compute unit is a set of processors that share a common memory (called *local memory*), invisible to other multi-processors. So every work-item in a same work-group can have access to this shared memory (as a work-group is processed by only one multi-processor). Using this local memory can avoid useless accesses to the global memory, and thus greatly improves performance as local memory latency is reduced by a factor of 100 compared to global memory. So different work-groups can have a major impact on performance because of this local memory.

On recent architectures (Fermi, Tahiti), hardware vendors have introduced a cache memory between the global memory and elementary processors. This cache allows a better programmability of this generation of GPUs: non-coalesced accesses have a lesser impact on performance, and therefore, local memory is less useful. But a better gridification can make a significant difference in performance because of memory access anyway.

But what is the link between gridification, architecture and performance?

In OPENCL the way of splitting nested loops into work-items and work-groups, also known as the gridification, greatly depends on the target architecture. For example, on a GPU target, it is more interesting to have a large number of small threads to load every elementary processor enough to hide latencies, as on this architecture, context switching is managed by hardware with nearly no overhead. If the target is a multi-core CPU, the problem will be a bit different as context switching costs a large number of cycles. For this architecture, it is better to keep a small number of work-groups (ideally the same number as the number of logical cores), that will process a more important number of work-items.

So, to determine the best gridification on a given architecture, a developer has to know this architecture very well (number of compute units, memory access strategy, *etc.*). And even in this case, there is not a secret recipe that could be applied each time on every kernel, so it can be tricky to find the best one. Hardware vendors themselves recommend doing experiments to find a good solution for gridification, as it is not as easy as it seems, and depends a lot on the kernel that is used. And even for a given kernel, gridification could be different depending on the NDRange.

To summarise, gridification is a key point for performance, but it can become a real headache in some cases. Indeed it is a complex puzzle to solve. And this work has to be done for every (or at least every compute intensive) kernel that is used in the application, and done each time a new kernel or a new target architecture is used. This step can be very time consuming, even for developers with significant experience.

SPEARDE suggests two automatic possible gridifications:

- a basic gridification that takes into account the execution platform and the number of work-items to be performed (quicker to obtain, usually for debug), according to vendor recommendation;

- an optimised gridification (targeting better performance), which takes into account the target architecture and produces the best work-groups for every kernel of a given application.

4.5.3 Tooling Support

The experience feedback shows that before having a code with a good acceleration factor, one initially has to port the code functionally onto the GPU, in order to validate the application on the GPU. Once this porting is done, optimisations can be realised.

4.5.3.1 Code Porting

According to the application complexity and the person who implements the application, the experience has shown that this stage can vary from several days to several weeks. Indeed, the re-writing of the (very verbose) *host* code is tedious and is error-prone. As the *host* implements kernels on the OPENCL device, in the case of a false result, the error can come from the writing of the *host* code as well as the *kernels* code.

Using SPEARDE brings an advantage: from an application graph, the tool can generate a *host* functional code. Hence the developer who is in charge of the porting only has to focus on the kernels porting. As kernels usually include weak number of lines, it can be done quite quickly.

This implementation enabled us to port existing applications on the GPU very quickly, sometimes within a day, because the only work to be supplied is the writing then the validation of kernels that are run on the GPU, the remaining work being automated.

4.5.3.2 Debug

A difficult point for the (manual) porting is that it is impossible, without suitable tooling, to directly debug OPENCL kernels because usual debug tools cannot directly access the GPU space memory. Some applications allow it but are available under Windows only, and are chargeable.

The SPEARDE tool generates code where some parts are reserved for helping to debug. When the code is produced, a related Makefile is also generated with some options that are deactivated by default. One of these options enables the collection of all the intermediate arrays (that are supposed to stay in the global memory) in the main computer memory; then to save these results in files or to compare them with reference values. This feature (available at the code generation step) allows one to gain a lot of time during the implementation of an application on GPU.

4.5.3.3 Profiling

SPEARDE offers two profiling features which can be useful for the GPU developer.

```
void Subtract(int bSize, Cplfloat matIn1[bSize][bSize],
  Cplfloat matIn2[bSize][bSize], Cplfloat matOut[bSize][bSize]) {
  int i, j;
  for (i = 0; i <bSize; i++) {
    for (j = 0; j <bSize; j++) {
      matOut[i][j] = matIn1[i][j] - matIn2[i][j];
    }
  }
}
```

Listing 4.2: C Subtract function

The first one is an option proposed in the Makefile, which allows one to draw at runtime the duration of a function run on the GPU by measuring - on the host - the spent time between the sending of the function in the related command queue, and the achievement of this function on the GPU. Thus this measurement includes the potential overhead of the call, the run time and the synchronisation time of the CPU by the GPU. Since it takes place on the host, the implementation of this feature imposes a synchronous processing of the GPU. It is useful to have a clear and quick outline of the time spent in every function (identification of hotspots for example).

The second enables greater analysis of what happens on the accelerator. The specification of the OPENCL language suggests functions allowing one to know exactly the moment of the command trigger in the command queue, the moment when the command was emitted towards the GPU, the moments of the starting and ending of the work. These functions rely on *events*, which are also used for the tasks synchronisation in asynchronous mode (see 4.5.1.2) and which are already generated by SPEARDE . The SPEARDE tool suggests getting back these events in an Excel file to perform a profiling of every kernel run on the GPU. If some board providers sell tools to do the same, these tools are different for every architecture. On the other hand the data supplied by SPEARDE are the same, whatever the running target is.

4.6   Kernels Generation

At the moment, SPEARDE does not propose automatic transformation of a C function into a GPU kernel. This porting is manually done; mostly a simple adaptation of the existing functions allows a functional code on a GPU, and enables one to reach a significant acceleration.

An example of a C function (loop nest structure) is shown in Listing 4.2. In this function, the atomic core is the subtraction of a complex number by another complex number. It is thus necessary to iterate $bSize \times bSize$ times to consume the whole input data. The offset in the input / output matrices depends on both i and j (loop indexes).

The OPENCL version of the same Subtract function is shown in Listing 4.3. In that case, the internal loops of functions do not appear any more in the kernel, but are outsourced so as to be able to be distributed on the multiprocessors of the execution platform (see 4.5.2.3). There are only the function core and a formula which allows

```
__kernel void oclSubtract(__private int bSize, __private int lineSize,
    __global float2* in1, __global float2* in2, __global float2* out) {
    int pos = get_global_id(1)*bSize + get_global_id(0);
    out[pos] = in1[pos] - in2[pos];
}
```

Listing 4.3: OPENCL Subtract function

one to find the position of the various values in the inputs/outputs matrices.

4.7   Code Optimisation Process

4.7.1   Host Optimisations

The SPEARDE tool generates the OPENCL *host* code without error and also implements the various optimisations detailed in Sections 4.5.1 and 4.5.2. These optimisations are applied at every OPENCL code generation, and do not require the user intervention.

The following sections describe some additional optimisations which depend on the user choice because, contrary to the previous ones, these optimisations are not always applicable.

4.7.1.1   Optimised Gridification

The partitioning described in Section 4.5.2.3 has a major importance to obtain good performances. Indeed a given kernel distributed in a inadequate way by the *host* code yields pitiful performances, sometimes worse than the ones when the code is not parallelised.

Finding the appropriate partitioning that brings the best performance often relies on the developer expertise knowing the target execution platform, and on the achievement of a series of tests. This optimal partitioning must be made for every application kernel so that the bad performance of only one does not degrade the global performance of the group.

Furthermore, when the user modifies the processing of a kernel or replaces it by another, it is again necessary to find the optimal partitioning for it. This process can sometimes be long, and is often boring.

SPEARDE offers a feature which allows one, for an application and given kernels, to determine with an extremely strong probability, the optimal partitioning for every application kernel; that is true for every OPENCL device used (even within the framework of a multi-GPUs application).

The only prerequisite for using this feature is the code generation on an execution platform that owns a GPU identical to the one which will be used for the final target.

4.7.1.2 Software Pipelining

Even with the optimisation of CPU / GPU transfers (so a maximal bandwidth), communication time remains an important part of the running time for embedded real-time applications; moreover the overlapping of some communications by computations is not still possible or not sufficient.

There is however a solution to minimise the communication / computation time by forcing the overlapping. This forcing is possible thanks to a *loop fusion* whose principle is explained below.

Notion of Fusion   A fusion is a repetition of work on different data, to partition a large amount of processing – on an important quantity of data – in several smaller processings that only deal with a part of this data set. So, instead of transferring the complete data onto the GPU, then running the global processing and finally getting back results to exploit them with the CPU, a partitioning is performed (with respect to data dependencies) in order to only process $1/n$ data and repeat this processing n times (see Figure 4.12).

As seen in 4.5.1.3, transfers can be delegated to a DMA controller while both the CPU and the GPU compute in parallel. If the computation / communication overlapping of is still not possible in the case of a sequential code, using fusions can make it workable. In that specific case, this overlapping of computations by communications is called *software pipelining*.

Software Pipelining   When the required resources are available, it is possible to build an overlapping as described in 4.5.1.4. For example, in the case of a GPU, it is possible to load a first data set, then to launch the computation on this data set, and to load the second data set in parallel and in an asynchronous way, and so on. The example of the third line of Figure 4.12 below well expresses the principle of this overlapping applied during a fusion. The purpose is to make the accelerator work as much as possible, without losing time waiting for the data to be present before starting computations (except for the first data set that suffers from an incompressible latency).

The last line of this figure shows what it is also possible to obtain by recovering communications in a direction with another one in the other direction. The gain of time for an equivalent work is obvious. On the last line which implements the full duplex on the PCI Express bus, the work on the GPU is continuous (accelerator fully loaded); which has as a direct consequence the shortest running time.

The SPEARDE interface enables one to select the various tasks to merge, in order to divide the processing into several parts. From this fusion, SPEARDE generates the code which allows this *software pipelining*, and thus wins in performance.

4.7.2   Application Profiling

Once kernels are ported and the *host* code is optimised, it can be relevant to extract an application profiling to know exactly the time spent by every kernel on the GPU and

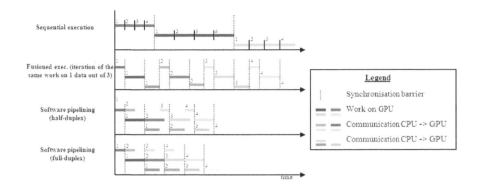

Figure 4.12: Fusion examples

which percentage of the global time of the application this time represents.

Sometimes some kernels, even if they are very badly written or a bit parallelised, are not very significant in the context of the global time of the application. It is completely useless to try to improve them because this improvement will be quasi-invisible at the level of global performances.

Also a kernel can represent an important part of the application. It is thus interesting to spend time to improve its behavior and thus its running time; which will have a major impact on the global running time of the application. Some methods to improve kernels are described in Section 4.8.3.

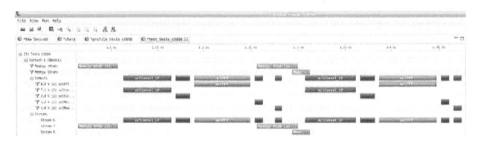

Figure 4.13: NVIDIA profiler

The time spent optimising a kernel can be a good investment because, contrary to the ultra-specific *host* code to a given application, kernels are often reused from one application to another. In other words, when this work has been done once, it will be capitalised in a library of functions.

Profiling can be performed either by a third tool (often a tool supplied by a board provider as the NVIDIA one on Figure 4.13), or by SPEARDE which can generate some profiling information in a file that can be used for any execution platform in the same way.

4.7.3   Kernel Optimisations

The kernels optimisation cannot be automatically done because some optimisations are really specific to the use case and to the application. However some rules are usually applicable:

- Avoid branches (if, switch / case, ...) because it may penalise performances (running time multiplied by the number of existing branches in a workgroup),

- Improve locality because, as the accesses to the global memory of a kernel are considerably more expensive than computations, it is better to avoid round trips between the global memory and registers when possible,

- When possible too, using the shared memory of multi-processors can also avoid accesses to the global memory,

- Outsourcing loop indexes of the function to be run in a way that these loops appear at the grid level in order to multiply the combinations of load balancing of multi-processors and to be sure to find the optimal size of workgroup,

- Make kernels sequentially read and write in the global memory in order to avoid additional and expensive memory transfers (*coalescing*),

- In some cases unrolling loops or the emphasis of some vectorial functions can bring additional information which enable the compiler to better optimise code.

Applying these optimisations, that are coupled with the optimisations at the *host* level, allow the achievement of good performances without too much effort, even by a developer who knows little of the target execution platform.

Sometimes a kernel raises a problem because it is weakly or not parallelisable. Thus one has to make a decision: if the communications cost makes possible its run on the CPU, it is maybe the best solution (otherwise it is crippling); or one may rewrite the kernel to bring to light the parallelism which is not obvious at first sight. On the other hand this scenario requires an expertise in terms of parallelism, as well as a knowledge of the many-core execution platforms to obtain an efficient kernel.

Important Points

- OPENCL being a standard which grows more and more, GPU board providers propose mostly kernels that are already optimised for their execution platforms; which makes any manual porting or optimisation useless. Also, more and more functions are available on the internet, and a community (larger than the CUDA one now) develops around this language.

- Coalescing is very important for the GPUs that do not include a data cache. However new generations of GPUs propose a memory cache which allows them to be less sensitive to coalescing. Thanks to this development, the writing of kernels seems to be facilitated.

4.8 Results

This section emphasizes our results according to three different execution platforms: NVIDIA, AMD and Intel (whose characteristics are mentioned in Table 4.1 (note that the maximum throughput in Single Precision for the Intel execution platform can be accelerated through the Turbo mode to reach 172.8 GFlops).

Execution platform characteristics	Intel Core-i7 980X	NVIDIA GeForce GTX 480	AMD Radeon HD 6970
Cores	6	480	384 vec4
Frequency (GHz)	3.33	1.4	0.88
GFlops max (SP)	159.84	1344.96	2703
Memory (GB)	12	1.536	2048
Bandwidth (GB/s)	25.6	177.4	176
Power consumption (W)	130 max	250	210

Table 4.1: Benchmarked execution platforms

To better understand the various optimisations that have been described in the previous sections, several incremental steps are detailed: the first one (Section 4.8.1) gives the initial performance (without any optimisation); Section 4.8.2 applies the optimisation at the *host* level; it is the same for 4.8.3 but at *kernel* level. Finally the complete optimisation (Section 4.8.4) achieves these experiments before the synthesis in Section 4.8.5.

For each of these steps, one adds the duration (in days) of the related manual porting to emphasize the productivity gain (knowing that our automatic code generation process lasts between some seconds to a couple of minutes).

4.8.1 Basic OPENCL Code Generation

This first step consists only of a basic code generation, that is without any optimisation: at *host* level, the partitioning in threads and blocks (gridification) is basic; at *kernel* level, all the functions preserve their atomic processing level (compared to the C version). For each execution platform, a comparison is given with the total time of the C application to establish the global speed-up of the whole application.

Time for manually generating code from C to OPENCL lasts **6 days** (validation of results included).

NVIDIA One can notice that this first (basic) code generation is already efficient when looking at the obtained speed-up in Table 4.2.

AMD It is also efficient on AMD as shown by Table 4.3 even if the computing time is a bit longer (compared to NVIDIA) whereas the theoretical computing power is

Time (ms)	Speed-up
47.377	4.386

Table 4.2: Without optimisation for the whole application on NVIDIA

greater. The fact that AMD supplies a SIMD architecture, not or badly exploited at the moment, certainly has an influence on this lesser performance.

Time (ms)	Speed-up
55.558	3.740

Table 4.3: Without optimisation for the whole application on AMD

Intel   On Intel, the speed-up also exists (Table 4.4), on a lesser scale however. But if we compare the difference of computation time with the power at the peak of every architecture, the 6 cores are proportionally better used than the GPUs with this basic code.

Time (ms)	Speed-up
79.743	2.607

Table 4.4: Without optimisation for the whole application on Intel

4.8.2   Host Optimisation

This second step (but the first stage of optimisation) aims at illustrating the improvements which can be applied at the *host* level, that is at the level of the CPU which orders the data and partitions the functions in blocks that will then be processed by the accelerator (gridification). Communications can be optimised at this level to improve the global processing time of the application and thus the global speed-up. Obviously no kernel is modified with regard to the previous version.

Time for applying the *host* optimisation lasts **4 days** (validation of results included).

For this first optimisation, we added additional information in the tables of results: the column Speed-up enables us to compare with the initial C application, while the column Speed-up2 is a comparison with the initial OPENCL code.

NVIDIA   Optimising the *host* calls towards the accelerator and partitioning the data in blocks to improve feed to the NVIDIA board has a major effect: the application henceforth runs almost four times as fast as the initial OPENCL code; the time of data communication (not reducible at the moment) represents approximately 40% of the global time of the application (what can potentially limit the margin of future progress).

With very basic kernels (Table 4.5), the NVIDIA board is now 16 times quicker than the reference C code. The optimisation of the OPENCL *host* code thus has a dominant role in obtaining performance on the Fermi architecture.

Time (ms)	Speed-up	Speed-up2
12.525	16.591	3.783

Table 4.5: Host optimisation for the whole application on NVIDIA

AMD A better gridification also yields an improvement in performance on the AMD achitecture. However this gain with regard to the basic OPENCL version is lower than on the NVIDIA execution platform (Table 4.6). The vec4 architecture of AMD processors seems to have an importance in the performance gain for which the *host* code optimisation alone cannot settle and the compiler alone does not succeed in optimising.

Time (ms)	Speed-up	Speed-up2
17.118	12.139	3.246

Table 4.6: Host optimisation for the whole application on AMD

Intel The new partitioning has less impact on the Intel processor (Table 4.7). As it has only six cores, distributing thousands of threads in a different manner has much less impact than on architectures that own hundreds of physical processors. On the other hand the communication optimisation takes more benefits from it.

Time (ms)	Speed-up	Speed-up2
68.670	3.027	1.161

Table 4.7: Host optimisation for the whole application on Intel

4.8.3 Kernel Optimisation

This third step (but only second in terms of optimisation) aims at illustrating the improvements which can be performed at the *kernel* level. These improvements show several aspects: improvement of data access (coalescing, constant or shared memory)

but also improvement of computations by a better usage of processors (vectorisation, loop unrolling).

The time for manually applying the kernel optimisation lasts **3 days** (validation of results included).

In order to measure the gain on every kernel, but also the impact of this step for every execution platform, the applied gridification will be the same as in 4.8.1. The column Speed-up enables comparison with the initial C application, whereas the column Speed-up2 is still a comparison with the initial OPENCL code (see 4.8.1).

NVIDIA   Even if the speed-up exists here (Table 4.8), it remains less than in the previous step. Given that the NVIDIA execution platform is scalar, optimisations probably are at the data access level, with a compiler which is certainly more efficient with vectors of float4 type (used in the vectorised functions).

Time (ms)	Speed-up	Speed-up2
20.413	10.180	2.321

Table 4.8: Kernel optimisation for the whole application on NVIDIA

AMD   The speed-up (Table 4.9) is a bit lower than the one obtained in 4.8.2 for AMD too, with an optimisation only concentrated on the three computation kernels that are the most costly. This optimisation effect also seems to be as efficient as the gridification; it can be explained by the fact that in some cases, the compiler did not succeed in exploiting the vec4 units in an optimal way without a code which facilitates its work. Using the shared memory also brings a performance gain.

Time (ms)	Speed-up	Speed-up2
21.345	9.735	2.603

Table 4.9: Kernel optimisation for the whole application on AMD

Intel   This is the only case where the optimisation of the computation kernels shows an effect greater than the partitioning one (Table 4.10). It can be explained by the fact that the kernel optimisation (vectorisation, loop unrolling) allows one to take advantage of vectorial units which are included into the CPU (SSEx.x). The gain seems to be limited but the parallelisation on several cores of the same processor and the usage of vectorial units yield a bottleneck at the level of the main memory (shared by all the processors) and the cache memory (common L3 and cache coherency).

Time (ms)	Speed-up	Speed-up2
65.204	3.188	1.223

Table 4.10: Kernel optimisation for the whole application on Intel

4.8.4 Complete Optimisation

The following results include both the *host* and *kernel* optimisations described in 4.8.2 and 4.8.3. They aim at demonstrating whether these two levels of optimisation are orthogonal (and thus complementary) and if there is any ascendancy of an optimisation on the other one.

The time for manually applying the complete optimisation lasts **1 day** (validation of results included).

The Speed-up column enables us to compare the results with the initial C application, while the Speed-up2 column is a comparison with the initial OPENCL code. Thus one can easily compare the gap in performance between the initial porting (6 days) and the complete optimisation of the application (7 days).

NVIDIA By applying both optimisations to the NVIDIA execution platform, the result obtained is better but not as much as the previous results let it hope (Table 4.11). As a matter of fact the total speed-up is very close to the speed-up obtained after the initial porting. However, this result is understandable due to the scalar architecture used in the NVIDIA GPUs, the cache use and the efficiency of the NVIDIA compiler (few overheads). These results may be very close to the maximum that can be reached on this execution platform without modifying the code of kernels in depth.

Time (ms)	Speed-up	Speed-up2
10.274	20.226	4.611

Table 4.11: All optimisations for the whole application on NVIDIA

AMD Contrary to what has been noticed on the NVIDIA execution platform, the speed-up obtained for the AMD execution platform (Table 4.12) corresponds almost to the sum of speed-ups obtained in Sections 4.8.2 and 4.8.3. In that case, optimisations are very orthogonal and thus complement each other to take advantage of the available power.

If the performance is less good than the one on NVIDIA, one can underline an overhead of almost 40% (approximately 5 ms on this application). This point remains a progress axis for AMD boards, whose software environment (drivers and tools) is less supplied and less stable than the competitor's one. Going from the SDK 2.2 to the SDK 2.3 and changing drivers (10.12 to 11.2) enabled a significant reduction in this overhead.

Time (ms)	Speed-up	Speed-up2
9.462	21.961	5.872

Table 4.12: All optimisations for the whole application on AMD

Intel Using OPENCL on the CPU shows the same limitation (Table 4.13) as on the NVIDIA execution platform; that is using both the *host* and *kernel* optimisations does not bring the cumulative gain of every optimisation taken individually. On the other hand in the case of the CPU, the *kernel* optimisation seems the most efficient. This limitation is probably due to the fact that all the cores access the same memory which is managed by a unique controller.

The final speed-up of 4.8 is completely correct if we take into account 6 physical cores, even if some technological tricks (such as the hyperthreading and the turbo mode) somewhat falsify the comparison (speed-up of 4.2 without).

Time (ms)	Speed-up	Speed-up2
32.476	6.401	2.455

Table 4.13: All optimisations for the whole application on Intel

4.8.5 Synthesis

NVIDIA The NVIDIA execution platform seems to be the easiest to program because its processors are scalar ones; hence vectorising is not necessary. That is why the optimisation at *host* level shows very good performance, in spite of running very basic kernels.

In Figure 4.14, the comparison of the various bars shows that there are few differences between the *host* optimisation and the *complete* one; hence a good performance can be reached with basic kernels (*host* optimisation). This execution platform seems to be a good candidate for automatic programming tools.

AMD The AMD execution platform is more complex due to its vec4 processors. Indeed benchmarks show that a stress must focus on the *kernel* level to take advantage of the available computing power. However a new version of compiler / drivers could improve things.

An automatic programming tool must be efficient on both levels (*host* and *kernel*); which makes the work more complex because of the vectorisation. Manual work will certainly be necessary.

In Figure 4.15, some functions (X_6, COR, DBF, DOP) have a speed-up notably lower than the one reachable by also optimising kernels. If we do not consider X_6 (whose the deviation between host and complete optimisations is of the order of

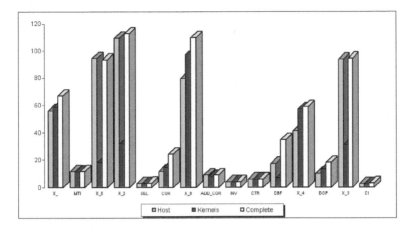

Figure 4.14: Speed-ups for each optimisation on NVIDIA

$3\mu s$, thus subject to the measurement error), the other functions perform numerous computations (> 500 instructions) and thus have to take advantage of vectorial units to reach good efficiency.

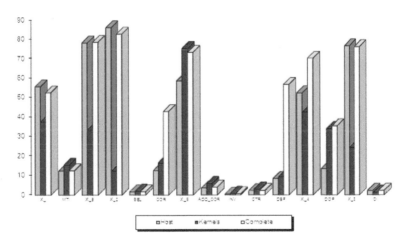

Figure 4.15: Speed-ups for each optimisation on AMD

Intel The CPU can be programmed easily in OPENCL in order to parallelise the processing on its physical cores. But an optimisation must be applied at the *kernel* level to exploit the available SIMD instructions, in particular for the heaviest computation functions which can largely take advantage of it.

Programming is close to the AMD model in the sense that an optimisation of both levels is necessary to better take advantage of the Intel architecture (see Figure 4.16) for some functions (COR, DBF, X_4, DOP). The compiler can thus use the vectorial units of the CPU (SSE, ...) if the computation functions are written to bring to light the vectorisables operations.

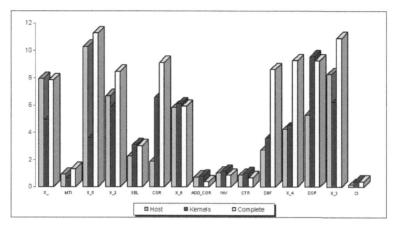

Figure 4.16: Speed-ups for each optimisation on Intel

4.9   Conclusion and Perspectives

These experiments demonstrated that a tooling approach is unavoidable when generating an efficient OPENCL code that yields good performances without wasting weeks or months. This approach takes advantage of a high level modeling: a unique data flow application model enables the generation of an efficient and suited code for several types of GPU targets (as well as other multi/many-cores). Different levels of optimisations are offered to the user.

As the tool generates the glue code (with respect to coding rules) that calls kernels (libraries), no maintainability has to be ensured to deal with the error-prone OPENCL *host* code. It allows the user to focus on smarter steps such as trying new application modeling or analysing several parallelisation schemes to improve performance. This iterative process generates the underlying code in several seconds in comparison with a manual coding (weeks to months).

Future work would consist of generating, thanks to the SPEARDE tool, functional kernels and thus implementing the whole chain of OPENCL code generation. We also aim to consolidate our approach by benchmarking an APU. Investigating an OPENMP / OPENCL hybrid programming is another research axis. Finally taking into account any optimisation that could decrease power consumption remains a relevant point to explore for high performance embedded systems.

References

[1] TOP500.org, "TOP500 — TOP 500 Supercomputer sites". top500.org

[2] HPC-Project, "Par4All — Single Source, Multiple Targets", 2012. www.par4all.org

[3] CAPS Entreprise, "HMPP — Hybrid Multicore Parallel Programming". www.caps-entreprise.com

[4] The Portland Group, "PGCL — PGI OpenCL Compiler for ARM". www.pgroup.com

[5] Cray, NVIDIA, PGI, CAPS, "OpenACC — Directives for accelerators". www.openacc-standard.org

[6] Gedae Inc., "Gedae". www.gedae.com

[7] E. Lenormand, G. Edelin, "An industrial perspective: a pragmatic high-end signal processing design environment at Thales", In proceedings of the Workshop on Systems, Architectures, Modeling and Simulation (SAMOS), 52-57, 2003.

[8] P. Bonnot, F. Lemonnier, G. Edelin, G. Gaillat, O. Ruch, P. Gauget, "Terapix: Definition and SIMD implementation of a multi-processing architecture approach on FPGA", In proceedings of Design, Automation & Test in Europe (DATE), 2008.

[9] A. Demeure, Y. Del Gallo, "Array-OL: An Approach for Signal Processing Design", In proceedings of SAME, System On Chip session, 1998.

©Saxe-Coburg Publications, 2014.
F. Magoulès, (Editor),
Patterns for Parallel Programming on GPUs
Saxe-Coburg Publications, Stirlingshire, Scotland, 111-148.

Chapter 5

Optimization methodology for Parallel Programming of Homogeneous or Hybrid Clusters

S. Vialle[1,3] and S. Contassot-Vivier[2,3]

[1] *Supelec & UMI GT-CNRS 2958, Metz, France*
[2] *Université Lorraine, Loria, UMR 7503, Nancy, France*
[3] *AlGorille INRIA Project Team, Nancy, France*

Abstract

This chapter proposes a study of the optimization process of parallel applications to be run on modern architectures (multi-core CPU nodes with GPUs). Different optimization schemes are proposed for overlapping computations with communications, and for computation kernels.

Development methodologies are introduced to obtain different optimization degrees and specific criteria are defined to help developers find the most suitable degree of optimization according to the considered application and parallel system. According to our experience in industrial collaborations, we analyze both performance and code complexity increase. This last point is an important issue, especially in the industry, as it directly impacts development and maintenance costs.

Complete experiments are performed to evaluate the different variants of a benchmark application that consists of a dense matrix product. In those experiments, different runtime parameters and cluster configurations are tested. Then, the results are analyzed to evaluate the interest of the different optimization degrees as well as to validate the interest of the proposed optimization methodology.

Keywords: message passing, multithreading on multicore, vectorization on GPU, communication-computation overlapping, computing kernel optimization, deployment.

5.1   Motivations and Objectives

During recent decades, parallel computing has known a great development. Great improvements have been made on the software side (efficient standard parallel libraries for communications [1] or thread management [2]) and on the hardware side (increase in the number of cores, development of new devices like GPUs).

However, with the emergence of new types of parallel architecture, whose complexity has increased with the levels of explicit hierarchies, and the never-ending demand for efficiency by users (for intensive computations like physical simulations and so on), computer scientists are still faced with the challenge of optimally exploiting the power of the latest systems.

According to our past experiences in parallel design and developments, and the numerous traps we have observed, we propose in this chapter a didactic study of the design and implementation of a common scientific application. Our case-study deals with the very classical matrix product. Our objective is to detail the main choices a developer would have to face for the design, implementation and optimal use of such an application on a modern cluster.

5.1.1   Programming Modern Distributed and Parallel Architectures

Modern parallel architectures are mainly clusters of complex and powerful nodes, typically multicore CPUs sometimes enhanced with hardware accelerators like GPUs (often denoted as hybrid nodes). Although these architectures are cheap, they can lead to very high performances. This is why they are extensively used in large parallel systems. However, they include two or three different parallelism grains that require as much parallel programming paradigms. For example, we can implement parallel algorithms using:

- MPI alone, deploying (approximately) one MPI process per CPU core,

- MPI with OpenMP, deploying at least one MPI process per node and several OpenMP threads per MPI process,

- MPI with CUDA, to program a cluster of GPUs, deploying at least one MPI process per node, and running some grids of CUDA threads on GPUs from the MPI processes,

- MPI with OpenMP and CUDA, to program a cluster of nodes including both multicore CPUs and GPUs, deploying at least one MPI process per node, some CPU threads per MPI process, and running grids of GPU threads from one or several CPU threads.

The last configuration is the most complex one but it allows for the implementation of codes that can run on both CPU and GPU cores of each node. Moreover, it enables the overlapping of CPU computations, GPU computations, CPU/GPU data transfers and inter-node communications. However, the cost of such advantages is a higher complexity to develop, debug and optimize a code including all these features. Finally, when running on some benchmark data sets, it can be very hard to validate and certify this type of codes. In the same way, the higher design, development and maintenance cost of such codes sometimes may be prohibitive in comparison to the gains obtained relative to a more simple (and thus cheaper) parallel software.

We propose in this chapter a methodology, composed of basic and generic development rules and implementation examples, to ease development of efficient multi-paradigm and multi-grain parallel codes on multicore CPU and manycore GPU clusters.

5.1.2 Benchmark Application

In order to ease the didactic description of our approach, we have chosen the very classical application of dense matrices product.

We denote A and B as two real square matrices of size $n \times n$ and we want to compute $C = A \times B$ on a parallel system containing P nodes. For this purpose, we adopt a classical algorithm on a ring topology of the nodes by distributing vertical strips of the B and C matrices (whose widths are n/P columns) over the nodes. In the same way, the A matrix is decomposed in horizontal strips (whose heights are n/P lines) that are initially distributed over the nodes. Then, on each node of the system, the local square sub-matrix of C (of size $\frac{n}{P} \times \frac{n}{P}$) corresponding to the local strips of A and B that are owned at that time is computed. Once this is done, the horizontal strips of A are cyclically shifted from one node to the following one in the ring, using MPI communications. Then, the local computations of other sub-matrices of C are done and so on until all the sub-matrices of C are computed. It can be deduced easily from the size of C ($n \times n$) and the number of nodes in the system (P), that P local multiplication and communication steps will be necessary to perform the whole computation of C and to return A in its initial state.

For clarity's sake, the initial distribution of the matrices is given in Figure 5.1, and the first four steps of the algorithmic process are illustrated in Figure 5.2.

In addition to that data distribution, the local part of matrix B on each node is transposed in order to optimize the memory accesses a little bit by having the same line size to parse between A and BT during the product. So, we obtain the basic algorithmic scheme, involving only CPU computations and synchronous communications, given in Algorithm 5.1.

In this algorithm, the communications are not explicitly described because there are several ways to implement such an operation, even in a synchronous/blocking mode. For example, with the MPI library, this can be efficiently achieved by the function `MPI_Sendrecv_replace`.

In fact, this point is one of the key issues in the optimization process of a parallel application. One aspect of the scope of this chapter is to look for the best option among the different possibilities either at the design level or at the implementation

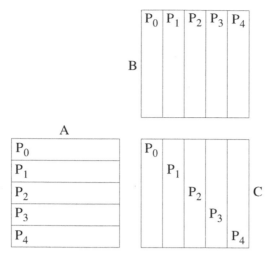

Figure 5.1: Initial distribution of the matrices over five nodes

---

Algorithm 5.1 Basic parallel algorithm for matrices product

Initial data: A, BT and C arrays are distributed over the nodes as in Figure 5.1.
  BT is the transposed version of the local part of B on the current node.

1: **for all** node $NodeId \in \{0, \ldots, P-1\}$ **do in parallel**
2: **for** $step = 0$ to $P - 1$ **do**
3:    // *Loop over the global steps as in Figure 5.2*
4:    $\text{LineOffset} \leftarrow \frac{n}{P} \times ((step + NodeId)\%P)$
5:    **for** $i = 0$ to $\frac{n}{P} - 1$ **do**
6:      // *Computation of a square sub-matrix within the local vertical strip of* C
7:      **for** $j = 0$ to $\frac{n}{P} - 1$ **do**
8:        $\text{val} \leftarrow 0$
9:        **for** $k = 0$ to $n - 1$ **do**
10:          $\text{val} \leftarrow \text{val} + A[i][k] \times BT[j][k]$
11:        **end for**
12:        $c[i + \text{LineOffset}][j] \leftarrow \text{val}$
13:      **end for**
14:    **end for**
15:    Synchronous communications for cyclically shifting the strips of A
      over the nodes by one position to the right
16:    // *The result of this operation is that:*
17:    // *- the current local strip of* A *is sent to node* $(NodeId + 1)\%P$
18:    // *- the new local strip of* A *is received from node* $(P + NodeId - 1)\%P$
19: **end for**
20: **end for all**

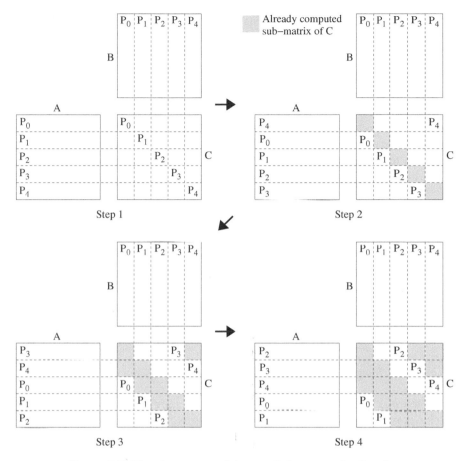

Figure 5.2: First four steps of the parallel process for 5 nodes

one. Before exploring the ways the communications can be performed in Section 5.2, we briefly describe in the next subsection the parallel system that has been used to obtain all the experimental results that are reported within the chapter.

5.1.3   Experimental Context

The parallel system that has been used for the entire set of experiments presented in this chapter is a cluster composed of 16 nodes each including an Intel Nehalem quad core at 2.67Ghz, 6 Gb RAM and a NVIDIA GeForce GTX480 GPU. The interconnection network is a Gigabit Ethernet with a DELL Power Object 5324 switch.

Concerning the software environment, the OS is a Linux Fedora 64bits. The C compiler is the GNU C version 4.5.1 and the CUDA version is 4.2.

5.2 Interest and Difficulties of Computations and Communications Overlapping

The problem of overlapping computations and communications in parallel applications has been extensively studied in the last two decades, see for example [3–5,11,16], and is still an active research topic [6,7,9,10,14].

The obvious advantage of such optimization, when it can be ideally realized, is to completely hide one of the two actions (computations or communications) behind the other one in terms of execution time. A simple example is given in Figure 5.3 where each box corresponds to the computation of its label.

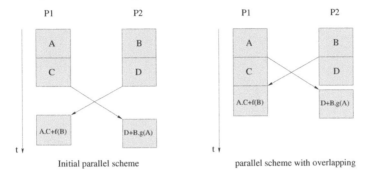

Figure 5.3: Simple case of overlapping of computations and communications

Nevertheless, the seizure of such gain often requires important modifications in the parallel algorithm and most often the overlapping is not complete but only partial. In some cases it is not even pertinent to try to overlap because the gains are much smaller than the effort of design and implementation. So, the first step when studying a potential overlapping of computations and communications is to check if it is worth doing it! This is what is discussed in the following paragraph.

5.2.1 Decision Criteria to Implement Overlapping

Ideally, when working on the development of a parallel application, one may want to obtain its maximal optimization in order to obtain the smallest execution time. However, in practice this is generally not what is done, save for simple cases where optimal designs and implementation are obvious. This is due to the ratio between the required effort to add a given enhancement and its gain over the application. Although this ratio is often a secondary criteria in academic research because fundamental studies aim at exploring all the potentiality of a given parallel problem, this becomes a major element in the industrial context. The main difference between these two contexts comes from the fact that the industry is directly linked to economic constraints. So, the difficulty to design, implement and maintain an application has an important impact over the cost of the application (conception time, number of people required and their competence level).

So, before bringing any improvement to an application, its level of pertinence must be measured. Moreover, the common approach (of good sense) consists of bringing the improvements with the highest gains in first and then following that with the improvements of decreasing gains. So, the improvements are sorted in decreasing order of their respective gains.

Now, let us define the optimization ratio of an application as 0% corresponding to no optimization (no improvement done) and 100% corresponding to the most efficient version of the application that can be made (all the possible improvements are done). According to our experience, we have been able to observe that when someone brings a series of improvements to an application by following their decreasing gain order, the difficulty tends to increase exponentially with the optimization ratio. Moreover, since the improvements are performed in decreasing order of their gains, the gain curve tends to slow down when increasing the optimization ratio. These facts are empirically illustrated in Figure 5.4.

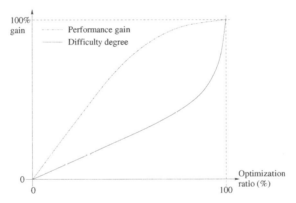

Figure 5.4: Difficulty degree and performance gain evolution in function of the optimization ratio

So, a decision criterion for bringing improvements to an application can be deduced by finding a specific threshold inside the optimization ratio interval where a satisfying trade-off between the difficulty degree and the overall gain is achieved. Another way to get a decision criterion is to consider each improvement separately and to compare its ratio between its estimated difficulty degree and its potential gain with a given threshold.

However, those criteria require achievement of a good idea of the difficulty and gain curves. Although it is quite subjective to evaluate the difficulty curve, the gain curve can be obtained quite easily by monitoring the time consumption of every part of the application and by ordering them in decreasing order.

In a parallel application, we can distinguish two main types of time consumption. The former is related to the computations and the latter concerns the communications. Concerning the computations, the monitoring generally consists of determining in which functions of the program the majority of the computation time is passed. This allows the designers/programmers to focus their optimization/parallelization effort on the most time consuming parts of the application. In the same way, the monitoring of the communications provides the time passed in each communication phase and this information directly influences the use of an overlapping technique.

Such an improvement will depend initially on external parameters like the available time/budget to design and implement such optimization and the importance degree of the application performances. Those criteria have to be considered before any analysis of the pertinence of including overlapping in the application. Then, parameters related to the development and exploitation contexts of the application will play a role during the analysis. We can cite for example the software environment, the parallel system architecture and the number of available nodes for production.

Once the external parameters have been considered, the pertinence of the overlapping should be evaluated according to two criteria. The first one checks that the measure of the maximum potential gain of the overlapping is large enough. That measure is obtained by selecting the minimum time consumption between computations and communications and by computing the ratio of this minimum to the total execution time of the application. The prior selection of the minimum comes from the fact that an ideal overlapping will at best completely *hide* (overlap) the shorter time consuming activity inside the other one. Thus, the time of that hidden activity will be removed from the total execution time. So, the potential gain is directly linked to the ratio between the computation and communication times. Its maximum value is reached when those two activities take approximately the same time. This is illustrated in Figure 5.5 where we consider, for clarity's sake, that there is no additional cost in the application other than the parallel computations and the communications. In this theoretical case, the maximum potential overlapping is 50% when both activities take the same time as their overlapping makes the application twice as fast (50% shorter). In real applications, the overall behaviour will be similar to the one depicted in this figure except that the maximum potential of overlapping will be under 50% due to constant additional costs in the application (initialization, post-treatments, termination, *etc.*).

For example, if we consider an application where the computation and communication times are equal and correspond to 40% of the total execution each. Then, although the potential gain will be maximal, it will be limited to 40% of the initial execution time. Now, let us imagine that the computation time of the application is 85% of its total execution time, and the communication time is only 1%. Then, although any ideal overlapping (if it exists) would completely hide the communications, it would obtain a maximal gain of only 1% of the total execution time. This is a very small gain according to the design/implementation effort required and the complexity increase of the source code. In such a case, it is very likely that the overlapping would be considered not pertinent.

In fact, that first criterion is fulfilled when the potential gain becomes large enough according to a given threshold, corresponding to the trade-off limit between optimization and design/implementation/maintenance cost. It provides an interesting filter but it is quite coarse due to the fact that it is totally theoretical and is based upon the hypothesis that an ideal overlapping can be found. However, this is generally not pos-

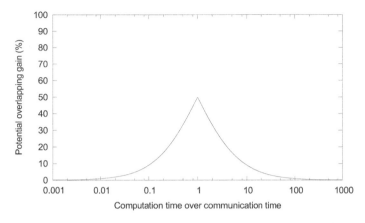

Figure 5.5: Potential overlapping gain according to the ratio between the computation time and the communication time in an application with no other costs

sible in practice and it is very common that only a part of the parallel computations and communications can actually be overlapped, reducing the final gain.

This is why a more subtle criterion is necessary once the first filter is passed. It is important to keep in mind that this second criterion should be checked only when the first criterion is verified because it requires a deeper analysis of the application algorithms and potentially a finer monitoring. It consists of evaluating the quality of the best overlapping scheme found by analyzing the parallel scheme of the application. This quality is measured by the percentage of the shortest activity that actually can be overlapped with the other activity. It represents, in some sense, the maximal degree of overlapping that can be achieved between computations and communications. The maximal quality (100%) corresponds to the case where one of the activities is completely overlapped by the other one.

Finally, the maximal global gain that can be expected (in percentage of the total execution time) is deduced by multiplying the first ratio (used in the first criterion) with that quality measure. The second criterion is fulfilled for sufficiently large values of this global gain.

For example, let us consider that 48% of the total execution time of an application is spent for computations and 46% for the communications. The first criterion is fulfilled since the ratio of the shortest activity is 46%. However, if the best overlapping scheme that is found can only overlap 10% of the communications with the computations (quality measure), then the actual maximal gain will be only $46\% \times 10\% = 4.6\%$, and the second criterion would probably not be satisfied.

In conclusion, we can say that the first criterion is used to decide whether a design analysis of the possible overlapping schemes has to be conducted or not, and the second one is used to decide whether it is worth implementing it or not.

If we apply this methodology to our matrices product application, we have to monitor the computation time, the communication time and the total execution time in order to check the first criterion. Such measures are given in Table 5.1 for a 4096×4096 matrix size and different numbers of nodes.

Number of nodes (P)	computation time (s)	communication time (s)	total exec time (s)	ratio of the shortest activity (%)
2	40.852	1.417	44.186	3.21
4	20.460	1.612	23.828	6.77
8	10.240	1.622	13.606	11.92
16	4.943	1.720	8.412	20.44

Table 5.1: Computation, communication and total times in the basic parallel matrices product for $n = 4096$, and potential gain of the overlapping

First of all, it can be observed that the communication time just increases slightly with the number of nodes. This is due to the fact that only the number of communications increases with the number of nodes but the global volume stays constant. This is not the same for the computation time as the parallelism is quite efficient and there is almost a linear decrease with the number of nodes. The total execution time shows a slower decrease than the computation time due to the inclusion of the communications, but also to the sequential parts of the program (initialization, finalization, *etc.*) that have generally near constant costs according to the problem size.

The very different behaviours of the computation and communication times imply that the ratio of the shortest activity (the communications in this case) increases with the number of nodes and reaches very significant percentages of the total execution time. According to these results, the pertinence of the overlapping is quite obvious for sufficiently large numbers of nodes. Effectively, an ideal overlapping should provide a gain of around 12% with 8 nodes and 20% with 16 nodes. Nevertheless, although this is not observable in these experiments, it must be kept in mind that there is always a threshold over the number of nodes beyond which the computation time becomes smaller than the communication time and, as explained in the first criterion description, the potential overlapping gain decreases.

At this point, the decision of implementing the overlapping still depends on the second criteria. A short analysis of the matrices product parallel algorithm (see Algorithm 5.1 and Figure 5.2) reveals that the communications performed at each step concern only some input data (a strip of A). So there is no strong constraint over the start time of those communications and they can be done during the computations of the C sub-matrices without involving any perturbation between the two activities. The only interaction between them may be concurrent read accesses on the A strip, but these types of accesses are quite efficiently managed by the current hardware and they would imply a negligible loss of time. Moreover, with the global communication time being smaller than the global computation time in Table 5.1 (a finer monitoring would confirm that it is also true when comparing them within each iteration of the global loop), it seems possible in this case to obtain an almost complete overlapping of the communications with the computations. Thus, the overlapping quality is close to 100% and the maximal actual gains are very close to the theoretical gains obtained in Table 5.1 (right column). So this parallel application is very well suited to the overlapping.

In the following paragraphs, we explore different overlapping strategies for our benchmark application. The MPI communication library is used in our implementations as it is currently the standard environment for parallel developments.

5.2.2 Attempting to Use Non-Blocking MPI Communications

When trying to implement overlapping in a parallel application, the first idea that comes to mind is to use the non-blocking communications that are available in the MPI library. The key idea in such communication operations is that they do not block till the communication is actually performed but they return immediately. It is a bit like a registering system in which the communications to be done are inserted on demand and removed as soon as they are performed. However, unlike the intuitive idea that the management of those asynchronous communications would be performed in an additional thread (and thus in parallel with the main process), the MPI standard does not specify any thread use for this and in general, the communications are managed explicitly at their initial request or whenever their completion is tested (including the waiting functions) [8]. So, in this context, the overlapping of communications and computations may not be fully parallel and thus may be inefficient.

According to our benchmark application, the overlapping scheme we obtain is given in Algorithm 5.2. As the communications are potentially performed during the computations, two versions of the local A matrix are required on each node to avoid concurrent read-write accesses. At each step, one version is used to perform the current computations and to send the current version of A to the next node while the other one is used for the reception of the next version of A from the previous node. For convenience in managing the two versions of A, they are placed in a global array of size two, implying an additional dimension (in first position) in the local array A. The "..." in the parameters of the call to the local computations function corresponds to additional parameters that are not relevant here.

In this version, we use persistent communications instead of the simple `Issend` and `Irecv` functions because this avoids multiple creations/releases of the involved MPI requests that would take place at each iteration of the main loop (over the `step` counter).

As mentioned above, although that overlapping scheme is operational, it may not provide the best performances (see Section 5.2.5) due to the fact that non-blocking communications are not multi-threaded. In the next subsection another scheme is proposed making use of separate threads for computations and communications.

5.2.3 Synchronous MPI Communications inside Dedicated Threads

In order to avoid the problem of the asynchronous MPI communications, a second possibility to implement the overlapping consists of using separate threads for the computations and the communications.

Algorithm 5.2 Overlapping scheme with non-blocking MPI communications

```
// Me is the number of the current node
// NbPE corresponds to P
// SIZE corresponds to n
// LOCAL_SIZE corresponds to n/P

// Status and requests for the non-blocking MPI communications
MPI_Status  StatusS[2];
MPI_Status  StatusR[2];
MPI_Request RequestS[2];
MPI_Request RequestR[2];

// Creation of persistent communications if more than one node
if (NbPE > 1) {
  MPI_Ssend_init(&A[0][0][0], LOCAL_SIZE*SIZE, MPI_DOUBLE, (Me+1)%NbPE, 0, ←
      MPI_COMM_WORLD, &RequestS[0]);
  MPI_Recv_init(&A[1][0][0], LOCAL_SIZE*SIZE, MPI_DOUBLE, (Me-1+NbPE)%NbPE, 0, ←
      MPI_COMM_WORLD, &RequestR[1]);

  MPI_Ssend_init(&A[1][0][0], LOCAL_SIZE*SIZE, MPI_DOUBLE, (Me+1)%NbPE, 0, ←
      MPI_COMM_WORLD, &RequestS[1]);
  MPI_Recv_init(&A[0][0][0], LOCAL_SIZE*SIZE, MPI_DOUBLE, (Me-1+NbPE)%NbPE, 0, ←
      MPI_COMM_WORLD, &RequestR[0]);
}

// Computation and circulation loop (same as line 2 in the basic scheme)
for (int step = 0; step < NbPE; step++) {

  // Index of the local version of A to use for the computations and sending
  int CurrentIdx = step%2;
  // Index of the local version of A to use for the reception
  int NextIdx = 1 - CurrentIdx;

  // Communications
  if (NbPE > 1) {
    MPI_Start(&RequestR[NextIdx]);
    MPI_Start(&RequestS[CurrentIdx]);
  }

  // Local computations
  KernelLocalProduct(step, CurrentIdx, ...);

  // Waiting for communications completion before going to next step
  if (NbPE > 1) {
    MPI_Wait(&RequestR[NextIdx], &StatusR[NextIdx]);
    MPI_Wait(&RequestS[CurrentIdx], &StatusS[CurrentIdx]);
  }
}

// Release of persistent communications requests
if (NbPE > 1) {
  MPI_Request_free(&RequestS[0]);
  MPI_Request_free(&RequestR[1]);

  MPI_Request_free(&RequestS[1]);
  MPI_Request_free(&RequestR[0]);
}
```

A simple and efficient way to do that is to use the OpenMP directives in conjunction with MPI. The principle is to place communications in one OpenOMP thread and the local computations in another one (possibly several for multi-core nodes). In the case of multiple computing threads, each of them performs only a part of the local computations. Similarly to the global distribution of the computations over the nodes, the local subdivision over the computing threads is done in horizontal strips of the square sub-matrix of C that has to be computed at the current step of the main loop. This decomposition is illustrated in Figure 5.6. In respect of the communications, since they are performed in a separate thread, they are implicitly executed in parallel with the computations and there is no need to use asynchronous communications. This is interesting because it reduces the code complexity (no MPI requests management).

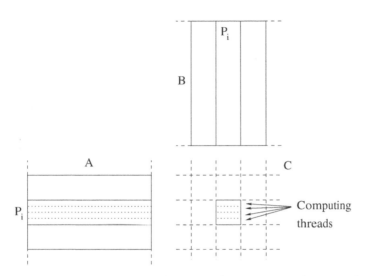

Figure 5.6: Decomposition of the local computations for multiple computing threads

In Algorithm 5.3 is given the most general version where there may be multiple computing threads. For each computing thread, the start and end indices (`infvalinc` and `supvalexc`) of its assigned horizontal sub-strip of C are computed. The synchronous `Sendrecv` MPI primitive is used in the communication thread.

In the two previous versions, only CPU computations are involved. However, it is currently possible to use additional devices such as GPU to speed up the computations. In the following subsection overlapping strategies in the context of GPU use are presented.

5.2.4 Overlapping MPI Communications and GPU Computations

The computations performed in our benchmark application are very well suited to the use of GPU due to their regularity. However, when using a GPU, data transfers are required to and from the GPU to the central memory of the node. As those transfers may influence the potential of the overlapping (whether it is included in it or not), we have added this information in our monitoring presented in Table 5.2. So there are two sub-columns for the computation time. The first one corresponds to the GPU

Algorithm 5.3 Overlapping scheme with separate computing and communication threads

```
MPI_Status status;

// Computation and circulation loop
#pragma omp parallel
{
  for (int step = 0; step < NbPE; step++) {
    int idx = step % 2;
    int nbthcalc = omp_get_num_threads()-1;

    // Computation threads
    if (omp_get_thread_num() < nbthcalc) {
      // Dynamic computation of the data range of the thread
      int q = LOCAL_SIZE / nbthcalc;
      int r = LOCAL_SIZE % nbthcalc;
      int infvalinc = q*omp_get_thread_num() + (omp_get_thread_num() < r ? ↩
          omp_get_thread_num() : r);
      int supvalexc = infvalinc + q + (omp_get_thread_num() < r ? 1 : 0);
      // Local computation
      KernelLocalProduct(step, idx, ... , infvalinc, supvalexc);

    // Input data circulation thread
    } else {
      if (NbPE > 1) {
        MPI_Sendrecv(&A[idx][0][0], LOCAL_SIZE*SIZE, MPI_DOUBLE, (Me+1)%NbPE, step,↩
            &A[1-idx][0][0], LOCAL_SIZE*SIZE, MPI_DOUBLE, (Me-1+NbPE)%NbPE, step, ↩
            MPI_COMM_WORLD, &status);
      }
    }

    // Synchronization barrier: wait all computation and comm achieved
    #pragma omp barrier
  }
} // end of parallel region
```

Number of nodes (P)	GPU computation time (s)		communica-tion time (s)	total exec time (s)	ratio of the shortest activity (%)	
	without transfers	including transfers			without transfers	including transfers
2	1.771	1.819	1.386	5.084	27.27	35.78
4	0.851	0.889	1.549	4.186	20.33	21.24
8	0.401	0.436	1.578	3.757	10.66	11.59
16	0.168	0.199	1.548	3.502	4.79	5.69

Table 5.2: GPU computation, communication and total times in the basic parallel matrices product for $n = 4096$, and potential gain from the overlapping

computation time without data transfers and the second one includes them. As a consequence, there are also two sub-columns for the ratio that respectively correspond to both variants of overlapping excluding or including the GPU data transfers.

Although the global behaviours of the computation and communication times are almost the same as in the initial version (see Table 5.1), the computation times are much smaller than with CPU computations. In fact, there is a nearly constant speed up around 25-23 (respectively without and with data transfers) between the CPU computations and the GPU ones according to the number of nodes. This has a double impact over the ratio of potential overlapping. Firstly, the total execution time is much smaller than with CPU computations whereas the communication times are almost the same. So, the proportion of the communications in the total time is implicitly increased. Secondly, the computation time becomes much smaller than the communication time when the number of nodes increases. This tends to decrease the ratio of potential overlapping, as can be seen in the ratio columns of Table 5.2.

From those results, we can conclude that the use of GPU is very interesting for absolute performances but it decreases the interest of overlapping when the number of nodes increases. In the case of our benchmark application, the first overlapping criterion may not be verified for 16 nodes and more. In practice, the decision to make a deeper analysis of the overlapping interest would depend, at this point, on the number of nodes planned to be used when exploiting the application. In the scope of our study, we consider a possible use of the application in any configuration of nodes. So, the analysis of the second criterion (maximal quality of the overlapping) is still pertinent due to the rather significant ratios obtained for small numbers of nodes.

In respect of the overlapping quality, an essential advantage of the GPU kernel calling mechanism in the context of overlapping lies in its naturally asynchronous nature. In fact, once the data have been transferred to the device, a kernel call from the CPU is non-blocking and allows it to perform other tasks during the kernel execution on the GPU without recourse to any additional thread. Obviously, this behaviour is possible because the CPU and the GPU are distinct and independent devices in terms of code execution (like any other co-processor like network or sound devices). Synchronization points can be explicitly inserted in the code if necessary. In respect of the inclusion of GPU transfers in the overlapping, the implementation is more complex and requires multiple threads (see Section 5.2.4.2), but it can also be achieved quite efficiently.

Finally, it appears that the actual quality of an overlapping of GPU computations with communications should be high, and the second criterion is verified.

In the following two subsections, we propose different versions of overlapping GPU computations with inter-node communications. As the parallel system used for the experiments contains NVIDIA GPUs, the CUDA API is used in the proposed source codes.

5.2.4.1 Natural Overlapping of GPU Computations with Blocking MPI Communications

The first overlapping scheme is quite simple as it only concerns the GPU computations. It mainly consists of executing at each step of the global process, the data transfer of the current A strip to the GPU, the call of the GPU kernel and the inter-nodes communications of A strips. The asynchronous (non-blocking) nature of the GPU kernel calls makes an implicit overlapping of the kernel execution and the inter-node communications.

The corresponding overlapping scheme is given in Algorithm 5.4. It can be seen that there is no explicit synchronization of the GPU in this code. In fact, this is not required in that case because a single stream is used by default on the GPU and within one stream, only one kernel or data transfer can be executed at a time. Moreover, GPU data transfers are implicitly synchronous. Asynchronous transfers are possible but they imply strong constraints on the involved memory banks that significantly increase the code complexity. So this solution is not pertinent in our context.

Finally, it appears that in our algorithm each GPU data transfer or kernel call will be blocked while the previous one is not finished. Hence, the kernel call in the loop will be executed only once the transfer of A is completed, and the transfer of A in the next iteration will only begin once the kernel call in the previous iteration is finished. This behaviour ensures a valid execution of the main loop of the parallel process while preserving a simple source code.

Algorithm 5.4 Overlapping scheme with implicit asynchronous GPU kernel call

---

```
MPI_Status status;

// Transfer of the local strip of B and the node id to the GPU
gpuSetDataOnGPU();
// Computation and circulation loop
for (int step = 0; step < NbPE; step++) {
  int idx = step%2;
  // Transfer of the current local strip of A from the CPU to the GPU
  gpuSetAOnGPU(idx);
  // Computation
  gpuKernelLocalProduct(step,GPUKernelId); // Async call of the GPU kernel
  // Input data circulation
  if (NbPE > 1) {
    MPI_Sendrecv(&A[idx][0][0], LOCAL_SIZE*SIZE, MPI_DOUBLE, (Me+1)%NbPE, step, &A↵
        [1-idx][0][0], LOCAL_SIZE*SIZE, MPI_DOUBLE, (Me-1+NbPE)%NbPE, step, ↵
        MPI_COMM_WORLD, &status);
  }
}
// Get back results from the GPU to the CPU
gpuGetResultOnCPU();
```

Although this version should provide very good performances, there are still some possible improvements according to the data transfers to the GPU. As mentioned above, the GPU invocations being exclusive within a single stream, we have seen that the computation kernel and the transfer of A are sequentially scheduled. This is exactly the same for the initial data transfer before the main loop and the transfer of A in the first iteration. Moreover, the use of a synchronous MPI primitive and synchronous GPU transfers prevent the overlapping of the inter-node communications with the transfer of A at the next iteration or with the final data transfer after the loop. So, data transfers to and from the GPU are not included in this overlapping scheme. As a last step towards the complete optimization of the overlapping, a final version including data transfers is proposed in the following subsection.

5.2.4.2 Inserting the CPU/GPU Data Transfers in the Overlapping Mechanism

As can be seen in Table 5.2, the inclusion of the GPU data transfers in the overlapping increases its interest a little bit. Although it is not a major factor in the decision, it may push back the interest threshold over the number of nodes. So, we propose a final overlapping scheme including those transfers.

For this final optimization, the use of multiple streams on the GPU does not help due to the sequential dependency between the data transfers of A and the kernel calls. Moreover, as mentioned in the previous subsection, asynchronous GPU transfers induce a more complex memory management due to specific constraints. Asynchronous MPI primitives could also be used but, as mentioned previously, they are less efficient than separate threads due to the blocking synchronous data transfers of A to the GPU. In fact, the progress of the MPI communication would not be effective during the transfer of A, thus preventing an actual overlap of those two activities. Moreover, the initial and final transfers respectively to and from the GPU (before and after the main loop) could not be overlapped in such a scheme.

A more convenient and efficient solution is to use separate threads to perform on one hand, the GPU transfers and computations, and on the other hand, the inter-node communications. Such a scheme, using the OpenMP directives, is presented in Algorithm 5.5. It is quite similar to Algorithm 5.3 involving the use of OpenMP. However, the number of OpenMP threads is explicitly set to two in this lastest version: one for the GPU management and one for the communications.

There are specific GPU management rules when running multiple threads. Although a GPU device can be used by several threads at a time, each thread can use only one GPU device at a time. It is worth mentioning that it is very delicate to use one GPU device from several threads simultaneously and this should be done only when necessary. Mutual exclusion can be imposed between the threads using a same GPU by using lower level CUDA contexts. However, such exclusion mechanisms are not useful in our scheme and are outside the scope of this chapter.

Conversely, the specification of the GPU device used by each thread managing GPU computations would be required in the presence of several GPU devices per node. In fact, the scheme proposed in Algorithm 5.5 should be extended in the presence of several GPU devices by decomposing the local computations according to the number of available GPU devices and by assigning one thread per GPU device to manage their respective computations and data transfers. So, similarly to the scheme presented in Algorithm 5.3, each computing thread would manage a part of the locally distributed computations. The main difference is that the threads would do their assigned computations on distinct GPU devices instead of distinct CPU cores. In this case, the function `cudaSetDevice` must be used to indicate which GPU device will execute all the subsequent CUDA invocations made by the calling thread. This function can be called several times by the same thread and allows it to use different GPUs during its execution. With the latest versions of CUDA (4.2), it is not necessary to explicitly assign the GPU device to a thread when there is a single device inside the node. By default, all the threads will use this device.

Algorithm 5.5 Overlapping scheme with multiple threads

```
MPI_Status status;      // MPI asynchronous communication status

// Explicit creation of two threads (more is useless)
omp_set_num_threads(2);

// Computation and circulation loop: creation of the threads
#pragma omp parallel
{
  int thId = omp_get_thread_num();

  for (int step = 0; step < NbPE; step++) {
    int idx = step % 2;

    switch (thId) {

    // Computation thread
    case 0 :
      // Initialize GPU usage at step 0
      if (step == 0) {
        cudaSetDevice(0);      // Indicates that thread 0 uses the GPU 0 (optional)
        gpuSetDataOnGPU();     // Data transfer to the GPU
      }
      // Transfer of the current local version of A to the GPU
      gpuSetAOnGPU(idx);
      // Local computation
      gpuKernelLocalProduct(step, GPUKernelId);
      // Finalize GPU usage from thread 0 at last step
      if (step == NbPE-1) {
        gpuGetResultOnCPU(); // Get back the results from the CPU
      }
      break;

    // Communication thread
    case 1 :
      if (NbPE > 1) {
        MPI_Sendrecv(&A[idx][0][0], LOCAL_SIZE*SIZE, MPI_DOUBLE, (Me+1)%NbPE, step↩
        , &A[1-idx][0][0], LOCAL_SIZE*SIZE, MPI_DOUBLE, (Me-1+NbPE)%NbPE, step↩
        , MPI_COMM_WORLD, &status);
      }
      break;
    }

    // Synchronization barrier: wait for termination of both computation and ↩
        communication
    #pragma omp barrier
  }
} // end of parallel region: end of the threads
```

In our scheme, we have explicitly included this action because it is not implicit in all versions of CUDA, but also in a pedagogic goal to help the reader to keep in mind that the device choice may be necessary with multiple GPU devices.

Finally, this last scheme realizes a potentially complete overlapping and should obtain slightly better performances than the previous one. A global performance comparison of the different versions is presented in Section 5.4. However, experimental results focused on the overlapping are given and analyzed in the next section.

5.2.5 Experimental Comparison and Analysis of the Overlapping Schemes

We present in Table 5.3, a small synthesis of the experimental results obtained with the four overlapping versions. The times (in seconds) reported in this table correspond to the duration of the main computation/communication loop. They are averages of five executions after a first warm up execution. In fact, it is not rare to observe in a series of executions that the first one takes more time than the following ones. This is generally due to automatic energy-saving settings that reduce the frequencies of unused devices (cores or GPUs). So, the first execution is penalized by the time for those previously unused devices to get back to their maximal performance capabilities.

Version	Algorithm 5.2	Algorithm 5.3	Algorithm 5.4	Algorithm 5.5
Comms	MPI async in main process	MPI sync in 1 thread	MPI sync in main process	MPI sync in 1 thread
Comps	1 CPU kernel using 8 threads	8 CPU kernels in 8 threads	1 GPU kernel with async call	1 GPU kernel + tansfers in 1 thread
# nodes (P)	Main computation-communication loop time (s)			
2	11.664	11.642	1.818	1.919
4	6.545	6.575	1.602	1.501
8	4.138	3.637	1.603	1.523
16	2.943	2.374	1.608	1.522

Table 5.3: Main loop time (s) for the four versions of overlapping with $n = 4096$

In connection with the first two schemes with CPU computations (Algorithms 5.2 and 5.3), several configurations are possible according to the number of computing threads used. In the table are presented the configurations providing the best performances. The first overlapping scheme uses a multi-threaded CPU kernel with 8 OpenMP threads and the second scheme uses 8 sequential CPU kernels in separate OpenMP threads plus another thread for the communications. It can be seen that the results between these two schemes are globally quite similar. However, the second scheme tends to be a bit more scalable when the number of nodes increases (up to 20% better). In fact, those two schemes have quite different behaviours.

As mentioned in Section 5.2.2, the overlapping of asynchronous MPI communications may be ineffective due to the lack of separation between the main process and the communications. In some cases, the communications are actually performed sequentially to the computations during the waiting task. A finer monitoring of this scheme has allowed us to observe that the total time of the main loop corresponds to the sum of the computation time and the communication waiting time at the end of the iterations. Moreover, the comparison with the total time of the main loop obtained with the basic version (Algorithm 5.1), in the same conditions, shows that they are practically identical. So there is no actual overlapping. A potential improvement would be to interleave asynchronous communication tests and computations as mentioned in [8]. Nevertheless, this cannot be a generic approach as it is not always possible to insert communication tests inside a computation kernel (typically when using a kernel from a library like BLAS).

The results of the second scheme are a bit better. Indeed, the loop times in this scheme are a little bit smaller than the ones in the first scheme and in the basic scheme, with a difference increasing with the number of nodes. This tends to indicate that there is an actual overlapping that seems to increase with the number of nodes. This behaviour can be explained by two reasons. The former is that for small numbers of nodes, the computation time is much longer than the communication time, yielding a low potential of overlapping and thus loop times similar to the first scheme. The latter, already pointed out in the comments of Table 5.1, is that computation times decrease faster than communication times when the number of nodes increases, thus increasing the potential of overlapping up to its maximum for a specific number of nodes (seemingly a little beyond 16 nodes for our first two overlapping schemes). Thus, when the number of nodes increases (up to some threshold not observable in our experiments) the potential overlapping in the second scheme becomes more and more important while there is still no actual overlapping in the first scheme. This explains the performance divergence of those two schemes.

In connection with the last two schemes in Table 5.3 (Algorithms 5.4 and 5.5), the first obvious result is that the use of GPUs provides an important gain in the computation time. Moreover, fine monitoring reveals that the overlapping is effective in both versions. This is mainly due to the practically complete hardware independence of the computation and communication activities, as they are performed on different devices. The two proposed schemes present very similar global behaviours and rapidly reach their performance limit with only four nodes. This comes from the fact that in these schemes, the computation time is smaller than the communication time for every multi-node configuration. Hence, their respective loop times are mainly governed by their communication times. Those times slightly decrease when the number of nodes increases due to the smaller data amount to send/receive on each node. But they rapidly reach their lower limit with just a few nodes. It is worth noticing that contrary to the overlapping schemes with CPU computations (Algorithms 5.2 and 5.3), the potential overlapping in these last two schemes (Algorithms 5.4 and 5.5) decreases when the number of nodes increases. The slight performance difference between these two schemes comes from the overlapping of the GPU transfers that is effective in Algorithm 5.5. Finally, the (bad) performance of this last scheme with two nodes is quite unexpected. The reasons of this phenomenon are not yet clear and should be the subject of further investigations.

These first experiments have allowed us to get a performance overview of the considered overlapping schemes and to analyze their respective global behaviours. A more detailed analysis of their efficiency is given in Section 5.4.2.

5.3 Impact of Optimization Degree in Computing Kernels

Optimizing computing kernels run on each computing node is a classic objective when developing a HPC code. On modern architectures it means: optimize serial code, parallelize the code on the different cores of a node, and attempt to use an accelerator (like GPU) when available. These optimization degrees are time consuming to develop, except when an adapted optimized library already exists. However, in any case, optimizing the computing kernel run on each node can have a great impact on distributed runs on a cluster.

5.3.1 Typical Degrees of Optimization

When running computations on modern CPU cores, we usually start designing a serial kernel, basically optimized (called *Ck0* in the following). Algorithm 5.1 illustrates the design of a basically optimized serial algorithm for one CPU core. We use a transposed TB matrix in order to improve cache memory usage and to decrease the number of cache misses. We achieve performance of 1.60 $Gflops$ on one core of our tested cluster (with Nehalem processors). But we can greatly increase this performance.

5.3.1.1 Optimization of CPU Computing Kernels

Algorithm 5.6 adds OpenMP multithreading to split the main computation loop run on each node (the loop over the lines of the local slice of A as in Figure 5.6). This is achieved very easily by adding just one compilation directive (one line) before the main loop. As mentioned in Section 5.2.2, two copies of A (indexed on the first dimension of the array) are used in order to avoid concurrent read-write accesses. Moreover, we introduced some local variables (PtA and PtB) to access A and TB elements with just one dimensional array indexes. However, this last optimization had no significant impact using the `gcc` compiler (that probably makes this type of optimization by itself).

This multithreaded version (named *Ck1*) achieves a performance close to 6.98 $Gflops$ on one node of our testbed cluster, running 8 threads. Different experiments have shown that best performances are achieved running 8 OpenMP threads on our Nehalem processor with 4 physical cores enhanced with hyperthreading. So, we have to run one thread per logical core (*i.e.* 8 threads).

Algorithm 5.7 is another version (named *Ck2*) that uses the matrix-matrix product of the famous BLAS library (`cblas_dgemm` routine) to perform on each node the computation of the local sub-matrix of C. The BLAS function call requires several parameters, specifying the storage format of the A, B and C matrices as well as their respective line and column sizes. This library is well known to the HPC community (that never redevelops a matrix-matrix multiplication), and is generally supplied by constructors or by specialized communities. We achieved a performance close to

Algorithm 5.6 Multithreaded CPU kernel (Ck1)

```
// Local slice of A matrix is stored in A[2][LOCAL_SIZE][SIZE].
// Local slice of transposed B Matrix is stored in TB[LOCAL_SIZE][SIZE].
// Local slice of resulting C Matrix is stored in C[SIZE][LOCAL_SIZE].

// At step "step", the processor compute the C block starting at line:
int OffsetLigneC = ((Me+step)*LOCAL_SIZE)%SIZE;

// OpenMP parallelization of the main loop on A[idx] lines
#pragma omp parallel for
for (int i = 0; i < LOCAL_SIZE; i++) {
    double *PtA = &A[idx][i][0];          // Ptr on the current A line
    for (int j = 0; j < LOCAL_SIZE; j++) {
        double *PtTB = &TB[j][0];         // Ptr on the current TB line
        double accu = 0.0;                // Local accumulator of a new result
        // Compute a new value of the resulting C matrix
        for (int k = 0; k < SIZE; k++) {
            accu += PtA[k] * PtTB[k];
        }
        // Store the new result in C matrix
        C[i+OffsetLigneC][j] = accu;
    }
}
```

Algorithm 5.7 Sequential BLAS CPU kernel (Ck2)

```
// idx: index of the 2D array of A[2][LOCAL_SIZE][SIZE] to read at current step.
// OffsetLigneC: starting line of the C block computed at current step.

cblas_dgemm(CblasRowMajor, CblasNoTrans, CblasNoTrans, LOCAL_SIZE, LOCAL_SIZE, ↩
    SIZE, 1.0, &A[idx][0][0], SIZE, &B[0][0], LOCAL_SIZE, 0.0, &C[OffsetLigneC][0], ↩
    LOCAL_SIZE);
```

$9.81 \, Gflops$ on one core of our testbed cluster. We used the ATLAS version of the
BLAS library, but with pure sequential implementation of each routine.

Finally, Algorithm 5.8 illustrates a computing kernel still based on a BLAS library
call, but applied to a subpart of the local slice of the A matrix: processing lines in the
range [InfValInc;SupValExc[(kernel *Ck3*). This computing kernel is called from
an OpenMP multithreaded algorithm (see Algorithm 5.3). Several OpenMP threads
are run, each thread computes its [InfValInc;SupValExc[range and calls the
Ck3 kernel. Experiments have pointed out that the most efficient way of using kernel
Ck3 was to run only one computing thread per physical core (and not relying on the
hyperthreading mechanism). We reached $36.30 \, Gflops$ on our testbed nodes.

Algorithm 5.8 BLAS CPU kernel to be used in a multithreaded scheme (Ck3)

```
// idx: index of the 2D array of A[2][LOCAL_SIZE][SIZE] to read at current step.
// OffsetLigneC: starting line of the C block computed at current step.
// InfValInc: index of the first line of A[idx] processed by the thread.
// SupValExc: index of the first line of A[idx] not processed by the thread.

cblas_dgemm(CblasRowMajor, CblasNoTrans, CblasNoTrans, (SupValExc - InfValInc), ↩
    LOCAL_SIZE, SIZE, 1.0, &A[idx][InfValInc][0], SIZE, &B[0][0], LOCAL_SIZE, ↩
    0.0, &C[OffsetLigneC+InfValInc][0], LOCAL_SIZE);
```

Algorithm 5.9 Basic GPU kernel (Gk0)

```
// Definition of the GPU computing kernel
__global__ void MatrixProductKernel_Gk0(int step)
{
  int lig = blockIdx.y;
  int col = threadIdx.x + blockIdx.x * BLOCK_SIZE_X_K0;
  double res = 0.0;

  if (col < LOCAL_SIZE) {
    for (int k = 0; k < SIZE; k++) {
      res += GPU_A[lig][k] * GPU_B[k][col];
    }
    GPU_C[lig+(((GPU_Me+step)*LOCAL_SIZE)%SIZE)][col] = res;
  }
}
// Call of the GPU computing kernel Gk0

// Description of a block of threads
Db.x = BLOCK_SIZE_X_K0;
Db.y = 1;
Db.z = 1;
// Description of a grid of blocks
Dg.x = LOCAL_SIZE/BLOCK_SIZE_X_K0 + (LOCAL_SIZE%BLOCK_SIZE_X_K0 ? 1 : 0);
Dg.y = LOCAL_SIZE;
Dg.z = 1;

// Run the grid of blocks of threads with Gk0
MatrixProductKernel_Gk0<<<Dg,Db>>>(step);
```

5.3.1.2 Optimization of GPU Computing Kernels

Using a GPU allows for the achievement of higher performance when the computations are adapted to the *vector-like* architecture and programming model. Details about GPU programming (using CUDA framework for NVIDIA cards) is beyond the scope of this study. However, we aim to show that there are similarities with CPU programming according to the optimization process of computing kernels.

Algorithm 5.9 shows the source code of a basic CUDA kernel *Gk0* (top) and the source code of this kernel call (bottom). This short code is composed of very classical operations in a CUDA program. It is quite simple as it uses only the *global memory* of the GPU and it accesses data without fully respecting their *coalescence*. Those omissions may induce a performance degradation as a part of the memory bus bandwidth of the GPU is wasted and the thread scheduling may not be optimal. We achieved a performance of $38.80\,Gflops$ on the GTX480 GPU board of each node of our testbed.

If we go a step further in the optimization process, Algorithm 5.10 introduces a medium optimized GPU computing kernel (*Gk1*). It uses the global memory of the GPU but also its *shared memory*: a fast memory used like a cache memory explicitly managed by the developer in the source code. In the previous GPU algorithm, another part of this fast memory was a real cache memory entirely managed by the GPU. Moreover, the Gk1 kernel has also coalescent data accesses that allow for a better scheduling of GPU threads. That kernel is to be used on a two-dimensional grid of thread blocks as presented in Algorithm 5.11. The `cudaFuncSetCacheConfig` function is used before the kernel call in order to increase the size of the shared mem-

---

Algorithm 5.10 GPU kernel using shared memory (Gk1)

```
__global__ void MatrixProductKernel_Gk1(int step)
{
    __shared__ double sh_A[BLOCK_SIZE_Y_K1][BLOCK_SIZE_X_K1]; // Local "cache" of A
    __shared__ double sh_B[BLOCK_SIZE_X_K1][BLOCK_SIZE_X_K1]; // Local "cache" of B
    double res = 0.0;                                          // Local result storage
    int ligC = threadIdx.y + blockIdx.y*BLOCK_SIZE_Y_K1;      // Coordinates of the C
    int colC = threadIdx.x + blockIdx.x*BLOCK_SIZE_X_K1;      // elt computed
    int colA = threadIdx.x;                                    // Initial indexes of
    int ligB = threadIdx.y;                                    // A column and B line

    // For each step: process BLOCK_SIZE_X_K1 elt of the required A line and B column
    for (int step = 0; step < SIZE/BLOCK_SIZE_X_K1; step++) {
        // Load A data into the shared sh_A array
        if (ligC < LOCAL_SIZE) {
            sh_A[threadIdx.y][threadIdx.x] = GPU_A[ligC][colA];
            colA += BLOCK_SIZE_X_K1;
        }
        // Load B data into the shared sb_B array
        if (colC < LOCAL_SIZE) {
            int ligShB = threadIdx.y;
            for (int sstep = 0; sstep < BLOCK_SIZE_X_K1/BLOCK_SIZE_Y_K1; sstep++) {
                sh_B[ligShB][threadIdx.x] = GPU_B[ligB][colC];
                ligB += BLOCK_SIZE_Y_K1;
                ligShB += BLOCK_SIZE_Y_K1;
            }
        }
        // Wait for all threads having updated the A and B "cache memories"
        __syncthreads();
        // Update C value using A and B data uploaded into the shared memory
        if (ligC < LOCAL_SIZE && colC < LOCAL_SIZE)
            for (int k = 0; k < BLOCK_SIZE_X_K1; k++)
                res += sh_A[threadIdx.y][k] * sh_B[k][threadIdx.x];
        // Wait for all threads having finished to use current values in the A and B ↩
            caches
        __syncthreads();
    }
    // Last step: process the remaining elts of the required A line and B colum
    if (SIZE % BLOCK_SIZE_X_K1 != 0) {
        // Cache a last value of A
        if (ligC < LOCAL_SIZE && colA < SIZE)
            sh_A[threadIdx.y][threadIdx.x] = GPU_A[ligC][colA];
        // Cache some last values of B
        if (colC < LOCAL_SIZE) {
            int ligShB = threadIdx.y;
            for (int sstep = 0; sstep < BLOCK_SIZE_X_K1/BLOCK_SIZE_Y_K1 && ligB < SIZE; ↩
                sstep++) {
                sh_B[ligShB][threadIdx.x] = GPU_B[ligB][colC];
                ligB += BLOCK_SIZE_Y_K1;
                ligShB += BLOCK_SIZE_Y_K1;
            }
        }
        // Wait for all threads having updated the A and B "cache memories"
        __syncthreads();
        // Update C value with the last A and B values uploaded in the shared memory
        if (ligC < LOCAL_SIZE && colC < LOCAL_SIZE)
            for (int k = 0; k < SIZE % BLOCK_SIZE_X_K1; k++)
                res += sh_A[threadIdx.y][k] * sh_B[k][threadIdx.x];
    }
    // Store the final computed value into the C matrix variable
    if (ligC < LOCAL_SIZE && colC < LOCAL_SIZE)
        GPU_C[ligC][colC] = res;
}
```

Algorithm 5.11 Gk1 GPU kernel call

```
// Description of a block of threads
Db.x = BLOCK_SIZE_X_K1;
Db.y = BLOCK_SIZE_Y_K1;
Db.z = 1;
// Description of a grid of blocks
Dg.x = LOCAL_SIZE/BLOCK_SIZE_X_K1 + (LOCAL_SIZE%BLOCK_SIZE_X_K1 ? 1 : 0);
Dg.y = LOCAL_SIZE/BLOCK_SIZE_Y_K1 + (LOCAL_SIZE%BLOCK_SIZE_Y_K1 ? 1 : 0);
Dg.z = 1;
// Maximize the size of the GPU shared memory for the Gk1 kernel
cudaFuncSetCacheConfig(MatrixProductKernel_Gk1, cudaFuncCachePreferShared);
// Run the grid of blocks of threads with the required kernel
MatrixProductKernel_Gk1<<<Dg,Db>>>(step);
```

---

ory that can be used by the kernel. This kernel source is longer and more complex than the first one. Not all developers can write or maintain this code. But it achieves a performance of 98.00 $Gflops$ on one node of our testbed (instead of 38.80 $Gflops$ with GK0 !).

Finally, Algorithm 5.12 introduces the usage of the highly optimized cuBLAS library: calling the routine `cublasDgemm` and a transposition kernel (user defined). The call to the cuBLAS library routine is close to the call to the BLAS library routine (on CPU), but the result is always stored in *column major* mode as in FORTRAN libraries. Then, it is necessary to transpose the resulting matrix at the end of each step before storing it in the entire local slice of the C matrix. This last GPU kernel is named *Gk2*. Calling the cuBLAS library is more complex than calling the BLAS library on a CPU, but it remains reasonable for GPU developers and it achieves a high performance of 154.00 $Gflops$ on one node of our testbed.

Algorithm 5.12 cuBLAS based GPU kernel (Gk2)

```
// Compute AxB calling cuBLAS library
cublasDgemm(handle, CUBLAS_OP_T, CUBLAS_OP_T, LOCAL_SIZE, LOCAL_SIZE, SIZE, &alpha,↩
    Adr_GPU_A, SIZE, Adr_GPU_B, LOCAL_SIZE, &beta, Adr_GPU_R, LOCAL_SIZE);
// Transpose Column Major result into a part of the C matrix
// Description of a block of threads
DbT.x = BLOCK_SIZE_XY_TK0;
DbT.y = BLOCK_SIZE_XY_TK0;
DbT.z = 1;
// Description of a grid of blocks
DgT.x = LOCAL_SIZE/BLOCK_SIZE_XY_TK0 + (LOCAL_SIZE%BLOCK_SIZE_XY_TK0 ? 1 : 0);
DgT.y = LOCAL_SIZE/BLOCK_SIZE_XY_TK0 + (LOCAL_SIZE%BLOCK_SIZE_XY_TK0 ? 1 : 0);
DgT.z = 1;
// Run the transposition kernel on the grid of blocks of threads
TransposeKernel_v0<<<DgT,DbT>>>(Adr_GPU_R, Adr_GPU_C + ((step+Me)%NbPE) * ↩
    LOCAL_SIZE * LOCAL_SIZE, LOCAL_SIZE, LOCAL_SIZE);
```

5.3.2 Experimental Highlighting of the Kernel Optimization

In Table 5.4 are presented the CPU kernels performances achieved on one node of our testbed, together with their respective speedups according to the first basic version (Ck0). A regular and significant improvement of the performance with the increase of the optimization degree can be seen. Moreover, we can observe that the C source code of the different CPU versions remains *reasonably simple*. Using the BLAS library is easy. So, it appears really interesting to develop these improvements on CPU, and specially the last one, calling a BLAS implementation and adding OpenMP multithreading. Theoretically, the Atlas implementation of the BLAS can be compiled in a multithreaded way in order to internally use the available cores on each node. However, our version of Atlas library was not multithreaded, and we had to explicitly manage multithreading via OpenMP.

CPU kernel version	Ck0 (basic optimization)	Ck1 (OpenMP multithreading)	Ck2 (Atlas/BLAS monothreaded)	Ck3 (Atlas/BLAS + OpenMP multithreading)
Gflops	1.60	6.98	9.81	36.30
Speedup	1.0	4.4	6.1	22.7

Table 5.4: Performances of the different CPU kernels

In Table 5.5 the performances obtained with the different GPU kernels are given. The optimized cuBLAS based kernel (*Gk2*) is 4.0 times faster than the basic GPU kernel, 4.2 times faster than the most optimized CPU kernel (based on the BLAS library and OpenMP multithreading), and 96.3 times faster than the basic and sequential CPU kernel. The final performance improvement of our matrix product kernel on one node is significant. However, it requires the learning of CUDA programming in order to use GPU accelerators. Moreover, if the problem to solve is more complex or more original than a simple dense matrix product, it is probable that no highly optimized libraries (like BLAS and cuBLAS) will be available. Then the developer will have to design and implement some highly optimized kernels by himself. This type of work requires a lot of expertise and a long development time, independently of the distribution on several computing nodes.

GPU kernel version	Gk0 (basic)	Gk1 (medium optimized)	Gk2 (cuBLAS)
Gflops	38.80	98.00	154.00
Speedup vs GPU-basic	1.0	2.5	4.0
Speedup vs CPU-optim	1.1	2.7	4.2
Speedup vs CPU-basic	24.3	61.3	96.3

Table 5.5: Performances of the different GPU kernels

In the next section we investigate the impact of kernel optimization over the performance of a distributed version on a cluster, and we attempt to identify the right couples (kernel optimization, parallel scheme optimization).

5.3.3 Decision Chain for Optimization of Computing Kernels

A computing kernel optimization process can lead to long and expensive development. To enter this kind of process is an important decision. A chain of decision criteria has to be considered.

As explained in Section 5.2.1, the first criterion is the ratio of the considered kernel in the entire application. It is not very useful to spend great effort on optimization in a kernel that takes only 1% or 2% of the total application time. On the other hand, if the kernel represents a significant part of the total execution time, then we have to study the criteria introduced in the following paragraphs.

5.3.3.1 Technical Criterion

When considering a computing kernel, the first criterion to evaluate before entering a new optimization development step is whether its performance can be theoretically optimized or not. A possible approach is based on counting the computing operations and the memory accesses achieved by the kernel. This approach uses the concept of *arithmetic intensity* introduced by NVIDIA in [15]. We partially studied this approach in [13] and more deeply in a collaboration with the EDF company [12].

The main steps are:

1. Counting the number of floating point operations achieved by the kernel: n_{ops}.

2. Counting the number of memory accesses achieved by the kernel. However, we need a model of the architecture, or at least some hypothesis about the hierarchy and speeds of the different memories. For example, we may count only accesses to the main memory, not to cache memories. So, we need to make assumptions about the cache size and cache management. Finally, we obtain a number of accesses in function of the architecture: $n_{a,archi}$.

3. Computing the *arithmetic intensity*: $i_a = n_{ops}/n_{a,archi}$, the average number of operations achieved per memory access.

4. Comparing this value to the *critic arithmetic intensity*: i_c, defined as the ratio between the processor speed (flops) and the memory access speed (bandwidth).

5. Deducing the theoretical minimal execution time:

    - If $i_a > i_c$, the kernel is *cpu-bound*: it is limited by the computing speed of the processor, and the theoretical minimal execution time is:
      $t_{ideal} = n_{ops}/(processor\_speed)$.

    - If $i_a < i_c$, the kernel is *memory-bound*: it is limited by the memory bandwith, and the theoretical minimal execution time is:
      $t_{ideal} = n_{a,archi}/(memory\_bandwidth)$.

When the experimental execution time is sufficiently larger than the theoretical minimal time, then it is interesting to attempt to optimize the kernel code. Moreover, it is sometimes possible to design new algorithms with an arithmetic intensity (i_a) closer to the critical one (i_c), in order to better exploit both computing and memory access capabilities of the processor.

5.3.3.2   Required Expertise Criterion

The first steps of the CPU kernel optimization are *standard* and require basic computer science knowledge. The usual optimization includes data structure and data access design in order to read and/or write contiguous memory locations and to avoid cache misses. Then, a simple access to multithreading via libraries like OpenMP is possible for loops performing independent iterations. A software developer with basic knowledge about processor architectures and multithreading libraries can achieve this degree of serial optimization and multithreading. However, the next steps are much more complex, and very few developers are able to design optimized code like BLAS libraries. Moreover, using multithreading leads to particular data storage and data access optimization, requiring specific knowledge.

When using GPUs, the required level of expertise increases quickly. Designing algorithms and codes with *coalescent* memory accesses is the basic training of a CUDA developer, and is usually well understood. But, developing explicit caching algorithms to exploit the fast *shared memories* of the NVIDIA GPUs requires a higher level of expertise. Many developers will never reach this second level of expertise. However, GPUs do not (yet) support a complex OS with various tasks. It is possible to monitor and to control what happens on a GPU, and finally to acquire a very high level of expertise and to achieve very optimized kernels.

In any case, achieving computing kernel optimization requires an adapted level of expertise, that takes time to acquire. So, an important decision criterion for starting an optimization process or not, is the availability (and the cost) of this expertise inside the development team or the company. Obviously, when an existing highly optimized library can be used in the kernel, like BLAS in our benchmark application, the right solution is to learn the usage of this library and to adapt the kernel to use it. It often allows the achievement of high performance with limited extra development efforts and a low expertise level.

5.3.3.3   Use Context Criterion

When the kernel code is used in a multi-node parallel context, the kernel time will be often compared to the communication time. When an overlapping of those two activities is possible, an efficient strategy is to reduce computation and communication times as much as possible so that they become of the same order. This maximizes the potential overlapping. However, it is shown in Section 5.4.2 that it is sometimes efficient to have communication times greater than computation times, in order to get an experimental gain close to the expected one (deduced from the potential overlapping).

Some software is designed for a long term exploitation and for intensive usage. In such cases, the development time remains smaller than the sum of the execution times ($T_{dev} << \sum(T_{exec})$) of the application during its lifetime. So, increasing the development time in order to decrease each execution time a bit may have a strong attraction. Nevertheless, if the application has a short life cycle, or if it is to be used rarely, the optimization effort may be more time consuming than the sum of the gained times in all the executions of the optimized version during its lifetime.

5.3.3.4 Complete Decision Chain

Finally, before investing into optimization effort of some computation kernels, one has to take care of:

(1) the ratio of this kernel in the total execution time of the application,

(2) the distance between the performance obtained and the theoretical performance of this kernel with the considered parallel architecture,

(3) the expertise level of the available developers or the existence of a suitable highly optimized library,

(4) the opportunity to overlap kernel computations with inter-node communications (in a multi-node architecture), and

(5) the estimated total amount of execution times of the application during its lifetime compared to the extra development time required.

5.4 Global Experiments and Analysis

The hardware and software components of the parallel system that has been used to perform the following experiments are detailed in Section 5.1.3.

5.4.1 Experimentation Strategy

The different versions of the benchmark application have been tested on different numbers of nodes of the cluster and with different computing variants (variable number of computing threads when relevant). As it is not reasonable (and not fully pertinent) to present the entire set of results obtained from those experiments in this chapter, two levels of selection have been applied. The first one concerns the application variants (overlapping scheme and computing kernel). Hence, Algorithm 5.2 is not selected as it has already been shown in Section 5.2.5 that this scheme is not efficient at all. The second selection level is related to the runtime configurations (number of computing threads). For each selected variant only the runtime configuration that has obtained the best performance is retained.

As mentioned in Section 5.2.5, each result is the average of five consecutive executions after an initial warm-up. Moreover, as a first analysis of the overlapping schemes

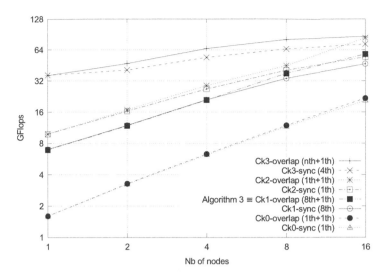

Figure 5.7: Performance curves of different CPU computing kernels with or without overlapping on a multi-core CPU cluster

already has been presented in that previous section, the current section is more dedicated to the analysis of the actual efficiency of the overlapping (according to the expected performance) as well as the efficiency of the computing kernels.

5.4.2   Experimental Results

For clarity's sake, the analysis is decomposed into two parts according to the type of computing kernel.

5.4.2.1   Performance on Multicore CPU Cluster

In Figure 5.7 are shown the performance curves achieved, with 1 to 16 nodes, by our different CPU kernels, with no overlapping or with the overlapping scheme in Algorithm 5.3. The two bottom curves correspond to the performance achieved with the *Ck0* CPU kernel that includes only some basic serial optimization (see Section 5.1.2 and algorithm 5.1) and that uses only one CPU core (no multithreading inside this kernel).

In the *Ck0* CPU kernel with no overlapping (*Ck0-sync* curve), the communication time ranges from 3.2% up to 20.4% of the entire application time respectively from 2 up to 16 nodes. Moreover, it is 3.4% up to 25.8% of the computation loop time. This computing kernel has limited performance, but when the number of nodes increases it becomes interesting to overlap communications with computations to save up to 25.8% of the computation loop time (see Section 5.2.1). Then we have implemented the overlapping scheme in Algorithm 5.3, using an explicit OpenMP thread to achieve MPI communications, and another thread to run the computation kernel (see Section 5.2.3). Finally, the performance curve *Ck0-overlap* stays quite similar to *Ck0-sync* but shows a small improvement on 16 nodes.

We have followed a very similar approach with the *Ck1* CPU kernel, that is a multi-threaded version of the previous one. Curves *Ck1-sync* and *Ck1-overlap* respectively show the performance achieved without and with overlapping. It has to be noticed that due to technical constraints in OpenMP, the actual implementation of the *Ck1-overlap* is Algorithm 5.3. However, these two schemes have the same semantics that consist of having several computing threads and one communication thread. The analysis of the curves shows that running 8 threads on the 4 hyperthreaded cores of our Nehalem processors has led to a significant decrease in the computation time. The communication time remains unchanged, and from 2 to 16 nodes it ranges from 12.1% to 35.1% of the application time, and from 14.1% to 55.8% of the computation loop time. In this context, the overlapping of computations with communications is highly attractive. With 8 and 16 nodes, the performance increase is significant and justifies the development effort of the overlapping.

The next curves concern the usage of a BLAS library kernel (Atlas implementation), identified as the *Ck2* CPU kernel in Figure 5.7. This is a sequential kernel using only one core, but with a very high degree of optimization. With this kernel, the communication time ranges from 13.5% to 37.1% of the application time, and from 16.5% to 62.6% of the computation loop time. The performance increase on the *Ck2-overlap* curve, compared to the *Ck2-sync* curve, starts as soon as 2 nodes are used and becomes surprisingly strong with 16 nodes. In fact, when using 16 nodes with this computing kernel, communications become longer than computations (in the computation loop): $T_{comm} = 1.7 \times T_{comput}$. Then, the loop computation time appears to be very close to the communication time: the time saved by the overlap is 93% of the expected one. On 8 nodes, the communication time is less than the computation time ($T_{comm} = 0.86 \times T_{comput}$), and the time saved by the overlap is only 22% of the expected one. It seems that overlapping inter-node communications with node computations is better when the computation time is smaller than the communication time. However, in this case the performance is bounded by the communications. Usually, designers of parallel codes try to get communications shorter than computations. See Section 5.4.3 for a detailed analysis of this phenomenon.

The last performance curves correspond to the variant of the application with the same sequential BLAS kernel, but called in parallel from different threads in order to use the available cores of the CPU. Parallel runs of the BLAS kernel have been tested with 2, 3, on up to 12 threads. With no overlapping, the number of threads providing the best performance is constant and corresponds to 4. With the overlapping, the best number of threads varies with the number of nodes (and so with the size of the sub-problem run on each node). With 2, 4 and 8 nodes the best performance is obtained with 8 computing threads (and one communication thread), while with 16 nodes only 4 computing nodes (and one communication thread) are necessary. These results are depicted by the *Ck3-overlap* curve. Compared to the *Ck3-sync* curve, the improvement in the overlapping is visible and significant from 2 to 16 nodes. In this context, the

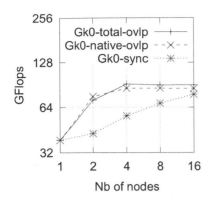

Figure 5.8: Performance of the basic Gk0 kernel on a GPU cluster

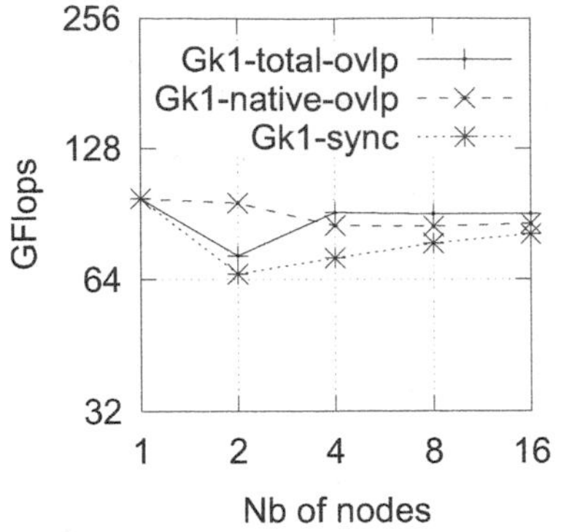

Figure 5.9: Performance of the optimized Gk1 kernel on a GPU cluster

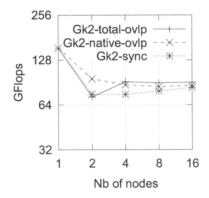

Figure 5.10: Performance of the highly optimized Gk2 kernel on a GPU cluster

communication time is greater than the computation time with 4, 8 and 16 nodes. However, the overlap is close to 100% of its expected value only with 16 nodes when $T_{comm} = 5.5 \times T_{comput}$.

5.4.2.2 Performance on GPU Cluster

We have experimented each of our three GPU kernels with three parallel variants: with no overlapping (Algorithm 5.1 with a GPU kernel), with a native overlapping mechanism (Algorithm 5.4), and with an overlapping including the CPU/GPU data transfers (Algorithm 5.5). In Figure 5.8 are given the three performance curves of the *Gk0* kernel, a basic GPU kernel not using the fast *shared memories* of the GPU but using only its *global memory* (and some registers). The bottom curve illustrates the performance of the version with no overlap of the inter-node communications, GPU computations and data transfers between CPUs and GPUs. We have enforced synchronization of the GPU kernel so that these operations do not overlap. From 1 to 2 nodes the performance increase is poor, and is stronger from 2 to 16 nodes. Using 2 nodes doubles the computing power, but inserting inter-node communications is a great penalty that seriously limits the impact of a second GPU. When increasing the number of nodes from 2 to 16, the communication time increases very slightly (from $1.39s$ to $1.58s$) while the computing power increases strongly. So the performance curve increases significantly up to 16 nodes. The upper performance curves correspond to the overlapping modes. The penalty of inter-node communications is not sensitive from 1 to 2 nodes, but on 4 nodes the computation time (on the GPU) is less than the inter-node communication time. So the overlapped execution time is limited by the communication time that remains approximately constant, and the performance reaches its limit. Our gigabit Ethernet interconnection network appears insufficient to support GPU nodes: they require and produce data faster than this network can route.

The highest curve shows the performance of the version overlapping inter-node communications with both GPU computations and CPU/GPU data transfers. This code is more complex to develop (see Section 5.2.4.2 and Algorithm 5.5), but it achieves slightly better performances from 4 to 16 nodes than the native overlapping version. However, performances are a little bit weaker on 2 nodes. As already mention in Section 5.2.5, this phenomenon is still under investigations.

The results obtained with the *Gk1* GPU kernel are given in Figure 5.9. This kernel code is more complex and uses the fast *shared memories* of the GPU like a cache memory explicitly managed by the developer at application level. With or without any overlap mechanism, we can observe that best performance is obtained on only 1 computing node. Performance of this computing kernel on one node is approximately three times greater than performance of the *Gk0* kernel, and computation times are smaller than communication times. So the communication times of our gigabit Ethernet network always compensate the computation times won by using several nodes, and the total execution time does not decrease. This phenomenon is more visible with the third GPU kernel (*Gk2*), using the highly optimized cuBLAS library. Figure 5.10 shows very high performance on only 1 node (close to $154Gflops$), and a strong performance decrease when using more nodes, even with a total overlap of the communications with both computations and data transfers.

5.4.3 Discussion

5.4.3.1 Assessment of Overlapping Strategy on CPU Clusters

Finally, overlapping communications with computations on a multicore CPU cluster is successful with the strategy based on an explicit thread running and managing the MPI communications (see Section 5.2.3). However, it is not obvious to reach the ideal execution time: usually we observe $T_{overlap} > max(T_{comput}, T_{comm})$. Considering that in the ideal case $T_{saved}^{ideal} = (T_{comput} + T_{comm}) - max(T_{comput}, T_{comm}) = min(T_{comput}, T_{comm})$, detailed experiments on our cluster have shown that:

- when $0 < \frac{T_{comm}}{T_{comput}} < 0.95$, we get: $T_{saved} < 0.30 \times T_{saved}^{ideal}$,

- when $1.0 < \frac{T_{comm}}{T_{comput}}$, we can achieve: $T_{saved} = T_{saved}^{ideal}$.

So, although obtaining $T_{saved} = T_{saved}^{ideal}$ seems attractive, usually it provides *inefficient* results as the communication times are longer than the computation ones. Even if the overlapping strategy can lead to achieving 100% of the expected gain, this gain is strongly limited by the small overlapping potential. Moreover, it may require a lot of resources for a limited extra-speedup. For example, the *Ck3-overlap* performance curve increases up to 16 nodes, but the minor increase from 8 to 16 nodes does not justify doubling the cluster size. It is important to know how to track and achieve overlapping to improve the performance, but not to track it at all costs.

5.4.3.2   Assessment of Overlapping Strategy on GPU Clusters

Our experiments show that an overlapping mechanism can lead to significant performance increase on a GPU cluster. We can evaluate the efficiency of the two overlapping strategies that have been implemented. The synchronous implementation of the computation loop can be modeled with:

$$T_{loop}^{sync} = T_{comp} + T_{trans} + T_{comm}$$

the execution time of the native overlap strategy is:

$$T_{loop}^{native-ovlp} = T_{trans} + max(T_{comp}, T_{comm})$$

and the execution time of the more complex and total overlap strategy is given by:

$$T_{loop}^{total-ovlp} = max(T_{comp}, T_{trans} + T_{comm})$$

As on the CPU cluster, we measured T_{comp}, T_{trans} and T_{comm} with the (strongly) synchronous version (no overlapping). Then, the ideal saved times that are expected for each overlapping strategy are computed and compared to the actual saved times obtained in the experiments. Finally, the ratios T_{comm}/T_{comp} (or $T_{comm}/(T_{comp} + T_{trans})$) and $T_{saved}/T_{saved}^{ideal}$ are deduced. We obtained very different results from the ones with the CPU kernels. With the *Gk0* kernel:

- with the native overlapping strategy we obtain:
  $0.75 < T_{comm}/T_{comp} < 8.4$, and $0.84 < T_{saved}/T_{saved}^{ideal} < 1.02$

- with the total overlapping strategy we obtain:
  $0.75 < T_{comm}/(T_{comp} + T_{trans}) < 7.8$, and $0.92 < T_{saved}/T_{saved}^{ideal} < 1.12$

Compared to the CPU kernel results, we have a greater ratio T_{comm}/T_{comp} due to the very high speed of the GPUs. Therefore communication times quickly exceed computation times (even when adding the transfer times). Moreover, the overlapping being very efficient in those contexts, the major part of the expected gain of the overlapping is actually achieved: at least 84% with the basic and native overlapping strategy. When using the total overlapping strategy, we have measured a gain of time greater than the expected one (110% of the expected time). Obviously, such results are not coherent with the theory. However, they can be explained (at least partially) by the additional GPU synchronization that had to be used in the basic version with no overlapping in order to force the CPU to wait for the GPU kernel termination. We remind the reader that by default a GPU kernel call is non-blocking. Such synchronization induces additional costs that may lead to measuring longer computation times than the real ones.

Anyway, independently of the problem of the exact correspondence of the monitored activities between two application variants, it appears that the native overlapping strategy on a GPU cluster is very easy to deploy, the total overlapping strategy is not so complex (see Section 5.2.4), and both are successful. We save almost 90% of the expected time with a T_{comm}/T_{comp} ratio around 1, and almost 100% with a higher ratio. However, as we claimed for CPU clusters, it is not interesting to run parallel programs with strongly dominant communication times. In Figure 5.8 a strong improvement when using overlapping mechanisms can be observed, but there is no global improvement when using more than 4 nodes with these mechanisms (using more resources is *useless*).

Analyses of the T_{comm}/T_{comp} and $T_{saved}/T_{saved}^{ideal}$ ratio for *Gk1* and *Gk2* kernels would lead to similar results to the *Gk0* ones. However, they have a limited interest. As explained previously, our interconnection network is not fast enough to use these kernels. A network upgrade would be required (towards Infiniband for example), or the use of benchmark requiring many more computations.

5.4.3.3   Looking for the Most Interesting Solution

Due to the limited capacity of our gigabit Ethernet interconnection network, the number of nodes providing the best performance of our benchmark problem decreases when the speed of the computing kernel increases. Table 5.6 summarizes the configurations most suited to the different kernels. With all the CPU kernels, it is interesting to use the 16 nodes of the cluster and to implement a multithreaded overlapping of computations with communications. However, when running the fastest CPU kernel, the performance increase from 8 to 16 nodes is small.

When running GPU kernels, the most interesting number of nodes decreases. With the basic *Gk0* GPU kernel (easy to design) it is better to use only 4 nodes, and to implement a total overlapping of communications with both computations and CPU/GPU data transfers. With faster GPU kernels, it is better to use only 1 node to run this benchmark problem. Then, no inter-node communication is required and it is not necessary to implement any overlapping mechanism.

Kernel	Most suited parallel scheme	Nodes	Gflops
Ck0	Overlapping (1 comp. thread and 1 comm. thread)	16	22
Ck1	Overlapping (8 comp. thread and 1 comm. thread)	16	58
Ck2	Overlapping (1 comp. thread and 1 comm. thread)	16	84
Ck3	Overlapping (n comp. thread and 1 comm. thread)	16	87
Gk0	Total overlapping (comm. *vs* comp. + trans.)	4	92
Gk1	Mono-node exec. (no comm.)	1	98
Gk2	Mono-node exec. (no comm.)	1	154

Table 5.6: Configurations providing the best performance for each computing kernel

Obviously, it could be interesting to run a larger benchmark, with bigger matrices. But problems to solve are not always *infinitely scalable*. Sometimes we have to solve a large but finite problem. Then, we can look for the fastest solution, with limited development time and with limited computing resources. If some adapted high performance libraries are available (like BLAS and cuBLAS in our example) it is highly recommended to (test and) use such libraries. When some problem-specific high performance kernels have to be developed, a pertinent trade-off between the development time (and cost) and the gain in execution time must be found. For example, we can track to:

- decrease the execution time under a fixed threshold, no more, no less,

- minimize the sum: $T_{dev} + \sum(T_{exec})$

When spending a lot of time (and money) to develop a very fast computing kernel, it is possible to exceed the capacities of the available interconnection network. Then, the application performance will be limited to the speed achieved with only a few nodes, or even only one node (if the problem size fits the memory size on one node). Then, it may be more interesting to spend less time developing the computing kernel, and to spend some time overlapping computations with communications in the parallel program. Another possibility is to decrease development time and cost, and to buy a better interconnection network. The most suited strategy depends on each use-case.

5.5   Conclusion

Due to the high hardware complexity of current processors, code optimization is mandatory for high performance computing codes. But an optimization process is, in some sense, an endless process that may lead to important extra development costs for only small performance improvements. A methodology is required to avoid this type of pitfall.

In this chapter we have investigated the optimization process of a toy application (a dense matrix product) on a multicore CPU/GPU cluster. Throughout this process, some methodologies have been proposed to develop optimized computing kernels and efficient overlapping of communications with computations, and to identify the most interesting configurations and deployments on CPU or GPU clusters. Following these methodologies, different possible degrees of optimization have been presented and several series of criteria have been proposed to help developers decide up to which degree of optimization the development effort has to be led.

Our study shows that even on a basic test application, a significant increase in the code complexity (especially in GPU kernels) can be observed with the increase of the optimization degree, requiring more expertise to develop and maintain and leading to longer development times.

The variants of the application obtained have been fully benchmarked with different runtime parameters (when pertinent) and different configurations of the test platform. Those benchmarks have pointed out that the highest optimization degrees may sometimes be useless as they bring no visible gain. Moreover, the experiments have also shown that a strong limitation that quickly appears with optimized codes comes from the interconnection network. In fact, current classical networks such as Gigabit Ethernet are not suited to the interconnection of powerful nodes running optimized computing kernels.

In the near future, we plan to achieve complementary benchmarks with different problem sizes and with different clusters, in order to confirm the generality of our analysis and methodology. Moreover, we aim at studying other overlapping schemes as well as CPU kernels using vector units (like SSE or AVX ones).

References

[1] "Open Source High Performance Computing". http://www.open-mpi.org

[2] "OpenMP multi-threaded programming API". http://www.openmp.org

[3] F. Baude, D. Caromel, N. Furmento, D. Sagnol, "Overlapping communication with computation in distributed object systems", in P. Sloot, M. Bubak, A. Hockstra, B. Hertzberger, (Editors), " High-Performance Computing and Networking", Lecture Notes in Computer Science, 1593, 744–753, Springer Berlin / Heidelberg, 1999. doi:10.1007/BFb0100635

[4] E.M. Daoudi, A. Lakhouaja, H. Outada, "Overlapping Computation/Communication in the Parallel One-Sided Jacobi Method", in H. Kosch, L. Böszörményi, H. Hellwagner, (Editors), "Euro-Par 2003 Conference", Lecture Notes in Computer Science, 2790, 844–849, Springer, 2003. doi:10.1007/978-3-540-45209-6_115

[5] L.D. de Cerio, M. Valero-García, A. González, "Overlapping Communication and Computation in Hypercubes", in L. Bougé, P. Fraigniaud, A. Mignotte, Y. Robert, (Editors), "Euro-Par '96 Conference, Vol. I", Lecture Notes in Computer Science, 1123, 253–257. Springer, 1996. doi:10.1007/3-540-61626-8_33

[6] G.I. Goumas, N. Anastopoulos, N. Koziris, N. Ioannou, "Overlapping computation and communication in SMT clusters with commodity interconnects",

CLUSTER, 1–10, IEEE, 2009. doi:10.1109/CLUSTR.2009.5289174

[7] R.L. Graham, S.W. Poole, P. Shamis, G. Bloch, N. Bloch, H. Chapman, M. Kagan, A. Shahar, I. Rabinovitz, G. Shainer, "Overlapping computation and communication: Barrier algorithms and ConnectX-2 CORE-Direct capabilities", IPDPS Workshops, 1–8, IEEE, 2010. doi:10.1109/IPDPSW.2010.5470854

[8] T. Hoefler, A. Lumsdaine, "Message Progression in Parallel Computing - To Thread or not to Thread?", CLUSTER, 213–222, IEEE, 2008. doi:10.1109/CLUSTR.2008.4663774

[9] T. Hoefler, A. Lumsdaine, "Overlapping Communication and Computation with High Level Communication Routines", IEEE International Symposium on Cluster Computing and the Grid, 572–577, 2008.

[10] J.B. White, J.J. Dongarra, "Overlapping Computation and Communication for Advection on Hybrid Parallel Computers", IPDPS, 59–67, IEEE, 2011. doi:10.1109/IPDPS.2011.16

[11] T.H. Kaiser, S.B. Baden, "Overlapping communication and computation with OpenMP and MPI", Sci. Program., 9(2,3), 73–81, Aug. 2001. http://dl. acm.org/citation.cfm?id=1239928.1239932

[12] W. Kirschenmann, "Towards sustainable intensive computing kernels - Vers des noyaux de calcul intensif perennes", PhD thesis, Lorraine University, 2012. (in French)

[13] W. Kirschenmann, L. Plagne, S. Vialle, "Parallel SP_N on Multi-Core CPUs and Many-Core GPUs", Transport Theory and Statistical Physics, 39(2), 255–281, 2010.

[14] V. Marjanovic, J. Labarta, E. Ayguadé, M. Valero, "Overlapping communication and computation by using a hybrid MPI/SMPSs approach", in T. Boku, H. Nakashima, A. Mendelson, (Editors), "ICS", 5–16, ACM, 2010. doi:10.1145/1810085.1810091

[15] NVIDIA, "NVIDIA CUDA C Programming Guide 4.0", 2011. http://developer.download.nvidia.com/compute/DevZone/ docs/html/C/doc/CUDA_C_Programming_Guide.pdf

[16] A.K. Somani, A.M. Sansano, A.K. Somani, A.M. Sansano, "Minimizing overhead in parallel algorithms through overlapping communication/computation", Technical report, Institute for Computer Applications in Science and Engineering, 1997.

©Saxe-Coburg Publications, 2014.
F. Magoulès, (Editor),
Patterns for Parallel Programming on GPUs
Saxe-Coburg Publications, Stirlingshire, Scotland, 149-169.

Chapter 6

Program Sequentially, Carefully, and Benefit from Compiler Advances for Parallel Heterogeneous Computing

M. Amini[1], **C. Ancourt**[2], **B. Creusillet**[3], **F. Irigoin**[2] and **R. Keryell**[1]

[1]*SILKAN Inc., Los Altos CA, USA*
[2]*MINES ParisTech/CRI, Fontainebleau, France*
[3]*SILKAN, Meudon, France*

Abstract

The current microarchitecture trend leads toward heterogeneity. This evolution is driven by the end of Moore's law and the frequency wall due to the power wall. Moreover, with the spreading of the smartphone, some constraints from the mobile world drive the design of most new architectures. An immediate consequence is that an application has to be executable on various targets.

Porting and maintaining multiple versions of the code base requires different skills and the efforts required in the process as well as the increased complexity in debugging and testing are time consuming, thus expensive.

Some solutions based on compilers emerge. They are based either on directives added to C like in OpenHMPP or OpenACC or on an automatic solution like POCC, Pluto, PPCG, or PAR4ALL. However compilers cannot retarget any program written in a low-level language such as unconstrained C in an efficient way. Programmers should follow good practices when writing code so that compilers have more room to perform the transformations required for efficient execution on heterogeneous targets.

This chapter explores the impact of different patterns used by programmers, and defines a set of good practices allowing a compiler to generate efficient code.

Keywords: parallel programming, automatic parallelization, coding rules.

6.1   Introduction

As mono-core processor technology has reached its limits, and as our computing needs are growing exponentially, we are facing an explosion of proposals in the current architectural trends, with more arithmetic units usable at the same time, vector units to apply similar operations on the elements of short vectors (such as SSE, AVX, NEON, *etc.*), several computing cores on the same processor die, several processors sharing or not the same memory, more heterogeneous architectures with hardware accelerators of specific functions, FPGA or massively parallel GPU.

As a consequence, an application has to be executable on various platforms, at a given time as well as during its whole life cycle. This execution has to meet some efficiency criteria, such as energy or computational efficiency, that may not be compatible. Thus the development and maintenance costs become crucial issues, and automatic optimization and parallelization techniques, whereas often considered as unrealistic silver bullets, are returning to the front stage as a partial solution to lower the development and maintenance cost.

Of course, automatic parallelization cannot be expected to produce miracles, as the problem is intractable in the general case. Reaching the highest possible performance for a given application on a specific architecture will always require some type of human intervention, sometimes ending up with a complete rewrite from scratch.

However, and fortunately, sufficiently *well-written* sequential programs can expose enough parallelism that automatic parallelizers can detect, and for which they can do a sufficiently good job. In particular, we advocate that, before any attempt at manual or automatic parallelization, programs should avoid sequential processor optimizations and stick as much as possible to the high-level semantics of the algorithms. Thus, instead of writing code for a specific class of architectures, programmers and more widely code generators must learn how to write sequential programs, efficiently targeting the current class of advanced compilers, namely compilers with loop optimizers, vectorizers and automatic parallelizers.

This chapter, based on the long experience of its authors in this area, mainly on the PIPS [1, 20] and PAR4ALL [2, 34] projects, details some good programming practices for imperative languages that are compliant with the current capabilities of automatic parallelizers, and more generally optimizers, to maximize the precision of analyses and thus help the tools in generating efficient code. As a preliminary clue, and not surprisingly, let us say that the more structured a program is, the easier it is to analyze.

Since parallelism is present at many levels in current architectures, even a program executed on a single core can benefit from being well written, for example by allowing the use of vector instruction sets or computing some parts at compile-time through partial evaluation.

In the remainder of this document, we focus mainly on the C language, and we assume that the reader is knowledgeable in the C99 programming language[1]. However,

---

[1] And more specifically the ISO/IEC 9899:TC3 WG14 standard. The last public draft can be found here: http://www.open-std.org/JTC1/SC22/WG14/www/docs/n1256.pdf. We could focus on C11, but this latest version is too recent to be widespread yet.

```
int kernel(int n, int m) {
  int a[n][m], b[n][m];
#pragma acc kernels
  {
    int i=0;
    while(i<n) {
      for(int j=0; j<m; j++) {
        a[i][j]=i+j;
        if(i==j)
          a[i][j]=i-j;
        b[i][j]=a[i][j];
      }
      i++;
    }
  }
}
```

Figure 6.1: OpenACC example with a while loop. The PGI compiler is able to parallelize this loop nest and schedule it on GPU

the principles can be generalized for other languages.

In this chapter, we give in Section 6.2 some advice on program structure and control flow. The Section 6.3 presents some points related to data structures and types. Then Section 6.4 introduces the concept of directives and pragmas to help the compiler in their quest to efficient parallel code. Section 6.5 recalls the interest of already parallelized libraries. Before concluding, Section 6.6 details some constraints related to object-oriented languages.

This work has been done within the OpenGPU project, where the authors have been involved in developing compilers for GPU, mainly related to C and DSL to OpenCL translation.

6.2 Program Structure and Control Flow

Most optimizers rely on the good properties of the program control flow to generate efficient results. Thereby, a program with poorly structured computational parts (which contains goto, break, continue, exit(), multiple returns, *etc.*) prevents further code transformations and automatic optimizations. Of course some tools such as PIPS [1, 20] or the PGI Compiler have some restructuring capabilities, as shown in the listing from Figure 6.1, but they have their limitations. So a good practice is to adopt a well-structured programming style, or at least to restrict the use of poorly structured code to inherently sequential parts. More generally well-structured programming has to be used in parallel parts, and if not, another way to express parallelism has to be used, for example by relying on hand-coded libraries as shown in Section 6.5 or by hiding messy code as in Section 6.2.3.

6.2.1   Well-Formed Loops...

Many advanced optimization techniques, such as automatic parallelization, traditionally focus on loops — which are usually the most intensive parts of the programs
— and more specifically on `for` loops with good properties, namely loops which are
similar to Fortran `do` loops: the loop index is an integer, initialized before the first iteration, and its value is incremented by a constant value and compared to loop-invariant
values at each iteration, and not changed by the loop body itself. The number of iterations is known before the loop is entered. Note that language extensions such as
OpenMP [28], OpenACC [26] and HMPP [8] provide parallel constructs for `do` and such
well-formed `for` loops, but not for general `for` or `while` loops.

Tools based on the polyhedral model [4,9,12,22,30] have long been historically very
strict, by also enforcing that the initial value, the lower and the upper bounds be affine
integer expressions of the surrounding loop indices and loop-invariant values, as well
as `if` conditions and array indices. This is also a requirement of several compilers
such as Cetus or the R-Stream compiler [33].

The polyhedral model has been extended to lift some of these conditions, and these
extensions are available in LooPo [15] and POCC [6,30]. It must also be noted that
applying a series of pre-processing transformations — such as constant propagation
or induction variable substitution — can raise the number of good candidates [5].
However, this is quite undesirable in source-to-source compilers.

So, even when these conditions are not compulsory, they are greatly encouraged, as
most tools take advantage of them to detect parallelism and/or generate more efficient
code. For instance, the following *manually optimized* piece of code

```
double a[n][m][l];
double * p = &a[0][0][0];
for(int i = 0; i < n*m*l; i++)
  p[i] = ...;
```

can be parallelized by the PAR4ALL OpenMP compiler [34], but the communications
cannot be generated accurately in the GPU version because of the non-linear loop
upper bound.

In most tools [9,29,31–33], loop transformations only target *well-formed* `for` loops,
while other compilers also deal with `while` loops [6,15]. In between, PIPS tries to
detect `for` and `while` loops which are equivalent to *well-formed* loops. For that
purpose, it is important to write these loops in such a way that they can be detected
as Fortran-like `do` loops. In particular, this implies using simple comparison and
increment expressions, and avoiding putting the `for` body code inside the increment
expression as in:

```
for (i=0; i<n; a[i] = i, i++);
```

Also, incrementing an integer index should be preferred to directly incrementing a
pointer:

```
for (p=a; p<a+n; p++)
  *p = ...;
```

should be replaced by:

```
for (int i = 0; i<n; i++)
    a[i] = ...;
p = &a[n]; // if the value of p is required later
```

6.2.2 ...and Loop Bodies

The conditions on the loop bodies characteristics depend on the tools capabilities. For instance the PGI Compiler used not to parallelize loops containing if conditions [36] in previous versions. Tools relying on fully polyhedral techniques historically require that internal if conditions be affine integer expressions [12, 22], but this restriction recently has been lifted [6, 30]. The R-Stream compiler lies somewhere in between, allowing some non-affine condition expressions. PIPS allows any internal control flow by using approximation techniques [10], provided that there is no jumping construct from and to the loop body. However, it must be kept in mind that, in most cases, the more information that is available to the optimizer, the more efficient it can be[2].

Most tools offer no or very limited interprocedural capabilities. For instance, ROSE and PGI Compilers [29, 32] do not parallelize loops with inner function calls, but this can be by-passed in a PGI compiler with the -Mconcur=cncall option that specifies that all loops containing calls can be safely parallelized, or by activating automatic *inlining*. The R-Stream compiler [33] assumes by default that functions have no side-effects, which may lead to incorrect code; but it provides a mechanism — called an *image function* — for the user to describe the side-effects of library functions using stub functions.

On the other hand, PIPS has been designed from the very beginning as an interprocedural parallelizer [20, 37], and uses interprocedural summarizing techniques to take into account memory accesses hidden in function calls. Cetus [31] also has some simple interprocedural capabilities, which allows some loops to be parallelized with function calls.

6.2.3 Testing Error Conditions

It is generally not possible to safely change the execution order of statements in a group involving calls to exit() or assert(): hence compilers do not even try to optimize or parallelize the surrounding loops. It is a good idea to avoid these calls inside portions of code which are good candidates for optimization. However, it may not be desirable in all cases, in particular during the development phase of the sequential version of the application.

In particular, asserts are very useful for debugging the sequential version, but they can be removed easily by passing the -DNDEBUG option to the pre-processor, even if some compilers such as PIPS can take into account some of the information they carry

---

[2]Sometimes large constant values may lead to information loss because of overflow errors in the abstractions used to represent the programs internally. Symbolic bounds can be useful, even when they are actually constant.

```
#include <assert.h>

int f(int m, int n) {
  int k = 0;
  assert(m >= 1 && n >= 1);
  /* From the previous assert,
     PIPS infers that m >= 1 and n >= 1 */
  for(int i = 0; i < m; i++)
    for(int j = 0; j < n; j++)
      k++;
  /* From the previous precondition after the assert,
     PIPS infers that k >= 1 at the function exit */
  return k;
}
```

Figure 6.2: Example of assert giving some semantics information in PIPS and PAR4ALL

as shown in Figure 6.2. It is important to test the bounds of the entry parameters and the data not only to prevent some errors but also because it may give clues to prove that some pieces of code are indeed parallel. Instead of simply removing the asserts, they should at least be replaced by some code that tests some conditions of soundness.

Exits are often used when testing error conditions, such as system calls return values. But since these tests do not affect the program semantics when there is a correct execution, a good practice would be to wrap system calls in dedicated macros or functions which would receive a simpler and non-blocking definition for the parallelizer, different from the real implementation that can be more complex, as discussed later in Section 6.5.2. Figure 6.3 gives an example for the `malloc()` function.

Another solution is to wrap error code between **#ifdef** ERROR_CONTROL ... **#endif** pairs to be able to remove such code on demand.

More generally, packaging this type of complex I/O code into libraries that also can be parallelized by some specialists is a solution, as explained in Section 6.5.1.

6.2.4 Declaration Scope

Even in interprocedural optimizers which can deal with parameter passing through global variables such as COMMON in Fortran, or with static local variables, global declarations may induce memory dependencies which prevent parallelization. Removing these dependencies requires interprocedural program transformations which are not always possible nor available. They consist of cloning a whole program sub-tree and adding the global variable as parameters to all functions and function calls in the cloned sub-tree, resulting in more expensive analysis and transformation cost.

Hence, global (and Fortran `common`) or static local variables must be avoided at least in program parts which are good candidates for parallelization, and, preferably, in the whole application since program analyses and transformations more and more tend to take the whole program behavior into account.

C99 offers the possibility of declaring data almost anywhere in the code. Paral-

```
// malloc wrapper with error testing
void * my_malloc(size_t size, int err_code,
                 const char * restrict err_mess)
{
  void * res = malloc(size);
  if (res == NULL) {
    /* This IO is an issue since it prevents
       parallelization: */
    fputs(err_mess, stderr);
    /* This global exit leads to an unstructured control
       graph, reducing optimization opportunities ... */
    exit(err_code);
  }
  return(res);
}

/* Wrapper provided to the parallelizer.
   Note that in case of a source-to-source parallelizer,
   yet another version may be given to the back-end
   compiler to take into account the targeted
   architecture characteristics. */
void * my_malloc(size_t size, int err_code,
                 const char * restrict err_mess)
{
  // No more IO or exit()!
  void * res = malloc(size);
  return(res);
}
```

Figure 6.3: Wrapping system calls

lelizers are unequally ready to accept this feature, which means that you may have to gather all data declarations at the beginning of a statement block. This is nevertheless a good practice to avoid declarations intermingled with jumping constructs, as this may render code restructuring and maintenance more difficult.

6.2.5 Interprocedural Control Flow

Automatic code generation tools more and more include more or less advanced interprocedural capabilities, such as the propagation of constant values, summaries of scalar or arrays read and written by function calls (Cetus and PIPS, and even mixes of structures and arrays for PIPS). This greatly enhances their parallelizing capabilities.

A common restriction in parallelizing compilers and standards such as HMPP [8] or OpenACC [26] is that recursive functions are forbidden. The iterative version is then to be preferred, and, in some cases, this may even expose some intra-procedural instruction parallelism which could not be exploited with the recursive version because such optimization does not cross function calls.

6.3 Data Structures and Types

The C language provides several basic data structures, which can be combined to create more complicated ones. Traditionally, parallelizing compilers have focused their efforts on arrays, and this is still their preferred target. However, some are broadening their range of action to deal with mixes of structures and arrays, pointers, *etc.* But it must be borne in mind that aggregating data may reduce the optimization opportunities or their efficiency.

For instance, grouping the application infrastructure values inside a structure may be practical to avoid passing several parameters to functions, but it may prevent the compiler from using them when testing memory dependencies without data transformations.

Dealing with arrays of structures is similarly not practical, and dependency analysis can be extended easily to deal with them. However, generating communications for heterogeneous targets is more difficult. Depending on the size of the structures, on the fields actually accessed during the exported computation, and on the communication costs, it may be more advisable to transfer a whole sub-part of the array, or to pack/unpack the desired fields to reduce the communication costs.

Notice also that unions are difficult to handle precisely. They create a discrepancy between memory usage and the actual semantics of the program since the same memory locations may be used to store completely unrelated objects. For safety reasons, the compiler must assume the dependencies, whereas the computations may be semantically independent. So unions, if needed, are to be kept in some purely sequential parts.

Finally, pointers are unequally handled. Analyzing and optimizing code using recursive data structures, such as linked lists or trees, is also still an active research area, for example with shape analysis. It may be useful to convert a linked list into an array if the processing cost is large enough. Another possibility for the compiler is to make use of speculative techniques to parallelize such codes.

The remainder of the section gives more specific advice on maximizing the optimization opportunities for applications using pointers and arrays.

6.3.1   Pointers

Pointers allow one to designate a single memory location using several names, or may designate several memory locations throughout their lifetimes: this is called *dynamic aliasing*. However practical it may be, it makes subsequent program analyses more complicated, as compilers must safely assume that two pointers are aliased whenever they cannot prove the contrary. Some compilers provide ways to turn off this behavior when the user is sure that there is no pointer aliasing. For instance, PAR4ALL provides a `--no-pointer-aliasing` command-line option. Other compilers such as the one from PGI requires the user to declare pointers with the C standard `restrict` qualifier. Basically, when using this qualifier, the programmer asserts that for the pointer lifetime, the pointed memory area is only accessed using this pointer. The compiler uses this information when optimizing code since no memory access using another pointer will generate a dependence with the accesses using the restricted pointer. For example the OpenACC code in Figure 6.4 can be parallelized by the PGI compiler only because the pointers are declared restricted.

```
void kernel(int n,
            float * restrict a,
            float * restrict r) {
#pragma acc region
   {
     for (int i = 0; i < n; ++i)
       r[i] = a[i]*2.0f;
   }
}
```

Figure 6.4: OpenACC example with the restrict qualifier required to allow parallelization

Here are some pieces of advice to maximize the benefits of using source-to-source
compilers allowing the use of pointers:

- Always use the same expression to refer to a memory location inside a function;
  for instance, avoid the following type of code:

```
my_parts = syst->domain[i]->parts;
my_parts[j] = ...;
```

  since `syst->domain[i]->parts` is designated by two different expressions: `syst->domain[i]->parts` of course and `my_parts`, which may
  confuse the compiler tracking the memory use.

- Do not assign two different memory locations to a pointer (that means that a
  pointer rather should be considered as a single assignment variable). For example in the code

```
if (cond())
   p = &a[f()];
else
   p = &b[g()];
*p = h();
```

  it is difficult for the compiler (and also a human being) to figure out which
  element of which array is really written.

- Do not use pointer arithmetic, or solely with great care. In particular do not use
  it if it leads to pointer aliasing (avoid p = p+i or p++ if p is a pointer). Note
  that this is a particular case of the previous point.

  For example avoid using pointers to perform a strength reduction on array accesses such as:

```
double a[N], b[N];
double *s = a, *d = b;
while (s<&a[N])
   *(d++) = *(s++);
```

  but prefer the following clearer version that reflects the original algorithm and
  exposes some trivial parallelism:

```
double a[N], b[N];
for(int i = 0; i < N; i++)
  b[i] = a[i];
```

- Reserve the use of pointers for the sole dynamic allocation of arrays and to function parameter passing (in C, to emulate the C++ reference concept). In C++, use references instead of pointers, when possible.

Note that you can have variable size arrays in C99 (as available in Fortran for decades), such as:

```
int n = f();
int m = g();
double a[3*n][m+7];
```

which can spare you the trouble of explicitly allocating and freeing pointers, or playing with `alloca()`.

- Avoid function pointers because, even when they are legal, they prevent precise interprocedural analyses and optimizations since it may be difficult to figure out which function is eventually called. This is also the case with a virtual function in C++: the underlying implementation involves a table of function pointers.

- Do not use recursive data structures such as linked lists, trees, *etc.* since it is often difficult to figure out what object is really pointed to, as explained previously in the introduction to the section.

- Be aware of the C standard constraints on pointer expressions, pointer differences, and more generally on pointer arithmetic.

6.3.2   Arrays

As array manipulations are often the source of massive parallelism, parallelizers often concentrate their efforts on them. However, their task can be made easier by following a number of coding guidelines which are detailed below.

6.3.2.1   Providing and Respecting Array Bounds

Parallelizing compilers often make the assumption that the program is correct, and in particular that array bounds are not violated. Otherwise, the behavior of the program may be undefined. This (bad) programming style is often used as array reshaping to iterate in a large global loop ranging over all the elements normally visited by a loop nest on all dimensions of an array, as shown in the next section. A modern compiler may figure out loop nest coalescing automatically to get maximum sequential performance anyway.

The bounds should be provided.

6.3.2.2 Linearization

In many automatic parallelizers, array references are represented using the integer polyhedron lattice; array reference indices must be affine integer expressions for the compiler to be able to study inter-iteration independencies, to propagate information over the program representation, and/or to generate communications.

For example `a[2*i-3+m][3*i-j+6*n]` is an affine array reference but `a[2*i*j][m*n-i+j]` is not (it is a polynomial of several variables).

This explains why you should not use array linearization to emulate accesses to multidimensional arrays with one-dimensional arrays, as in:

```
double a[n][m][l];
double * p = a;
for(int i = 0; i < n; i++)
  for(int j = 0; j < m; j++)
    for(int k = 0; k < l; k++)
      p[m*l*i + l*j + k] = ...;
```

The cleaner understandable following version should be used instead:

```
double a[n][m][l];
for(int i = 0; i < n; i++)
  for(int j = 0; j < m; j++)
    for(int k = 0; k < l; k++)
      a[i][j][k] = ...;
```

In the first cluttered version, the polynomial array index expression cannot be represented in a linear algebra framework; this type of loop is usually not parallelized, and communications on GPU cannot be generated.

Some compilers (see [13, 25]) try to *delinearize* this type of array accesses. But this transformation is not always successful.

6.3.2.3 Successive Array Element References

To reduce the analysis complexity, some compilers compute summaries of array element accesses in sets. For instance, PIPS array region analyses [2, 11] gather array elements in sets represented by convex polyhedra. This means that non-convex sets of array elements are approximated by sets that contain elements which do not belong to the actual set, and are thus imprecise. Of course, further analyses and transformations are more likely to succeed and produce efficient code if array region analyses are more precise. Therefore, in case of successive accesses to array elements, it is recommended to group them as much as possible so that two consecutive accesses in the program flow can be represented by a convex set. As an example, the version in Figure 6.5 is preferable to the version in Figure 6.6.

6.3.3 Casts

Casts are somewhat tricky to analyze because they induce translating a data memory layout into another one, and this may be very difficult in the general case, especially

```
/* In the following statement sequences and expression,
   all reference to a and b are made in a following way.
   So first the region with a[i-1] and a[i] is built,
   which is compact, and the a[i+1] reference is added,
   leading still to a compact region. */
tmp = a[i-1] + a[i] + a[i+1];
b[i-1] = ...;
b[i]   = ...;
b[i+1] = ...;
```

Figure 6.5: Consecutive array accesses

```
/* The array region access is first computed from a[i-1]
   and a[i+1] which is non compact and then the a[i]
   element is added */
tmp = a[i-1] + a[i+1] + a[i];
/* The same for b */
b[i]   = ...;
b[i+1] = ...;
b[i-1] = ...;
```

Figure 6.6: Disjoint array accesses leading to imprecise array region analysis in PIPS and PAR4ALL

for source-to-source tools which try to preserve the initial aspect of the program, and as the memory layout may be architecture-dependent.

Hence the effects of the cast operator on the analyses may lead to a loss of precision: it is recommended to use it sparingly, out of the *hot* spots, and only when it does not impact the memory layout.

6.4   Directives and Pragma (OpenMP ...)

Fashionable extensions to sequential languages are hints expressed as pragma or directives hidden into comments in the source code to inform the compiler that some parts can be executed in parallel, offloaded to an accelerator or with data and computation distributed on a distributed-memory massively parallel computer. The extensions we are interested in here are those which do not modify the sequential semantics of a program. For example, expressing that a sequential part is parallel does not change the semantics of the sequential part and this extension can be ignored by a compiler and the program remains correct[3].

OpenMP [27, 28] and HPF [17, 18] are old standards based on this principle, but with different targets and paradigms. OpenMP targets shared-memory multiprocessors whereas HPF is more ambitiously oriented towards distributed-memory massively parallel machines with deeper compiler support. Unfortunately, only OpenMP has been successful in its achievements, even if HPF had some impact on the development of

---

[3]Actually the fine operational semantics may change because for example of the non-associativity of floating-point computations or some signed integer operations resulting from various rounding.

```
/* This is executed by several threads concurrently */
#pragma omp parallel for
  for (i = 0; i < n; i++)
      // Iterations are distributed between the threads
      x[i] += y[i];
  // Implicit synchronization here

// Launch all the threads
#pragma omp parallel
{
  /* But the following is run on only one thread,
     with its own copy of p */
  #pragma omp single private(p)
  {
    // Iterate on the elements of a list from the head
    p = listhead;
    while (p) {
      /* While there is still an element, launch a new
         task asynchronously to process it in parallel */
      #pragma omp task
      {
        process (p);
      }
      // Look at next element
      p = next(p);
    }
  }
}
```

Figure 6.7: Small example of C language with OpenMP extension

```
! Explain that Anew is to be allocated to the accelerator.
! A has a copy also allocated to the accelerator and
! is initialized with the value of A from the host:
!$acc data copyin(A), create(Anew)
iter = 0
do while ( err .gt. tol .and. iter .gt. iter_max )
  iter = iter + 1
  err = 0.0
  ! The following loop nest is parallel and to be outlined
  ! for execution on the accelerator with some scheduling
  ! parameters.
  ! Instruct also the compiler there is a reduction done
  ! on the err variable
  !$acc kernels loop reduction(max:err), gang(32), worker(8)
  do j=1,m
    do i=1,n
      Anew(i,j) = 0.25 * ( A(i+1,j ) + A(i-1,j ) &
                           A(i, j-1) + A(i, j+1) )
      err = max( err, abs(Anew(i,j) - A(i,j)) )
    end do
  end do
  !$acc end kernels loop
  if ( mod(iter, 100) .eq. 0 ) print *, iter, err
  ! This affectation can be done in parallel,
  ! as with HPF workload:
  !$acc parallel
  A = Anew
  !$acc end parallel
end do
!$acc end data
```

Figure 6.8: Example of OpenACC with Fortran 90 commented after [16]

parallel models and languages [21]. Figure 6.7 shows an example of OpenMP.

More modern extensions such as HMPP [8] or OpenACC [26] are developed for C, C++ and Fortran to extend these concepts to other domains, such as heterogeneous computing or even to embedded systems with SME-C [3]. An example of the OpenACC Fortran program is found in Figure 6.8.

The interesting aspect is that even if the compiler dealing with this extension is not or no longer available, the sequential program remains and is not lost. It can still be optimized and parallelized later, manually or automatically with other tools.

It is an interesting path toward incremental manual parallelization without losing the investments in the source code that remains sequential. But the sequential sources need to be reorganized to express parallelism exploitable by the tools. Thus this extension takes advantage of the good practices described in this chapter.

6.5 Using Libraries

6.5.1 Relying on Efficient Libraries

An easy way to parallelize part of the execution in a sequential program is to use some libraries that are already parallelized, such as linear algebra libraries (MKL, BLAS, LAPACK, PETSc) or other mathematical libraries (FFTW [14] to compute various fast Fourier's transforms).

Even I/O operations exist as parallel libraries, which is of great importance since computer performance increases more quickly than I/O latency reduction and bandwidth improvement.

In this way, a programmer can benefit from highly parallelized and optimized expertise packaged in libraries (ScaLAPACK, PLASMA, MAGMA, CuBLAS, PETSc) without having to invest time in the parallelization phase.

Unfortunately, not all the parts of an application exist as libraries, and if so, may not be combined. Furthermore, they may not be directly usable with some automatic parallelizers, as explained in the following section.

6.5.2 Quarantined Functions: Stubs

Using complex functions can stress some compilers too much or sometimes, parallelizing a program globally needs the whole program source but the source of the libraries is not available or definitely too complex or irrelevant to be retargetable.

In this case, two different compilers may be needed: one to do the automatic parallelization on a code with some functions hidden from it and another more robust non parallelizing compiler to compile the problematic functions. Afterwards, the two programs are linked together to produce a global program.

But there may be still an issue: if the parallelization is performed by program comprehension, for example by using some abstract interpretation as in PIPS, the whole program source has to be analyzed, with all the library functions which are unfortunately unavailable. A description of the behaviors of these functions is needed for automatic parallelization.

This can be provided by some external ways such as a contract description in an XML files such as with SPEAR tools [23], by using some `#pragma` in HMPP [8] or OpenACC [26], directives or attributes such as in Fortran (`intent(in)`, `intent(out)` or `intent(inout)` specifying some arguments are read or/and written by a function).

Another way is to provide the parallelizer with a stub function that mimics the behavior needed by the parallelizer to know what is needed for a parallelism analysis. For example in PAR4ALL, which is based on PIPS, the memory accesses to the memory are analyzed to see if there are conflicts or not between pieces of code, scalar variable values are tracked by semantic analysis for improving the dependency test and applying various optimizations, input/output effects are tracked to avoid unfortunate parallelism of input/output and so on. So for PAR4ALL, stub functions with these effects are needed.

The advantage of this last solution is that no language extension or `#pragma` is needed. The drawback is that some simple functions have to be written instead and the global compilation flow has to be adapted to provide the stub functions to the parallelizer and to substitute the real functions afterwards in the final executable.

6.6 Object Oriented Programming

Although we focus in this chapter on the C and Fortran languages, object-oriented programming gains momentum even in high-performance computing, with C++ which is an object-oriented extension of the C language, or even more logically Fortran 2003 and 2008 versions that include directly object-oriented concepts.

Object-oriented languages have some interesting high-level aspects allowing conciseness and abstraction with the drawback that it may difficult to understand what is really executed on the target, by comparison with simpler languages such as C, closer to a high-level macro-assembler.

As for languages that are not object-oriented , a simple general rule is to avoid using constructs that lead to unstructured code (such as exceptions and object creation/deletion) and unpredictable code (such as virtual functions) in compute intensive parts with some parallel potential such as heavy loop nests.

Using virtual functions in C++ means that the choice of the real function to be used is made only at execution time, which is costly (equivalent to using a function pointer in C) and difficult to analyze by a parallelizer compiler.

When possible, using advanced templates (which can be seen as a type of high-level C preprocessor) replaces virtual functions by compile-time specialization with simpler function overloading which are plain function calls. They can even be in-lined.

Furthermore, using C++ well-known templates, for example from the STL or BOOST libraries, may be recognized by the compiler. For example, by understanding its semantics, a loop iterating on a `std::vector` is replaced by some parallel constructs [24]. There are even some direct implementations of the algorithms from STL that are directly parallel, such as the MCSTL [35] or STAPL [7], or variations with some specialized parallel template libraries such as TBB [19].

Pointers used in C to pass arguments in functions can be replaced by references (&) in C++ to establish the programmer intentions and to let the parallelizer be able to find parallelism.

Working with expressions on objects in C++ is quite powerful but may create many temporary objects with much time spent in object creation and deletion, content copy. This may spoil memory bandwidth and electrical power, but also have some side effects preventing the parallelization. A nice feature from C++11 is that there are some move constructors that may avoid some useless object copy or creation with their side effects.

Exceptions (or arbitrary jump) are other side effects to avoid in the parallel sections of a program. Even if they are caught locally, it is equivalent to unstructured control flow that may impair the parallelism. More generalized use of exceptions that may be caught interprocedurally for example can be seen as non-local **goto**[4] which is inherently challenging but question the parallelism itself: what are the semantics of a parallel loop with an exception in an iteration? Do we rollback all the loop in a transaction way? Do we execute all the iterations but not the trouble-making one? Do we execute all the iterations up to the exception-throwing one to emulate sequential semantics?

6.7 Conclusion

Never send a human to do a machine's job.

Agent SMITH, in *Matrix* (Andy & Larry WACHOWSKI, 1999).

Because of the current and foreseen technological constraints, parallelism is the only way to go for speed and energy efficiency. Unfortunately, parallel programming has been a real challenge for more than 50 years now.

Parallelizing compilers are promising tools to generate code for a variety of architectures. Of course, the generated code is often not as efficient as hand-programming by specialists, nor as clean as a new development in a pure parallel programming language, but is an interesting trade-off relative to the time-to-market advantage for legacy code.

Automatic parallelization is no magic bullet and has been a research area for 40 years. Unfortunately it has not become mainstream, perhaps because of too high expectations. Parallelization is an intractable issue in general and one cannot expect an automatic tool to solve intractable problems better. Fortunately, providing some rules are obeyed when writing an application, parallelism becomes easier to detect by parallelizing compilers. Low hanging fruits must be picked first.

---

[4]Like `setjmp()` and `longjmp()` in C.

Even if the rules presented here have been devised based upon experience with PIPS and PAR4ALL, they are far more general and even applicable to modern compilers targeting sequential targets that have more and more parallelism anyway, such as SIMD instruction sets.

Basically, the application code should be as structured as possible. At least the unstructured parts should be segregated into some parts not to be parallelized, to keep the time-consuming parallelized parts large enough.

Easy parallelized parts often use regular **for** loops like Fortran **do** loops, in preference to **while** loops. Loop nest candidates for parallelization should not contain I/O or debug or error control code, or there should be an easy way to switch them off.

Automatic parallelization implies some type of program comprehension and everything that uselessly obfuscates the program design is to be banned. Using clear data types, without type casts, local declaration instead of long-life data structures, explicit argument passing instead of global variable side effects are some of the basic rules to follow.

Since pointers are often not well managed by a compiler because of the difficulty in tracking what is really pointed to, pointer use has to be minimized as has the use of recursive data structures, function pointers or virtual function in object-oriented languages. As a particular case, avoid array linearization and casting, but prefer using the data as they are declared. Modern compilers no longer need this type of manual optimization to get good sequential performance, so good sequential programming does not usually impact execution times.

If some of these recommendations cannot be applied, then try to group the non-compliant code outside loop nests which are good candidates for parallelization or, more generally speaking, outside the most computational-intensive parts of the program. This is good practice, for instance, for heap allocations.

In some cases, the programmer has some knowledge on the program that is difficult to figure out automatically. Attributes in some languages, decoration or pragmas can be used to help the compiler to parallelize the code. When these pragmas do not change the sequential semantics as with OpenMP, OpenHMPP or OpenACC, this is an efficient pragmatic attitude to take further into a parallel execution without losing the sequential program, and thus without having to maintain different alive program versions.

But before launching heavy parallel developments, relying on some libraries already parallelized by some experts for a large range of platforms is definitely the way to begin. Unfortunately the original application may not be structured to use an existing library but this restructuring should be worth the investment.

Actually, most of the previous rules are common sense rules that have become more and more common with the development of recent new languages or even with recent versions of existing languages, such as C++11 or Fortran 2008. Good programming for parallelism begins with good sequential programming.

Even if these programming rules seem to be constraining, they are often considered as sound programming rules even for classical sequential programming. That means that (re)writing an application to ease parallelization can be a good opportunity for code cleaning and modernization by reengineering.

From a higher point of view, program parallelization implies some language and tool choices. Since the program sources are the real value of the applications, one should use standard approaches, if possible Open Source, to be more confident in the life duration of the environment and not to being hijacked by some companies and be bound to their future. When parallelizing a program, the entry cost is often important, because the program has to be fitted into some new constructs, and may be rewritten in a new language with a new high-level architecture. But if some of the tool used disappears for some reason, the exit cost may be considerably worse, because reverse engineering the optimizations that have been made to fit the former environment, before even beginning to port all the application to a new environment, can be a nightmare.

For these reasons, a milder approach involving some coding rules and automatic parallelization, with some optional pragmas or directives and some use of parallel libraries, seems a good compromise between efficiency, time-to-market and technology continuity.

Acknowledgments

This work is supported by the OpenGPU project with funding from the French Systém@TIC Research Cluster.

We would like to thanks all the PIPS and PAR4ALL team, mainly at MINES ParisTech and SILKAN, and all the members of the OpenGPU project for their fruitful discussions and comments.

References

[1] M. Amini, C. Ancourt, F. Coelho, B. Creusillet, S. Guelton, F. Irigoin, P. Jouvelot, R. Keryell, P. Villalon, "PIPS Is not (just) Polyhedral Software", in First International Workshop on Polyhedral Compilation Techniques (IMPACT 2011), Chamonix, France, Apr. 2011.

[2] M. Amini, B. Creusillet, S. Even, R. Keryell, O. Goubier, S. Guelton, J.O. McMahon, F.X. Pasquier, G. Péan, P. Villalon, "Par4All: From Convex Array Regions to Heterogeneous Computing", in 2nd International Workshop on Polyhedral Compilation Techniques (IMPACT 2012), Paris, France, Jan. 2012.

[3] R. Barrère, M. Beemster, R. Keryell, "SME-C — C99 with pragma and API for parallel execution, streaming, processor mapping and communication generation", Technical report, SMECY Project, 2012.

[4] M.M. Baskaran, U. Bondhugula, S. Krishnamoorthy, J. Ramanujam, A. Rountev, P. Sadayappan, "A compiler framework for optimization of affine loop nests for GPGPUs", in Proceedings of the 22nd annual international conference on Supercomputing, ICS, 225–234, ACM, New York, NY, USA, 2008.

[5] C. Bastoul, "Improving Data Locality in Static Control Programs", PhD thesis, Université Paris VI, Dec. 2004.

[6] M.W. Benabderrahmane, L.N. Pouchet, A. Cohen, C. Bastoul, "The polyhedral model is more widely applicable than you think", in Proceedings of the 19th joint European conference on Theory and Practice of Software, international conference on Compiler Construction, CC'10/ETAPS'10, 283–303, Springer-Verlag, Berlin, Heidelberg, 2010. doi:10.1007/978-3-642-11970-5_16

[7] A. Buss, Harshvardhan, I. Papadopoulos, O. Pearce, T. Smith, G. Tanase, N. Thomas, X. Xu, M. Bianco, N.M. Amato, L. Rauchwerger, "STAPL: standard template adaptive parallel library", in Proceedings of the 3rd Annual Haifa Experimental Systems Conference, SYSTOR '10, 14:1–14:10, ACM, New York, NY, USA, 2010. doi:10.1145/1815695.1815713

[8] CAPS Entreprise, "HMPP Workbench", 2010. http://www.caps-entreprise.com

[9] C. Chen, J. Chame, M. Hall, "CHiLL: A framework for composing high-level loop transformations", Technical Report 08-897, University of Southern California, June 2008.

[10] B. Creusillet, "Array Region Analyses and Applications", PhD thesis, École des Mines de Paris, Dec. 1996. http://www.cri.ensmp.fr/doc/A-295.ps.gz

[11] B. Creusillet, F. Irigoin, "Interprocedural analyses of Fortran programs", Parallel Computing, 24(3–4), 629–648, 1998. http://citeseer.ist.psu.edu/creusillet97interprocedural.html

[12] P. Feautrier, "Dataflow Analysis of Array and Scalar References", International Journal of Parallel Programming, 20(1), 23–53, Sept. 1991.

[13] B. Franke, M. O'Boyle, "Array recovery and high-level transformations for DSP applications", ACM Trans. Embed. Comput. Syst., 2(2), 132–162, May 2003. doi:10.1145/643470.643472

[14] M. Frigo, S.G. Johnson, "The Design and Implementation of FFTW3", Proceedings of the IEEE, 93(2), Special issue on "Program Generation, Optimization, and Platform Adaptation", 216–231, 2005.

[15] M. Griebl, "The mechanical parallelization of loop nests containing while loops", PhD thesis, Passau, 1997.

[16] M. Harris, "An OpenACC Example (Part 2)", 2012. http://developer.nvidia.com/cuda/openacc-example-part-2

[17] High Performance Fortran Forum, "High Performance Fortran Language Specification", Version 1.0 CRPC-TR 92225, Center for Research on Parallel Computation, Rice University, Houston, USA, May 1993. http://hpff.rice.edu/versions/hpf1

[18] High Performance Fortran Forum, "High Performance Fortran Language Specification", Version 2.0, Center for Research on Parallel Computation, Rice University, Houston, USA, Jan. 1997. http://hpff.rice.edu/versions/hpf2

[19] Intel, "Intel Threading Building Blocks for Open Source (Intel TBB)", 2012.

http://threadingbuildingblocks.org

[20] F. Irigoin, P. Jouvelot, R. Triolet, "Semantical Interprocedural Parallelization: An Overview of the PIPS project", in International Conference on Supercomputing, 144–151, June 1991.

[21] K. Kennedy, C. Koelbel, H. Zima, "The rise and fall of high performance Fortran", Communications of the ACM, 54(11), 74–82, Nov. 2011. doi:10.1145/2018396.2018415

[22] C. Lengauer, "Loop Parallelization in the Polytope Model", in Proceedings of the 4th International Conference on Concurrency Theory, CONCUR '93, 398–416, Springer-Verlag, London, UK, 1993.

[23] E. Lenormand, G. Édelin, "An industrial perspective: A pragmatic high-end signal processing design environment at THALES", in International Conference on Embedded Computer Systems: Architectures, MOdeling and Simulation (SAMOS), 2003.

[24] C. Liao, D.J. Quinlan, J.J. Willcock, T. Panas, "Extending Automatic Parallelization to Optimize High-Level Abstractions for Multicore", in Proceedings of the 5th International Workshop on OpenMP: Evolving OpenMP in an Age of Extreme Parallelism, IWOMP '09, 28–41, Springer-Verlag, Berlin, Heidelberg, 2009. doi:10.1007/978-3-642-02303-3_3

[25] V. Maslov, "Delinearization: an efficient way to break multiloop dependence equations", SIGPLAN Not., 27(7), 152–161, July 1992. doi:10.1145/143103.143130

[26] OpenACC Members, "The OpenACC^{TM} Application Programming Interface", Version 1.0, Nov. 2011. http://www.openacc-standard.org

[27] OpenMP Architecture Review Board, "OpenMP Standard, 1.0", Oct. 1997. http://www.openmp.org

[28] OpenMP Architecture Review Board, "OpenMP Standard, 3.1", July 2011. http://www.openmp.org

[29] The Portland Group, "PGI Compiler User's Guide", 2012.

[30] L.N. Pouchet, "PoCC: the Polyhedral Compiler Collection Package", 2012.

[31] Purdue University, "The CETUS Compiler Manual", 2011. http://cetus.ecn.purdue.edu/Documentation/manual

[32] D. Quinlan, C. Liao, T. Panas, R. Matzke, M. Schordan, R. Vuduc, Q. Yi, "ROSE User Manual: A Tool for Building Source-to-Source Translators, Draft User Manual", Lawrence Livermore National Laboratory, June 2012.

[33] Reservoir Labs, Inc., "R-Stream Parallelizing C Compiler, Power User Guide", 2012.

[34] SILKAN, "Par4All — Single Source, Multiple Targets", 2012. http://par4all.org

[35] J. Singler, P. Sanders, F. Putze, "MCSTL: The Multi-core Standard Template Library", in A.M. Kermarrec, L. Bougé, T. Priol, (Editors), "Euro-Par 2007 Parallel Processing", 4641, Lecture Notes in Computer Science, 682–694, Springer Berlin / Heidelberg, 2007. doi:10.1007/978-3-540-74466-5_72

[36] E. Stoltz, "Effective Compiler Utilization", in Linux Supercluster Users Confer-

ence, Sept. 2000.

[37] R. Triolet, P. Feautrier, F. Irigoin, "Direct Parallelization of Call Statements", in ACM SIGPLAN Symposium on Compiler Construction, 176–185, 1986.

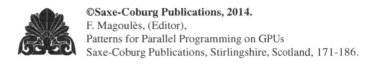

©Saxe-Coburg Publications, 2014.
F. Magoulès, (Editor),
Patterns for Parallel Programming on GPUs
Saxe-Coburg Publications, Stirlingshire, Scotland, 171-186.

Chapter 7

Using MELT to Improve or Explore your GCC-Compiled Source Code

B. Starynkevitch

CEA, LIST, Software Reliability Lab, Gif-sur-Yvette, France

Abstract

This paper introduces the MELT framework and domain-specific language to extend the GCC compiler. It explains the major internal representations (*Gimple*, *Tree*-s, *etc.*) and the overall organization of GCC. It shows the major features of MELT and illustrates why extending and customizing the GCC compiler using MELT is useful (for instance, to use GPGPUs through OPENCL). It gives some concrete advice and guidelines for development of such extensions with MELT.

Keywords: compilation, GCC, domain-specific language, high-performance computing, GPGPU, OpenCL, MELT, Gimple.

7.1 Introduction to MELT

7.1.1 GCC and MELT

MELT [8,9] (see http://gcc-melt.org/ for code and documentation) is a high-level domain specific language[1] to extend or customize the GCC compiler. GCC (see http://gcc.gnu.org for more) is the major free software compiler for many languages (C, C++, Ada, Fortran, Go, Objective C ...), target processors (x86, ARM, Sparc, MIPS, PowerPC) and systems (Linux, AIX, Android).

---

[1]The MELT implementation is free software (GPLv3+ licensed) available from http://gcc-melt.org/ as a plugin for GCC (4.6, 4.7 or better).

The GCC compiler is a large legacy software with more than 5 million source lines [2], which provides (notably in its 4.6 release of March 2011, and its 4.7 release of March 2012) a plugin machinery to extend it. But coding plugins for GCC in plain *C* is quite difficult (because *C* is not a language specially suited for symbolic processing, like the one happening inside compilers). MELT is a *domain specific language* designed to ease the development of specific GCC extensions, for tasks aimed at specific applications or libraries like: specialized warnings, specific optimizations, coding rules validation *etc.*

A GCC compilation reads the user source code, then transforms it in specific GCC internal representations, notably *Tree*-s (for declarations and operands) and *Gimple*-s (for instructions). The bulk of an optimizing GCC compilation is made of more than 250 GCC passes operating on its internal representations. GCC uses many internal representations, notably *Gimple*-s ("normalized" elementary abstract instructions, representing elementary steps of the compiled code, such as the addition of a temporary "variable" with a constant going into another temporary) and *Tree*-s (elementary abstract syntax trees, notably operands of *Gimple*-s, *e.g.* temporary, local or global variables, formals and constants).

MELT can be used to take advantage of GCC powerful representations and processing by customizing it suitably to the (advanced) user's needs. It is implemented as a "meta"-plugin for GCC, which generates *C* code operating on GCC internal representations, then compiles that generated *C* into MELT modules and dynamically loads these modules. MELT can be executed on GNU/LINUX systems[3] having a GCC compiler supporting plugins.

Working inside GCC enables access to the internal representations of the compiler. This has several benefits: it is more precise than textual based tools (for instance, it is quite easy to find all functions with two formal double arguments without requiring their definition's signature to fit on a single line); since it is working on some current internal representations in the compiler, it can profit from prior work already done by the compiler (parsing -for various source languages-, previous optimization and inlining passes) and could improve its future work (remaining optimization or code generation passes).

7.1.2   A Glimpse into *Gimple*

Let us consider the classical square matrix multiplication code in *C*, with each matrix represented by an array of double precision IEE754 numbers. The *C* source code is given by Figure 7.1 (and is an obvious candidate to use the GPU, for large enough matrix size n). From the compiler's point of view, this code might not be parallelizable, *e.g.* when m and a matrixes are physically overlapping in memory, and we should declare the formals as `double* restrict m` *etc.* to tell the compiler that they cannot

---

[2]Measuring the source code size of GCC is already a challenge. Some tools may give nearly 10 million lines of source code lines as the computed code size of the same version of GCC.

[3]MELT should be easily ported to any operating system providing the POSIX `dlopen` and `dlsym` functions for loading dynamic shared libraries, and supporting GCC plugins.

```
void matmul(int n, double*m, double *a, double *b)
{
  for (int i=0; i<n; i++)
    for (int j=0; j<n; j++)
    {
      double s=0.0;
      for (int k=0; k<n; k++)
        s += a[i*n + k]   *   b[k*n + j];
      m[i*n + j] = s;
    }
}
```

Listing 7.1: Matrix multiplication `matmul.c`

overlap or alias.

This simple code is transformed considerably inside the GCC compiler. Very quickly, it gets "gimplified", that is transformed into *Gimple* instructions. To obtain a textual dump of internal representations after most passes of GCC, invoke it as `gcc-4.7 -std=c99 -O2 -Wall -fverbose-asm -fdump-tree-all -c matmul.c`; this gives a lot of (arbitrarily[4] numbered) dump files, including `matmul.c.004t.gimple` Listing 7.2, which shows that the *Gimple* form contains much more elementary instructions, and many temporary variables like *e.g.* `D.1603`; the compiler introduces these to break complex instructions into simpler operations. Control flow operations are broken up into many jump labels *e.g.* `<D.1591>` and elementary tests with `goto`-s.

After "gimplification", many other GCC optimization passes transform that high-level *Gimple* representation into lower-level *Gimple/SSA* (for *Static Single Assignment*). This is a form in which every variable is assigned once (so can be understood as defined once with a sort-of equality, so is "simpler" to handle through formal methods). For instance, our matrix multiplication is later optimized into the dump file `matmul.c.086t.phiopt2` of 91 lines, including Listing 7.3, which illustrates that the *Gimple/SSA* form uses several SSA versions (*e.g.* j_{33} and j_{44}) of the same Gimple variable (here j). When a basic block (like `<bb 7>` of Listing 7.3) is reachable from several defining assignments (in different blocks) for a variable, a Φ [function] assignment statement explicits that fact by "merging" the several origins of that variable's value, so `i_41 = PHI<i_34(6), 0(2)` means that the versioned SSA name i_{41} gets its value either from i_{34} computed in `<bb 6>` or from 0 when coming from `<bb 2>`.

Notice that coding the same algorithm in the different programming languages understood by GCC produces very similar *Gimple/SSA* forms inside the GCC compiler, even when using high-level *C++11* constructs like nested `std::vector` or

---

[4]The numbers in dump file names are unique, but sadly don't order these dump files in chronological executions of passes.

```
matmul (int n, double * m, double * a, double * b)
{
  int D.1595;
  int D.1596;
  long unsigned int D.1597;
  long unsigned int D.1598;
  double * D.1599;
  double D.1600;
  int D.1601;
  int D.1602;
  long unsigned int D.1603;
  long unsigned int D.1604;
  double * D.1605;
  double D.1606;
  double D.1607;
  int D.1608;
  long unsigned int D.1609;
  long unsigned int D.1610;
  double * D.1611;
  {   int i;
    i = 0;
    goto <D.1592>;
    <D.1591>:
    {   int j;
      j = 0;
      goto <D.1589>;
      <D.1588>:
      {       double s;
        s = 0.0;
        {       int k;
          k = 0;
          goto <D.1586>;
          <D.1585>:
          D.1595 = i * n;
          D.1596 = D.1595 + k;
          D.1597 = (long unsigned int) D.1596;
          D.1598 = D.1597 * 8;
          D.1599 = a + D.1598;
          D.1600 = *D.1599;
          D.1601 = k * n;
          D.1602 = D.1601 + j;
          D.1603 = (long unsigned int) D.1602;
          D.1604 = D.1603 * 8;
          D.1605 = b + D.1604;
          D.1606 = *D.1605;
          D.1607 = D.1600 * D.1606;
          s = D.1607 + s;
          k = k + 1;
          <D.1586>:
          if (k < n) goto <D.1585>;
          else goto <D.1587>;
          <D.1587>:
        }
        D.1595 = i * n;
        D.1608 = D.1595 + j;
        D.1609 = (long unsigned int) D.1608;
        D.1610 = D.1609 * 8;
        D.1611 = m + D.1610;
        *D.1611 = s;
      }
      j = j + 1;
      <D.1589>:
      if (j < n) goto <D.1588>;
      else goto <D.1590>;
      <D.1590>:
    }
    i = i + 1;
    <D.1592>:
    if (i < n) goto <D.1591>;
    else goto <D.1593>;
    <D.1593>:
  }
}
```

Listing 7.2: Gimplification of matrix multiplication `matmul.c.004t.gimple`

```
  # s_51 = PHI <s_25(3), 0.0(5)>
  # k_52 = PHI <k_26(3), 0(5)>
  D.1595_10 = i_41 * n_6(D);
  D.1596_11 = D.1595_10 + k_52;
  D.1597_12 = (long unsigned int) D.1596_11;
  D.1598_13 = D.1597_12 * 8;
  D.1599_15 = a_14(D) + D.1598_13;
  D.1600_16 = *D.1599_15;
  D.1601_17 = k_52 * n_6(D);
  D.1602_18 = D.1601_17 + j_44;
  D.1603_19 = (long unsigned int) D.1602_18;
  D.1604_20 = D.1603_19 * 8;
  D.1605_22 = b_21(D) + D.1604_20;
  D.1606_23 = *D.1605_22;
  D.1607_24 = D.1600_16 * D.1606_23;
  s_25 = D.1607_24 + s_51;
  k_26 = k_52 + 1;
  if (n_6(D) > k_26)
    goto <bb 3>;
  else
    goto <bb 4>;

<bb 4>:
  # s_40 = PHI <s_25(3)>
  D.1595_27 = i_41 * n_6(D);
  D.1608_28 = D.1595_27 + j_44;
  D.1609_29 = (long unsigned int) D.1608_28;
  D.1610_30 = D.1609_29 * 8;
  D.1611_32 = m_31(D) + D.1610_30;
  *D.1611_32 = s_40;
  j_33 = j_44 + 1;
  if (n_6(D) > j_33)
    goto <bb 5>;
  else
    goto <bb 6>;


<bb 5>:
  # j_44 = PHI <j_33(4), 0(7)>
  goto <bb 3>;

<bb 6>:
  i_34 = i_41 + 1;
  if (n_6(D) > i_34)
    goto <bb 7>;
  else
    goto <bb 8>;

<bb 7>:
  # i_41 = PHI <i_34(6), 0(2)>
  goto <bb 5>;
```

Listing 7.3: Excerpt of `matmul.c.086t.phiopt2` - *Gimple/SSA* form

`std::valarray` templates, `std::for_each` application, and `<functional>` standard header with anonymous functions; the standard *C++11* library is nicely optimized by GCC, but that library is still implemented through usual *C++11* constructs.

7.1.3   MELT Features

MELT is a high-level domain specific language designed to ease the extension of GCC for customization purposes. It is implemented in a free-licensed (GPLv3) GCC plugin (and MELT infrastructure), has the following features:

- The MELT language has a Lisp-like syntax and design : every MELT phrase is an expression producing some result[s]. Every expression (called S-expr) is in parenthesis, starting with the operator or keyword, and followed by operands. Case in identifiers (called *symbols*, as in Lisp or Scheme) is not significant. Identifiers may contain non-letter characters. So the sum of 2 and x is expressed as (+i x 2) where +i is a symbol denoting the addition (of two raw integers) primitive. Parenthesis are highly significant; every non-trivial MELT expression is parenthesized, except some traditional syntactic sugar [5].

- MELT is translated to *C* code (through a translator itself implemented in MELT); that generated *C* code[6] may then be compiled into a shared object on the fly, then dynamically loaded with `dlopen`, all during the same single execution of GCC augmented by MELT. This enables MELT code to contain some small *C code chunks* which can call external libraries, or low-level GCC internal functions.

- MELT deals with "high-level" dynamically typed *values* (objects, lists, closures, tuples, boxed numbers, boxed *Gimple*-s, etc...) and raw GCC *stuff* (*e.g.* raw `long`, raw *Gimple*, raw *Tree*-s, raw basic blocks), and enables reflective [6] and functional programming styles.

- a runtime (implemented as the `melt.so` GCC plugin) provides many utilities, notably an efficient MELT generational copying garbage collector (tuned for frequent allocation of many temporary MELT values), built above the GCC mark and sweep garbage collector (which is quite primitive, and expects most *Gcc* material to live quite a long time), and a dynamic loader for MELT modules.

- the MELT system has an extensible *pattern matching framework*: extensions written in MELT use many patterns and can easily filter the internal representations of GCC (notably *Gimple* and *Tree*-s) through a high-level declarative syntax.

---

[5] The MELT reader parses `'1` exactly as `(quote 1)`, and `?(cstring_same "fflush")` exactly as `(question (cstring_same "fflush"))`, *etc.*

[6] The GCC compiler (version 4.7) is itself in transition, aiming to be progressively and partly rewritten in *C++* code. MELT actually is translated to the common subset of *C* and *C++* code which is acceptable inside GCC plugins. If and when GCC would be re-written in idiomatic *C++* code, the MELT translator would be adapted to that.

- the MELT implementation is layered: the runtime is used by all the MELT system; the translator parses MELT code (from file, memory, or even sockets) into s-expressions, which are then macro-expanded, normalized, generated an internal representation of the emitted *C* code, at last pretty-printed to generated *C* files, compiled into a shared object, dynamically loaded. Each layer is quite modular and can be extended by an advanced user. For instance, user-specific language constructs can be provided (through the macro machinery).

- the MELT system is able to deal with asynchronous textual messages[7] (in MELT S-expr syntax); this enables passes coded in MELT to communicate with external processes (*e.g.* graphical interfaces, web servers, *etc.*) through asynchronous textual protocols, in messages which might be handled at nearly any time inside passes provided in MELT (but not inside existing GCC passes, which would not react to them).

The MELT plugin release 0.9.5 (available on `http://gcc-melt.org/`, free software, GPLV3+ licensed, of April 2012) for GCC 4.7 has a MELT runtime of 23KLOC (thousands of lines of source code, counted with `wc`), including nearly 6KLOC of MELT generated code, the MELT (to C or C++) translator has 46KLOC (giving 1629KLOC of generated *C* code, which is also distributed), and nearly 8KLOC of MELT code providing a foundation for user provided MELT extensions.

7.2 MELT Usage for HPC Customization

HPC (High-Performance Computing) should become a preferred domain for compiler customization, and MELT can be the right tool for that.

7.2.1 Traversing GCC Internal Representations with MELT

Working inside the GCC compiler enables access to the exact internal representations used by the compiler. In particular, MELT permits one to navigate on the code, as worked on by GCC, *e.g. after function inlining*.

To give a simple toy example (Algorithm 7.1)[8], Figure 7.4, one might want to catch all calls like `fflush(NULL)` (used to flush all `<stdio.h>` files) inside every function whose name starts with `bar` and do that search *after inlining*. This simple query cannot be handled by simple textual tools (like `perl` or `awk`, *etc.*) because it needs to know what functions are inlined by GCC (and inlining decisions are not easily predictable). The relevant internal GCC representation is *Gimple/SSA*.

The MELT code of Listing 7.4 illustrates several traits of the MELT programming language. Pattern matching is done with `match` expressions (beginning lines 3 and 10), containing matching clauses starting with patterns (prefixed with a question mark

---

[7]Since version 0.9.5 of April 2012 of the MELT plugin for GCC 4.7
[8]This is `ex05` of `melt-examples` on GitHub.

Algorithm 7.1: Finding `fflush(NULL)` inside any `bar` function

---

for *each function* `cfun` **do**

    if `cfun`*'s name start with* `bar` **then**

        for *each basic block* `bb` *of* `cfun` **do**

            for *each gimple* `g` *inside* `bb` **do**

                if `g` *is a call to* `fflush` *with one argument, constant* `0` **then**

                  | inform the user of the location of `g`

                end

            end

        end

    end

end

`?`, *e.g.* `?_` for the wildcard pattern). Iterative constructs (beginning lines 1, 6 and 8), conventionally named with `each` or `with` in their names, have input arguments [perhaps an empty list `()` if none is required] followed by local formals. So the `eachgimple_in_basicblock` expression starting line 8 can be understood as: iterate inside the raw basic block `bb`, and for each *Gimple* inside, bind it to local variable `g` whose type `:gimple`, *i.e.* raw *Gimple* stuff of GCC, then evaluate the body sub-expression[s] (here, a `match` on `g`) from lines 10 to 16.

This example illustrates the power of pattern matching, when analyzing (or transforming) GCC internal *Gimple* representations : filtering internal code representation is an essential operation when working inside a compiler. The `match` of line 10 of Figure 7.4 filters a given gimple instruction `g` to find if it is a call to `fflush` with a constant `0` argument (since `NULL` is macro expanded to *e.g.* `(void*)0`). it is filtered as a *Gimple* call instruction with one argument (with the `gimple_call_1` matcher) to a function, represented as a *Tree* in *Gimple*, whose declaration (matching the `tree_function_decl_named` matcher) refer to a name matching the sub-pattern `?(cstring_same "flush")`, filtering strings equal to the literal `"flush"`. Actually, this is not the most efficient way to find call to the standard `fflush` function; a more clever way would be to filter all the functions declarations to find out and store the *Tree* for that `fflush` and filter for it.

Pattern matching in MELT can also *extract* components from filtered data; hence a pattern like:

```
?(gimple_assign_plus
  ?(tree_ssa_name ?var ?_ ?lvers ?_)
  ?(tree_ssa_name ?var ?_ ?rvers ?_)
  ?(tree_integer_cst ?rincr))
```

will filter all *Gimple/SSA* statements adding the *same* variable `var` (with two different *SSA* versions: `lvers` on the left side, `rvers` on the first right side of the assignment) to some integer constant `rincr`; the extracted pattern variables `var lvers rvers rincr` are available inside the body of that matching clause. The pattern is non-linear,

```
669 │ (with_cfun_decl ()
670 │   (:tree cfundecl)
671 │   (match cfundecl
672 │     ( ?(tree_function_decl_named
673 │          ?(cstring_prefixed "bar") ?_)
674 │        (each_bb_current_fun ()
675 │            (:basic_block bb)
676 │            (eachgimple_in_basicblock (bb)
677 │               (:gimple g)
678 │               (match  g
679 │                 ( ?(gimple_call_1  ?_
680 │                     ?(tree_function_decl_named
681 │                       ?(cstring_same "fflush") ?_)
682 │                     ?(tree_integer_cst 0))
683 │                   (inform_at_gimple g
684 │                        "found fflush(NULL)"))
685 │                 ( ?_ ())))))))
686 │     ( ?_ ()))))
```

Listing 7.4: MELT example - seeking `fflush(NULL)` *after inlining* inside functions
        `bar*`

since the same pattern variable `?var` appears twice in it. When matching its second
occurrence (for the first right hand operand of the assignment), it should be compared
to the data already found.

7.2.2 Taming HPC Parallelism with GRAPHITE and MELT

An important issue in HPC is to improve parallel computation. This is a very ambitious and a very long-term goal. Within the GCC compiler, many efforts have been
invested for that goal, notably through the GRAPHITE project [10, 11], which uses
polyhedral techniques to detect parellelization opportunities in *Gimple*.

Using GPGPU for the highly parallel and data regular parts of the computation is
possible, notably with the CUDA proprietary language and with the OPENCL industry
standard [5]. Both are specialized *C*-like dialects and runtime infrastructures designed
to take advantage of GPGPUs. However, they require recoding of the crucial parts
(*i.e.* numerical kernels) of an HPC application in another language (*e.g.* OPENCL or
CUDA)

Experimental code has been developed to translate *Gimple* to *OpenCL* using the
GRAPHITE infrastructure within the GRAPHITE-OPENCL project [1]. However, all
GPGPU related effort within GRAPHITE is (or was) still *highly experimental*, so is
not yet integrated inside the released GCC *compiler*. Since MELT is targeting official

GCC releases[9], it is not possible to use this experimental GRAPHITE-OPENCL work from MELT. And the GRAPHITE component of released GCC compilers does not even provide any plugin hooks, so cannot be easily extended (either in MELT or through any GCC plugin coded in *C*). Because MELT is extending `gcc-4.7` as released, it can only use the public interfaces provided by GCC.

However, the `graphite` pass of GCC 4.7 is able to detect parallelizable loops, and this detection can be used by MELT extensions. MELT knows about GCC `loop` material and provides a primitive `loop_can_be_parallel` to query if GRAPHITE has detected if a given loop is parallelizable. Once such a loop is found, a MELT pass has to recompute some information that GRAPHITE has computed for its own internal purpose, without providing an API to query it. In particular, each parallelizable loop has some induction variable, but GRAPHITE is not publishing it, so MELT has to recompute it.

Hence, re-doing in MELT what has been done in *experimental prototypes* related to GCC is not easy, because the released GCC compilers do not provide the interface to do that, so a significant amount of code has to be re-written (or we need to wait until some future release of GCC provides the relevant plugin hooks or public API, or gets a newer GRAPHITE merged inside.). And merging into MELT the experimental GRAPHITE is as difficult as merging it into the GCC trunk[10] (we leave that task to the developers of GRAPHITE). Furthermore, the experimental MELT branch is very often merged with the current GCC trunk.

Hence, generating of simple OPENCL variant from the internal *Gimple* is not yet achieved (in April 2012) within the MELT project. And when tentatively running, it would only translate very simple cases of parallisable algorithms. A production-level OPENCL generator would have to be tightly integrated inside GRAPHITE.

A practical issue, when generating OPENCL, is to estimate the size of the arrays (and the number of iterations inside loops). In very simple cases (*e.g.* a loop with a compile-time constant bound), GCC may already have such an estimate. In real cases, even as simple as the trivial matrix multiplication of Listing 7.1, determining the bounds from the *Gimple* representation of *Gimple* code from Listing 7.2 is not that simple. Concretely, running the matrix multiplication on the GPGU is worthwhile only for a large enough (*e.g.* $n > 200$ perhaps) dimension of the matrix. The exact threshold -which is highly system and machine specific- should probably be computed by machine learning techniques [3].

Many other tools to take advantage of GPGPU exist. Some tools, in particular STARPU [2], extend GCC with appropriate pragmas to ease integration with "codelets" running on the GPGPU.

---

[9]The official GCC releases are evolving significantly fast enough, so integrating experimental *Graphite* work is not reasonable for a single person outside of the small *Graphite* developers' community, and integrating some of their code into GCC releases (*i.e.* the current trunk) is already a challenge for *Graphite* people.

[10]The GCC trunk is the actively developed GCC branch, which will become the next release.

7.2.3 Why HPC needs GCC Extensions and Customizations?

High performance computing may profit from *specific* GCC extensions and customizations, like:

- navigation or refactoring tools for large scientific (legacy) code

- dynamically choosing an implementation of some classical numerical library (*e.g.* a GPU or a CPU variant of LAPACK [11], *etc.*)

- application specific pragmas (or compiler builtins)

- customized optimizations, in particular when mathematical knowledge may suggest them (*e.g.* replacing the addition of some matrix M with itself [12] by a scalar multiplication by 2)

- "domain specific profiling" could be achieved by *automatically* inserting "profiling instructions" (perhaps as simple as incrementing a profiling counter) within the *Gimple* code

- *etc.*

```
/* GIMPLE_RETURN <RETVAL> represents return statements.

   RETVAL is the value to return or NULL.  If a value is returned it
   must be accepted by is_gimple_operand.  */
DEFGSCODE(GIMPLE_RETURN, "gimple_return", GSS_WITH_MEM_OPS)

/* GIMPLE_PHI <RESULT, ARG1, ..., ARGN> represents the PHI node

   RESULT = PHI <ARG1, ..., ARGN>

   RESULT is the SSA name created by this PHI node.

   ARG1 ... ARGN are the arguments to the PHI node.  N must be
   exactly the same as the number of incoming edges to the basic block
   holding the PHI node.  Every argument is either an SSA name or a
   tree node of class tcc_constant.  */
DEFGSCODE(GIMPLE_PHI, "gimple_phi", GSS_PHI)
```

Figure 7.1: Two cases of *Gimple* from `gcc/gimple.def`

The main insight is that some important HPC software could consider *customizing* the GCC compiler for *their own purposes*, and MELT can be the right tool for such an approach. However, extending GCC (even with MELT) has some human cost, because the GCC internal representations are intrinsically complex: *Gimple* has 38 cases (of which 14 are specific to OPENMP) listed in file `gcc/gimple.def` of GCC (see

---

[11]http://www.netlib.org/lapack
[12]While a good numerical scientist would probably never write code like $M + M$ (where M is some big matrix) himself, some preprocessing or macro-expansion could bring such occurrences, and handling them inside the compiler can be worthwhile.

Figure 7.1), and *Tree* has nearly 200 cases, listed in file `gcc/tree.def` (see Figure 7.2). A given GCC compiled application is very likely to use the majority of these cases, which have to be handled individually. Notice that some *Tree* cases cannot appear at *Gimple/SSA* level (*e.g.* RETURN_EXPR, which is rendered by a GIMPLE_RETURN instruction) while others (like SSA_NAME) are specific to *Gimple/SSA*.

```
/* All pointer-to-x types have code POINTER_TYPE.
   The TREE_TYPE points to the node for the type pointed to.  */
DEFTREECODE (POINTER_TYPE, "pointer_type", tcc_type, 0)

/* Contents are in TREE_REAL_CST field.  */
DEFTREECODE (REAL_CST, "real_cst", tcc_constant, 0)

/* Pointer addition.  The first operand is always a pointer and the
   second operand is an integer of type sizetype.  */
DEFTREECODE (POINTER_PLUS_EXPR, "pointer_plus_expr", tcc_binary, 2)

/* & in C.  Value is the address at which the operand's value resides.
   Operand may have any mode.  Result mode is Pmode.  */
DEFTREECODE (ADDR_EXPR, "addr_expr", tcc_expression, 1)

/* RETURN.  Evaluates operand 0, then returns from the current function.
   Presumably that operand is an assignment that stores into the
   RESULT_DECL that hold the value to be returned.
   The operand may be null.
   The type should be void and the value should be ignored.  */
DEFTREECODE (RETURN_EXPR, "return_expr", tcc_statement, 1)

/* Variable references for SSA analysis.  New SSA names are created every
   time a variable is assigned a new value.  The SSA builder uses SSA_NAME
   nodes to implement SSA versioning.  */
DEFTREECODE (SSA_NAME, "ssa_name", tcc_exceptional, 0)
```

Figure 7.2: some cases of *Tree* from `gcc/tree.def`

7.3   Some Hints and Advice for Taming GCC with MELT

Extending GCC is challenging, mostly because of the complexity of compiler technology (so extending other industrial strength free software compilers like OPEN64 or LLVM/CLANG would also be difficult).

Customizing GCC (with MELT) raises several issues:

- understanding the intricate GCC internal representations, including *Gimple* instructions (*i.e.* the `gimple` data) and *Tree*-s (`tree` pointers), but also `gimple_seq` (a sequence of gimple instructions), `basic_block` (an elementary block of instructions, containing a `gimple_seq`, entered only at its start, and jumping to other basic blocks or returning to the caller function), `edge` (an arrow between `basic_block`-s, with GCC knowing each side of it), or even `function`-s or `cgraph`-s. Furthermore, all these data types are not available at all times in GCC (some passes are run when some data is not computed yet).

- understanding the numerous GCC internal passes (there are ≈ 250 of them!), and what kind of new passes should be written, and where to insert them. There are no obvious coding rules relating a pass appearing in the GCC source code, to its name.

- understanding the MELT domain specific programming language and its interface to GCC (if coding a GCC plugin in *C*, understanding the coding conventions and GCC plugin interface to *C* is also challenging).

- choosing what pass[es] should be added into GCC; the pass manager (in function `init_optimization_passes` from file `gcc/passes.c` of the GCC source code) is organizing the passes into several kinds (see file `gcc/tree-pass.h`)

    - `GIMPLE_PASS` for "simple Gimple passes" working on one function at a time;

    - `RTL_PASS` for back-end "Register Transfer Language" passes (which are target-processor specific, so probably not relevant here);

    - `SIMPLE_IPA_PASS` for "simple Inter-Procedural Analysis" passes;

    - `IPA_PASS` for full "Inter-Procedural analysis" passes.

Passes are described by `struct opt_pass` data structures, containing the type and name of the passes, and some function pointers, notably the *gate* function pointer (often null) which decides if the pass has to be executed, and the *execute* function which does the real job of the pass.

A pass of a given type can only be inserted near other passes of the same kind.

- choosing which GCC internal representations should be used; this choice also depends of the considered pass; for instance, *Gimple/SSA* is not always available, or on the contrary may be required before some pass.

7.3.1 Choosing the Right Passes

The order and set of executed passes (within some given compilation by GCC) depends upon the actual code compiled by GCC and also of the optimizations requested at compilation time (*e.g.* is different with `-o1` and with `-o3`). Passes whose name starts with a letter can give *dump files* (a textual file dumping some internal representation handled by the pass, *e.g.* the *Gimple* code). The GCC program option `-fdump-tree-all` produces all the dump files; unfortunately the name (*e.g.* `matmul.c.004t.gimple`) of the dump file is not very meaningful (because the contained number *e.g.* `004` is *not* a chronological ordering of passes).

A possible way of understanding the concrete passes executed by GCC is to add a MELT hook with the `register_pass_execution_hook` function provided by MELT. The registered closure gets the pass name and number and is invoked before each pass.

Most MELT extensions involve insertion of additional passes (coded in MELT). Here are some guidelines for choosing where to insert such passes:

- if your pass needs only *Gimple* instructions without a control flow graph, consider inserting it after the `gimple` pass.

- if your pass needs *Gimple/SSA* instructions, insert your pass after the `ssa` pass at least.

- if your pass needs inlining to have been done, consider inserting it after the `phiopt` pass

- if your pass requires GRAPHITE to have detected parallelizable loops, insert it after `graphite` pass

- *etc.*

Choosing the right place to insert your pass is still a difficult issue, notably when interprocedural optimizations are required (or are useful).

7.3.2   Using the Available Representations

GCC has many internal data types and representations: the `gengtype` utility, which generates[13] marking routines for the GCC garbage collector, handles more than 1900 types with GTY annotations. So GCC has many more internal representations than just `tree`-s and `gimple`-s.

MELT is in principle able to access any such GTY-ed data type: part of the MELT runtime is generated, notably the layout of boxed values (*e.g.* boxed `gimple` or `edge` values) and their low level *C* support code (*e.g.* for allocating such values, and for copying or scanning them in the MELT garbage collector). Each GCC material known to MELT is described in a *C-type* instance: so the `loop` GCC data is described in a `ctype_loop` descriptor (giving the `:loop` "keyword" to annote material of that type in MELT code), *etc.* So adding a new *C-type* is a matter of providing its descriptor and then regenerating all MELT generated code (inside the MELT branch).

The GCC compiler does not provide any direct means to add specific data *inside* existing representations (like `gimple`, *etc.*). To associate their own data to such existing representations, GCC plugins and the MELT extension have to manage this association outside the internal representations. A convenient way is to keep in some hash-table, keyed by GCC representations like `gimple`, `tree`, *etc.* the association between internal GCC representations and MELT (or GCC plugins') extensions. Hence, every *C-type* provides not only boxed values (so a boxed *Tree* is a MELT value containing a `tree` pointer), but also homogeneous hash-tables: *e.g.* a map of *Tree*-s is an hash-table, itself a MELT value, having `tree`-s as keys, and arbitrary non-null MELT values associated with each of them.

---

[13] The GCC compiler has more than a dozen specialized internal *C* code generators: `gengtype` generating garbage collection marking routines; `genattr` generating attribute information in the back-end from machine description; `genautomata` for pipeline hazards, *etc.* Most generators are not available to plugins.

With the *Gimple/SSA* representation, GCC manage also the "use-def" information: when *trssa* is some raw `tree` of an *SSA* name from some *Gimple/SSA* instruction, the `walk_use_def_chain_depth_first` and `walk_use_def_chain_breadth_first` MELT primitives apply a given MELT closure to a given value and to every `tree` and `gimple` defining (*i.e.* setting) or using the variable under *trssa*.

7.4   Conclusion and Future Work

This chapter should suggest developers of important scientific high performance computation software consider extending and customizing the GCC compiler suite for their specific needs. This could in particular be useful to take advantage of GPGPUs and other specialized hardware.

Diving into GCC is an intimidating experience (because of the complexity and size of the `gcc` legacy software), but this paper gave some practical hints to make it easier.

Extending or customizing GCC has the decisive advantage of leveraging on the powerful internal representations and transformations already provided by GCC. These assets are the main reasons to build your extensions above GCC. In addition, extending GCC is adequate when implementing custom optimizations or code transformations.

Future work on MELT (if compatible with available funding) may include interfacing additional GCC features, more OPENCL related extensions, a Web interface to MELT, analysis to help drive energy-consumption related facilities.

High performance computing is a major potential application of compiler customizations. MELT extensions should be "easily" prototyped to implment such specific enhancements.

Acknowledgments

Work on MELT has been possible through French public funding from DGCIS of GlobalGCC and OpenGPU projects.

References

[1] A. Kravets, A. Monakov, A. Belevantsev, "Graphite-OpenCL: Generate OpenCL code from Parallel Loops", GCC Summit, 2010.

[2] C. Augonnet, S. Thibault, R. Namyst, P.A. Wacrenier, "StarPU: A Unified Platform for Task Scheduling on Heterogeneous Multicore Architectures", Concurrency and Computation: Practice and Experience, Special Issue: Euro-Par 2009, 23, 187–198, Feb. 2011. http://hal.inria.fr/inria-00550877

[3] G. Fursin, O. Temam, "Collective optimization: A practical collaborative approach", ACM Transactions on Architecture and Code Optimization, 7, 20:1–20:29, Dec. 2010. doi:10.1145/1880043.1880047

[4] GCC, "GCC internals doc.", Mar. 2012. http://gcc.gnu.org/onlinedocs/gccint/

[5] K. Karimi, N.G. Dickson, F. Hamze, "A Performance Comparison of CUDA and OpenCL", Read, cs.PF(1):12, 2010. `http://arxiv.org/abs/1005.2581`

[6] J. Pitrat, "Artificial Beings (the conscience of a conscious machine)", Wiley / ISTE, Mar. 2009.

[7] B. Starynkevitch, "MELT code [GPLv3] within GCC", 2006-2012. `http://gcc-melt.org/` and `svn://gcc.gnu.org/svn/gcc/branches/melt-branch`

[8] B. Starynkevitch, "Middle End Lisp Translator for GCC, achievements and issues", GROW09 workshop, within HIPEAC09, Paphos, Cyprus, Jan. 2009. `http://www.doc.ic.ac.uk/~phjk/GROW09/`

[9] B. Starynkevitch, "MELT - a Translated Domain Specific Language Embedded in the GCC Compiler", DSL2011 IFIP conf., Bordeaux, France, Sept. 2011. `http://adsabs.harvard.edu/abs/2011arXiv1109.0779S`

[10] K. Trifunovic, A. Cohen, "Enabling more optimizations in GRAPHITE: ignoring memory-based dependences", Proceedings of the 8th GCC Developper's Summit, Ottawa, Canada, Oct. 2010. `http://hal.inria.fr/inria-00551509`

[11] K. Trifunovic, A. Cohen, D. Edelsohn, F. Li, T. Grosser, H. Jagasia, R. Ladelsky, S. Pop, J. Sjödin, R. Upadrasta, "GRAPHITE Two Years After: First Lessons Learned From Real-World Polyhedral Compilation", GCC Research Opportunities Workshop (GROW'10), Pisa, Italy, Jan. 2010. `http://hal.inria.fr/inria-00551516`

©Saxe-Coburg Publications, 2014.
F. Magoulès, (Editor),
Patterns for Parallel Programming on GPUs
Saxe-Coburg Publications, Stirlingshire, Scotland, 187-207.

Chapter 8

OpenCL: A Suitable Solution to Simplify and Unify High Performance Computing Developments

J. Passerat-Palmbach and D.R.C. Hill

ISIMA, Aubière, France
LIMOS, Université Blaise Pascal – CNRS UMR 6158, Clermont-Ferrand, France

Abstract

Manycore architectures are now available in a wide range of HPC systems. Going from CPUs to GPUs and FPGAs, modern hardware accelerators can be exploited using heterogeneous software technologies. In this chapter, we study the inputs that OpenCL offers to high performance computing applications, as a solution to unify developments. In order to overcome the lack of native OpenCL support for some architectures, we survey the third-party research works that propose a source-to-source approach to transform OpenCL into other parallel programming languages. We use FPGAs as a case study, because of their dramatic OpenCL support compared to GPUs for instance. These transformation approaches could also lead to potential works in the model driven engineering (MDE) field that we conceptualize in this work. Moreover, OpenCL's standard API is quite rough, thus we also introduce several APIs from the simple high-level binder to the source code generator that intend to ease and boost the development process of any OpenCL application.

Keywords: OpenCL, abstraction layers, survey, source-to-source, transformation, manycore.

8.1 Introduction

At the end of the last decade we entered more seriously into the era of hybrid computing, where different types of processors are used in a common computing system.

Modern accelerators are now available as commercial off the shelf (COTS), we can buy and or design our own high performance hybrid architecture. Manycore central processing units (CPUs), general-purpose graphical computing units (GPGPUs) and more recently the AMD accelerated processing units (APUs) are gaining more and more interest. FPGAs also have been considered to be elements of a general purpose High Performance Computing system, they are used in some of the best architectures (like the one proposed by Cray Inc.) [5]. Nowadays, the high performance computing (HPC) community tends to champion GPU architectures to speed-up applications, but according to [16], FPGAs offer better performances than GPUs when faced with some integer arithmetic operations. In addition to impressive performances, the FPGA approaches have many advantages including small footprint with very low energy costs. Most of FPGA logic is configurable, and this architecture is saving the processing power since we only design the specific features that will be used. If we can reuse the same silicon for different functions, we also have the advantage of an easy mapping of different operations to different silicon thus allowing massive parallelism. Long before the GPGPU boom, in 2004, companies joined to establish the FPGA high performance computing alliance (FHPCA). This alliance is dedicated to the use of Xilink FPGAs for high end real-world industrial applications. Since the advent of the Virtex 4 (and now with much larger devices) the use of FPGAs for general purpose numerical computing has become a reality. Even if it was not really noticed in the Top500 at that time, the University of Edinburgh supercomputing centre proposed in 2007 an FPGA based supercomputer named "Maxwell".

The case of FPGAs in HPC is particularly significant. Given the advantages previously exposed, the question is why don't we have more FPGAs in HPC? The main cause in our opinion is that the programming model problem is neither mature nor accessible to the scientific community. Common HPC developers are not used to programming in hardware description languages (HDLs, such as VHDL) for FPGAs, and the problem is not just learning a new language, since it is mainly a design issue. Indeed, we do not design circuits as we design programs. Even if predefined libraries are available, they do not compensate for the fact that there is no real standard hardware. The point is that we need a technology that can be understood by the heterogeneous HPC community, allowing them to address the wide range of hardware accelerators at their disposal.

Since its introduction in June 2008, the OpenCL™ (open computing language) standard has been specifically designed to address the challenge of executing HPC applications on heterogeneous systems consisting of multi-core processors, GPGPUs and FPGAs. OpenCL is based on the C programming language but it provides additional features to leverage highly-parallel hardware accelerators. OpenCL allows the programmer to explicitly specify and control parallelism.

Though numerous accelerator vendors started to support OpenCL for CPUs and GPUs, fewer efforts were given to supporting hybrid systems with FPGAs. Recent advances from the Altera Corporation, make us confident that the OpenCL programming model will propose advantageous solutions to common problems that limited the adoption of FPGAs for HPC. While native tools are not reliable yet, we can still focus on third-party developments that act as converters from OpenCL to HDL without the need for any further development from FPGAs vendors.

Part of this work actually considers FPGAs as a case study of the ability to take advantage of OpenCL on platforms that do not officially support this technology. We have chosen to tackle this problem through FPGA-aimed proposals, since this community has been very productive in terms of solutions to detach from vendors. Still, the same conclusions could be applied to other architectures lacking OpenCL support, the most notable being Intel Sandy/Ivybridge GPU parts, when used under the Linux OS (operating system).

Vendor-agnostic approaches should democratize the use of OpenCL for HPC developments, and promote GPU computing at the same time as the main platform offering OpenCL support. However, OpenCL suffers from a highly verbose and constrained API. Thus, this study also surveys software solutions assisting OpenCL development.

In this chapter, we:

- State the need for an abstraction layer for OpenCL;

- Survey the propositions to provide OpenCL support for any architecture through a source-to-source transformations approach;

- Study the most significant application programming interfaces (APIs) to ease OpenCL development and compare their features;

- Recall the inputs of the OpenCL technology in High Performance Computing applications, and especially for GPUs.

8.2 On the Need for an Abstraction Layer for OpenCL

8.2.1 OpenCL in Brief

OpenCL is a standard proposed by the Khronos group that aims to unify developments on various types of hardware accelerators architectures like CPUs, GPUs and FPGAs. It provides programming constructs based upon C99 to write the actual parallel code (called the kernel). Kernels execution is executed by several work-items, that will be mapped to different execution units depending on the target: for instance, GPUs will associate them to local threads. For scheduling purposes, work-items are then bundled into work-groups each containing an equivalent amount of work-items.

They are enhanced by application programming interfaces (APIs) used to control the device and the execution. At the time of writing, the latest version of the API is 1.2 [7] that has been released in November, 2011. OpenCL programs execution relies on specific drivers issued by the manufacturer of the hardware they run on. The point is OpenCL kernels are not compiled with the rest of the application, but on the fly at runtime. This allows specific tuning of the binary for the current platform.

OpenCL brings three major inputs to HPC developments: as a cross-platform standard, it allows development of applications once and for all for any supported architecture. It is also a great abstraction layer that allows developers to concentrate on the parallelization of their algorithm, and leave the device specific mechanics to the driver.

8.2.2 OpenCL: A Constrained API

In the introduction we have evoked the major problem of OpenCL: its complicated API. Concretely this lies in three major problems that will be detailed hereafter: bloated source code, double calls and risky constructs. First, when kernel functions that execute on the hardware accelerator remain concise and thus fully expressive, host API routines result in verbose source code where it is difficult for an external reader or for a non-regular developer, to determine the purpose of the application among all those lines. Second, some design choices of the API make it even more verbose when trying to write portable code that can run on several hosts without any change. For instance, OpenCL developers are used to calling most of the API query functions twice. Indeed, a first call is often required to determine the number of results to be expected, and a second actually gets the right amount of elements. We will designate these two subsequent invocations of the same routine as the **double-call** pattern hereafter. Finally, such verbose constructs discourage developers from checking the results of each of their calls to the API. At the same time, the OpenCL API is very permissive with regard to the type of the parameters its functions accept. Now imagine that two parameters have been awkwardly swapped in an API call, it is very likely that the application keeps quiet about this error if the developer has not explicitly checked the error code returned by this call. In an heterogeneous environment such as OpenCL, where the parallel part of the computation will be relocated on hardware accelerators, runtime errors that only issues error codes are not the easiest bugs to remove.

All these drawbacks make it clear that although the OpenCL standard is a great tool offering portability in high performance computing, it does not meet the higher level APIs expected by parallel developers to help them avoid common mistakes, and to produce efficient applications in a reasonable lapse of time.

8.3   OpenCL Support on Various Platforms: The FPGAs Case Study

Enabling OpenCL for a particular FPGA architecture can be achieved in two major ways. The first relies on vendors who need to provide an OpenCL driver implementation for their particular device. While both NVIDIA and ATi provide OpenCL drivers for their GPU products, Intel has recently enabled a large set of its processors to support OpenCL. However the driver implementation solution is still in its infancy across the FPGA community. Altera is known for their FPGA products, but is also an active member of the Khronos Group, responsible of the OpenCL standard. The company has announced the development of an OpenCL framework, and presents encouraging results of a Monte-Carlo Black Scholes simulation implementation in [1].

Researchers' initiatives have led us to consider another way of thinking that does not involve any intervention from the FPGA's vendor, but relies on third-party developments to provide OpenCL support for FPGAs. The main advantage of these solutions is that they can be applied to any platform lacking OpenCL support. In this section, we study the most promising solutions from the literature, focusing on FPGAs, as long as this community has been in need of a unified programming model for a long time now, and consequently proposed more tools to meet their expectations.

8.3.1 Source-to-Source Transformation Approach

Supporting the whole OpenCL standard can become a long and costly operation for a vendor, while its community might not perceive the benefits of switching to OpenCL developments, or simply do not require high performance. That being said, another strategy comes into play to bypass vendors decisions: offer OpenCL support for a range of devices from a third-party effort. Such projects are all based on the same principle that consists of transforming the OpenCL source code into a language already supported by the target platform. In this section, we will survey the most interesting proposals of source-to-source compiling aiming at similar goals.

8.3.1.1 At the Beginning, there was CUDA

At the moment, OpenCL is mostly known to be a unified solution to program GPUs from various origins, and to compete with NVIDIA's CUDA technology in the GPU computing domain. Being almost two years older than OpenCL, CUDA has been targeted by research works earlier than its counterpart, particularly when considering the opportunities to have it running on other devices than NVIDIA GPUs. Most of these approaches make use of the same principle as the strategy we identified to provide OpenCL support for an FPGA architecture from a third-party initiative: *i.e.* source-to-source transformation.

In 2008, Stratton *et al.* proposed MCUDA, a tool intended to execute CUDA code on a multi-core CPU [15]. This chapter brings up the fundamental problems that will be encountered when attempting to set up such a code generation approach, and even puts forward efficient solutions. Let us recall that CUDA relies on the single instruction, multiple thread (SIMT) paradigm, so the application logic is placed at the thread level. Threads perform the same operations on different input data, but sometimes, an operation needs to access data that have been processed by another thread. In such a case, CUDA developers have to synchronize their threads at the particular step of the algorithm dealing with shared data to make sure the data they are processing is up to date.

Before parallelizing the application among CPU threads, MCUDA first serializes the CUDA input in order to analyse it more simply. MCUDA tries to identify independent code parts in terms of data within the newly serialized code. When such parts are detected, they are bounded by what is called a thread-loop. Thread-loops induce implicit synchronization points at their boundaries. Thus, an explicit request to synchronize threads in the original CUDA source code will result in two thread-loops: one embracing the code before the synchronization point and the other one after.

Instead of basing the computation on logical threads, MCUDA rises to a block of logical threads level. This strategy excludes semantic losses since blocks are independent along a classical CUDA execution. They contain logical threads that will perform the same operations with no constraint on the order in which the blocks are processed. MCUDA behaves identically, since after being serialized, blocks are executed by OS threads created by OpenMP directives, and thus rely on the underlying scheduling policy for their order of execution to be determined.

Now that the code is serialized and that the synchronization points are respected, MCUDA treats memory accesses. The most important point of this step is to understand that CUDA, such as OpenCL, defines several data areas mainly to take advantage of the different caching mechanisms available in a GPU architecture. As long as CPUs display a single cached memory space, MCUDA maps any type of memory to the unique memory space of the CPU. Still, memory areas also bring information on the scope of the data they store, forcing MCUDA to apply another conversion step that again prevents semantic losses in the output code. For example, when variables shared by all the logical threads of a block can be replaced by a single variable, elements declared as private to a thread have to be duplicated. To do so, MCUDA introduces arrays containing the particular value of a given thread in the cell corresponding to its identifier. We will see further on that the same pondering about memory spaces must be observed when thinking about an FPGA implementation.

Basically, the philosophy of MCUDA lies in two main steps:

1. Group local-thread based computations and express them at a block level (SIMT → SIMB);

2. Parallelize the execution of independent blocks with a pool of worker threads.

More generally, the purpose is to obtain first independent elements before executing them concurrently following an arbitrary scheduling. This mechanism is classical and can also be found in other works involving CUDA and GPU architectures such as [13]. This implies two major choices when implementing an OpenCL converter: first, you need to figure out how the work-items will be mapped on the target architecture, and second, how the memory hierarchy will be represented on your FPGA.

One year later, some of the authors of MCUDA applied their conclusions to FPGA architectures and proposed FCUDA: a tool to compile CUDA kernels onto FPGAs. FCUDA's philosophy is quite similar to MCUDA's in the fact that its main purpose is to translate CUDA SIMT code into SIMB independent blocks that are ready to be transformed. Now, when MCUDA spreads those blocks on multiple CPU cores through OpenMP threads, FCUDA will synthesise FPGA cores according to the register transfer level (RTL) design corresponding to the kernel function.

The way FCUDA deals with memory is quite interesting and thoroughly described in the paper [12], wherein authors make concrete proposals concerning the memory locations of the FPGA assigned to their CUDA counterparts. For instance, they propose to take advantage of direct memory access (DMA) burst mode in order to implement constant memory.

Additionally, the workflow allowing FCUDA to transform CUDA code into FPGA hardware description language (HDL) requires an intermediate stage where C code is produced and passed to a third-party software. This step enables developers to tune the resulting code before it is synthesized into a RTL design. However, we need to note that FCUDA displays some drawbacks, indeed it only handles kernels and does not take into account the host API.

8.3.1.2   Then comes OpenCL

The MCUDA way to deal with parallel applications was pursued by several recent studies, this time generating HDL for a given FPGA from OpenCL source code. In 2011, Owaida *et al.* introduced SOpenCL (Silicon OpenCL) a source-to-source transformation process that converts OpenCL code into HDL to build FPGA-enabled hardware accelerators [11]. Just like MCUDA, SOpenCL first applies a serialization step on the kernel in order to join logical threads from a given work-group into independent execution environments. SOpenCL uses the fact that work-groups are actually three-dimensional containers of local-threads to insert a triple-nested loop that will pass on each local-thread thanks to its x, y, z coordinates in the kernel to compute the data it was assigned.

Barriers and synchronization points are also handled in a similar way. Whenever a synchronization point must be set up, the loop around the current statement is split into two sub-loops: the first deals with the part of the statement before the synchronization point, while the second handles the remaining part. This process is called **loop fission**.

Finally, memory areas are also treated in a way close to MCUDA. The idea is to figure out the lifetime of a variable to state whether it can be reused across loops or not. Concerning the variables' scope, each logical-thread is provided with a private copy of the variable only if the latter is meant to be used in several sub-loops, which would potentially overwrite its content. The final location of variables in memory is bound to the targeted FPGA, but we have seen previously that no semantic information was lost during this stage.

What makes SOpenCL original is its template-based approach when the time comes to generate HDL code. SOpenCL proposes a hardware accelerator template including both the Data Path and Stream Units that will be involved in the computation. Taking advantage of the LLVM compiler framework [9], the hardware generation flow results in synthesisable HDL for the accelerator following an architectural template, instead of issuing an unpredictable output code.

In 2010, Jääskeläinen *et al.* [6] proposed another work inspired from MCUDA. However, this OpenCL-based design methodology differs from other proposals by exploring the extension feature offered by the OpenCL standard. As we have seen previously, OpenCL allows vendors to add specific extensions of their own to exploit their hardware a bit further than the sole standard API would. The main advantage of this capacity is that it does not imply rewriting code when switching from an extension-enabled architecture to a standard one. Thus, vendors can allow the specificities of their hardware to leverage, while remaining compliant with others'. As long as extensions availability can be checked at source level, one can adapt its algorithm behaviour to take advantage of the extensions only when possible. In an FPGA approach, this feature appears crucial since it allows hardware designers to provide custom architectures synthesized on an FPGA platform. Clients can then choose to benefit from these particular developments or not, and even try both solutions in the blink of an eye without having to revise their entire source.

In conclusion, we have seen that no matter the source-to-source tool we studied, the implementation choices are roughly the same. The process follows a common skeleton that is summed up hereafter:

1. Serialize work-groups by executing their local-threads sequentially;

2. Eliminate barriers and synchronization points thanks to loop fission;

3. Analyse variables livelihood to determine which can be shared and which should be copied in a private area for each local-thread;

4. Convert the resulting source code to an HDL, taking work-groups as the base unit for the computation.

8.4   High-Level APIs for OpenCL: Two Philosophies

8.4.1   Ease OpenCL Development through High-Level APIs

8.4.1.1   Standard API C++ Wrapper

The OpenCL standard not only describes the C API that any implementation should meet, but also the C++ wrapper that comes along with it. This wrapper provides both C++ bindings of the OpenCL calls, and also two restricted declinations of the Standard Template Library (STL) from genuine C++: the string and vector classes. These two classes have been rewritten for the purpose of the OpenCL wrapper as a subset of their counterparts but are mostly compliant. The idea is to get rid of STL's bloated classes, which *std::string* is nothing but the best example. As long as they display an interface close to the original classes, the OpenCL versions, stored in the *cl* namespace, can be swapped with the matching STL class thanks to a single macro.

Another C++ mechanism nicely leveraged by the OpenCL C++ wrapper is exceptions. OpenCL errors are handled in a low-level way with error codes to be compared to 0 to assess whether the previous call is completed successfully. Obviously this technique is not quite adapted to develop with higher level languages, because it inflates source codes with non-effective lines. Moreover, it forces developers to be very careful and to explicitly check the returning code of their invocations, and, in the case of problems, to retrieve the corresponding error. In our case, this painful process is handled by the exception mechanism that forces developers to catch the exception and treat it consequently.

The remaining elements of this binding are dedicated to ease the OpenCL API for developers. The most significant example of this is the double call pattern foreseen in our short introduction to OpenCL in Section 8.2.2. Using the traditional OpenCL C API, one needs to perform two successive calls to the same function to first figure out the number of results to be stored in an array provided for this purpose, before actually filling it through a second call requesting the exact number of elements to store in the array of results subsequently. The C++ wrapper here greatly facilitates the process since a single call is needed to obtain the results, while *cl::vector* is used instead of dynamically allocated arrays.

Listing 8.1 shows an example of the wrapper syntax. Although efforts can be noticed to provide a simple API, the result remains quite verbose since Listing 8.1 only lists GPU devices and creates a dummy kernel from a source file in the context of the discovered device.

8.4.1.2 QtOpenCL

Used to provide nice bindings for C++ development tools going from database drivers to concurrency, the Qt library developed by Nokia [10] now also offers its own OpenCL wrapper as a set of extensions named QtOpenCL. At the time of writing, we would like to insist on the fact that QtOpenCL is neither included in the stable Qt 4.7 release, nor in the future 4.8 version according to Nokia's roadmap. However, QtOpenCL is freely available for download as an extension and is compatible with Qt 4.6.2 and Qt 4.7 frameworks.

As an OpenCL wrapper, QtOpenCL aims to break down three main barriers that we already identified as OpenCL drawbacks: initialization phase, memory management and kernel execution. To assist users in the initialization phase, and particularly to compile the external OpenCL source code, QtOpenCL automatically handles OpenCL source files reading through a single method. Memory management receives as much consideration so that buffers can be created more simply. Moreover, their object oriented interface allow users to call methods such as *read()* directly on buffers to retrieve results from a hardware accelerator.

The third point of the QtOpenCL intentions targets kernel executions. This aspect is handled "à la Qt" thanks to the *QFuture* class, well-known by developers using Qt for their CPU developments involving concurrency.

QFuture is an event returned when a kernel is run through the *QtConcurrent::run* method, and allows one to wait for the kernel to complete. In addition, *QFuture* is compatible with the *QFutureWatcher* class that uses the signal/slot mechanism which Qt is based upon. The latter mechanism is an implementation of the Observer design pattern that causes a routine to be called when a particular event occurs. In our case, the event signals the completion of the associated kernel and can raise an update of

```
try {
  // Place the GPU devices of the first platform into
     a context
  cl::vector<cl::Platform> platforms;
  cl::vector<cl::Device> devices;

  cl::Platform::get(&platforms);
  platforms[0].getDevices(CL_DEVICE_TYPE_GPU, &devices
     );
  cl::Context context(devices);

  // Create and build program
  std::ifstream programFile("kernel.cl");
  std::string programString(std::istreambuf_iterator<
     char>(programFile),
        (std::istreambuf_iterator<char>()));
  cl::Program::Sources source(1, std::make_pair(
     programString.c_str(),
        programString.length()+1));
  cl::Program program(context, source);
  program.build(devices);

  // Add kernel to progam
  cl::Kernel fooKernel(program, "foo");

  // Create kernel
  cl::vector<cl::Kernel> allKernels;
  program.createKernels(&allKernels);
}
catch(cl::Error e) {
  std::cerr << e.what() << std::endl;
}
```

Listing 8.1: GPU devices listing and kernel creation using the C++ wrapper API
            (adapted from [14])

```
// context creation
QCLContext context;
if ( !context.create() ) {
  std::cerr << "Error in context creation for the GPU"
      << std::endl;
  return 1;
}

const int vectorSize = 1024000;
QCLVector<int> inVector = context.createVector<int> (
    vectorSize );
QCLVector<int> outVector = context.createVector<int> (
    vectorSize );

for (int i = 0; i < vectorSize; ++i) {
  inVector[i] = i;
}

// kernel build
QCLProgram program = context.
    buildProgramFromSourceFile ( "./kernel.cl" );
QCLKernel kernel = program.createKernel ( "foo" );

// enqueue and run kernel
kernel.setGlobalWorkSize ( vectorSize );
kernel ( inVector, outVector );
```

Listing 8.2: GPU context creation kernel enqueueing using QtOpenCL

the graphical user interface (GUI) of the application for example.

Listing 8.2 presents how to enqueue a dummy kernel that takes a vector of integers as a parameter and outputs another one, using QtOpenCL.

8.4.1.3 PyOpenCL

PyOpenCL is a research initiative developed at the same time as its CUDA counterpart PyCUDA [8]. Both approaches rely on a concept called GPU run time code generation (RTCG) that intends to solve common problems encountered when harnessing hardware accelerators. In PyOpenCL, this translates into a flexible code generation mechanism that can adapt to new requirements transparently. In the end, programmers can summon kernels as if they were methods from the program instance they have just built.

Apart from those dynamic features, PyOpenCL displays the classical inputs from an OpenCL wrapper developed in a high level language such as Python. The latter being well-known for its concision and simplicity, PyOpenCL directly benefits from this

```
programFile = open ( 'foo.cl', 'r' )
programText = programFile.read ( )
program = cl.Program ( context, programText )
program.build ( )
```

Listing 8.3: GPU program building using PyOpenCL

characteristic. This is achieved widely because of Python's dynamic typing system that delegates an important part of the work to the interpreter. Finally, OpenCL source code reading takes advantage of Python file handling capacities, so that a program can be read from source and built using no more than four lines, as can be seen in Listing 8.3.

8.4.2   Generating OpenCL Source Code from High-Level APIs

8.4.2.1   ScalaCL

ScalaCL is a project, part of the free and open-source Nativelibs4java initiative, led by Olivier Chafik [4]. The Nativelibs4java project is an ambitious bundle of libraries trying to allow users to take advantage of various native binaries in a Java environment.

From ScalaCL itself, two projects have recently emerged. The first one is named Scalaxy. It is a plugin for the Scala compiler that intends to optimize Scala code at compile time. Indeed, Scala functional constructs might run slower than their classical Java equivalents. Scalaxy deals with this problem by pre-processing Scala code to replace some constructions by more efficient ones. Basically, this plugin intends to transform Scala loop-like calls such as map or foreach by their while loops equivalents. The main advantage of this tool is that it is applicable to any Scala code, without relying on any hardware.

The second element resulting from this fork is the ScalaCL collections. It consists of a set of collections that support a restricted amount of Scala functions. However, these functions can be mapped at compile time to their OpenCL equivalents. A compiler plugin dedicated to OpenCL generation is called at compile time to normalize the code of the closure applied to the collection. Functional programming usually defines a closure as an anonymous function embedded in the body of another function. A closure can also access the variables from the calling host function. The resulting source is then converted to an OpenCL kernel. At runtime, another part of ScalaCL comes into play, since the rest of the OpenCL code, like the initializations, is coupled to the previously generated kernel to form the whole parallel application. The body of the closure will be computed by an OpenCL processing element (PE), which can be a thread or a core depending on the host where the program is being run. Listing 8.4 presents a simple closure that computes the apply the cosine function to every element of an array. Only the execution of the closure's body is deported to the hardware accelerator targeted by OpenCL.

The obvious asset of ScalaCL is its ability to generate OpenCL at compile time.

```
import scalacl._
import scala.math._

implicit val context = new ScalaCLContext

val range = (0 to 1000000).cl
val rangeArray = r.toCLArray

// Runs asynchronously on the GPU via OpenCL
val mapResult = rangeArray.map ( v => cos(v).toFloat )
```

Listing 8.4: Computing cosine of the 1000000 first integers through ScalaCL

It means that we could enhance ScalaCL by adding an extra step to tune the issued OpenCL kernel at compile time and take advantage of GPU vendor specific extensions for instance.

8.4.2.2 Aparapi

Aparapi [2] is a project initiated by AMD and recently freed under an MIT-like open source licence. It intends to provide a way to perform OpenCL actions directly from a pure Java source code. This process involves no upstream translation step, and is then wholly carried out at runtime. To do so, Aparapi relies on a Java native interface (JNI) wrapper of the OpenCL API that hides complexity from developers.

Basically, Aparapi proposes to implement the operations to be performed in parallel within a Kernel class. The kernel code takes place in an overridden *run()* abstract method of the Kernel class that sets the boundaries of the parallel computation. At the time of writing, only a subset of Java features are supported by Aparapi, it means that *run()* can only contain a restricted amount of features, data types, and mechanisms. Concretely, primitive data types, except char, are the sole data elements that can be manipulated within Aparapi's kernels.

For years, Java has been used to managing concurrency problems thanks to a Thread class whose implementation makes use of the native thread of the underlying operating system where the Java virtual machine (JVM) runs. Thread implements the Runnable interface that only consists of providing a *void run()* method that will be called when the thread is launched. This mechanism is widely adopted in the Java world, and most of the frameworks offering an abstraction layer to Thread employ it in order to remain compliant between each other. At first, it seems that Aparapi follows the same path given that it designates a *run()* method to contain the parallel code. However, Aparapi's source code does not involve Runnable at any moment. A simple example of using Aparapi is set up in Listing 8.5 to square an array of 8 integers.

This design choice seems rather awkward when taking into consideration that the parallel tasks are assigned to a pool of CPU worker threads, the Java thread pool (JTP), when no accelerator can be found on the host platform. In fact, several imple-

```
final int[] inArray = new int[] {1, 2, 3, 4, 5, 6, 7,
    8};
final int[] outArray = new float[input.length];

Kernel kernel = new Kernel ( ) {
  public void run() {
      outVector [ getGlobalId() ]  = inArray [
          getGlobalId() ] * inArray [ getGlobalId() ];
  }
}

kernel.execute(inArray.length);
```

Listing 8.5: Squaring an array of integers using Aparapi

mentations of a JTP are now shipping with the Java standard development kit (SDK) like Executors or Fork/Join, and have proved to be both efficient and user-friendly. Software design fosters reutilization as much as possible and being compliant with standard tools not only fastens development but it also strengthens it.

Additionally, it is interesting to note that Aparapi is not fully cross-platform, albeit being written in Java. The JNI bindings used to perform the calls to the OpenCL API make the Java package of Aparapi bound to native binaries. Thus, Aparapi cannot be shipped as a single package and depends on the ability of its underlying platform to run native code. This aspect can become a problem in terms of simplicity of use by clients, since it forces them to have a C++ tool-chain installed on each platform they want to run Aparapi on, so that the native part of the library can be recompiled for their particular platform. Still, native code dependency is not a major drawback for Aparapi given that there are few chances that a platform cannot execute the compiled-side of the JNI part of the library. This means that Aparapi can mostly be considered as a cross-platform tool that requires little effort from the client to be effective.

The first versions of Aparapi came with a slight limitation: AMD constrained the library to run on its devices only! Systems where AMD devices could not be found used to fall back to the JTP instead. Thanks to the open-source licence that protects this tool, a third-party developer was able to remove that latter constraint. In fact, execution is locked on a particular set of devices, here AMD GPUs, only by comparing the OpenCL platform identifier to the string identifying an AMD OpenCL platform. The removal of this software restriction makes Aparapi a potential high-level API to design HPC application.

8.4.3   A Complete Solution: JavaCL

JavaCL is an open source initiative that targets a smooth integration of OpenCL in Java applications. Like ScalaCL that we have studied in the previous section, JavaCL is part of the Nativelibs4java project developed by Olivier Chafik. The JavaCL library displays two interesting aspects that we will describe hereafter.

The first input from this library is to ease OpenCL development from the host side. In order to be easily integrated in Java code, the OpenCL 1.1 API [7] has been fully wrapped in Java classes. Every element required to perform OpenCL computations can now be handled directly in Java. This allows us to write nothing but the kernel using the C OpenCL API.

JavaCL is issued as a single *jar* file containing all the dependencies needed to be executed on any platform, including native libraries in charge of being the bridge between Java and the OpenCL platform. This way, it is perfectly independent from its underlying platform, and can be shipped easily by several ways. The most convenient one in our opinion is a Maven repository. Maven [3] is a build tool targeting Java applications that allows the projects it constructs to declare dependencies located in remote repositories. When a dependency is encountered for the first time, the maven client installed on the host system building the project downloads the dependency, and stores it in a local repository, so that it can be reused in a further build.

Functions intending to query an OpenCL installation have been designed to provide the most information in a single call. This completeness leads to an invocation pattern well-known by OpenCL developers: the double-call pattern foreseen in Section 8.2.2. For instance, a function such as *clGetPlatformIDs* will return a list of the available OpenCL platforms in an array passed as a parameter along with its size. This array must have been allocated upstream and its size is consequently the maximum amount of results it can store. In addition to filling the array with the available platforms, *clGetPlatformIDs* also returns the total number of platforms in the system. Consequently, an application needs to invoke *clGetPlatformIDs* twice in order to figure out dynamically the amount of platforms on a given system: first, the function is called to determine the number of platforms and allocate an array according to this result, second, the function is summoned to actually fill the array. Such a design is widely used in the OpenCL API, and developers often have to call the same function twice in a row to make their code portable. The whole process results in bloated source files, whose real behaviour might become difficult to comprehend. JavaCL answers this awkwardness through its API that automatically issues a filled array as a result.

When platforms have been identified, it is time for an OpenCL application to list their related devices and to create a context combining some of them. As long as a high-performance computing application's main purpose is to speed up computation time, developers usually select the most efficient devices to form the OpenCL context in which their application will run. Once again, JavaCL takes care of this step by providing a *createBestContext* method that creates a context with the device containing the most work units.

The two previous features focused on increasing the ease of use of the OpenCL API. Moreover, JavaCL also enhances OpenCL development thanks to the Java language capabilities. Let us now examine the characteristics that make JavaCL really more than a simple OpenCL wrapper.

As we have seen in our introduction to OpenCL, the latter stores data that are to be treated on the device into buffers. The main concern with these buffers is that whatever data they contain, they are represented by the sole *cl_mem* type. This is a potential source of harm since the compiler has no way to check that you are passing a wrong buffer type as parameter to a kernel for example. On the other side, object oriented languages such as Java are used to encapsulating data in dedicated containers. JavaCL does so by providing a different class for each data type that contains a buffer. Thanks to Java generics, a *CLBuffer* class can be parameterised with the primitive data type the buffer actually contains. Not only is expressive containers a nice feature for developers who have to correct a source code they did not write, but it is a particularly good point that helps compilers find errors. Strong static typing prevents errors encountered when buffers from any type are accepted as parameters, which can appear dramatic when programming devices such as GPUs or FPGAs. To sum up, the JavaCL API allows the compiler to check little programming errors at compile time, before they turn into malicious bugs at runtime.

Being compiled at runtime, within the host program, OpenCL sources might lead to compiling errors as any program would. However, due to on-the-fly compiling, errors are a bit more tedious to take into account than in a usual program. Developers have to explicitly request the compilation error log through the classical double call syntax inherent in the OpenCL API query system. This is not particularly suited to solve problems efficiently, and one has to make sure correctly to handle the output of the compiler anytime he builds a kernel through the C API. In the Java world, runtime errors are traditionally handled by exceptions. The exceptions mechanism is cleverly adapted by JavaCL so that any kernel build will raise a *CLBuildException* that can be caught, and whose content can be printed easily.

In the same way, enqueued tasks errors are also wrapped in JavaCL exceptions. An exception hierarchy has been designed to cover the scope of potential errors issued by an OpenCL-enabled application. Explicit exceptions matching the most wide-spread OpenCL errors can be cast throughout the application lifetime; for example, memory-bound errors corrupting the command queue are covered by *CLException.InvalidCommandQueue*. Once again, this JavaCL feature avoids the developer having to deal with involved error codes, while the way Java handles exceptions ensures that errors will be reported at one time or another.

Last but not least, the most promising part in our opinion is the Generator. All the previous features introduced in this section either wrapped OpenCL calls or enhanced the API with type and error checking capabilities for example. The interesting point with the JavaCL generator is its ability to parse a pure OpenCL source file containing one or several kernels, and to issue a corresponding Java source file. The latter contains a class that associates a method per kernel present in the source file. In order to smoothly integrate in the host application, the automatically generated Java class is named after the source file name, whereas each of its methods bears the name of a kernel parsed in the file. Two aspects need to be distinguished to fully understand the inputs the generator brings to OpenCL development.

First, it widely contributes to simplifying OpenCL development: while JavaCL wrappers already make OpenCL on-the-fly compilation comfortable, the Generator allows developers to skip this step by reading the source code at compile time and

```
CLContext context = JavaCL.createBestContext();
CLQueue queue = context.createDefaultQueue();

final int vectorSize = 36864;
Pointer<Integer> inPtr = allocateInts (vectorSize);

for (int i = 0; i < vectorSize; ++i) {
    inPtr.set(i,i);
}

CLBuffer <Integer> inVector = context.createIntBuffer(
    Usage.Input, inPtr);

// Create an OpenCL output buffer
CLBuffer<Integer> outVector = context.createIntBuffer(
    Usage.Output, width*height*8);

// Read the program sources and compile them
MyKernel kernel = new MyKernel(context);

CLEvent addEvt = kernel.foo(queue, inVector,
    vectorSize, vectorSize / 192);

// Blocks until the kernel finishes
Pointer<Integer> outPtr = outVector.read(queue, addEvt
    );
```

Listing 8.6: Squaring an array of integers using JavaCL

generating a corresponding class whose methods can be called to launch the associated kernel.

Second, applications safety is again enforced given that kernel parameters are now typed. Traditionally, kernel parameters need to be set once and for all before enqueueing the kernel. JavaCL brings a first improvement to this process by allowing parameters all to be passed at once as a list of Objects. However, this behaviour might lead to runtime errors since the type and order in which parameters are passed cannot be verified at compile time, each of them being identified by a reference to an Object. Here, the Generator enables an earlier detection of this type of error since the prototype of the method acting as a proxy of the kernel to be enqueued will only match the right type and order of the parameters. Listing 8.6 displays the execution of an instance of the kernel *MyKernel*, the corresponding class of which was generated upstream by the JavaCL Generator.

Finally, the combination of an enhanced wrapping API and a generation mechanism proves that JavaCL goes further than the other APIs studied here.

8.4.4 Summary Table of the Solutions

In Table 8.1, we compare the APIs studied in this work according to the availability of three features: high-level wrapper, code generation facility, and cross-platform portability of the resulting binary that will run on the host.

API	Wrapper	Code-generator	Cross-platform
C++ Wrapper	Yes	No	No
QtOpenCL	Yes	No	No
PyOpenCL	Yes	Yes	Yes
ScalaCL	Yes	Yes	Yes
Aparapi	Yes	Yes	No
JavaCL	Yes	Yes	Yes

Table 8.1: Comparison of the studied APIs according to three criteria

Table 8.1 states that although C++ is one of the most wide-spread language in the HPC community, it suffers from poor APIs to abstract OpenCL.

8.5 Perspectives

Source-to-source solutions might lead to interesting works in the field of model driven engineering (MDE). MDE is a modelling approach that emphasises two main aspects: the first are models and meta-models that allow one, for instance, to represent domain specific modelling languages (DSML), and are generally expressed in the UML formalism. The second element guiding MDE are transformation engines and code generators, they bring a dynamic part to MDE. Their role is to define how meta-models are bound together, and how specific code can be generated from the information they contain. We observe at least a three-level hierarchy often presented as a pyramid, where meta-models are at the top level (M2), classical models at the intermediate one (M1), and the lowest level represents the real world (M0). In our case, we can consider both OpenCL as a meta-model of kernel functions. We can say that kernels are conform OpenCL. On the other side, programming constructs such as VHDL, NVIDIA PTX or Intel SSE instructions are three equivalent types of model describing concrete binaries or RTL designs, *i.e.* the real world. These languages obviously display specificities but their final purpose is the same, so their common aspects can be factored in a meta-model to which they conform. Let us call this meta-model Meta-Language. Given that OpenCL and Meta-Language are two meta-models, MDE allows us to transform elements of the same level automatically, provided valid transformations are available from one meta-model to another. Thus, this modelling way would provide a base when enabling new targets to support source-to-source compilation of OpenCL applications, allowing developers to save lots of time and to simply follow the guidelines contained in the transformation rules.

Figure 8.1 sums up the potential skeleton of an MDE approach to handle OpenCL source-to-source conversion to other languages:

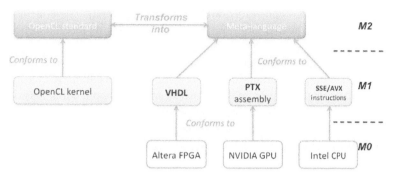

Figure 8.1: Skeleton of an MDE approach to transform OpenCL into any programming language

8.6   Conclusion

In this chapter we have attempted to show that the OpenCL standard was a great tool offering portability in high performance computing and authorizing a wider usage of GPUs, FPGAs, and other manycore platforms. We have seen that a raw usage of OpenCL does not meet the comfort of higher level APIs that parallel developers expect to help them avoid common mistakes, and to produce efficient applications in a reasonable amount of time. We have presented different approaches enabling software reuse and even more portability with features that avoid the developed code to be bound to the intrinsic characteristics of hardware platforms. Thus developers can base their developments upon reliable software components that have been tested many times and across several architectures. This consideration opens a new scope on the benefits of OpenCL for HPC. Using a cross-platform standard gives new testing perspectives. Indeed, such a feature obviously profits heterogeneous computing approaches where FPGA can now be integrated among CPUs and GPUs using OpenCL. Not only do we have at our disposal abstraction levels much more understandable for developers not used to HDL-enabled codes, but we have seen in the previous sections that many APIs intend to bind OpenCL to widespread high-level languages such as C++ or Java. At the same time, legacy codes written in these languages can now benefit from the horsepower of manycores, without having to mix several programming languages in order to enable an application to exploit new hardware accelerators.

On the sole FPGA development side, OpenCL can also bring interesting features thanks to its ability to rely on the compiler, and the vendor driver to produce the hardware dependent part of the application. By doing so, migrations to a new FPGA version do not rely on developers anymore but rather on the vendor's drivers. The application involved should consequently scale smoothly requiring no or few interventions from developers.

Last but not least, an abstraction layer that automatically generates low-level code changes the way FPGA applications are developed. Although several intellectual property (IP) cores are available for various purposes such as the support of Ethernet, they still need to be routed to be enabled. In the same way, developers might spend much valuable time designing state machines that will rule the computation on the FPGA. Albeit being important for a successful development, these considerations distract developers from the principal purpose of any HPC application: speed-up!

As a conclusion, delegating low-level tasks that can be automated to the backend of an abstraction layer should improve the quality of the parallel developments, since they will take up a larger place in the roadmap of an application.

Acknowledgements

The authors would like to thank D. S. Hill, Khaled Benkrid and Wim Vanderbauwhede for their careful reading and useful suggestions on the draft. This work was partly funded by the Auvergne Regional Council.

References

[1] Altera Corporation, "Implementing FPGA Design with the OpenCL Standard", Technical report, Altera Corporation, 2011.

[2] AMD, "Aparapi", 2011. `http://code.google.com/p/aparapi/`

[3] Apache Software Foundation, "Apache Maven Project", 2002. `http://maven.apache.org/`

[4] O. Chafik, "ScalaCL", 2011. `http://code.google.com/p/scalacl/`

[5] S. Craven, P. Athanas, "Examining the viability of FPGA supercomputing", EURASIP Journal on Embedded systems, 1, 8, Research Article ID 93652, 2007.

[6] P. Jääskeläinen, C. de La Lama, P. Huerta, J. Takala, "OpenCL-based design methodology for application-specific processors", in 2010 International Conference on Embedded Computer Systems (SAMOS), 223–230. IEEE, 2010.

[7] Khronos OpenCL Working Group, "The OpenCL Specification 1.2", Specification 1.2, Khronos Group, November 2011.

[8] A. Klöckner, N. Pinto, Y. Lee, B. Catanzaro, P. Ivanov, A. Fasih, "PyCUDA and PyOpenCL: A Scripting-Based Approach to GPU Run-Time Code Generation", Parallel Computing, 38(3), 157–174, 2012.

[9] C. Lattner, V. Adve, "LLVM: A compilation framework for lifelong program analysis & transformation", in International Symposium on Code Generation and Optimization, CGO 2004, 75–86, IEEE, 2004.

[10] Nokia, "QtOpenCL", 2010. `http://doc.qt.nokia.com/opencl-snapshot/`

[11] M. Owaida, N. Bellas, K. Daloukas, C. Antonopoulos, "Synthesis of platform architectures from opencl programs", in IEEE 19th Annual International Sympo-

sium on Field-Programmable Custom Computing Machines (FCCM), 186–193, IEEE, 2011.

[12] A. Papakonstantinou, K. Gururaj, J. Stratton, D. Chen, J. Cong, W. Hwu, "FCUDA: Enabling efficient compilation of CUDA kernels onto FPGAs", in IEEE 7th Symposium on Application Specific Processors, SASP'09, 35–42, IEEE, 2009.

[13] J. Passerat-Palmbach, J. Caux, P. Siregar, D. Hill, "Warp-Level Parallelism: Enabling Multiple Replications In Parallel on GPU", in Proceedings of the European Simulation and Modeling Conference 2011, 76–83, 2011.

[14] M. Scarpino, "OpenCL in Action", Manning Publications, Shelter Island, NY, 2011.

[15] J. Stratton, S. Stone, W. Hwu, "MCUDA: An efficient implementation of CUDA kernels for multi-core CPUs", Languages and Compilers for Parallel Computing, 16–30, 2008.

[16] J. Williams, A. George, J. Richardson, K. Gosrani, S. Suresh, "Computational density of fixed and reconfigurable multi-core devices for application acceleration", 2008.

©Saxe-Coburg Publications, 2014.
F. Magoulès, (Editor),
Patterns for Parallel Programming on GPUs
Saxe-Coburg Publications, Stirlingshire, Scotland, 209-225.

Chapter 9

Parallel Preconditioned Conjugate Gradient Algorithm on GPU

F. Andzembe and J. Koko

LIMOS, Université Blaise Pascal – CNRS UMR 6158, Clermont-Ferrand, France

Abstract

We are proposing a parallel implementation of the preconditioned conjugate gradient algorithm on a GPU-platform. The preconditioning matrix is a first order approximate inverse derived from the SSOR preconditioner. Used through sparse matrix-vector multiplication, the proposed preconditioner is well-suited for massively parallel architectures like GPUs. Compared to CPU implementation of the conjugate gradient algorithm, our GPU preconditioned conjugate gradient implementation is up to 16 times faster (8 times faster at worst).

Keywords: preconditioned conjugate gradient, parallel computing, graphics processing unit.

9.1 Introduction

In recent years, *graphics processing units* (GPUs) have evolved into a very flexible and powerful many-core processor. Indeed, the modern GPUs are specialized for compute-intensive, massively parallel computation, *e.g.* rendering a real-time realistic three-dimensional environment. The fast-growing video game industry exerts strong economic pressure that forces constant innovation. The massively parallel architecture offers tremendous performance in many high-performance computing applications. Numerical algorithms can be significantly accelerated if the algorithms map well to the characteristic of the GPU.

In this chapter we focus on the numerical solution of the generalized Poisson equation. The Poisson equation arises in many applications in computational fluid dynamics, electrostatics, magnetostatics, image processing, *etc.* Numerical solution of the Poisson equation, through finite element or finite difference discretization, leads to large sparse linear systems usually solved by iterative methods instead of direct methods (Gaussian elimination or Cholesky factorization).

The conjugate gradient (CG) algorithm is one of the best known iterative methods for solving linear systems with a symmetric, positive definite matrix. The method is easy to implement and, for the Poisson equation, can handle complex domains and boundary conditions. The CG method can be adapted easily for linear systems with a symmetric, semi-definite positive matrix (see *e.g.* [15]). With a suitable preconditioner, the performance can be dramatically increased. The preconditioned conjugate gradient (PCG) has proved its efficiency and robustness in a wide range of applications.

Preconditioning consists of replacing the original linear system by one which has the same solution, but which is likely to be easier to solve with an iterative solver. Our goal is to develop a suitable and flexible PCG algorithm for the GPU architecture. Standard preconditioning techniques like incomplete factorizations or symmetric successive over-relaxation (SSOR) are hard to parallelize because of their strongly serial processing due to the forward/backward substitutions. Simple preconditioners like Jacobi have a limited impact on the efficiency and robustness of the method. The approximate inverse preconditioners have attractive features for GPU. First, the columns or rows of the approximate inverse matrix can be generated in parallel. Second, the preconditioner matrix is used in PCG through matrix-vector multiplications, easier to parallelize than forward/backward substitutions. But the approximate inverses techniques suffer from lack of robustness.The fully parallel technique does not guarantee that the resulting approximate inverse is either symmetric or positive definite. The efficient preconditioning has been largely ignored in previous work, except in [1] where a heuristic approximate inverse, based on an SSOR preconditioner, is proposed as the preconditioner for the PCG algorithm. The approximate inverse is derived on a rectangular domain with a regular grid (finite difference method). Our approximate SSOR inverse is derived rigorously using a first order approximation and is independent of the discretization method (finite element or finite difference method). The SSOR approximate inverse is computed with its natural sparsity instead of the sparsity of the matrix of the linear system [14]. The PCG algorithm presented in this chapter then can be used for any linear system with a positive definite matrix (not necessarily arising from discretization of the Poisson equation).

The chapter is organized as follows; In Section 9.2 we present the preconditioned conjugate gradient algorithm. The derivation of the SSOR approximate inverse preconditioner is described in Section 9.3. The implementation of the algorithm on GPU is presented in Section 9.4, followed by numerical experiments in Section 9.5.

9.2   Conjugate Gradient Algorithm

The solution of large sparse linear systems is an important problem in computational mechanics, atmospheric modelling, geophysics, biology, circuit simulation, *etc.* In general, these linear systems are solved using iterative methods.

9.2.1 Motivation

Let Ω be a bounded, open domain in $\mathbb{R}^d$, $d = 2, 3$. We consider the generalized Poisson equation

$$\alpha u - \nabla \cdot (\nu \nabla u) = f \quad \text{in } \Omega \tag{9.1}$$

where

- α is a non negative real constant;

- $\nu - \nu(x) > 0, \forall x \in \Omega$.

A solution u of (9.1) must satisfy boundary conditions (Dirichlet, Neumann or Cauchy). Equation (9.1) arises in a wide range of physical problems (computational fluid dynamics, magnetostatics, electrostatics, electronic device simulation, *etc.*).

Another field of applications of the results of the chapter is linear elasticity. Let Ω be an elastic solid (in $\mathbb{R}^d$, $d = 2, 3$) with Lamé coefficients λ and μ and subjected to external forces f. Assuming that the elastic body is fixed in a part Γ of its boundary, the displacement field $u \in \mathbb{R}^d$ satisfies

$$\begin{aligned} -\nabla \cdot \sigma(u) &= f \quad \text{in } \Omega \\ u &= 0 \quad \text{on } \Gamma \end{aligned} \tag{9.2}$$

where σ is the stress tensor

$$\sigma(u) = \lambda \text{tr}(\epsilon(u))\mathbb{I}_2 + 2\mu\epsilon(u)$$

with $\epsilon(u)$ the strain tensor

$$\epsilon(u) = \frac{1}{2}(\nabla u + \nabla u^T)$$

A discretization of (9.1) and (9.2) (using finite element or finite difference) leads to the linear system

$$Ax = b \tag{9.3}$$

where A is real, symmetric and positive definite. Many solution methods exist:

- direct methods (Gaussian elimination, Cholesky decomposition), [11, 16, 19]

- iterative methods (Jacobi, conjugate gradient, *etc.*), [11, 17–19, 21]

For sparse linear systems, the direct methods proceed in three phases. First, pre-ordering is applied to minimize fill-in (*i.e.* nonzero elements introduced during the elimination process in positions which were initially zeros). Second, a factorization (or elimination) is performed. Finally, the forward/backward substitution are executed for each different right-hand side. Due to filling-in, the data structures used in the direct methods are therefore complicated. If the matrix A is large the direct methods become impracticable. Moreover, the main serial loop inherent in such methods restricts their parallelization.

Iterative methods, starting with an initial guess, work by repeatedly improving an approximate solution until it is accurate enough. These methods access the coefficient matrix A of the linear system (9.3) through the matrix-vector multiplication $y = A \cdot x$. Thus one need only supply a routine for computing the sparse matrix-vector multiplication y which allows full exploitation of the sparsity of A. There are two families of iterative methods:

- stationary methods (Jacobi, Gauss-Seidel, SOR, SSOR) are older, simpler to understand and implement, but generally not efficient;

- nonstationary methods (conjugate gradient, minimum residual, generalized minimum residual, biconjugate gradient, *etc.*) are relatively recent; harder to understand, but they can be highly efficient.

Nonstationary methods differ from stationary methods in that the computation involves information that changes at each iteration.

9.2.2 Conjugate Gradient

The conjugate gradient (CG) is one of the best known iterative methods for solving sparse symmetric positive definite linear systems. The method is flexible, easy to implement and converges (theoretically) in a finite number of steps. Furthermore, its implementation requires only matrix-vector multiplications. The conjugate gradient algorithm is presented in Algoritm 9.1.

Algorithm 9.1: Conjugate gradient (CG) algorithm

$k = 0$: Initialization: x_0 and $\varepsilon > 0$ given.

$$p_0 = r_0 = b - Ax_0$$

$k \geq 0$: While $\dfrac{r_k^T r_k}{r_0^T r_0} > \varepsilon^2$

1. $q_k = Ap_k$

2. $\alpha_k = \dfrac{r_k^T r_k}{p_k^T q_k}$

3. $x_{k+1} = x_k + \alpha_k p_k$

4. $r_{k+1} = r_k - \alpha_k q_k$

5. $\beta_k = \dfrac{r_{k+1}^T r_{k+1}}{r_k^T r_k}, \qquad p_{k+1} = r_{k+1} + \beta_k p_k$

Each iteration requires one matrix-vector product and two inner products. All the necessary operations can be found in a standard library (*e.g.* BLAS). In addition to the matrix A and the approximate solution x^k, we have to store three auxiliary vectors $(r^k, p^k$ and $q^k)$.

Define the A-inner product by

$$(x, y)_A = x^T A y$$

and the corresponding A-norm (or *energy norm*)

$$\| x \|_A = \sqrt{x^T A x}$$

A speed of convergence can be given in terms of A-norm and condition number $\kappa = \kappa_2(A) = \lambda_{max}/\lambda_{min}$, where λ_{max} and λ_{min} are the greatest and the lowest eigenvalues of A, respectively. If x^* is the solution of (9.3), then the sequence $\{x_k\}$ generated by Algorithm 9.1 is such that (see *e.g.* [18, 21])

$$\| x^* - x_k \|_A \leq 2 \| x^* - x_0 \|_A \left(\frac{\sqrt{\kappa} - 1}{\sqrt{\kappa} + 1} \right)^k \tag{9.4}$$

We see that the number of iterations to reach a relative reduction of ε in the error is proportional to $\sqrt{\kappa}$. In industrial applications, like computational fluid dynamics or electronic device simulation, the matrix A can have a large condition number, *i.e.* $\kappa_2(A) \gg 1$. For example, for $\Omega = (0\ 1)^2$, $\alpha = 0$, $\nu = 1$ and using a finite difference scheme of size $h = 1/(n + 1)^2$, the condition number of the resulting matrix is approximately

$$\kappa(A) = O(h^{-2}) \approx n^2$$

We expect then a number of iterations proportional to h^{-1}, *i.e.* n. Using *preconditioning*, the convergence of the CG algorithm can be achieved in a number of iterations considerably less that n. This "fast" convergence property is more attractive than the convergence in a finite number of iterations, when working with large size matrices.

9.2.3   Preconditioned Conjugate Gradient

As shown in (9.4), the convergence rate of Algorithm 9.1 depends on spectral properties of the matrix A. Preconditioning is transforming the linear system (9.3) into one that is equivalent in the sense that it has the same solution, but that has more favorable spectral properties. A *preconditioner* is a matrix that realizes such a transformation.

Let M be a symmetric positive definite matrix. The idea behind preconditioning is to replace (9.3) by

$$M^{-1} A x = M^{-1} b \tag{9.5}$$

for a left preconditioner, or

$$A M^{-1} y = b, \quad x = M^{-1} y \tag{9.6}$$

for a right preconditioner. The matrix M must be such that $\kappa_2(M^{-1}A) \ll \kappa_2(A)$ or $\kappa_2(AM^{-1}) \ll \kappa_2(A)$, and $Mz = r$ is inexpensive to solve. The preconditioned version of the conjugate gradient algorithm is presented in Algorithm 9.2.

Algorithm 9.2: Preconditioned conjugate gradient (PCG) algorithm

$k = 0$: Initialization: x_0 and $\varepsilon > 0$ given

$$r_0 = b - Ax_0, \quad Mz_0 = r_0, \quad p_0 = z_0$$

$k \geq 0$: while $\dfrac{r_k^T r_k}{r_0^T r_0} > \varepsilon^2$

    1. $q_k = Ap_k$

    2. $\alpha_k = \dfrac{z_k^T r_k}{p_k^T q_k}$

    3. $x_{k+1} = x_k + \alpha_k p_k$

    4. $r_{k+1} = r_k - \alpha_k q_k$

    5. $Mz_{k+1} = r_{k+1}$

    6. $\beta_k = \dfrac{z_{k+1}^T r_{k+1}}{z_k^T r_k}, \quad p_{k+1} = z_{k+1} + \beta_k p_k$

The additional cost is one linear system per iteration (to compute z_{k+1}). This sequence of computations is valid for both right and left preconditioners. The left preconditioned CG algorithm with M-inner product is mathematically equivalent to the right preconditioned CG algorithm with M^{-1}-inner product.

9.3 Preconditioners

There are two families of preconditioners

- the matrix M that approximates A, and for which solving a system is easier than solving one with A;

- the matrix M that approximates A^{-1}, so that only multiplication by M is needed.

The majority of preconditioners fall in the first family. But for parallelization on GPU, the second family is preferable. Further discussion on preconditioners can be found in [3, 11, 19, 21].

9.3.1 Incomplete Factorizations

For the left-preconditioner (9.6), one of the simplest ways is to perform an incomplete (LU or Cholesky) factorization, see *e.g.* [3, 19, 21]. The factorization is incomplete if during the factorization process certain fill elements, *i.e.* nonzero elements in the factorization in the position where the original matrix had a zero, have been ignored.

This incomplete factorization is rather easy and inexpensive to implement. Incomplete factorization preconditioners are generally given in factored form $M = LU$ or $M = RR^T$. The linear system in Step 5 of Algorithm 9.2 then reduces to forward/backward substitutions. But this leads to strongly serial loops, not suitable for modern GPUs.

9.3.2 Jacobi Preconditioner

For a symmetric positive definite matrix, the simplest preconditioner consists of just the diagonal of this matrix, *i.e.*

$$m_{ij} = \begin{cases} a_{ii} & \text{if } i = j \\ 0 & \text{otherwise} \end{cases}$$

The Jacobi preconditioner can be used without any extra storage beyond that of the matrix itself. A block version of the Jacobi preconditioner can be obtained by a partitioning of the variables. If the index set $S = \{1, \ldots, n\}$ is partitioned as $S = \cup S_i$ with the subsets S_i mutually disjoint, then

$$m_{ij} = \begin{cases} a_{ij} & \text{if } i \text{ and } j \text{ are in the same index subset} \\ 0 & \text{otherwise} \end{cases}$$

Block Jacobi preconditioners are particularly interesting in the case of elliptic PDEs in a rectangular domain discretized using finite difference (see *e.g.* [7, 10]). In this case, the matrix A is naturally block tridiagonal. For the general matrix, partitioning of the variables is itself a non trivial problem.

9.3.3 Approximate Inverses

To avoid solving linear systems, one possible way is to try to find a preconditioner that does not require solving a linear system. This can be done by computing M as a direct approximation to the inverse of A (see *e.g.* [5, 12, 21]). This problem can be formulated as the following minimization problem

$$\min_M F(M) = \frac{1}{2} \parallel I - AM \parallel_F^2 \tag{9.7}$$

for the right-approximate inverse, see *e.g.* [5, 12]. If we set $M = [x_1 \cdots x_n]$, *i.e.* x_i is the ith column of M, then the function F becomes separable

$$F(M) = \sum_{i=1}^{n} \frac{1}{2} \parallel e_i - Ax_i \parallel_2^2$$

where e_i is the ith canonical vector and the minimization problem (9.7) can be rewritten as

$$\min_M F(M) = \sum_{i=1}^{n} \min_{x_i} \frac{1}{2} \parallel e_i - Ax_i \parallel_2^2 \tag{9.8}$$

The parallelizability of (9.8) is obvious: the columns of M are generated in parallel. But it is difficult to predict whether the resulting approximate inverse is symmtric or non singular. Theoretically, it cannot be proved that the approximate inverse M obtained by (9.7) is non singular unless the approximation is accurate enough. But one of the requirements, for a "good" preconditioner, is to keep M sparse.

9.3.4   SSOR Preconditioner

An approximate (and sparse) inverse can be obtained easily using *symmetric successive over-relaxation* (SSOR). Assume that the matrix A is decomposed as follows

$$A = L + D + L^T$$

where D is the diagonal matrix of diagonal elements of A and L the lower triangular part of A. The SSOR preconditioner is defined by

$$M = KK^T \tag{9.9}$$

where

$$K = \frac{1}{\sqrt{2-\omega}}(\bar{D}+L)\bar{D}^{-1/2} \tag{9.10}$$

where $\omega > 0$ and $\bar{D} = (1/\omega)D$. The optimal value of the parameter ω will reduce the number of iterations to a lower order. Indeed, for a second order elliptic problem, a condition number $\kappa(M_{\omega_{opt}}^{-1}) = O(\sqrt{\kappa(A)})$ is reachable, [2]. But, as noted in Subsection 9.3.1, the factorized form (9.9) is not suitable for GPU since it leads to strongly serial loops.

By contrast to the previous preconditioning techniques, we can compute an approximate inverse of K explicitly. The factor K can be rewritten as

$$K = \frac{1}{\sqrt{2-\omega}}\bar{D}(I + \bar{D}^{-1}L)\bar{D}^{-1/2}$$

such that

$$K^{-1} = \sqrt{2-\omega}\,\bar{D}^{1/2}(I + \bar{D}^{-1}L)^{-1}\bar{D}^{-1}$$

Define $\rho(A)$, the spectral radius of a matrix A. Assuming that $\rho(\bar{D}^{-1}L) < 1$, then the inverse of $I + \bar{D}^{-1}L$ can be given by the Neumann expansion

$$(I + \bar{D}^{-1}L)^{-1} = I - \bar{D}^{-1}L + (\bar{D}^{-1}L)^2 - (\bar{D}^{-1}L)^3 + \cdots \tag{9.11}$$

or the Euler expansion

$$(I + \bar{D}^{-1}L)^{-1} = (I - \bar{D}^{-1}L)(I + (\bar{D}^{-1}L)^2)(I - (\bar{D}^{-1}L)^3)\cdots \tag{9.12}$$

Using (9.11) or (9.12), a first order approximate inverse of K is given by

$$K^{-1} \approx \sqrt{2-\omega}\,\bar{D}^{1/2}(I - \bar{D}^{-1}L)\bar{D}^{-1} = \sqrt{2-\omega}\,\bar{D}^{-1/2}(I - L\bar{D}^{-1}) =: \bar{K} \tag{9.13}$$

$\bar{K}$ can be computed easily using A and reciprocal operations in each diagonal element of A. Moreover, $\bar{K}$ has the same sparsity pattern as A. Indeed,

$$\bar{K}_{ij} = \sqrt{2 - \omega} \left(\frac{\omega}{a_{ii}} \right)^{1/2} \left(\delta_{ij} - \omega \frac{a_{ij}}{a_{jj}} \right), \quad j \leq i$$

The SSOR approximate inverse (SSOR-AI) preconditioner is therefore

$$\bar{M} = \bar{K}^T \bar{K} \tag{9.14}$$

and Step 3 in Algorithm PCG is replaced by $z_{k+1} = \bar{M} r_{k+1}$. Note that $\bar{M}$ can be computed with a prescribed sparsity pattern (*e.g.* the one of A) to reduce the computational cost, [14].

Another strategy is to keep $\bar{M}$ in its factorized form (9.14). The preconditioning step of Algorithm 9.2 becomes

$$y_{k+1} = \bar{K} r_{k+1} \tag{9.15}$$

$$z_{k+1} = \bar{K}^T y_{k+1} \tag{9.16}$$

Computing (9.16) in parallel, using the current standard storage format for sparse matrices (*i.e.* the CSR format) is not straightforward. In general computing the transpose of a matrix is expensive. Indeed, the communication and the synchronization overhead for computing a small loop in parallel is much larger than the execution time of the few operations required for matrix column/vector multiplication. Since the sparsity pattern of $\bar{K}$ is the same as the one of the lower triangular part of A, the sparsity pattern of $\bar{K}^T$ is the one of the upper triangular part of A.

Remark 1. *In [1], Ament et al. propose the following approximate inverse preconditioner (obtained using a heuristic approach)*

$$\widetilde{M} = (I - LD^{-1})(I - D^{-1}L) \tag{9.17}$$

They called it the incomplete Poisson (IP) preconditioner. Note that for $\omega = 1$, (9.13) is

$$\bar{K} = D^{-1/2}(I - LD^{-1})$$

such that

$$\widetilde{M} = D^{1/2} \bar{K} \bar{K}^T D^{1/2}$$

9.4 GPU Implementation

9.4.1 Matrix Storage

To take advantage of the large number of zeros in matrices issuing from the discretization of PDEs, special storage formats are required. The main idea is to keep only non-zero elements, while allowing common matrix operations. For our numerical experiments, we adopt the *compressed sparse row* (CSR) format (see *e.g.* [9, 21]). In the CSR format, a $n \times n$ sparse matrix A, with nnz non-zero elements, is stored via three arrays:

AA (array of length nnz) contains the non-zero entries of A, stored row by row;

JA (array of length nnz) contains the column indices of the non-zero entries stored in AA;

IA (array of length $n + 1$) contains the pointers (indices) to the beginning of each row in the arrays AA and JA.

The following matrix

$$A = \begin{bmatrix} 2 & 0 & 1 & 3 & 0 \\ 0 & 4 & 0 & 0 & 1 \\ 1 & 0 & 0 & 2 & 4 \\ 0 & 1 & 1 & 2 & 4 \\ 5 & 0 & 1 & 0 & 3 \end{bmatrix}$$

is stored in CSR format by

IA : | 1 | 4 | 6 | 9 | 13 | 16 |

JA : | 1 | 3 | 4 | 2 | 5 | 1 | 4 | 5 | 2 | 3 | 4 | 5 | 1 | 3 | 5 |

AA : | 2 | 1 | 3 | 4 | 1 | 1 | 2 | 4 | 1 | 1 | 2 | 4 | 5 | 1 | 3 |

The CSR format is one of the most popular storage formats for sparse general matrices. It is particularly suitable for performing matrix-vector products. Further discussion on sparse matrix formats can be found, *e.g.* in [3,21].

9.4.2   CUDA

CUDA stands for *Compute Unified Device Architecture* and is a new hardware and software architecture for using NVIDIA *Graphics Processing Units* (GPUs) as a data-parallel computing device. CUDA is a parallel programming model [6,20] consisting of a sequential *host program*, running on a CPU host, and a *kernel program*, running on a parallel GPU device. The host program sets up the data and transfers it to and from the GPU while the kernel program processes the data using a potentially large number of parallel threads. The threads of a kernel are grouped into a grid of *thread blocks*. The threads of a given block share a local-store and may synchronize via barriers. Threads in different thread blocks cannot be synchronized. A modern NVIDIA GPU is built around an array of shared memory multiprocessors. Each multiprocessor is equipped with 8 scalar cores and 16KB of high-bandwidth low-latency memory. The CUDA programming guide [6] provides tips for maximizing performance.

The parallelization of update operations (for x, r and p) is straightforward. In our code, update operations represent about 15% of GPU time. The crucial problem in the parallelization of the Algorithms 9.1-9.2, on GPU, concerns the inner product and the matrix-vector multiplication.

The inner-product seems inherently sequential but there is an efficient parallel algorithm even for GPU architecture: the *parallel prefix sum (scan)*. The GPU implementation of this algorithm is provided through the NVIDIA technical report [13]. For general discussion on parallel prefix operations, see *e.g.* [8].

```
__global__ void
spmvCSRscalar(const int  n,
              const int  *ia,
              const int  *ja,
              const float *aa,
              const float *x,
                   float *y)
{
   int i = blockDim.x * blockIdx.x + threadIdx.x;
   if (i < n){
        float dot = 0.0f;
        int i1 = ia[i];
        int i2 = ia[i+1];
        for (int jj = i1; jj < i2; jj++){
          int ii=ja[jj];
          dot += aa[jj] * x[ii];
        }
        y[i] = dot;
   }
}
```

Listing 9.1: Scalar sparse matrix vector multiplication ($y = Ax$) kernel

Sparse matrix-vector operations represent the dominant cost in the PCG algorithm (and in many iterative algorithms) for solving large-scale linear systems. If dense matrix-vector operations are regular and often limited by floating point throughput, sparse matrix-vector operations are much less regular in their access pattern and, consequently, are generally limited by bandwidth.

In [4], Bell and Garland propose two implementations of sparse matrix-vector multiplication for the CSR format: the first using one thread per row, Listing 9.1, and the second using a 32-thread warp per matrix row. A version of the latter with an 8-thread warp per matrix row is shown in Listing 9.2 and was used in [14]. The vector version gives best performances with a fine tuning of the number of warp threads. The main drawback of the vector version is that its performance strongly depends on the average number of nonzero elements per matrix row and the tuning cannot be done dynamically. Indeed, the average number of nonzero element per matrix row must be known *a priori*.

Another implementation of the sparse matrix-vector multiplication $y = Ax$ is to split multiplications and additions operations as follows

$$z_{ij} = A_{ij}x_j, \quad \forall(i,j) \tag{9.18}$$

$$y_i = \sum_j z_{ij}, \quad \forall i \tag{9.19}$$

Numerical experiments show, in [14], that the performances of this sparse matrix-vector multiplication are almost stable for any matrix size. CUDA implementations of (9.18)-(9.19) are shown in Listing 9.3-9.4.

```
__global__ void
spmvCSRvector8(const int n,
                const int  *ia,
                const int  *ja,
                const float *aa,
                const float *x,
                    float *y)
{
    __shared__ float vals[512];
    //global thread index
    int thread_id = blockDim.x * blockIdx.x + threadIdx.x;
    //global warp index
    int warp_id   = thread_id / 8;
    //thread index within the warp
    int lane      = thread_id & (8-1);

    // one warp per row
    int i = warp_id;

    if (i < n){
        int i1 = ia[i];
        int i2 = ia[i+1];

        //compute running sum per thread
        vals[threadIdx.x] = 0;
        for (int jj = i1 + lane; jj < i2; jj+=8){
            vals[threadIdx.x] += aa[jj] * x[ja[jj]];
        }
        if (lane < 4)  vals[threadIdx.x] += vals[threadIdx.x + 4];
        __syncthreads();
        if (lane < 2)  vals[threadIdx.x] += vals[threadIdx.x + 2];
        __syncthreads();
        if (lane < 1)  vals[threadIdx.x] += vals[threadIdx.x + 1];

        //first thread writes result
        if (lane == 0) y[i] = vals[threadIdx.x];
    }
}
```

Listing 9.2: Vector sparse matrix vector multiplication ($y = Ax$) kernel with 8-thread warp per matrix row

```
__global__ void
spmvCSReprod(const int nnz,
            const int   *ja,
            const float *aa,
            const float *x,
                float *ycsr)
{
    unsigned int i = blockDim.x * blockIdx.x + threadIdx.x;
    if (i < nnz) ycsr[i]=x[ja[i]]*aa[i];
}
```

Listing 9.3: CUDA kernel for (9.18)

```
__global__ void
spmvCSRrsum(const int n,
            const int *ia,
            const int *ja,
            const float *ycsr,
                  float *y)
{
    //one thread per matrix row
    int i = blockDim.x * blockIdx.x + threadIdx.x;
    if ( i < n){
        float dot = 0.0f;
        int i1 = ia[i];
        int i2 = ia[i+1];
        for (int jj = i1; jj < i2; jj++){
            dot += ycsr[jj];
        }
        y[i] = dot;
    }
}
```

Listing 9.4: CUDA kernel for (9.19)

9.5 Numerical Experiments

For the numerical experiments, we used the following processors:

CPU Intel Xeon Quad-Core 2.66GHz, 12GB RAM (using gFortran),

GPU NVIDIA Tesla T10, 240-core, 4GB RAM (using CUDA).

All reals are of the *float* type in both Fortran and CUDA codes. We used the sparse matrix-vector multiplication (9.18)-(9.19), *i.e.* Listings 9.3-9.4. In all algorithms, we started with $x_k = 0$ and we iterated until $\| r_k \| \| b \|^{-1} < 10^{-5}$.

We investigated the behaviour of our SSOR-AI preconditioner on a matrix arising from a Poisson equation (9.1) (with $\alpha = 0$, $\nu = 1$ and $f = 1$) on a unit disc discretized by the finite element method, Figure 9.1. The resulting matrix A is symmetric, positive definite, Table 9.1.

Problem	matrix size (n)	Number of nonzero elemens
Mat1	130009	908357
Mat2	265345	1853863
Mat3	525849	3677445
Mat4	755681	5285531
Mat5	1063159	7435047
Mat6	2105137	14728973

Table 9.1: Matrix size and number of nonzero elements

In our numerical experiments, we used only $\bar{M}_A$ as preconditioner (with $\omega = 1.1$) to reduce the computational cost. Indeed, performing matrix-matrix multiplication is

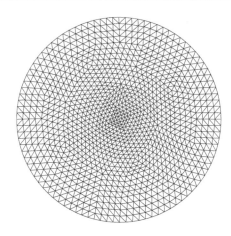

Figure 9.1: Unit circle discretized by nonuniform finite element

much less costly if the sparsity pattern of the resulting matrix is known.

Problems	CG/CPU Time (Sec.)	CG/GPU Time (Sec.)	Speed-up
Mat1	8.75	1.70	5.14
Mat2	33.37	5.02	6.64
Mat3	118.55	12.75	9.28
Mat4	211.71	23.10	9.16
Mat5	381.36	37.58	10.14
Mat6	1059.66	101.62	10.42

Table 9.2: Conjugate gradient Algorithm 9.1: CPU versus GPU

In Table 9.2 we compare the conjugate gradient Algorithm 9.1 implemented on GPU
with its CPU counterpart. We can notice that without preconditioning, the CG algorithm on the GPU is about up to 10 times faster than its CPU implementation. In
Table 9.3 we report the performances of the preconditioned conjugate gradient Algorithm 9.2 using the Jacobi preconditioner. We notice again that the GPU implementation is up to 10 times faster than the CPU implementation. Note that the Jacobi
preconditioned conjugate gradient is about 10% faster than the original conjugate gradient Algorithm 9.1.

In Table 9.4 we report the performances of the SSOR-AI preconditioned conjugate
gradient algorithm. We notice first that on the CPU, the saving of computational
time is not significant. For the largest problem, the SSOR-AI preconditioned CG is
even lower than the unpreconditioned version. This is due to the additional cost of
preconditioning operations (9.15)-(9.16). On a GPU the preconditioning operations
(9.15)-(9.16) are done using parallel kernels. As a result, the speed-up obtained with
the GPU implementation is significant: 18 times for the largest problem. Note that,

Problems	PCG/CPU Time (Sec.)	PCG/GPU Time (Sec.)	Speed-up
Mat1	8.75	1.59	5.4
Mat2	29.99	4.46	6.72
Mat3	106.17	11.56	9.18
Mat4	196.59	20.26	9.70
Mat5	336.33	32.27	10.4
Mat6	944.97	92.83	10.17

Table 9.3: Jacobi preconditioned conjugate gradient Algorithm 9.2: CPU versus GPU

Problems	PCG/CPU Time (Sec.)	PCG/GPU Time (Sec.)	Speed-up
Mat1	9.95	1.11	8.96
Mat2	28.35	3.02	9.38
Mat3	106.89	7.60	14.06
Mat4	210.56	14.61	14.41
Mat5	366.31	23.12	15.84
Mat6	1196.78	63.60	18.81

Table 9.4: SSOR-AI preconditioned conjugate gradient Algorithm 9.2: CPU versus GPU

for the largest problem, the SSOR-AI PCG algorithm is 15 times faster than the Jacobi PCG, and 16 times faster than the original CG algorithm.

9.6   Conclusion

We have presented a parallel implementation, on GPU, of the preconditioned conjugate gradient algorithm for linear systems with a symmetric, positive definite matrix. Our preconditioner, derived from the standard SSOR, is an approximate inverse and can therefore be used in the PCG algorithm through a sparse matrix-vector multiplication. Numerical experiments show that the speed-up obtained with our PCG on a GPU, with respect to the CPU implementation of the CG algorithm, is between 8 and 16.

We plan to investigate another SSOR approximate inverse (*e.g.* using second order approximation in (9.11) or (9.12)) as well as another sparse matrix storage format (*e.g. block compressed sparse row*) Our PCG algorithm is currently designed for 1-GPU platform. A multi-GPU implementation is under study to improve scalability.

Acknowledgments

This work was funded by *Bourse Innovation*, Conseil Régional d'Auvergne – UE Fonds FEDER.

References

[1] M. Ament, G. Knittel, D. Weiskopf, W. Strasser, "A parallel preconditioned conjugate gradient solver for the Poisson Problem on a multi-GPU platform", in Proc. 18th Euromicro Conference on Parallel, Distributed and NetWork-Based Computing, 583–592, Pisa, Italy, Febrary 17-19 2010.

[2] O. Axelsson, A. Barker, "Finite Element Solution of Boundary Value Problems. Theory and Computation", Academic Press, Orlando, Fl., USA, 1984.

[3] R. Barret, M. Berry, T.F. Chan, J. Demmel, J. Donato, J. Dongarra, V. Eijkhout, R. Pozo, C. Romine, H. Van der Vorst, "Templates for the Solution of Linear Systems: Building Blocks for Iterative Methods", SIAM, Philadelphia, PA, USA, 1994.

[4] N. Bell, M. Garland, "Efficient Sparse Matrix-Vector Multiplication on CUDA", Technical Report NVR-2008-04, NVIDIA, 2008.

[5] E. Chow, Y. Saad, "Approximate inverse preconditioners via sparse-sparse iterations", SIAM J. Sci. Comput., 19, 995–1023, 1998.

[6] NVIDIA Corporation, "NVIDIA CUDA Programming Guide", Technical report, NVIDIA, 2008.

[7] J. Demmel, "The condition number of equivalence transformations that block diagonalize matrix pencils", SIAM J. Numer. Anal., 20, 599–610, 1983.

[8] J.W. Demmel, M.T. Heath, H.A. van der Vorst, "Parallel numerical linear algebra", Acta Numerica, 2, 111–198, 1993.

[9] I.S. Duff, A.M. Erisman, J.K. Reid, "Direct Methods for Sparse Matrices", Clarendon Press, Oxford, 1986.

[10] L. Elsner, "A note on optimal block-scaling of matrices", Numer. Math., 44, 127–128, 1984.

[11] G.H. Golub, C.F. Van Loan, "Matrix Computations", The John Hopkins University Press, Baltimore, 1989.

[12] M.J. Gorte, T. Huckle, "Parallel preconditioning with sparse approximate inverses", SIAM J. Sci. Comput., 18, 838–853, 1997.

[13] M. Harris, "Parallel Prefix (Scan) Sum with CUDA", Technical report, NVIDIA, 2008.

[14] R. Helfenstein, J. Koko, "Parallel preconditioned conjugate gradient on GPU", J. Comput. Appl. Math., 236, 3584–3590, 2012.

[15] E.F. Kaasschieter, "Preconditioned Conjugate gradients for solving singular systems", J. Comput. Appl. Math., 24, 265–275, 1988.

[16] P. Lascaux, R. Théodor, "Analyse numérique matricielle appliquée à l'art de l'ingénieur", Volume 1, Masson, Paris, 1994.

[17] P. Lascaux, R. Théodor, "Analyse numérique matricielle appliquée à l'art de l'ingénieur", Volume 2, Masson, Paris, 1994.

[18] D. Luenberger, "Linear and Nonlinear Programming", Addison Wesley, Reading, MA, 1989.

[19] G. Meurant, "Computer Solution of Large Systems", Studies in Mathematics and its Applications, North Holland, 1999.

[20] J. Nickolls, I. Buck, M. Garland, K. Skadron, "Scalable parallel programming with CUDA", Queue, 6(2), 40–53, 2008.

[21] Y. Saad, "Iterative Methods for Sparse Linear Systems", SIAM, Philadelphia, 2003.

©Saxe-Coburg Publications, 2014.
F. Magoulès, (Editor),
Patterns for Parallel Programming on GPUs
Saxe-Coburg Publications, Stirlingshire, Scotland, 227-248.

Chapter 10

Solving Sparse Linear Systems with CG and GMRES Methods on a GPU and GPU Clusters

R. Couturier and L. Ziane Khodja

FEMTO-ST Institute, University of Franche-Comte, Belfort, France

Abstract

In this chapter, we aim to exploit the computing power of GPUs for solving sparse linear systems. Therefore, we have chosen two different iterative solutions to implement and to test their performances on GPUs. The conjugate gradient method is used for solving symmetric linear systems, and the generalized minimal residual method is used, more precisely, for solving unsymmetric linear systems. First, we have adapted the sequential algorithm of each method to the GPU architecture, by using the CUDA programming environment. We noticed that computations of both methods were faster on a GPU than on a CPU. Then, we parallelized algorithms of both iterative methods on a GPU cluster in order to solve large sparse linear systems. The performances of these parallel algorithms were tested on GPU clusters and on CPU clusters. We can notice that a GPU cluster is faster than a CPU cluster for solving sparse linear systems, but it is more efficient when these linear systems are large size ones.

Keywords: sparse linear systems, CG and GMRES methods, CUDA, GPU clusters.

10.1 Introduction

Linear systems are used in many computational problems and many fields of research such as mathematics, engineering, biology or physics [1]. Solving these problems involves solving these linear systems. Iterative methods are widely used for solving sparse linear systems that arise in most numerical applications. They are often more suitable than their counterpart, direct methods. In fact, a direct method requires a fill-in operation in the factorization step of the sparse matrix. However the fill-in operation is expensive in terms of computation time and memory space, and more specifically, for large sparse matrices. In contrast, an iterative method computes an approximation of the solution by executing successive iterations of the same block of elementary operations. Different computing platforms, sequential and parallel computers, are used for solving sparse linear systems with iterative solutions. Nowadays, graphics processing units (GPUs) have become attractive for solving these linear systems, due to their computing power and their ability to compute faster than traditional CPUs.

In this present chapter, we provide the main key points of the GPU implementations of two well-known iterative methods, which are the conjugate gradient method and the generalized minimal residual method. In addition, we compare the performances of these methods obtained on GPUs with those obtained on CPUs. First, we describe in Section 10.2 the computing principle of the algorithm of each method for solving sparse linear systems. Then in Section 10.3, we show how to efficiently implement the algorithms of these methods on a GPU. Finally in Section 10.4, we present the parallel implementations of these algorithms on a cluster of GPUs for solving large sparse linear systems.

10.2   Iterative Methods

Let us consider the following large sparse system of n linear equations in $\mathbb{R}$:

$$Ax = b \tag{10.1}$$

where $A \in \mathbb{R}^{n \times n}$ is a sparse nonsingular square matrix, $x \in \mathbb{R}^n$ is the solution vector, $b \in \mathbb{R}^n$ is the right-hand side and $n \in \mathbb{N}$ is a very large integer number. Iterative methods for solving the large sparse linear system (10.1) proceed by successive iterations for the same block of operations, during which a sequence of approximations to the solution, $\{x_k\}_{k \geq 0}$, is generated. From an initial guess x_0, they compute an approximate solution x_k which gradually converges, at each iteration $k \geq 1$, to the exact solution x^*:

$$x^* = \lim_{k \to \infty} x_k = A^{-1}b \tag{10.2}$$

The number of iterations necessary to achieve the exact solution is not known beforehand and can be infinite. In practice, the computations of an iterative solver are stopped after a fixed number of iterations, and/or when an approximate solution $\tilde{x}$ satisfying the following criterion is found:

$$\|b - A\tilde{x}\| < \varepsilon \tag{10.3}$$

where $r = b - A\tilde{x}$ is the residual of the computed solution $\tilde{x}$ and $0 < \varepsilon < 1$ is the residual tolerance threshold. Thus, an iterative method is called convergent if for any choice of the initial guess the norm of the residual of the solution is sufficiently small.

Some of the main iterative methods that have proved their efficiency for solving large sparse linear systems are those of the Krylov subspaces [2]. The main idea of these methods is to generate a Krylov subspace $\mathcal{K}_k$ spanned by a basis of successive pairwise orthogonal vectors, based on the sparse matrix A and the initial residual r_0:

$$\mathcal{K}_k(A, r_0) \equiv span\{r_0, Ar_0, A^2 r_0, \cdots, A^{k-1} r_0\} \tag{10.4}$$

Then, the sequence of successive approximate solutions, $\{x_k\}_{k \geq 1}$, are computed in $\mathcal{K}_k(A, r_0)$ as follows:

$$x_k \in x_0 + \mathcal{K}_k(A, r_0) \tag{10.5}$$

which is equivalent to

$$x_k = x_0 + q_{k-1}(A)r_0, \quad k \in \mathbb{N}^* \tag{10.6}$$

by imposing the orthogonality of the residual with the vectors of $\mathcal{L}_k$

$$b - Ax_k \perp \mathcal{L}_k \tag{10.7}$$

where q_{k-1} is a polynomial of degree $k - 1$ and $\mathcal{L}_k$ is a *kth* order Krylov subspace of constraints constructed using $\mathcal{K}_k$ according to the method. The formula (10.7) is called the Galerkin condition when $\mathcal{L}_k = \mathcal{K}_k$ and otherwise it is called the Petrov-Galerkin condition. This orthogonality constraint allows us to compute an approximate solution x_k which minimizes the residual over the generated Krylov subspace $\mathcal{K}_k$.

The convergence of Krylov subspace methods is generally fast, but it is not often ensured and it strongly depends on the properties of the sparse matrix (symmetry, sparsity, definite or indefinite positive, *etc.*). In practice, Krylov methods are usually used in combination with preconditioners that allow improvement and/or speed up of their convergence. The preconditioning process involves the replacement of (10.1) by one of the following sparse linear systems:

$$M^{-1}Ax = M^{-1}b \tag{10.8}$$

or

$$AM^{-1}\hat{x} = b, \quad x = M^{-1}\hat{x} \tag{10.9}$$

where M is the preconditioner. It is chosen such that matrices $M^{-1}A$ and AM^{-1} are better conditioned than A. So the left preconditioned system (10.8) and the right preconditioned system (10.9) are more easily solved than the linear system (10.1). The two best-known Krylov methods, presented in what follows, are the conjugate gradient method (CG) and the generalized minimal residual method (GMRES). The CG method gives good results only for symmetric sparse linear systems. In contrast, the GMRES method is well-suited to solving unsymmetric sparse linear systems.

10.2.1   Conjugate Gradient Method

The CG method was initially developed by Hestenes and Stiefel in 1952 [3]. It is one of the main iterative methods used for solving large sparse linear systems, and it can

---

Algorithm 16: Preconditioned conjugate gradient method

Input: Choose an initial guess x_0, a residual tolerance threshold ε and a maximum number of iterations max

1   $r_0 \leftarrow b - Ax_0$;
2   $convergence \leftarrow false$;
3   $k \leftarrow 1$;
4 **repeat**
5     $z_k \leftarrow M^{-1}r_{k-1}$;
6     $\rho_k \leftarrow (r_{k-1}, z_k)$;
7   **if** $k = 1$ **then**
8        $p_k \leftarrow z_k$;
9   **else**
10       $\beta_k \leftarrow \rho_k/\rho_{k-1}$;
11       $p_k \leftarrow z_k + \beta_k \times p_{k-1}$;
12   **end**
13     $q_k \leftarrow A \times p_k$;
14     $\alpha_k \leftarrow \rho_k/(p_k, q_k)$;
15     $x_k \leftarrow x_{k-1} + \alpha_k \times p_k$;
16     $r_k \leftarrow r_{k-1} - \alpha_k \times q_k$;
17   **if** $(\rho_k < \varepsilon)$ **or** $(k \geq max)$ **then**
18       $convergence \leftarrow true$;
19   **else**
20       $k \leftarrow k + 1$;
21   **end**
22 **until** $convergence$;

---

also be adapted to solve nonlinear problems of optimization. However, it should be applied to problems with symmetric/Hermitian positive definite matrices.

The CG is a Krylov method which produces, from an initial guess x_0, a sequence of successive approximate solutions $x_k \in x_0 + \mathcal{K}_k(A, r_0)$, satisfying the Galerkin condition (10.7) such that $\mathcal{L}_k = \mathcal{K}_k$. In fact, it is based on finding a set of at most n successive direction vectors $\{p_k\}_{k \in \mathbb{N}}$, that are mutually A-conjugate (A-orthogonalized vectors):

$$p_i^T A p_j = 0, \quad i \neq j \tag{10.10}$$

So in each iteration k, the approximate solutions x_k are computed by recurrence using the direction vectors p_k:

$$x_k = x_{k-1} + \alpha_k p_k, \quad \alpha_k \in \mathbb{R} \tag{10.11}$$

correspondingly, the residuals r_k are computed in the same way as follows:

$$r_k = r_{k-1} - \alpha_k A p_k \tag{10.12}$$

If all residuals r_k are nonzero, the direction vectors p_k can be chosen in order to verify the recurrence

$$p_0 = r_0, \quad p_k = r_k + \beta_k p_{k-1}, \quad \beta_k \in \mathbb{R} \tag{10.13}$$

The scalars α_k are chosen to minimize the A-norm of errors $\|x_* - x_k\|_A$ over Krylov subspace $\mathcal{K}_k$ spanned by direction vectors $\{p_k\}_{k \geq 0}$, and the scalars β_k are chosen to ensure that these direction vectors are mutually A-conjugate (equivalent to residuals are orthogonal). Thus the assumption that matrix A is symmetric and the recurrences (10.12) and (10.13) allow one to deduce that

$$\alpha_k = \frac{r_{k-1}^T r_{k-1}}{p_k^T A p_k}, \quad \beta_k = \frac{r_k^T r_k}{r_{k-1}^T r_{k-1}} \tag{10.14}$$

The operations of the left preconditined CG method are presented in algorithm 16. M is the preconditioning matrix and the operation $(\cdot, \cdot)$ defines the dot product of two vectors in $\mathbb{R}$. In each iteration k, the algorithm 16 seeks for a direction vector p_k (from line 7 to line 12 in the algorithm), such that the direction vector is orthogonal to the current preconditioned residual z_k and to all direction vectors $\{p_j\}_{0 < j < k}$ previously computed. Next, it computes the approximate solution x_k by a multiple α_k of the direction vector p_k (line 15). Then, it updates the residual r_k of the computed solution (line 16). The CG method converges at most after n iterations. However in practice, it terminates when the maximum number of iterations and/or the residual tolerance threshold ε are reached.

10.2.2 Generalized Minimal Residual Method

GMRES is an iterative method designed by Saad and Schultz in 1986 [4] as a generalization of the minimal residual method (MNRES) [5]. In addition to positive definite symmetric problems, it gives good results for solving unsymmetric, non Hermitian and indefinite symmetric problems. Therefore, it is considered as one of the best suited iterative methods for solving most large sparse linear systems.

GMRES is a Krylov method, which seeks for an approximate solution x_k minimizing the residual r_k over a Krylov subspace $\mathcal{K}_k$ spanned by

$$\mathcal{K}_k(A, v_1) \equiv span\{v_1, Av_1, \cdots, A^{k-1}v_1\} \tag{10.15}$$

where the Petrov-Galerkin condition is imposed

$$r_k \perp \mathcal{L}_k, \quad \mathcal{L}_k = A\mathcal{K}_k \tag{10.16}$$

It uses the Arnoldi's method [6] to form the orthonormal basis $V_k = \{v_1, v_2, \cdots, v_k\}$ of the Krylov subspace $\mathcal{K}_k$ and an upper Henssenberg matrix $\bar{H}_k = V_k^T A V_k$, such that $v_1 = r_0/\|r_0\|_2$, $v_k = A^{k-1}v_1$ and r_0 is the initial residual. Then at iteration k, an approximate solution x_k is computed in the Krylov subspace $x_0 + \mathcal{K}_k(A, v_1)$ as follows:

$$x_k = x_0 + V_k y \tag{10.17}$$

with $y \in \mathbb{R}^k$ as a vector of real scalars minimizing the Euclidean norm of the residual r_k

$$r_k = r_0 - AV_k y \quad \Rightarrow \quad \min_{y \in \mathbb{R}^k} \|r_k\|_2 = \min_{y \in \mathbb{R}^k} \|\beta e_1 - \bar{H}_k y\|_2 \tag{10.18}$$

where $\beta = \|r_0\|_2$ and $e_1 = (1, 0, \cdots, 0)$ is the first vector of the standard basis of $\mathbb{R}^k$.

The GMRES method is guaranteed to converge in at most n iterations (n is the size of the sparse matrix). However in the case of large sparse linear systems (more than ten thousand unknowns), the full GMRES would generate a large Krylov subspace if it requires many iterations for convergence. In order to avoid a huge memory storage of the Krylov subspace, the size of the orthonormal basis V_k is restricted to $m \ll n$ vectors and the GMRES method is restarted at each m iterations with the last solution x_m as an initial guess.

Algorithm 17 shows the main key points of the restarted GMRES method. It solves the left preconditioned sparse linear system (10.8), such that M is the preconditioning matrix and the integer m is the size of the generated basis V_m. At each iteration until convergence, GMRES uses the Arnoldi process (from line 7 to line 16 in algorithm 17) to produce a Krylov subspace basis V_m and a $(m+1) \times m$ upper Hessenberg matrix $\bar{H}_m$. Then, it solves the least-squares problem at line 17, to find the y_m which minimizes $\|r_m\|_2$. Finally, it computes the approximate solution x_m at line 18. The GMRES computations terminate when the residual norm is sufficiently small and/or the maximum number of iterations is reached.

10.3   Sequential Sparse Linear Solvers on a GPU

In this section, we present how to accelerate the computations of the CG and GMRES algorithms on a GPU for solving sparse linear systems. First, we give the main key points of their GPU implementations. Then, we present their performances obtained on a GPU compared to those obtained on a CPU.

10.3.1   GPU Implementation

For good GPU programming, and thus, for a good use of its computing power, one must, first of all, know the properties of the GPU architecture well. Indeed, a GPU is composed of a set of multiprocessors and a hierarchy of memories [7]. So, the functions of an algorithm executed on a CPU equipped with a GPU are launched by the host (CPU) and computed by the device (GPU) as kernels. Then, a kernel is concurrently executed on the device by thousands (or even millions) of GPU threads, organized in different thread-blocks and distributed among the GPU multiprocessors. Threads of the same kernel can cooperate among themselves through synchronization barriers and the shared memory, to give the final result of the kernel computations.

Moreover in order to adapt an algorithm to GPUs, the parallel and sequential codes of this algorithm must be determined. Indeed, operations that can be parallelized must be computed by the device in order to accelerate the computations. In contrast, all

---

Algorithm 17: Preconditioned generalized minimal residual method with restarts

---

Input: Choose an initial guess x_0, a residual tolerance threshold ε and a maximum number of iterations max

1   $convergence \leftarrow false$;
2   $k \leftarrow 1$;
3   $r_0 \leftarrow M^{-1}(b - Ax_0)$;
4   $\beta \leftarrow \|r_0\|_2$;
5   **while** $\neg convergence$ **do**
6      $v_1 \leftarrow r_0/\beta$;
7   **for** $j = 1$ **to** m **do**
8          $w_j \leftarrow M^{-1}Av_j$;
9   **for** $i = 1$ **to** j **do**
10             $h_{i,j} \leftarrow (w_j, v_i)$;
11             $w_j \leftarrow w_j - h_{i,j}v_i$;
12   **end**
13          $h_{j+1,j} \leftarrow \|w_j\|_2$;
14          $v_{j+1} \leftarrow w_j/h_{j+1,j}$;
15   **end**
16   Set $V_m = \{v_j\}_{1 \leq j \leq m}$ and $\bar{H}_m = (h_{i,j})$ a $(m+1) \times m$ upper Hessenberg matrix;
17   Solve a least-squares problem of size m: $min_{y \in \mathbb{R}^m}\|\beta e_1 - \bar{H}_m y\|_2$;
18      $x_m \leftarrow x_0 + V_m y_m$;
19      $r_m \leftarrow M^{-1}(b - Ax_m)$;
20      $\beta \leftarrow \|r_m\|_2$;
21   **if** $(\beta < \varepsilon)$ **or** $(k \geq max)$ **then**
22          $convergence \leftarrow true$;
23   **else**
24          $x_0 \leftarrow x_m$;
25          $r_0 \leftarrow r_m$;
26          $k \leftarrow k + 1$;
27   **end**
28 **end**

---

sequential codes (that cannot be parallelized) and operations that require data dependencies or perform recursive computations must be executed by a single thread or by the host, according to the size of the problem. In fact, the waiting of a thread for other threads, while they complete their computations, dramatically affects the performances of the GPUs.

We have implemented the CG and GMRES algorithms on a GPU by using the CUDA programming environment (Compute Unified Device Architecture) version 4.0, which is an extension of the C language developed by Nvidia, and the CUBLAS library (Basic Linear Algebra Subprograms of CUDA) to carry out the vector operations. As with most Krylov subspace methods, CG and GMRES iterations are mainly based on vector operations: matrix-vector multiplications, inner products, scalar-vector products, Euclidean norms, AXPY operations and so on. These vector operations are often easy to parallelize and are more efficient on parallel architectures when they work on large vectors. So in GPU implementations of CG and GMRES algorithms, vector operations are performed by the device, such that they are computed in parallel by a large number of GPU threads so that each thread i is in charge of computing its ith atomic operation.

The most important operation in both CG and GMRES algorithms is the sparse matrix-vector multiplication (SpMV). It is the most time-consuming operation and it requires to take care of the storage structures of sparse matrices in the memory. Indeed, the naive storage row-by-row (or column-by-column) of a sparse matrix is extremely wasteful of memory space and execution time, furthermore the zero elements of the matrix are stored whereas the results of the SpMV atomic operations involving them are useless. Besides, using sparse matrix storage leads to irregular memory accesses to nonzero elements, which slows down even more the SpMV multiplication. In addition, GPUs require coalesced memory accesses to their device memories in order to achieve maximum memory bandwidth, therefore naive storages of sparse matrices lead to very poor performances. One of the most efficient data structures for sparse matrices products on a GPU is the hybrid format (HYB) [8]. It is a combination of ELLpack (ELL) and Coordinate (COO) formats. Indeed, it stores a typical number of nonzero elements per row in ELL format and the remaining entries of exceptional rows in a COO format. It combines the efficiency of ELL due to the regularity of its memory accesses and the flexibility of COO which is insensitive to the matrix structure.

In CG and GMRES implementations, we use the HYB kernel [9], developed by Nvidia, to perform the SpMV multiplication. For vector operations, we use CUBLAS functions (dealing with double floating point): `cublasDdot()` for dot products, `cublasDnrm2()` for Euclidean norms and `cublasDaxpy()` for AXPY operations ($y \leftarrow ax + y$). For the remaining parallel operations, we coded their kernels in CUDA. For the CG algorithm 16, we developed a kernel for the XPAY operation ($y \leftarrow x + ay$, line 11). And for the GMRES algorithm 17, we developed a kernel for the scalar-vector products (lines 6 and 14), a kernel to solve the least-squares problem (line 17), which is an inexpensive operation for a small value of m and must be computed sequentially by one GPU thread, and a kernel for the solution vector updates of x (line 18).

Before any computations of CG and GMRES methods, data of the sparse linear system to be solved, which is the sparse matrix A, the initial guess x_0, the right-hand side b and the preconditioning matrix M, must be transferred from the CPU memory to the GPU device memory, because GPUs work only on data off-loaded onto their memories. Then, the CPU process acts as a controller of the main loop of the CG algorithm (the GMRES algorithm respectively) and the GPU executes all kernels inside the main loop. Each kernel of a parallel operation is launched by the

CPU process, by providing the execution configuration in the GPU: the number of threads per block $NbThreads$ and the number of thread-blocks $NbBlocks$ which can be computed as follows:

$$NbBlocks = \frac{n + NbThreads - 1}{NbThreads} \tag{10.19}$$

where n is the size of the sparse linear system. In this way, each GPU thread is in charge of one matrix row and/or one vector element.

10.3.2 Performances on a GPU

We tested the performances of both CG and GMRES methods on a Quad-Core Xeon E5620 CPU running at 2.4 GHz, and equipped with a Tesla C2070 GPU. The CPU provides 12 GB of RAM with a memory bandwidth of 25.6 GB/s, and the GPU contains 448 streaming processors, running at 1.15 GHz, and a device memory of 6 GB with a memory bandwidth of 144 GB/s.

All tests are made on double precision data and for a residual tolerance threshold $\varepsilon = 10^{-12}$, a maximum number of iterations $max = 500$, a restart limit of the GMRES method $m = 16$, a right-hand side b filled with 1.0 and an initial guess x_0 filled with 0. For the sake of simplicity, we have chosen the preconditioner M as the main diagonal of the sparse matrix A. Indeed it allows us to easily compute the required inverse matrix M^{-1} and it provides a relatively good preconditioning for not too ill-conditioned matrices.

To achieve more realistic results, we tested the CG and GMRES algorithms on sparse matrices of the Davis's collection [10], that arise in a wide spectrum of real-world applications. We chose six symmetric sparse matrices and six unsymmetric ones from this collection. In Figure 10.1 we show the structures of these matrices, and in Table 10.1 we present their main characteristics which are the number of rows, the number of nonzero elements and the matrix bandwidth.

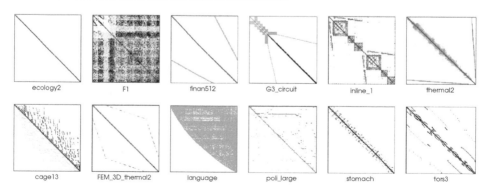

Figure 10.1: Sketches of sparse matrices chosen from the Davis collection

Matrix type	Matrix name	# rows	# nonzeros	bandwidth
	ecology2	$999,999$	$4,995,991$	$2,001$
	F1	$343,791$	$26,837,113$	$343,782$
Symmetric	finan512	$74,752$	$596,992$	$74,725$
	G3_circuit	$1,585,478$	$7,660,826$	$1,219,059$
	inline_1	$503,712$	$36,816,342$	$502,407$
	thermal2	$1,228,045$	$8,580,313$	$1,226,629$
	cage13	$445,315$	$7,479,343$	$318,788$
	FEM_3D_thermal2	$147,900$	$3,489,300$	$117,827$
Unsymmetric	language	$399,130$	$1,216,334$	$398,622$
	poli_large	$15,575$	$33,074$	$15,575$
	stomach	$213,360$	$3,021,648$	$20,284$
	tors3	$259,156$	$4,429,042$	$216,854$

Table 10.1: Main characteristics of sparse matrices from the Davis collection

Matrix name	$time_{cpu}$	$time_{gpu}$	τ	# iter.	prec.	Δ
ecology2	0.324s	0.029s	10.90	13	$5.06e-09$	$1.11e-16$
F1	1.146s	0.129s	8.85	15	$4.46e-11$	$1.35e-20$
finan512	0.029s	0.006s	4.75	12	$3.52e-09$	$2.22e-16$
G3_circuit	0.700s	0.064s	10.97	16	$4.16e-10$	$5.55e-16$
inline_1	1.316s	0.146s	9.04	15	$9.80e-12$	$6.78e-21$
thermal2	0.778s	0.081s	9.64	15	$5.11e-09$	$3.33e-16$

Table 10.2: Execution times in seconds of the sequential CG method on a CPU core
and on a GPU

Tables 10.2 and 10.3 show the performances of the sequential CG algorithm and
those of the sequential GMRES algorithm, respectively, for solving linear systems
associated with the sparse matrices presented in Table 10.1. However in Table 10.2,
the performances are presented only for symmetric sparse matrices due to the inability
of the CG method to solve unsymmetric matrices. In both tables, we take into account
the relative gains, τ, that can be obtained from a method implemented on the GPU
compared to the same method implemented on the CPU. The relative gains, given in
the fourth column of each table, are computed as ratios between the execution times
spent on the CPU, $time_{cpu}$, and those spent on the GPU, $time_{gpu}$:

$$\tau = \frac{time_{cpu}}{time_{gpu}} \tag{10.20}$$

From these ratios, we can notice that both CG and GMRES methods are more efficient
on the GPU than on the CPU for solving sparse linear systems. In fact, the GPU
can be considered as an accelerator for the data-parallel operations, such that each
operation is executed by a high number of GPU threads at a time. Typical relative

Matrix name	$time_{cpu}$	$time_{gpu}$	τ	# iter.	prec.	Δ
ecology2	1.451s	0.093s	15.63	21	$4.30e-13$	$9.28e-14$
F1	2.901s	0.299s	9.68	32	$2.96e-17$	$1.69e-20$
finan512	0.101s	0.015s	6.77	17	$3.21e-12$	$5.55e-16$
G3_circuit	2.519s	0.157s	16.03	22	$1.04e-12$	$2.37e-14$
inline_1	3.093s	0.307s	10.08	29	$1.90e-17$	$1.35e-20$
thermal2	2.251s	0.165s	13.66	21	$6.58e-12$	$3.33e-16$
cage13	1.076s	0.088s	12.23	26	$3.37e-11$	$1.75e-14$
FEM_3D_thermal2	1.039s	0.098s	10.59	64	$3.87e-09$	$1.82e-12$
language	2.781s	0.226s	12.29	90	$1.18e-10$	$1.16e-10$
poli_large	0.071s	0.036s	1.94	69	$5.00e-11$	$1.36e-12$
stomach	2.820s	0.255s	11.07	145	$2.20e-10$	$7.10e-15$
tors3	4.377s	0.373s	11.74	175	$2.69e-10$	$1.78e-14$

Table 10.3: Execution times in seconds of the sequential GMRES method on a CPU core and on a GPU

gains on the GPU for the CG method are about 9 and those for the GMRES method are about 11. The CG method is obviously more efficient (about 3 times faster) than the GMRES method for the symmetric sparse linear systems on both CPU and GPU implementations. However, we can see that ratios τ of the GMRES method are better than those of the CG method, because this last one is based on vector operations less complicated and easier to compute on the CPU than those of the GMRES method.

In addition to the execution times and the relative gains, we give in Tables 10.2 and 10.3 the number of iterations performed to solve the sparse linear system, the precision $prec$ of the solution computed on the GPU, and the difference Δ between the solution computed on the CPU and that computed on the GPU. Both parameters $prec$ and Δ allow us to validate and to check the accuracy of the solution computed by the GPU. They are computed as follows:

$$\Delta = max|x^{cpu} - x^{gpu}| \tag{10.21}$$
$$prec = max|M^{-1}r^{gpu}| \tag{10.22}$$

where Δ is the maximum element, in absolute value, of the difference between both solutions $x^{cpu}, x^{gpu} \in \mathbb{R}^n$ computed on the CPU and on the GPU, respectively; and $prec$ is the maximum element of the residual $r^{gpu} \in \mathbb{R}^n$ computed on the solution x^{gpu}. So we can see for both methods that the solutions computed on the GPU are almost the same as the solutions computed on the CPU, with an error varying from 10^{-12} to 10^{-21}, and their precisions, which are sufficient, are about 10^{-10}.

Finally, we can also notice that the GPU is less efficient for solving small sparse linear systems. For example in Tables 10.2 and 10.3, the relative gains for matrices *finan512* and *poli_large* are less than 5, because small sizes of sparse matrices do not allow best exploitation of the resources and the computing power of GPUs. In the next section, we study the performances of CG and GMRES algorithms on large sparse matrices by exploiting more than one GPU.

10.4   Parallel Sparse Linear Solvers on GPU Clusters

In this section, we aim at harnessing the computing power of multiple GPUs for solving large sparse linear systems, exceeding ten million of unknown values. First, we present the parallelization of CG and GMRES algorithms on a GPU cluster, and then, we present the performances and the scalability of their parallel implementations.

10.4.1   Parallel Implementation on GPU Clusters

The parallelization of both CG and GMRES algorithms requires a partitioning of data among the computing nodes of the GPU cluster. Let p denote the number of the computing nodes on the GPU cluster, such that a computing node is a couple of a CPU core, holding a MPI process, and a GPU. Before starting the parallel computations, all matrices and vectors involved in CG or GMRES algorithms are decomposed in p portions as in the example shown in Figure 10.2, such that each computing node i holds a portion of $\frac{n}{p}$ elements of each vector, a rectangular portion of the sparse matrix A_i of size $(\frac{n}{p} \times n)$ and a square portion of the preconditioning matrix M_i of size $(\frac{n}{p} \times \frac{n}{p})$. After the partitioning operation, each computing node i transfers its local data (the initial guess $x_{0,i}$, the sparse matrix A_i, the right-hand side b_i and the preconditioning matrix M_i) from the CPU memory to the GPU memory.

Afterwards, all computing nodes solve in parallel their own portions of the sparse linear system, $A_i x_i = b_i$, $0 \leq i < p$, using the same CG algorithm or the same GMRES algorithm adapted to GPUs described in Section 10.3. However in order to solve the complete sparse linear system (10.1), synchronizations must be performed between the local computations of the computing nodes over the GPU cluster. Indeed at each iteration, each computing node must communicate its local results to its neighbours. Therefore in both parallel CG and GMRES algorithms, we define two different points of synchronization: the reduction operation after any dot product and Euclidean norm, and the data exchange of the shared vector parts before any SpMV multiplication. We perform these synchronizations by using the communication operations of the OpenMPI library version 1.3.3. We use the MPI_Allreduce() routine for the reduction operations, and the MPI_Alltoallv() routine for the data exchanges of the shared vector elements between neignbors [11].

We give a special attention to the SpMV mutiplication in both parallel CG and GMRES algorithms. Besides its costly computations, the parallel SpMV multiplication requires data transfers between neighbours in order to construct the global vector needed for this operation. A computing node i builds its global vector, x_i, using its local vector, x_i^{local}, and portions of vectors, x_i^{shared}, shared with its neighbours, as is shown in Figure 10.2. The shared vectors are obtained before the SpMV multiplication, by performing data transfers over the GPU cluster as follows:

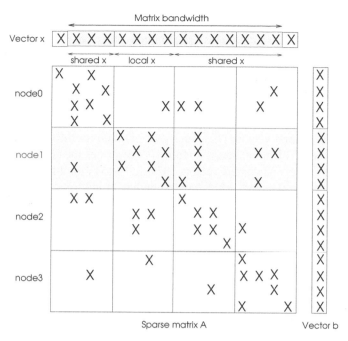

Figure 10.2: Data partitioning of the sparse matrix A, the solution vector x and the right-hand side b into four portions

- The local vectors x^{local} are transferred from the GPU memory to the CPU memory,

- Then, the shared vectors are exchanged between neighbouring MPI processes,

- Finally, the shared vectors x^{shared} received from neighbours are transferred from the CPU memory to the GPU memory.

In a GPU cluster, the synchronizations of the GPU computations are performed through the CPUs, since the GPUs cannot exchange data between them. So data communications must be performed between GPUs and CPUs before and after the data exchanges. We perform the GPU/CPU data transfers by using CUBLAS communication functions. We use the `cublasGetVector()` function for data transfers from the GPU to the CPU, and we use the `cublasSetVector()` function for data transfers from the CPU to the GPU.

It is interesting to note that communications of large data over a GPU cluster are more time-consuming than GPU computations, and more precisely, those of data transfers between GPUs and CPUs. We can notice that, in each iteration, the CG algorithm 16 performs the SpMV multiplication only once at line 13, whereas the GMRES algorithm 17 performs this multiplication m times at line 8, to build the Krylov basis V, and once at line 19, to check the convergence and to initialize parameters of the next iteration. However, the SpMV multiplication requires data communications between CPUs and GPUs, and data transfers of large vectors can penalize the resolution of sparse linear systems with the GMRES method.

We can notice that a SpMV multiplication does not often need all shared vector elements. In Figure 10.2, $node1$ only needs one vector element from $node0$, two vector elements from $node2$ and two vector elements from $node3$. So we can reduce the communication overheads over the GPU cluster by using compression and decompression operations on the shared vectors [12], such that only the useful vector elements are exchanged between GPU neighbours. Figure 10.3 describes the compression and decompression operations on shared vectors. The full SpMV multiplication on $node1$ needs the local vector elements, x_1^{local}, corresponding to indices 4, 5, 6, 7, and vector elements of indices 1, 8, 9, 13, 14 in local vectors x_0^{local}, x_2^{local}, x_3^{local} of $node0$, $node2$ and $node3$ respectively. So GPUs of neighbouring nodes $node0$, $node2$ and $node3$ perform the compression operation on vector parts required by $node1$. Then, these compressed vectors are transferred from the CPUs of these neighbouring nodes to the CPU of $node1$. Finally, the GPU of $node1$ decompresses the shared vectors received from its neighbours, so that each vector element is copied to the corresponding index in the global vector x_1.

In order to accelerate the computations, we developed in CUDA a kernel for the compression operation `compress()` and a kernel for the decompression operation `decompress()` to be performed by GPUs. The piece of code in Figure 10.4 presents the parallel SpMV multiplication on a GPU cluster, where the compression/decompression operations and the data transfers, for the construction of the global vector, are performed before the SpMV multiplication.

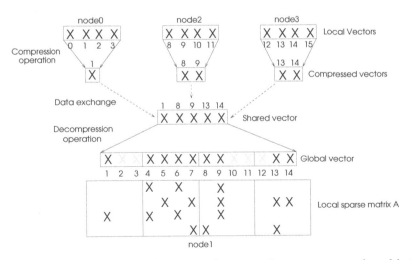

Figure 10.3: Compression and decompression operations on vectors shared between $node1$ and its neighbours $node0$, $node2$ and $node3$

```
/*Compression of shared vectors on the GPU*/
compression<<<NbBlocks,NbThreads>>>();

/*Copy of compressed vectors from the GPU to the CPU*/
cublasGetVector();

/*Data exchanges between neighbouring CPUs*/
MPI_Alltoallv();

/*Copy of received vectors from the CPU to the GPU*/
cublasSetVector();

/*Decompression of shared vectors received from neighbours on the GPU*/
decompress<<<NbBlocks,NbThreads>>>();

/*Sparse matrix-vector multiplication on the GPU*/
SpMV<<<NbBlocks,NbThreads>>>();
```

Figure 10.4: Code of the parallel sparse matrix-vector multiplication on a GPU cluster

10.4.2 Performances on a GPU Cluster

The performance evaluation of the parallel CG and GMRES algorithms are done on a cluster composed of six Xeon E5530 CPUs connected with an 20Gbps InfiniBand network. Each CPU is a Quad-Core running at 2.4 GHz and providing 12 GB of RAM with a memory bandwidth of 25.6 GB/s. In order to accelerate the performances of this cluster, two Tesla C1060 GPUs are connected to each Quad-Core CPU. A Tesla C1060 GPU contains 240 streaming processors running at 1.3 GHz, and it provides a device memory of 4 GB with a memory bandwidth of 102 GB/s. Each GPU is connected to its host via a PCI-Express 16x Gen 2.0 interface with a throughput of 8 GB/s. Hence, the communications that can be carried out between a GPU and its host in this cluster are about 12 times slower than the GPU memory bandwidth.

Matrix name	time$_{cpu}$	time$_{gpu}$	τ	# iter.	prec.	Δ
ecology	0.021s	0.013s	1.61	13	$5.06e-09$	$8.33e-17$
F1	0.259s	0.163s	1.59	15	$4.46e-11$	$1.02e-20$
finan512	0.003s	0.010s	0.30	12	$3.52e-09$	$1.66e-16$
G3_circuit	0.089s	0.073s	1.22	16	$4.16e-10$	$4.44e-16$
inline_1	0.195s	0.096s	2.03	15	$9.80e-12$	$5.08e-21$
thermal2	0.079s	0.069s	1.44	15	$5.11e-09$	$3.33e-16$

Table 10.4: Execution times in seconds of the parallel CG method on a cluster of 24 CPU cores and on a cluster of 12 GPUs

In Tables 10.4 and 10.5, we report the performances obtained by solving linear systems associated to the sparse matrices of Table 10.1, by using the parallel CG algorithm and the parallel GMRES algorithm, respectively. Both parallel algorithms are tested on a cluster of 24 CPU cores and then on a cluster of 12 GPUs. We can notice that it is not interesting to use multiple GPUs for solving small sparse linear systems,

Matrix name	$time_{cpu}$	$time_{gpu}$	τ	# iter.	prec.	Δ
ecology	0.069s	0.029s	2.38	21	$4.30e-13$	$4.38-15$
F1	0.558s	0.346s	1.61	32	$2.96e-17$	$1.69e-20$
finan512	0.007s	0.018s	0.39	17	$3.21e-12$	$4.99e-16$
G3_circuit	0.180s	0.113s	1.59	22	$1.04e-12$	$1.99e-15$
inline_1	0.394s	0.186s	2.12	29	$1.90e-17$	$6.78e-21$
thermal2	0.152s	0.104s	1.46	21	$6.58e-12$	$2.77e-16$
cage13	0.174s	0.115s	1.51	26	$3.37e-11$	$2.66e-15$
FEM_3D_thermal	0.051s	0.063s	0.81	64	$3.87e-09$	$9.09e-13$
language	0.262s	0.239s	1.10	90	$1.18e-10$	$8.00e-11$
poli_large	0.013s	0.060s	0.22	69	$4.98e-11$	$1.14e-12$
stomach	0.137s	0.152s	0.90	145	$2.20e-10$	$1.06e-14$
tors3	0.246s	0.218s	1.13	175	$2.69e-10$	$1.78e-14$

Table 10.5: Execution times in seconds of the parallel GMRES method on a cluster of 24 CPU cores and on a cluster of 12 GPUs

and for some matrices, it is better to solve them on a cluster of CPUs. As previously mentioned, GPUs are not efficient for applications dealing with a small amount of data. Indeed, the processors of GPUs are idle for a significant amount of time during computations. This fact is a waste of resources and it has a negative impact on GPU performances. In addition, the communications necessary to synchronize the computations over the cluster increase the idle times of GPUs, and thus, they slow down the parallel computations further.

In order to solve large sparse linear systems, we developed in C language a generator of large sparse matrices of sizes exeeding ten million rows. This generator is executed in parallel by all MPI processes before starting the solving computations. It is based on sparse matrices of the Davis's collection to build large sparse matrices with a banded structure. According to the desired size of the linear system to be solved, n, and the number of computing nodes in the cluster, p, each MPI process i computes the size of its part of the linear system, n_i, and its offset in the sparse matrix, $offset_i$, as follows:

$$n_i = \frac{n}{p} \tag{10.23}$$

$$offset_i = \begin{cases} 0 & if\ i=0 \\ offset_{i-1} + n_{i-1} & otherwise \end{cases} \tag{10.24}$$

The offsets and the sizes of the sub-matrices on the cluster allow a process to determine which processes own the unknown values needed for the full SpMV multiplication. Then, each MPI process i builds its sub-matrix A_i of size n_i by performing several copies of the same real sparse matrix chosen from the Davis's collection. It places all these copies on its part of the main diagonal of the global sparse matrix A, in order to generate matrices of banded structure as is shown in Figure 10.5. In addition, the empty spaces between consecutive copies on the main diagonal are fulfilled by small copies, *left_part* and *right_part*, of the same initial real matrix.

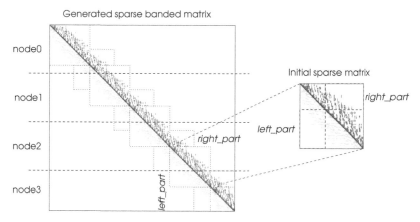

Figure 10.5: A large sparse banded matrix generated by four processes from a real matrix of the Davis collection

We test the parallel CG and GMRES algorithms on the GPU cluster for solving large sparse linear systems of 25 million unknowns. The associated sparse matrices are generated from those presented in Table 10.1, and their main characteristics are given in Table 10.6. We report the performances of the parallel CG and GMRES algorithms in Table 10.7 and in Table 10.8, respectively, obtained on a cluster of 24 CPUs and on a cluster of 12 GPUs. We can see that the relative gains τ obtained on the GPU cluster compared to the CPU cluster are about 4 for solving symmetric linear systems with the CG method, and about 5 for solving both symmetric and unsymmetric linear systems with the GMRES method. For solving large sparse linear systems, the GPU cluster is more efficient than the CPU cluster, in contrast to what is observed in Tables 10.4 and 10.5 for solving small linear systems. Indeed, a large size of linear systems allows us to avoid the idle processors and to harness the best resources of GPUs.

We also tested the performances of parallel CG and GMRES algorithms on a heterogeneous GPU cluster. We connected to the GPU cluster, previously described, two new computing nodes, each consisting of a Quad-Core Xeon E5620 CPU equipped with a Tesla C2070 GPU. The performances obtained on a cluster of 32 CPU cores and those obtained on a cluster of 14 GPUs are reported in Table 10.9 for the parallel CG algorithm and in Table 10.10 for the parallel GMRES algorithm. We can notice from these tables that the GPU cluster remains more efficient than the CPU cluster for solving large sparse linear systems, even if the cluster is composed of heterogeneous GPUs. Relative gains obtained from parallel algorithms on the GPU cluster are slightly less efficient than those obtained from sequential algorithms on one GPU (Tables 10.2 and 10.3). Indeed, parallel computations require synchronizations, and thus, data transfers between different components of the GPU cluster. However, the

Matrix type	Matrix name	# rows	# nonzeros	Bandwidth
	ecology2	25, 000, 000	12, 4948, 019	2, 002
	F1	25, 000, 000	2, 638, 821, 634	548, 731
Symmetric	finan512	25, 000, 000	278, 175, 945	123, 900
	G3_circuit	25, 000, 000	125, 262, 292	1, 891, 887
	inline_1	25, 000, 000	2, 010, 313, 852	867, 175
	thermal2	25, 000, 000	175, 300, 284	2, 421, 285
	cage13	25, 000, 000	435, 770, 480	352, 566
	FEM_3D_thermal2	25, 000, 000	595, 266, 787	206, 029
	language	25, 000, 000	76, 912, 824	398, 626
Unsymmetric	poli_large	25, 000, 000	53, 322, 580	15, 576
	stomach	25, 000, 000	354, 851, 028	34, 445
	tors3	25, 000, 000	433, 795, 264	328, 757

Table 10.6: Main characteristics of generated sparse matrices from those of the Davis collection

Matrix name	time_{cpu}	time_{gpu}	τ	# iter.	prec.	Δ
ecology2	0.694s	0.120s	5.78	15	$3.75e - 10$	$1.11e - 16$
F1	8.667s	2.582s	3.36	18	$4.01e - 12$	$2.71e - 20$
finan512	0.998s	0.261s	3.82	14	$1.04e - 10$	$2.77e - 16$
G3_circuit	1.085s	0.271s	4.00	17	$1.10e - 10$	$5.55e - 16$
inline_1	5.169s	1.375s	3.76	17	$1.57e - 12$	$1.35e - 20$
thermal2	1.191s	0.298s	3.99	16	$1.67e - 09$	$3.88e - 16$

Table 10.7: Performances of the parallel CG method on a cluster of 24 CPU cores and on a cluster of 12 GPUs

performances on the cluster of 14 GPUs are slightly better than those obtained on the cluster of 12 GPUs (Tables 10.7 and 10.8). In heterogeneous GPU clusters, we should continue studying the data partitioning and the load balancing between the different GPUs, for example in our heterogenous GPU cluster, we should take into account that a Tesla C2070 GPU is more efficient than a Tesla C1060 GPU.

In a last series of experiments, we tested the scalability of parallel CG and GMRES algorithms on a GPU cluster. The tests are performed on a large sparse linear system of 15 million unknowns. The sparse matrix associated to this linear system is generated from the symmetric sparse matrix *thermal2* of the Davis's collection. It contains 105, 166, 557 nonzero elements and its bandwidth is 2, 421, 285. In Figure 10.6, we report the execution times in seconds of the parallel CG and GMRES algorithms for different number of GPUs. We can see that both parallel algorithms are quite scalable. However, it is interesting to recall that GPUs are efficient for large sizes of problems, and the exploitation of multiple GPUs for small problems is a waste of resources. This

Matrix name	time$_{cpu}$	time$_{gpu}$	τ	# iter.	prec.	Δ
ecology2	2.205s	0.311s	7.09	21	$4.88e - 13$	$2.08e - 14$
F1	17.096s	4.323s	3.95	32	$3.25e - 17$	$2.71e - 20$
finan512	2.294s	0.429s	5.35	17	$3.22e - 12$	$8.86e - 14$
G3_circuit	2.640s	0.495s	5.33	22	$1.04e - 12$	$4.99e - 15$
inline_1	10.377s	2.530s	4.10	29	$2.06e - 17$	$1.35e - 20$
thermal2	2.751s	0.527s	5.22	21	$8.89e - 12$	$3.33e - 16$
cage13	3.985s	0.803s	4.96	26	$3.29e - 11$	$1.59e - 14$
FEM_3D_thermal	10.726s	2.063s	5.20	64	$3.88e - 09$	$1.82e - 12$
language	10.727s	1.833s	5.85	89	$2.11e - 10$	$1.60e - 10$
poli_large	7.302s	1.075s	6.79	69	$5.05e - 11$	$6.59e - 12$
stomach	20.306s	3.560s	5.70	145	$2.19e - 10$	$8.88e \quad 15$
tors3	26.452s	4.634s	5.71	175	$2.69e - 10$	$2.66e - 14$

Table 10.8: Performances of the parallel GMRES method on a cluster of 24 CPU cores and on a cluster of 12 GPUs

Matrix name	time$_{cpu}$	time$_{gpu}$	τ	# iter.	prec.	Δ
ecology2	0.640s	0.104s	6.15	15	$3.75e - 10$	$1.11e - 16$
F1	7.592s	1.896s	4.00	18	$4.01e - 12$	$2.71e - 20$
finan512	0.899s	0.228s	3.94	14	$1.04e - 10$	$2.77e - 16$
G3_circuit	1.115s	0.259s	4.30	17	$1.10e - 10$	$5.55e - 16$
inline_1	4.451s	1.144s	3.89	17	$1.57e - 12$	$1.35e - 20$
thermal2	1.151s	0.286s	4.02	16	$1.67e - 09$	$3.88e - 16$

Table 10.9: Performances of the parallel CG method on a cluster of 32 CPU cores and on a cluster of 14 GPUs

is why the two curves in Figure 10.6 tend to stabilize towards the end, since the size of the sparse linear system to be solved (15 million unknowns) is not large enough for these numbers of GPUs.

10.5 Conclusion

In this chapter, we have aimed at harnessing the computing power of GPUs for solving sparse linear systems. Therefore, we have studied how to adapt the algorithms of two well-known Krylov subspace iterative methods to GPU architectures. The first iterative method is the gradient conjugate method (CG), well-known for its efficiency to solve symmetric linear systems, and the second one is the generalized minimal residual method (GMRES), which is developed for solving more precisely unsymmetric linear systems.

First, we have shown the main key points to be considered in order to adapt an al-

Matrix name	$time_{cpu}$	$time_{gpu}$	τ	# iter.	prec.	Δ
ecology2	1.944s	0.270s	7.20	21	$4.88e-13$	$2.08e-14$
F1	15.008s	3.528s	4.25	32	$3.25e-17$	$2.71e-20$
finan512	2.027s	0.375s	5.40	17	$3.22e-12$	$8.86e-14$
G3_circuit	2.510s	0.456s	5.50	22	$1.04e-12$	$4.99e-15$
inline_1	8.942s	2.084s	4.29	29	$2.06e-17$	$1.35e-20$
thermal2	2.533s	0.492s	5.15	21	$8.89e-12$	$3.33e-16$
cage13	3.586s	0.689s	5.20	26	$3.29e-11$	$1.59e-14$
FEM_3D_thermal	9.427s	1.764s	5.34	64	$3.88e-09$	$1.82e-12$
language	9.589s	1.562s	6.14	89	$2.11e-10$	$1.60e-10$
poli_large	6.434s	0.931s	6.91	69	$5.05e-11$	$6.59e-12$
stomach	18.189s	3.056s	5.95	145	$2.19e-10$	$8.88e-15$
tors3	23.706s	3.977s	5.96	175	$2.69e-10$	$2.66e-14$

Table 10.10: Performances of the parallel GMRES method on a cluster of 32 CPU cores and on a cluster of 14 GPUs

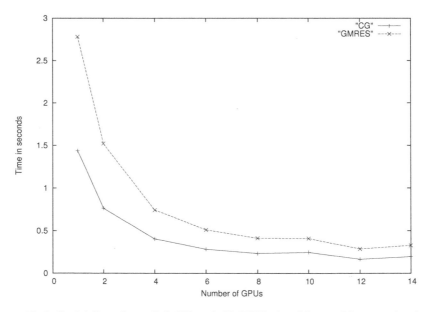

Figure 10.6: Scalabilty of parallel CG and GMRES algorithms with a matrix size of 15 million

gorithm for GPU architectures. So, we have described the implementation on one GPU of the sequential algorithms of the CG and GMRES methods. Then, we have tested these GPU implementations on one CPU equipped with a Tesla GPU. We have noticed that solving sparse linear systems with the GPU version of the CG method and/or the GMRES method is faster than the CPU version of the same method. Obviously, we have also noticed that the CG method is the most efficient for solving sparse symmetric linear systems, and the GMRES method is more efficient for solving the unsymmetric ones, whether they are implemented on the CPU or on the GPU.

Then, we have shown how to efficiently parallelize algorithms of CG and GMRES methods on a GPU cluster in order to solve sparse linear systems of large sizes. We have compared the performances of these parallel algorithms obtained on GPU clusters with those obtained on CPU clusters. We have noticed that solving large sparse linear systems is more efficient on a GPU cluster than on a CPU cluster. The parallel algorithms of CG and GMRES methods on a cluster of 14 GPUs are about 4 times and about 5 times, respectively, faster than the same parallel algorithms implemented on a cluster of 32 CPU cores for solving sparse linear systems of size 25 million unknowns. We have also noted that, even if the parallel algorithms are scalable, GPU clusters are efficient for large amounts of data, and in contrast, their use for solving small sparse linear systems does not give good performances and it can be considered as wasteful of resources.

It would be interesting to study the performance behavior and the scalability of other iterative methods for solving large sparse linear systems on GPU clusters. Moreover, the application of these iterative methods on other structures of sparse matrices (other than banded matrices) would have an impact on the communications over a GPU cluster, and it is interesting to study how to reduce these communication overheads. Finally, it would also be interesting to implement and to test the performances of parallel asynchronous algorithms on geographically distant GPU clusters.

References

[1] J. Bahi, S. Contassot-Vivier, R. Couturier, "Parallel Iterative Algorithms: from sequential to grid computing", Numerical Analysis & Scientific Computing, Chapman & Hall/CRC, 2007.

[2] Y. Saad, "Iterative Methods for Sparse Linear System", Society for Industrial and Applied Mathematics, Philadelphia, PA, USA, 2nd edition, 2003.

[3] M.R. Hestenes, E. Stiefel, "Methods of Conjugate Gradients for Solving Linear Systems", Journal of Research of the National Bureau of Standards, 49(6), 409–436, 1952.

[4] Y. Saad M.H. Schultz, "GMRES: a Generalized Minimal Residual Algorithm for Solving Nonsymmetric Linear Systems", SIAM J. Sci. Stat. Comput., 7(3), 856–869, 1986.

[5] C.C. Paige, M.A. Saunders, "Solution of Sparse Indefinite Systems of Linear Equations", SIAM Journal on Numerical Analysis, 12(4), 617–629, 1975.

[6] W. Arnoldi, "The Principle of Minimized Iteration in the Solution of the Matrix Eigenvalue Problem", Quart, Appl.Math., 9, 17–29, 1951.

[7] Nvidia, "NVIDIA CUDA C Programming Guide", Version 4.0, 2011.

[8] N. Bell, M. Garland, "Implementing Sparse Matrix-Vector Multiplication on Throughput-Oriented Processors", In SC09, 1–11, 2009.

[9] CUSP Library. `http://code.google.com/p/cusp-library/`

[10] T. Davis, Y. Hu, "The University of Florida Sparse Matrix Collection", 1997.
     `http://www.cise.ufl.edu/research/sparse/matrices/`

[11] R. Couturier, F. Jézéquel, "Solving large sparse linear systems in a grid environment using Java", In PDSEC'10, 11-th IEEE Int. Workshop on Parallel and Distributed Scientific and Engineering Computing, joint to IPDPS'10, ACM/IEEE Int. Parallel and Distributed Processing Symposium, Atlanta, United States, 2010.

[12] J. Bahi, R. Couturier, L. Ziane Khodja, "Parallel Sparse Linear Solver GMRES for GPU Clusters with Compression of Exchanged Data", Euro-Par Workshops, 1, 471–480, 2011.

©Saxe-Coburg Publications, 2014.
F. Magoulès, (Editor),
Patterns for Parallel Programming on GPUs
Saxe-Coburg Publications, Stirlingshire, Scotland, 249-279.

Chapter 11

Bioinformatics of Non-Coding RNAs and GPUs, A Case Study: Prediction at Large Scale of MicroRNAs in Genomes

F. Tahi[1], V.D. Tran[1], S. Tempel[1] and E. Mahé[2]

[1]*IBISC-IBGBI, University of Evry-Val d'Essonne/Genopole, France*
[2]*Minds Planet, France*

Abstract

Non-coding RNAs are functional RNAs that are not translated into proteins. Computational studies of non-coding RNAs have recently become an important challenge in bioinformatics, including their identification and structure prediction. We introduced in our EvryRNA platform several algorithms for those purposes: *P-DCFold*, *SSCA*, *Tfold*, *miRNAFold*, *ncRNAclassifier* and *BoostSVM*.

With the development of next-generation sequencing technologies, huge amounts of genomic and RNA sequences data have been produced. A parallelization of such tools is thus required to overcome the long execution time issue. GPU computing has appeared as an effective way for realizing parallel tasks. *miRNAFold*, an algorithm we developed for the search for microRNAs in genomic sequences, and initially written in C, was implemented in CUDA, which allows the use of GPUs, to search at large scale for microRNAs in genomic sequences.

Keywords: genomics, bioinformatics, non-coding RNA, microRNA, RNA structure, ncRNA prediction, GPU, CPU.

11.1   Introduction

Since the sequence of the first living organism in 1995, the number of sequenced genomes has significantly increased each year. There are currently several thousand genomes that have been sequenced. Recently, a new generation of sequencers (NGS) have been developed. Compared to the traditional Sanger sequencing, these new techniques can produce billions of nucleotides (Gigabases) in a single use. NGS creates an enormous amount of data, and thus parallel algorithms and high performance computing (HPC) are needed for processing such data. However, most research laboratories (public as well as private) cannot afford to equip large clusters of CPU calculations. Therefore, the use of computers containing graphics processor units (GPUs) is a realistic alternative to PC clusters for large computing power with a reasonable hardware cost.

With the advent of new broadband sequencing technologies, it is important to have fast and efficient *in silico* methods for analyzing large-scale genomic sequences. Among the biological objects targeted in genomes, non-coding RNAs (ncRNAs) are some of the most important ones, as they are involved in many biological processes. ncRNAs are genes that do not encode functional proteins, and possess structures that imply specific functions. Among these RNAs, transfer RNAs and ribosomal RNAs were discovered first and play a crucial role in protein synthesis in all organisms. Since their discovery, many ncRNAs have also been explored, such as the microRNAs (miRNAs). These are small ncRNAs which play important roles in biological processes, as they are implicated in the regulation of gene expression by targeting messenger RNAs (mRNAs) via translational inhibition or message degradation. The dysregulation of miRNAs causes a wide range of diseases such as hereditary progressive hearing loss, growth and skeleton defects, cancers, heart diseases, Alzheimer disease, *etc.* Thus, the prediction of ncRNA (including miRNA) structures and their identification in genomes are very important tasks for both biological and medical sciences.

Here we present our research work in the domain of bioinformatics applied to ncRNAs. We developed several algorithms and software for ncRNA structure prediction and analysis (*P-DCFold* [1], *SSCA* [2], *Tfold* [3], *miRNAFold* [4], *ncRNAclassifier* [5] and *BoostSVM* [6]), which are available through the EvryRNA web server (http://EvryRNA.ibisc.univ-evry.fr). Among these algorithms, we have an efficient and fast tool called *miRNAFold* for miRNAs searching in genomes. In the context of OpenGPU project, this algorithm has been parallelized for a use on GPUs, which allows optimizing the execution time of *miRNAFold* and thus presenting a software that enables miRNA searching at a large scale in genomes.

This chapter is structured as follows: in the next section, we present and describe our biological object of study, *i.e.* the ncRNAs. In Section 11.3, we present some bioinformatics domains related to ncRNAs, before presenting in the following section the bioinformatics platform EvryRNA we developed for RNAs, containing our different algorithms for predicting, searching and analyzing ncRNAs. Each of these algorithms is briefly described, except for *miRNAFold*, which is described in more detail in Section 11.5. The GPU version of *miRNAFold* is given in Section 11.6 and finally, in the last section, we present some related works on the use of GPUs in bioinformatics applications.

11.2 The World of Non-Coding RNAs

The knowledge of structures, interactions and associations of macromolecules is at the heart of understanding the working of living organisms. We usually think first about protein structures when mentioning structural biology, but had long forgotten the important role of ncRNAs that also adopt a three-dimensional structure (Figure 11.1), and are thus involved through their structural interactions in many biological processes. ncRNAs are genes that do not encode proteins. They play many important functional roles in cells. In the 1980s, the discovery of catalytic RNAs revolutionized our perceptions of the origin of life and led to the development of research into RNAs. Thus, the knowledge and understanding of RNA structures, their folding process, evolution and catalysis have currently almost reached the level achieved in the field of proteins.

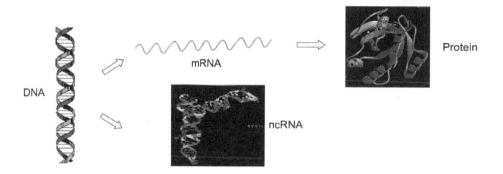

Figure 11.1: Biological functions are expressed through two ways: proteins and RNAs. Proteins are encoded from mRNAs; ncRNAs having their own structures do not encode proteins

11.2.1 ncRNA Structure

The structure of an RNA can be decomposed into different structural elements which allow a description of it with some level of precision. There exist three fundamental structural levels for ncRNAs (Figure 11.2):

- The primary structure is the sequence itself, which is composed of a polymer of nucleotides: adenine (A), cytosine (C), guanine (G) and uracil (U).

- The secondary structure represents the folding of the sequence by Watson-Crick (A-U and G-C) and wobble (G-U) base pairing. These pairs are formed through hydrogen bonds between corresponding nucleotides.

- The tertiary structure is the tridimensional conformation of the nucleotide chain, through which RNA molecules perform their diverse functions.

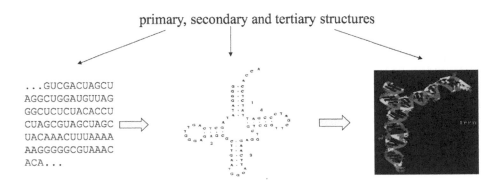

Figure 11.2: The three structure levels of ncRNAs

The secondary structure of an RNA is composed of several elements: stems (which are a succession of base pairings A-U, G-C and G-U), internal loops (that can be symmetrical or not), bulges and terminal loops, as shown in Figure 11.3.

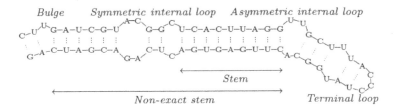

Figure 11.3: Components of ncRNA secondary structures

The structure given in Figure 11.3 is a particular structure called a hairpin structure or stem-loop structure. Small RNAs often possess a hairpin structure, while bigger RNAs are composed of several hairpins (multi-hairpin structure), as we can see below. Some ncRNAs contain some particular substructures called pseudoknots. A pseudoknot is composed of two stems that overlap each other and thus form a sort of knot (Figure 11.4).

Experimental observations have suggested a role for pseudoknots as conformational switches or control elements in several biological functions [7]. In molecules that lack

Figure 11.4: An example of a pseudoknot in an RNA secondary structure

an overall three-dimensional conformation, pseudoknots are locally folded and their positions along the sequence then reflect their functions [8]. For example, pseudoknots that are folded at the 5'-end of mRNAs are frequently involved in translational controls whereas those at the 3'-end maintain signals for replication.

11.2.2   Examples of ncRNAs

The first ncRNA discovered was transfer RNA (tRNA), followed by ribosomal RNA (rRNA) [9–11]. tRNAs and rRNAs play crucial roles in protein synthesis and are highly conserved across all genomes, not only in terms of structure, but also in function. Since these primary discoveries, many types of ncRNAs that regulate the transcription and translation of genes have been found, especially miRNAs and small nucleolar RNAs.

11.2.2.1   Transfer RNA

Transfer RNA (tRNA) contains 73 to 93 nucleotides, and is employed in the conversion of genetic codes or codons (three consecutive nucleotides) into twenty-letter codes of amino acids [11, 12]. Each tRNA is associated to an amino acid which corresponds to a genetic code. The tRNA is characterized by a cloverleaf secondary structure (see Figure 11.2) where the bottom loop is called an anticodon. tRNAs create a three-nucleotide pair between the anticodon and the mRNA codon, then provide its corresponding amino acid to the rRNA that will elongate the protein chain. tRNAs are present in all living organisms (bacteria, archaebacteria, fungi, plants, and animals).

11.2.2.2   Ribosomal RNA

Ribosomal RNA (rRNA) is the main component of ribosome in all living organisms. The ribosome contains two sub-units, a small and a large one. The small subunit is composed of 16S rRNA in prokaryote organisms and 18S rRNA in eukaryote organisms. It reads the mRNA and checks the compatibility between the mRNA codon and the tRNA anticodon. The large subunit is composed of 5S and 23S rRNAs in prokaryotes, while 5S and 28S rRNAs are found in eukaryotes. It allows the creation of the peptide bond between the amino acids [13].

Ribosomal RNAs have various sizes. The largest existing RNA is 23S rRNA, which is composed of more than 2900 nucleotides, while 16S rRNA contains around 1500 nucleotides and 5S rRNA has around 120 nucleotides (Figure 11.5).

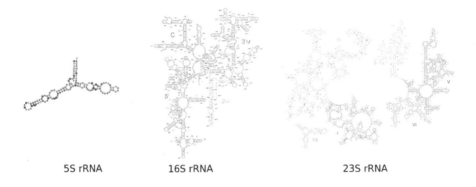

        5S rRNA   **16S rRNA**   **23S rRNA**

Figure 11.5: Examples of 5S, 16S, and 23S ribosomal RNA secondary structures

11.2.2.3   Small Nucleolar RNA

Small nucleolar RNAs (snoRNA) containing between 60 and 1 000 nucleotides exist in a hairpin structure [14, 15]. snoRNAs are mainly classified into two classes: C/D box and H/ACA box, which are conserved motifs in genomes. The C/D snoRNAs are involved in the 2'-O-ribose methylation of ribosomal RNAs and the H/ACA snoRNAs are implicated in the pseudouridylation of ribosomal RNAs [16]. Furthermore, each class of these conserved motifs has its characteristic secondary structure. Recently, different studies have shown that snoRNAs can also target mRNAs and process them as miRNAs [17].

11.2.2.4   MicroRNA

MiRNAs are ncRNAs which have about 21-25 nucleotides in sequence and are present in all sequenced higher eukaryotes [18, 19]. According to the current understanding of miRNA biogenesis, miRNA genes are first transcribed as long primary miRNAs (pri-miRNAs), and then are cleaved into 60-900 nucleotide long miRNA precursors (pre-miRNAs) by the Drosha/Pasha complex (see Figure 11.6). A pre-miRNA, which is structured as a hairpin, is transported into the cytoplasm by Exportin-5 and cleaved by Dicer into the mature miRNA [18]. In the RISC complex, a miRNA binds to a specific mRNA transcript and leads to the cleavage or the degradation of the mRNA. It is involved as a negative regulator of gene expression at the post-transcriptional level by binding to specific mRNA targets whose translations are inhibited or down-regulated [19, 20]. MiRNAs were first detected in the Caenorhabditis elegans genome [18], but seem to be present in all higher eukaryotes.

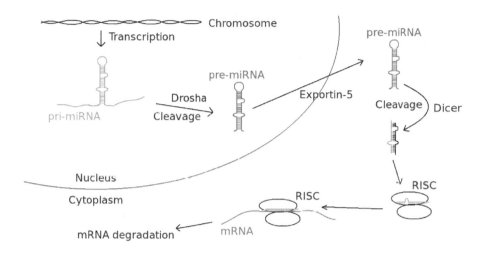

Figure 11.6: Biogenesis of miRNA. The pri-miRNA is cleaved by Drosha protein into pre-miRNA. The pre-miRNA is transferred in cytoplasm by Exportin-5 and cleaved by Dicer into mature miRNA. In the RISC complex, a miRNA binds to a target mRNA transcript and leads to the degradation of the mRNA

11.3 Bioinformatics and Non-Coding RNAs

ncRNAs, and more particularly ncRNA structures, are some of the most important biological objects which are largely studied in bioinformatics. The experimental techniques (X-ray crystallography, nuclear magnetic resonance (NMR), electron microscopy, mass spectrometry, *etc.*) to determine the structure of macromolecules have been considerably developed in recent years. Nonetheless, those techniques are still difficult, time-consuming and relatively expensive. Meanwhile, with the advent of new rapid sequencing technologies, massive amounts of RNA sequence data have been produced. The amount of experimentally determined ncRNA structures is thus lagging far behind the accumulation of ncRNA sequence data. The computational methods to model and predict their structures have become an essential step in order to identify the candidate structures, which can be studied further.

11.3.1   ncRNA Secondary Structure Prediction

The prediction of ncRNA secondary structures is of interest to biologists since the first publication in 1965 by Holley *et al.* on the structure of the alanine-encoding tRNA. The knowledge on this structural level may reveal the biological significance of RNA molecules. This is a simple and clear step towards solving the more complex tertiary structure of ncRNAs.

Two main approaches have been developed for predicting ncRNA secondary structures: thermodynamic and comparative approaches. The thermodynamic approach is based on the minimization of free energy using experimentally measured thermodynamic parameters. It is assumed that the naturally stable structure exists in its minimum free energy. Most algorithms implementing the first approach use thermodynamic parameters defined by the Turner Lab [21]. The limitations of this approach are partly due to the uncertainty of the energy model which is applied. Indeed, although it is recognized that the real structure has a relatively low energy, it is generally not the one of lowest energy as the RNA folding is also affected by its surroundings. This method usually produces combinatorial problems with a complexity higher than or equal to $\mathcal{O}(n^3)$. Among the proposed algorithms, we can refer *Mfold* [22], the best known and most widely used software for predicting the secondary structure from a given sequence. It is based on dynamic programming and has a complexity of $\mathcal{O}(n^3)$, where n is the sequence length.

Meanwhile, the comparative approach searches for conserved regions of aligned homologous sequences which belong to different species. It allows the determination of nucleotide covariation between species and thus proposes a common secondary structure. This method has yet been little automated. It is firstly due to the small amount of available sequences, as the method requires many homologous sequences to be effective. A poor alignment produced makes it difficult to assess the nucleotide covariation. Secondly, the existing algorithms that implemented this approach usually have high complexities (more than $\mathcal{O}(n^3)$). However, this comparative method has been shown to be more or less effective and allowed manually resolving structures of large RNAs, such as the 16S and 23S ribosomal RNAs. Among algorithms using multiple sequences, we can mention *Pfold* [23], based on context-free grammars, with a complexity of $\mathcal{O}(n^3)$. We can also cite *RNAalifold* [24], which integrates thermodynamic and phylogenetic information in a modified energetic model for predicting a common secondary structure of a set of homologous sequences with a complexity in time of $\mathcal{O}(n^3)$.

11.3.2   ncRNA Pseudoknot Prediction

An RNA secondary structure without pseudoknots is a planar structure (two-dimensional). This planar conformation is lost when it contains pseudoknots. Therefore, the pseudoknots are often considered as part of the tertiary structure, though the connections involved in pseudoknots are of the same nature as those of the secondary structure, *i.e.* simple base pairings AU, GC, and GU.

For a long time, proposed RNA secondary structure prediction algorithms have not predicted pseudoknots. Nonetheless, more and more studies have discovered a significant role for pseudoknots, especially in the regulation of several biological processes. The main reasons are the computational costs of the pseudoknot prediction. In [25], it was proved that the general problem of predicting RNA secondary structures containing pseudoknots is NP-hard for a large class of plausible models of pseudoknots. Most existing studies have searched for certain specific types of pseudoknots. An iterative stem-adding strategy can help reduce the search space and deal with pseudoknotted structures [26, 27]. For instance, *ILM* [27], which employed this strategy, is based on dynamic programming and allows the search for pseudoknots with an average complexity in time of $\mathcal{O}(n^3)$ and the worst complexity of $\mathcal{O}(n^4)$.

11.3.3 ncRNA Tertiary Structure Prediction

A limited number of methods have been proposed to predict the RNA tertiary structures from its sequence. The fragment assembly methods construct plausible conformations by gathering together short fragments obtained from experimental structures [28–30]. They can be enhanced by a probabilistic model that is used as a proposal distribution and an energy term enforcing realistic local conformations [31]. The discrete molecular dynamics simulations, which make use of discrete step function potentials, have been applied also for rapid conformational sampling [32]. Besides, the refinement of predicted secondary structures to accommodate the insertion of RNA three-dimensional motifs in an integer programming framework can allow generating complete 3D structures of large RNA molecules [33]. Nevertheless, all of those algorithms still have very high complexities in time.

11.3.4 ncRNA Identification

Detecting ncRNAs in genomic sequences makes an important step in sequence annotation. The *in silico* identification is realized via properties of short-read sequences from genomes. These properties can be intrinsically determined on a given sequence and its corresponding structure, such as composition of the sequence, motifs in its secondary structure, thermodynamic folding energy, *etc.* On the one hand, they may form a filter to exclude sequences that are unlikely to contain the ncRNA of interest. On the other hand, they can be used as features for classification using machine learning techniques, such as Naïve Bayes classifier, hidden Markov model, random forest, neural networks, support vector machine, *etc.* The functionality of ncRNAs often depends heavily on their secondary structure, which makes gene discovery very different from protein-coding RNA genes [34]. The structure prediction thus acts as a crucial preliminary element in ncRNA identification.

Several works have been carried out for identifying ncRNAs in genomes, based on three principal approaches: comparative genomics, homology-based and *ab initio* approaches. Comparative genomics methods employ the nature of phylogenetic conservation of certain ncRNAs in their primary sequence or secondary structure to screen for ncRNA genes using multiple sequence alignment. Homology-based approaches consist of searching for ncRNAs that are homologous to already known ncRNAs, considering the information on both sequence and structure. Finally, *ab initio* methods allow identification of non-homologous ncRNAs in new genomes, based on their intrinsic and physicochemical features.

For example, Jung *et al.* [35] tried to detect novel ncRNAs using profiles of short-read sequences based on the features of tag-contigs. *De novo* predictors have been developed also to identify ncRNAs in genomics sequences [36]. Rivas *et al.* [37] used probabilistic models of expected mutational patterns in pairwise sequence alignments to describe a computational comparative genomic screen for ncRNA genes. Comparative genome analysis was also attempted in other studies for a number of particular species [38–40].

11.3.5   ncRNA Structure Comparison

Structure comparison or alignment of ncRNAs has appeared as an effective method to identify their functions. Despite several attempted studies on RNA structure alignment, the function prediction of ncRNA molecules based on structural information is still a challenging problem in computational biology [41, 42]. The comparison of RNA secondary structures allows for RNA classification and phylogeny, as the secondary structures are often better conserved than the sequences themselves. Several computational tools have been proposed recently for RNA secondary structure pairwise comparison [43], using alignment and edit distance on labelled ordered trees (RNAforester [44], MiGaL [45], TreeMatching [46]), arc annotated sequences (Gardenia [47]), *etc.* Such a comparison helps group RNA structures into a small number of clusters, and then computes a representative folding for each cluster.

11.4   EvryRNA Bioinformatics Platform

We developed several algorithms for structure prediction, identification and analysis of ncRNAs, which are available via our bioinformatics plateform EvryRNA (`http://EvryRNA.ibisc.univ-evry.fr/`) (see Figure 11.7):

- *P-DCFold*: algorithm for predicting RNA secondary structures including pseudoknots [1].

- *SSCA*: algorithm for selecting homologous sequences for secondary structure prediction by the comparative approach [2].

- *Tfold*: algorithm for predicting RNA secondary structures combining *SSCA* and *P-DCFold* [3].

- *miRNAFold*: algorithm for searching for miRNAs in genomes [4].

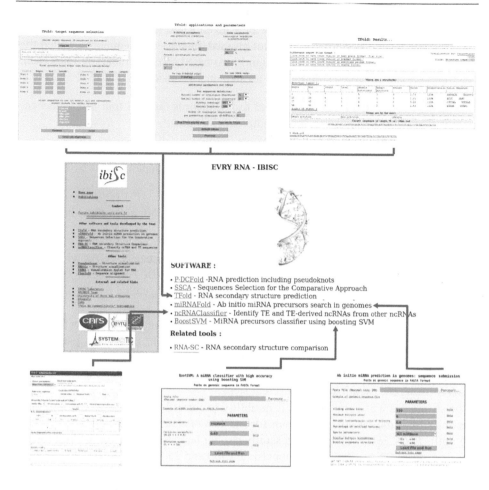

Figure 11.7: EvryRNA bioinformatics platform (http://EvryRNA.ibisc.univ-evry.fr/)

- *ncRNAclassifier*: algorithm for classifying ncRNA sequences based on their relationship with transposable element sequences [5].

- *BoostSVM*: algorithm for classifying real and pseudo miRNAs [6].

11.4.1 *P-DCFold* Algorithm

We developed an algorithm for prediction of ncRNA secondary structures using comparative modeling. The algorithm, called *DCFold* [48], is mainly based on a "divide and conquer" approach, where the stems are detected, from the more "relevant" to the less "relevant". This relevance is defined by different criteria, including the length and the nucleotide covariation. The originality of this algorithm is mainly:

- It predicts the secondary structure of a given RNA sequence, called target sequence, taking into account a set of aligned homologous sequences, called the test sequences. In other existing algorithms based on the comparative approach, one seeks a common structure for all sequences considered.

- It needs a relatively low number of test sequences (around four test sequences for a target sequence of a few hundred nucleotides).

- It searches in the target sequence for successions of pairings that form stems, rather than searching for all possible pairings, as is done in most existing prediction algorithms.

- The complexity in time of *DCFold* is $\mathcal{O}(n^2)$, while other algorithms have complexities of higher than or equal to $\mathcal{O}(n^2)$.

DCFold achieved very good prediction results on different ncRNAs. As with almost all existing RNA secondary structure prediction algorithms, *DCFold* does not take into consideration pseudoknots. We then developed an extension, called *P-DCFold*, which proposes a possibility for prediction of pseudoknots [1, 49].

P-DCFold allows a search for all pseudoknots, regardless of their types, with a complexity in time of $\mathcal{O}(n^2)$. The characteristics of *P-DCFold* is that the pseudoknot identification is carried out after predicting the pseudoknot-free RNA structure with the approach described above (*DCFold*). In other words, it looks for each of the two stems forming the pseudoknot at different steps.

The strong point of our algorithm is its ability to correctly predict a secondary structure in a short time, less than 2 seconds for an RNA of around one hundred nucleotides in length. *P-DCFold* is able to successfully predict large RNA structures like 16S and 23S ribosomal RNAs, that are composed of 1500 and 2500 nucleotides, respectively (see Section 11.2). This cannot be achieved with almost any other RNA secondary structure algorithms in the literature.

11.4.2   *SSCA* Algorithm

One major shortcoming of the comparative approach is the dependence of result quality upon considered homologous sequences and their alignment. To overcome this difficulty, some algorithms have realized the prediction of the structure along with the alignment. This approach seems efficient, but its drawback is the high complexity, which becomes greater than $\mathcal{O}(n^3)$.

We proposed an original approach that consists of selecting upstream of the prediction the homologous sequences that are best suited for searching the conserved structure. We developed the algorithm *SSCA* (Sequences Selection in Comparative Approach), which used ideas based on evolutionary models of RNA sequences with structural constraints [2, 50], in order to select the homologous sequences.

The comparative approach consists of identifying mutations from homologous sequence alignments. The sequences must have enough covariation in order to get compensatory mutations. However, the comparison becomes difficult if they are too different from each other. Hence, the choice of homologous sequences is critical, *i.e.* those that provide good prediction must be identified. While many possible combinations of homologous sequences may be used for prediction, only a few will give good structure prediction. This can be due to a poor-quality alignment in stems or high variability of certain sequences.

The problem is then to select the most relevant homologous sequences for the comparative approach. In the $SSCA$ algorithm, the selection is based on the idea that structure constraints skew the substitution matrices in stems. We defined three selection models $\mathcal{M}_{gu}$, $\mathcal{M}_{gc}$, and $\mathcal{M}_{gc+gu}$, then compared those three with the currently used model (M_{HC}) by predicting the structures of two RNA sequences. All three models improved significantly the probability of obtaining good prediction results, from around 0.01 without selection to an average of 0.32. The three models, $\mathcal{M}_{gu}$, $\mathcal{M}_{gc}$, and $\mathcal{M}_{gc+gu}$, also gave better results than the model M_{HC} since the percentage of good predictions was improved from 13.3% to 32.05%. Our models thus increased three times the chance of obtaining good predictions.

The results of the $SSCA$ algorithm were evaluated on predictions made with the *P-DCFold* algorithm. The $SSCA$ enabled us to choose good sets of homologous sequences that gave better predictions, compared to arbitrarily chosen sets of homologous sequences.

11.4.3 *Tfold* Algorithm

Tfold is an algorithm for predicting ncRNA secondary structures [3]. This algorithm efficiently combined $SSCA$ and *P-DCFold* described above. The general principle of *Tfold* is as follows: *Tfold* takes as input an RNA sequence S, called the "target sequence", from which one aims to predict the secondary structure, and a set A of aligned homologous sequences, called "test sequences". The first step is to get from A the best sequences for predicting the secondary structure of S. Then, for each combination of N sequences among those, a secondary structure is predicted for the target sequence. N represents the number of homologous sequences needed for identifying stems in the target sequence S. Finally, the last step of *Tfold* consists of selecting the stems which occur in a minimum number of predictions, in order to obtain the optimal structure.

Tfold has several characteristics: (i) it considers, besides length, conservation and covariation criteria, new stem selection criteria based on simplified and empirical stability rules; (ii) it can return several alternative structures, when there are "rival" stems (overlapping stems) with close scores; (iii) it allows errors (insertions, deletions and substitutions) in stems in the homologous sequences; (iv) it can take into account stems already known (if there are any) provided by the user, which are then considered as anchoring points, thus allowing an improvement in the prediction.

All these characteristics make *Tfold* competitive in terms of result quality and complexity in time ($\mathcal{O}(n^2)$). *Tfold* was tested on several ncRNAs (tRNA, 5S RNA, U1 RNA, srp RNA, tmRNA, RNAse P, 16S RNA and 23S RNA), with lengths varying from 76 to 2904 nucleotides. The predictions have an average sensitivity of around 80% and an average precision (PPV) of around 90%, which means that *Tfold* finds 8 pairings among 10, and when a pairing is predicted, it has 9 chances in 10 to be a good one. An important quality of *Tfold* compared to other existing tools is that *Tfold* is robust in both result quality and execution time. The results are globally homogeneous for any kind of considered RNA sequences: small or long sequences, conserved or very variable sequences, structures with or without pseudoknots, *etc.*

11.4.4   *ncRNAclassifier* Algorithm

Recent studies have shown that the entire genomes of higher eukaryotes are transcribed, whereas genes represent only a few percent of these genomes. Non-genic regions are mainly composed by ncRNAs and transposable elements (TEs), which represent a significant portion of many eukaryotic genomes. For example, about 50% of the human genome is derived from sequences of TEs [51]. TEs are present in most genomes that have been studied to date and in some cases, they represent the majority of the genome. They move or are copied from one genomic location to another [52].

Short non-autonomous TEs and some ncRNA precursors such as pre-miRNAs are characterized by a similar size and a hairpin secondary structure (see Figure 11.8).

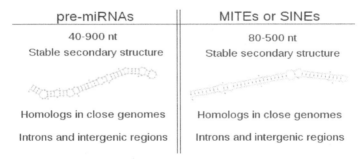

pre-miRNAs	MITEs or SINEs
40-900 nt	80-500 nt
Stable secondary structure	Stable secondary structure
Homologs in close genomes	Homologs in close genomes
Introns and intergenic regions	Introns and intergenic regions

Figure 11.8: Non-autonomous TEs and inverted repeat genes share common biological features (the structures given here correspond to CEL-LET-7 pre-miRNA in nematode and an occurrence of MADE1 TE in human genome)

Criteria to annotate miRNAs were proposed in 2003 and evolved to take into account the data produced using massively parallel sequencing technologies [53]. However, some studies showed that some miRNA genes were mis-annotated.

We considered small ncRNAs from the point of view of TEs and proposed a classification tool to sort the former according to their similarities to TE sequences [5]. We developed an automatic method called *ncRNAclassifier* for classifying ncRNA precursors into three categories based on the percentage of TEs in their sequence and their dispersion in the genome: *bona fide* pre-ncRNAs (or ncRNA genes), TE-derived ncRNAs and mis-annotated ncRNAs.

Our method is based on the observation that a pre-ncRNA with several occurrences widespread in the genome has a high probability of being either derived from a TE or being mis-annotated as being a pre-ncRNA while it is a TE. The first step of the *ncRNAclassifier* is to calculate the number of occurrences of the candidate, the number of chromosomes containing the different occurrences and the distance between the occurrences. Then, the second step calculates a consensus sequence from the ten most similar occurrences to the ncRNA sequence. Finally, the last step checks if the consensus sequence corresponds to a TE in RepBase TE database [54].

Using the *ncRNAclassifier*, we analyzed pre-miRNA sequences from several genomes: frog, human, mouse, nematode, rat, and sea squirt from the miRBase database (www.mirbase.org) [53]. We found that hundreds of human and mouse pre-miRNAs, and some frog, nematode, rat, and sea squirt pre-miRNAs can be classified as being derived from TEs. We also observed numerous examples of pre-miRNAs completely corresponding to TEs, which should therefore be re-annotated as TEs.

11.4.5 *BoostSVM* Algorithm

Methods allowing the distinguishing of miRNA from non-miRNA precursors constitute an important step in miRNA discovery. Machine learning has appeared as a promising approach for this classification problem. Nevertheless, the learning-based classification of pre-miRNAs faces the problem of imbalanced training data, as the available data are far from equal, where the number of determined non-miRNAs is much higher than that of identified pre-miRNAs. This causes a bias in the prediction result towards the more abundant samples and considerably restricts the performance of machine learning techniques [55]. However, the imbalanced data issue has not received much attention in existing studies.

We introduced *BoostSVM* [6] which uses a boosting technique with weakened support vector machine (SVM) component classifiers to deal with imbalanced training data in pre-miRNA classification. Boosting is an ensemble method in which weak component classifiers are subsequently added to an ensemble in such a way that they emphasize the samples misclassified by the existing classifiers in the ensemble. AdaBoost, the most popular boosting technique formulated by [56], was applied in our work. The core of AdaBoost procedure is to construct appropriate weak component classifiers. Each weak classifier is adaptively built with a favor to the samples misclassified by previous classifiers via weights associated to training samples. A weak classifier is the one which performs slightly better than a random guess. SVM, as a relatively strong classifier, does not seem to be suitable for the principle of boosting and may lead to performance degradation [57]. However, the use of a weakened SVM model is still efficient, as shown in [58–61].

In this work, we would like to enhance the weakness notion of component classifiers by implying a lower bound of $1/2 - \delta$, for some small δ, and an upper bound of $1/2$ on their training error. The SVM classifiers were weakened by training on subsets of the whole dataset. We selected the training subsets in such a way that the training errors on the whole dataset are bounded between $1/2 - \delta$ and $1/2$. We implemented the weighted C-SVM instance from LIBSVM [62], which allows the penalizing of the imbalance among training samples via their different weights. The boosting with such weakened SVM classifiers could improve the computation time of the training algorithm, as the training was realized on a smaller dataset and required a smaller number of support vectors.

We used different sets of positive data and negative data to perform the cross validation on mouse, human, and cross-species genomes. The positive data were taken from the miRBase database [53]. The negative data were extracted from various genomic sequences that did not contain pre-miRNAs. For feature selection, we studied in total 187 features, which gave information on structure and sequence of pre-miRNAs. To select the consistent and non-redundant features for each dataset from these 187 ones, we exploited the feature selection algorithms proposed by the WEKA workbench [63], including best first, linear forward selection, greedy stepwise, scatter search, and genetic search. The union of the features discovered by these five methods for each dataset was then used in our algorithm. It resulted in 18 features for the mouse data, 21 features for the human data, and 10 features for the cross-species data.

BoostSVM performed favorably in comparison with the state-of-the-art methods with over 90% accuracy, 0.87 F-score, 0.81 MCC, and 0.90 g-mean on mouse, human, and cross-species data. The classification results, as well as the execution time, were favorably comparable to those given by existing methods. Such a rapidity makes it a potential tool for genome-scale prediction.

11.4.6   *miRNAFold* Algorithm

miRNAFold is a fast algorithm for identifying pre-miRNAs in genomic sequences [4]. This algorithm is described below in the following section.

11.5   Search for miRNA Precursors in Genomes

11.5.1   Introduction

The identification of pre-miRNAs is difficult, expensive and time-consuming with experimental techniques. *In silico* prediction becomes a useful tool to identify potential pre-miRNAs, which can be experimentally studied further. Several methods have been developed recently for detecting pre-miRNAs, including comparative genomics, homology-based and *ab initio* approaches.

Comparative genomics and homology-based approaches cannot detect unknown families of pre-miRNAs and pre-miRNAs without known homologues. In addition, comparative approaches do not work on new genomes that have no related species sequenced. *Ab initio* methods are thus necessary to predict new pre-miRNAs in genomes.

To our knowledge, there are very few *ab initio* methods for identifying pre-miRNA structures in whole genomes. Those methods are usually specific to one or more genomes. Most existing algorithms called *ab initio* perform classification of pre-miRNAs. They take as input a candidate sequence for a pre-miRNA and calculate, often by learning methods, the probability for this sequence to be a pre-miRNA. This is the case with our algorithm BoostSVM presented above. In addition, the very few algorithms that make the search for pre-miRNAs in a genomic sequence are limited by the length of the considered sequence.

11.5.2 *miRNAFold* Method

11.5.2.1 The Approach

We developed a new *ab initio* method called *miRNAFold* for the structure prediction of pre-miRNAs in genomes [4]. Our goal was to design an algorithm that is able to find efficiently pre-miRNAs in whole genomes in a reasonable time. For this purpose, we adopted the following approach, which was motivated by different observations we made on pre-miRNAs from miRBase.

We consider a sliding window of a given size L that is sufficiently long to contain a pre-miRNA, in which we try to detect pre-miRNA hairpin structures. In a first step, we search for long exact stems that verify some criteria. These are then considered as anchors of possible hairpins. In a second step, we extend the selected stems in order to obtain the longest non-exact stems (see Section 11.2 and Figure 11.3) satisfying some constraints. Each selected non-exact stem can be considered as a good approximation of a pre-miRNA hairpin, and thus provides the hairpin position. Possible pre-miRNA hairpins are then tracked, considering the middle position of the non-exact stem as the middle position of the hairpin. Hairpins justifying some criteria are then selected. Thus, our approach consists of three main steps applied on each window subsequence:

1. Search for the longest exact stems.

2. Extend the selected stems and select the longest non-exact stems.

3. Predict the secondary structure of the hairpins corresponding to the selected non-exact stems.

11.5.2.2 The Algorithm

Given a genomic sequence of any size, for each subsequence delimited by the sliding window, a triangular base pairing matrix M is built as:

$$M(i,j) = \begin{cases} M(i-1, j-1) + 1 & \text{if M(i) and M(j) form a basepair} \\ 0 & \text{otherwise} \end{cases}$$

The algorithm then performs the following three main steps (illustrated in Figure 11.9).

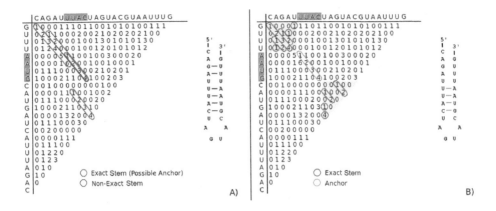

Figure 11.9: (A) Example of a matrix for determining exact and non-exact stems in a given genomic subsequence. The three longest stems are selected (surrounded by a blue circle). One of the three stems has been extended to a non-exact stem (surrounded by a red circle). (B) Search for hairpins. The anchor (surrounded by an orange circle) of the non-exact stem shown in (A) is positioned in the matrix, and then is extended to left and right sides (green areas) on different diagonals, in order to allow bulges and internal loops

Longest Exact Stem Searching   The longest stems validating a certain percentage (set by default to 70%) of criteria are identified in the matrix. The ten longest ones among them are then selected. For example, in Figure 11.9(A), the selection of three stems (surrounded by blue) is shown.

Longest Non-Exact Stem Searching   When an exact stem is selected, it is used as an "anchor" for finding a non-exact stem. The extension of the exact stem is achieved by considering only the diagonal containing the exact stem. For example, in Figure 11.9(A), a non-exact stem is indicated in red and corresponds to two exact stems. Once a non-exact stem is extended, it is selected if it justifies a certain percentage of criteria. Each selected non-exact stem is considered as a good approximation of a pre-miRNA hairpin, and gives the hairpin position. The possible pre-miRNA hairpin is then searched for in the subsequence associated to the selected non-exact stem.

Hairpin Formation   The hairpins are predicted from selected non-exact stems. The anchor of the considered non-exact stem is positioned in the matrix. It is then extended to left and right sides(see Figure 11.9(B), green areas) on different diagonals. This is for including bulges and internal loops into the hairpins. The stem-loop structures determined from the matrix must then verify a set of criteria in order to be selected.

11.5.3 Results

miRNAFold was tested on several genomic sequences. It was also compared to *CID-miRNA* [64], *miRPara* [65], and *VMir* [66], the unique algorithms in the literature that enable the search for pre-miRNAs in long genomic sequences. Our algorithm succeeded in predicting most known pre-miRNAs in genomes of different species. It gave better or at least similar sensitivity and selectivity to *CID-miRNA*, *miRPara* and *VMir*. *miRNAFold* is the only one that always gives a sensitivity of greater than 90%. Unlike the other programs, its sensitivity is homogeneous and stable regardless of the input genomic sequence.

An important advantage of our method compared to the existing ones is the execution time. The average running time of *miRNAFold* is at least 60 times faster than the fastest tested algorithm, *i.e. VMir*. On the tested sequences, *miRNAFold* took less than 30 seconds for a sequence of one million nucleotides, while *VMir* took more than 30 minutes, *miRPara* took about 20 hours, and *CID-miRNA* took more than 55 hours. This reveals that our method is currently the only one that can deal with a whole genome study in an acceptable time.

Despite its high speed, *miRNAFold* is still too long for the prediction of miRNAs on large genomes. The use of HPC techniques, including GPUs, is therefore a very important issue.

11.6 Search at Large Scale for miRNA Precursors in Genomes: Use of GPUs

Since the sequencing of the $\Phi X174$ bacteriophage in 1977 [67] and the sequencing of the first living organism, the bacteria *Haemophilus influenzae* [68], the number of sequenced genomes has always been increasing each year (see Figure 11.10). There are in total 3 173 sequenced genomes and 10 479 sequencing genome projects [69], as shown in the Genomes OnLine Database (www.genomesonline.org), which proposes a collection for all sequenced genomes and all sequencing genome projects.

Recently, next-generation sequencing (NGS) or high-throughput technologies have been introduced and widely exploited. Compared to the traditional Sanger shotgun technique, these new technologies can produce many Gigabases from a single instrument run [70]. With an enormous amount of data generated by NGS, it is essential to parallelize the bioinformatics algorithms. As the huge cost for a big computer cluster is unaffordable for most laboratories, while most personal computers contain graphics processing units, GPU becomes useful in treating those data thanks to its low-cost powerful parallelism. In 2007, NVIDIA created a compute unified device architecture (CUDA) language that allowed the use of GPUs in general-purpose computing (www.nvidia.com/object/cuda_home_new.html).

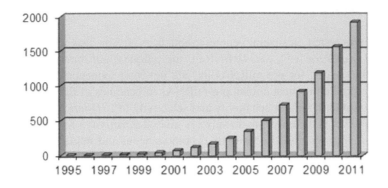

Figure 11.10: Number of completed sequenced genomes each year

11.6.1   The GPU Version of *miRNAFold* Algorithm

miRNAFold was written in the C language. To facilitate the conversion of the CPU code of *miRNAFold* into a GPU code, we chose the CUDA language, which allows using C codes inside CUDA instructions. Another reason of our choice is that we were provided with a Nvidia Quadro 5000 and a Nvidia NVS 4200M, and this language is suitable for a Nvidia GPU card.

The *miRNAFold* algorithm splits the input sequence into small subsequences and calculates a base pairing matrix for each subsequence, where pre-miRNA candidates are then investigated (see Section 11.5.2.2). Since the pre-miRNA candidates are independent of each other, their prediction operations are independent, and thus the base pairing matrices are also independent of each other. Therefore, the preliminary steps of the *miRNAFold* algorithm, *i.e.* splitting into subsequences and calculating the diagonals of the base pairing matrix, can be easily parallelized in CUDA (see Figure 11.11). We parallelized these two algorithmic levels into two hardware levels on Nvidia cards: blocks and threads.

Given an input sequence, *miRNAFold* calculates the number of subsequences required for identifying all possible pre-miRNAs in the sequence. This number is defined as the size of the sequence divided by the size of the shift of each sliding window, usually equal to 10 nucleotides. *miRNAFold* was developed to search for pre-miRNAs in whole chromosomes. With an average eukaryotic chromosome size of one hundred million nucleotides, *miRNAFold* should create 10 million subsequences. On the other hand, the subsequence size corresponds to the maximal size of searched pre-miRNAs. This maximal size varies from 50 to 300 nucleotides [53].

The number of diagonals in the matrix is two times as large as the size of the corresponding subsequence (Figure 11.11). The number of diagonals and the number of subsequences correspond to two different scales: from some thousand to some million for the number of subsequences; from 100 to 1 000 for the number of matrix diagonals. There are also two scales on GPU cards: the number of available threads and the

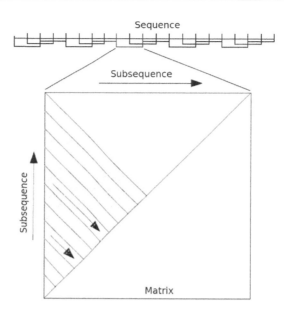

Figure 11.11: Overview of the independent steps in the *miRNAFold* algorithm. Firstly, *miRNAFold* splits the sequence into subsequences. Then for each subsequence, *miRNAFold* calculates a base pairing matrix where each diagonal is calculated independently

number of available blocks. The maximal number of available threads is 1 024, that is higher than the number of pre-miRNAs in all animals, but much lower that the average number of subsequences. The maximal number of available blocks on GPU cards is $65\,536\times65\,536\times1\,024$ that corresponds to about 4 000 billions possible blocks. This number is higher than the number of subsequences (an eukaryotic chromosome has about 10 million subsequences) and of course higher than the number of diagonals. To modify the CPU algorithm of *miRNAFold* into the GPU algorithm, a thread will correspond to the diagonal of the base pairing matrix and the block will correspond to the subsequence that also corresponds to the set of diagonals.

The three main steps of pre-miRNA candidate selection (base pairing operations and selection of stems; extension and selection of non-exact stems; creation and selection of hairpins) can be independently calculated. However, we demonstrate that the data flow between the hard disk and the GPU memory in the two first steps of the algorithm takes more time than using sequential processing.

The original function that calculates the base pairing matrix used a two-dimensional table. Except for three-dimensional textures, CUDA cannot use this data structure. We used a one-dimensional table for each structure that corresponds to each diagonal of the matrix. A thread then calculates from the base pairing diagonal the stem and the non-exact stem. The GPU card only memorizes the stems and the non-exact stems that validate a minimal percentage of parameters. Finally, to optimize the GPU instructions, we changed mostly multiple "if else" conditions into "switch" conditions.

11.6.2   Results Obtained by the GPU Version of *miRNAFold*

After checking that the GPU algorithm of *miRNAFold* gave the same output as the CPU algorithm, we compared the execution time of the two algorithms. We tested our algorithms on two computers with two GPU cards as follows:

- Computer 1; CPU Intel Xeon W3565, 3.2 GHz

- Computer 1; GPU Nvidia Quadro 5000, 352 CUDA Cores 1026 MHz

- Computer 2; CPU Intel i7 2760QM, 2.4 GHz

- Computer 2; GPU Nvidia NVS 4200M, 48 CUDA Cores 810 MHz

In Figure 11.12 the four cases of execution time on the two computers are shown. The execution time is linear to the sequence size: the larger the sequence, the longer the running time. The increase of speed between the GPU and CPU execution is constant: $1.34\times$ for the NVS 4200M GPU card and $9.12\times$ for the Quadro 5000 GPU card. For a sequence shorter than 50 000 nucleotides, the difference of execution time between the CPU and GPU algorithms is not significant because the data transfer from hard disk to the GPU memory and vice versa takes some time. For a sequence longer than 50 000 nucleotides, the difference of execution time becomes considerable. For example, the execution time of a sequence of 5 million nucleotides is 25 seconds on the CPU Intel Xeon W3565 and 3 seconds on GPU Nvidia Quadro 5000. These results show that the GPU algorithm is much faster than the CPU algorithm.

As we can see in Figure 11.12, the GPU algorithm is limited to 2-million-nucleotide sequence on the GPU Nvidia NVS 4200M. It is also limited to 120-million-nucleotide sequence on the GPU Nvidia Quadro 5000. These limitations come from the limit of available memories on GPU cards. To surmount these limitations, it would be necessary to modify the GPU algorithm by using multiple GPU cards or using asynchronous data flow, *e.g.* split the sequence into small parts and run each part alternatively.

We also used the Nvidia GeForce GTX 580 for the final test. This GPU card is actually one of the best Nvidia GPU card. The GPU card was plugged into computer 2. The speed increase between the GPU and the CPU running time is again constant: $16.75\times$ for the GeForce GTX 580 GPU card.

11.6.3   Conclusion

The results of the *miRNAFold* algorithm on GPU reveal that GPU cards could be used on such applications. The running times on GPU show that a GPU card increases 9 times the speed of the *miRNAFold* algorithm for a low cost (average price of a GPU card is 500 euros) and a small investment on CUDA programming. Our algorithm,

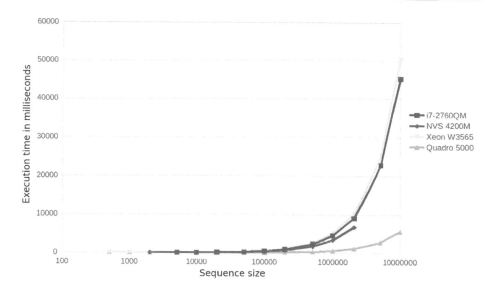

Figure 11.12: Comparison between the time execution of *miRNAFold* on CPU and GPU. The graph uses logarithmic scales. Different lines correspond to the different CPU and GPU execution time

which was already the fastest algorithm existing in the literature for the prediction of pre-miRNAs in genomes, can now be applied on large genomic sequences or entire genomes in an acceptable time for users.

The increase in speed between the Nvidia GTX 580 GPU card and the Nvidia Quadro 5000 is 2 times. These results disclose the importance of the GPU card for the running time of the algorithm. In October 2012, a new generation of the Nvidia GPU card will be available. Using this card will intensify again the speed factor of the GPU algorithm. Moreover, the modification of the hairpin creation algorithm and its selection for a better use on GPU should also enlarge the speed factor. These modifications can help realize the identification of miRNAs in whole genomes in a short time and will therefore be very useful for the scientists and users working on genome analysis and miRNAs in academic bioinformatics and biology laboratories, as well as in biotechnologies and pharmaceutical industries.

11.7 GPU Application in Bioinformatics

Bioinformatics has emerged as a primary application domain for the use of GPU computing. This is mainly due to huge amounts of available data on sequences, expressions and structures. These data will even explosively grow further as a result of advances in high-throughput technologies. Several research areas in bioinformatics have exploited GPUs, including sequence alignment, database search, phylogenetic

reconstruction, gene expression, microarray, gene regulatory networks, structure prediction, computational genomics and proteomics, next-generation sequencing and its
applications, *etc.*

11.7.1   Next Generation Sequencing

The new technologies of sequencing, called NGS (next-generation sequencing) can
produce many Gigabases of reads from a single instrument run [70]. For example,
the Illumina method can generate up to 100 million reads in a single run with a read
length of 36-100 nucleotides (see Table 11.1). However, the length of produced reads
is significantly shorter than that of the Sanger method.

	Average size of reads	Execution time (days)	Gb/run
Roche/454' GS	330	0.35	0.45
Illumina/Solexa GA_{II}	36 to 100	4	18
Life/AGP's Solid 3	50	7	30
Polonator G.007	26	5	12
Helicos BioScience	32	8	7

Table 11.1: Examples of sequencing methods and read capacity [71]

Short read alignment is an essential step for sequence assembly, *i.e.* deducing the
genomic sequence from the reads generated by sequencers. Different tools were developed for mapping reads against reference genomes, such as MAQ [72], RMAP [73],
SOAP [74], SOAP2 [75], *etc.* These methods are nevertheless really time-consuming.
For instance, 30 000 hours is required on one CPU to align the reads generated from
an Illumina run [70]. The use of parallel technologies, hence GPUs, which is specialized for parallel execution of several small tasks, becomes a crucial choice. For
instance, Ashwin *et al.* [76] proposed GPU-RMAP by making a parallel version for
RMAP; Liu *et al.* [77] developed SOAP3 by adapting SOAP2 into GPUs; Blom *et*
al. [78] developed SARUMAN, a mapping approach that returns all possible alignment positions of a read in a reference sequence using CUDA. *De novo* assembly is
usually more intensive in terms of complexity and time than mapping assembly [79].
It includes various methods, such as greedy algorithms VCAKE [80], graph oriented
approach that finds Eulerian tours [81], Minimus [82], Velvet [83], PASHA [84]. To
make use of the parallelism of GPUs, Mahmood *et al.* [85] introduced GPU-Euler,
a graph-based sequence assembly tool which also applied the CUDA programming
interface.

11.7.2   Sequence Identification

Sequence identification is an important challenge in bioinformatics study. Sequence
database searches are exploited to find the similarity between a new sequence and

known sequences in the database. The dynamic programming-based Smith-Waterman (SW) algorithm allows the detection of sequence similarities [86]. However, the cost of this approach is relatively expensive in terms of computing time and memory space. Some heuristic solutions, such as BLAST [87], have been proposed to improve the execution speed. However, aligning these sequences with the current algorithms requires very high-performance computers which are currently only available at the largest sequencing and bioinformatics centers [88].

Many versions of GPU for CUDA BLAST are now available. MUMmerGPU is one of the first GPGPU DNA alignment software that utilizes the NVIDIA CUDA [88]. The current version of MUMmerGPU (MUMmerGPU 2.0) is 13 times faster than the CPU version [88], but cannot perform inexact alignments [89]. Manavski *et al.* created a CUDA version of the exact Smith-Waterman algorithm, which is 3 times quicker than the heuristic BLAST in CPU [90]. BLAST is 40 times more rapid than the Smith-Waterman algorithm [91]. GPU-BLAST, which was created from NCBI-BLAST code, has the same options, produces the same results and is 4 times faster than the optimized NCBI-BLAST [92]. CUDASW++ and CUDASW++ 2.0, created by Lui *et al.*, are other versions of BLAST based on CUDA [93, 94].

11.7.3   RNA Structure Prediction

The high computational complexity in RNA structure prediction also demands a solution in parallelism. The Zuker algorithm is one of the most popular methods for RNA secondary structure prediction. To our knowledge, two methods based on the Zuker algorithm were created on GPU card [95, 96]. Rizk *et al.* used the same algorithm and function as Unafold [97]. They implemented in CUDA language and obtained a 17 times speed-up with the same outputs [96]. Lei *et al.* created a CPU-GPU hybrid computing system that accelerates 15.93 times more than the CPU implementation [95].

Acknowledgements

We would like to thank the Council of Essonne Region for funding this work in the context of OpenGPU project (Pôle de compétitivité System@tic, FUI 8), as well as all our collaborators.

References

[1] F. Tahi, S. Engelen, M. Régnier, "P-DCFold or How to Predict all Kinds of Pseudoknots in RNA Secondary Structures", Int. J. Artif. Intell. Tools, 14(5), 703–716, 2005.

[2] S. Engelen, F. Tahi, "Predicting RNA secondary structure by the comparative approach: how to select the homologous sequences", BMC Bioinf., 8, 464, 2007.

[3] S. Engelen, F. Tahi, "Tfold: efficient in silico prediction of non-coding RNA secondary structures", Nucleic Acids Res., 38(7), 2453–66, 2010.

[4] S. Tempel, F. Tahi, "A fast ab-initio method for predicting miRNA precursors in genomes", Nucleic Acids Res., 40(11), e80, 2012.

[5] S. Tempel, N. Pollet, F. Tahi, "ncRNAclassifier: a tool for the detection of transposable element sequences in RNA hairpins and their classification", BMC Bioinfomatics, 13:246, 2012, doi: 10.1186/1471-2105-13-246.

[6] V.D. Tran, B. Zerath, S. Tempel, F. Zehraoui, F. Tahi, "BoostSVM: A miRNA classifier with high accuracy using boosting SVM", in Proc. JOBIM, 259–266, 2012.

[7] P. Schimmel, "RNA pseudoknots that interact with components of the translation apparatus", Cell I, 58(1), 9–12, 1989.

[8] R. Mans, C. Pleij, L. Bosch, "Transfer RNA-like structures: Structure, function and evolutionary significance", Eur. J. Biochem., 201(2), 303324, 1991.

[9] R. Holley, J. Apgar, G. Everett, J. Madison, M. Marquisee, S. Merrill, J. Penswick, A. Zamir, "Structure of a ribonucleic acid", Sci., 147(3664), 1462–1465, 1965.

[10] A. Klug, J. Robertus, J. Ladner, R. Brown, J. Finch, "Conservation of the molecular structure of yeast phenylalanine transfer RNA in two crystal forms", PNAS, 71(9), 3711–15, 1974.

[11] S. Kim, J. Sussman, F. Suddath, G. Quigley, A. McPherson, A. Wang, N. Seeman, A. Rich, "The general structure of transfer RNA molecules", PNAS, 71(12), 4970–4974, 1974.

[12] F. Crick, "The origin of the genetic code", J. Mol. Biol., 38(3), 367–379, 1968.

[13] P. Nissen, J. Hansen, N. Ban, P. Moore, T. Steitz, "The structural basis of ribosome activity in peptide bond synthesis", Sci., 289(5481), 920–930, 2000.

[14] G. Dieci, M. Preti, B. Montanini, "Eukaryotic snoRNAs: A paradigm for gene expression flexibility", Genomics, 94(2), 83–88, 2009.

[15] J. Bachellerie, J. Cavaille, A. Huttenhofer, "The expanding snoRNA world", Biochim., 84(8), 775–790, 2002.

[16] R. Taft, E. Glazov, T. Lassmann, Y. Hayashizaki, P. Carninci, J. S.M., "Small RNAs derived from snoRNAs", RNA, 15(7), 1233–1240, 2009.

[17] A. Saraiya, C. Wang, "snoRNA, a novel precursor of microRNA in Giardia lamblia", PLoS Pathog., 4(11), e1000224, 2008.

[18] D. Bartel, "MicroRNAs: genomics, biogenesis, mechanism and function", Cell, 116(2), 281–197, 2004.

[19] L. He, G. Hannon, "microRNAs: small RNAs with a big role in gene regulation", Nat. Rev. Genet., 5(7), 522–531, 2004.

[20] Y. Lee, M. Kim, J. Han, K. Yeom, S. Lee, S. Baek, V. Kim, "microRNA genes are transcribed by RNA polymerase II", EMBO J., 23(20), 4051–4060, 2004.

[21] D. Mathews, J. Sabina, M. Zuker, D. Turner, "Expanded sequence dependence of thermodynamic parameters improves prediction of RNA secondary structure", J. Mol. Biol., 288, 911–940, 1999.

[22] D. Mathews, D. Turner, M. Zuker, "RNA secondary structure prediction", Curr. Protoc. Nucleic Acid Chem., 11, 1–10, 2000.

[23] B. Knudsen, J. Hein, "Pfold: RNA secondary structure prediction using stochas-

tic context-free grammars", Nucleic Acids Res., 31(13), 3423–3428, 2003.

[24] I. Hofacker, M. Fekete, C. Flamm, M. Huynen, S. Rauscher, P. Stolorz, P. Stadler, "Automatic detection of conserved RNA structure elements in complete RNA virus genomes", Nucleic Acids Res., 26, 3825–3836, 1998.

[25] R. Lyngso, C. Pedersen, "Pseudoknots in RNA secondary structures", in Proc. RECOMB, 201–209, 2000.

[26] X. Chen, S. He, D. Bu, F. Zhang, Z. Wang, R. Chen, W. Gao, "FlexStem: improving predictions of RNA secondary structures with pseudoknots by reducing the search space", Bioinf., 24(18), 1994–2001, 2008.

[27] J. Ruan, G. Stormo, W. Zhang., "An iterated loop matching approach to the prediction of RNA secondary structures with pseudoknots", Bioinf., 20, 58–66, 2004.

[28] K.T. Simons, C. Kooperberg, E. Huang, D. Baker, "Assembly of protein tertiary structures from fragments with similar local sequences using simulated annealing and Bayesian scoring functions", J. Mol. Biol., 268(1), 209–225, 1997.

[29] R. Das, D. Baker, "Automated de novo prediction of native-like RNA tertiary structures", PNAS, 104(37), 14664–14669, 2007.

[30] M. Parisien, F. Major, "The MC-Fold and MC-Sym pipeline infers RNA structure from sequence data", Nat., 452(7183), 51–55, 2008.

[31] J. Frellsen, I. Moltke, M. Thiim, K.V. Mardia, J. Ferkinghoff-Borg, T. Hamelryck, "A probabilistic model of RNA conformational space", PLoS Comput. Biol., 5(6), e1000406, 2009.

[32] S. Sharma, F. Ding, N.V. Dokholyan, "iFoldRNA: three-dimensional RNA structure prediction and folding", Bioinf., 24(17), 1951–1952, 2008.

[33] V. Reinharz, F. Major, J. Waldispühl, "Towards 3D structure prediction of large RNA molecules: an integer programming framework to insert local 3D motifs in RNA secondary structure", Bioinf., 28(12), i207–i214, 2012.

[34] A. Machado-Lima, H.A. del Portillo, A.M. Durham, "Computational methods in noncoding RNA research", J. Math. Biol., 56(1-2), 15–49, 2008.

[35] C.H. Jung, M. Hansen, I. Makunin, D. Korbie, J. Mattick, "Identification of novel non-coding RNAs using profiles of short sequence reads from next generation sequencing data", BMC Genomics, 11(1), 77, 2010.

[36] J. Gorodkin, I.L. Hofacker, E. Torarinsson, Z. Yao, J.H. Havgaard, W.L. Ruzzo, "De novo prediction of structured RNAs from genomic sequences", Trends Biotechnol., 28(1), 9–19, 2010.

[37] E. Rivas, R.J. Klein, T.A. Jones, S.R. Eddy, "Computational identification of noncoding RNAs in E. coli by comparative genomics", Curr. Biol., 11(17), 1369–1373, 2001.

[38] J.P. McCutcheon, S.R. Eddy, "Computational identification of non-coding RNAs in Saccharomyces cerevisiae by comparative genomics", Nucleic Acids Res., 31(14), 4119–4128, 2003.

[39] S. Steigele, W. Huber, C. Stocsits, P.F. Stadler, K. Nieselt, "Comparative analysis of structured RNAs in S. cerevisiae indicates a multitude of different functions", BMC Biol., 5, 25, 2007.

[40] B. Voss, J. Georg, V. Schon, S. Ude, W.R. Hess, "Biocomputational prediction of non-coding RNAs in model cyanobacteria", BMC Genomics, 10, 123, 2009.

[41] A. Huttenhofer, "RNomics: identification and function of small non-protein-coding RNAs in model organisms", Cold Spring Harb. Symp. Quant. Biol., 71, 135–140, 2006.

[42] L. Zheng, L. Qu, "Computational RNomics: structure identification and functional prediction of non-coding RNAs in silico", Sci. China Life Sci., 53(5), 548–562, 2010.

[43] J. Allali et al., "BRASERO: A Resource for Benchmarking RNA Secondary Structure Comparison Algorithms", Adv. Bioinf., 2012.

[44] M. Hochsmann, T. Toller, R. Giegerich, S. Kurtz, "Local similarity in RNA secondary structures", in Proc. IEEE Comput. Soc. Bioinf. Conf., 2, 159–168, 2003.

[45] J. Allali, M.F. Sagot, "A multiple layer model to compare RNA secondary structures", Softw. Pract. Exper., 38(8), 775–792, 2008.

[46] A. Ouangraoua, P. Ferraro, L. Tichit, S. Dulucq, "Local similarity between quotiented ordered trees", J. Discrete Algorithms, 5(1), 23–35, 2007.

[47] G. Blin, A. Denise, S. Dulucq, C. Herrbach, H. Touzet, "Alignments of RNA structures", IEEE/ACM Trans. Comput. Biol. Bioinf., 7(2), 309–322, 2010.

[48] F. Tahi, M. Gouy, M. Regnier, "Automatic RNA Secondary Structure Prediction with a Comparative Approach", Comput. Chem., 26(5), 521–530, 2002.

[49] F. Tahi, S. Engelen, M. Régnier, "A Fast Algorithm for RNA Secondary Structure Prediction Including Pseudoknots", in Proc. IEEE Symp. Bioinf. Bioeng. (BIBE), 11–17, 2003.

[50] S. Engelen, F. Tahi, "An Open Problem in RNA Secondary Structure Prediction by the Comparative Approach", in Proc. Int. Conf. Math. Eng. Tech. Med. Biol. Sci. (METMBS), 293–299, 2004.

[51] E. Lander et al., "Initial sequencing and analysis of the human genome", Nat., 409(6822), 860–921, 2001.

[52] N.L. Craig, R. Craigie, M. Gellert, A.M. Lambowitz, Mobile DNA II, ASM Press, 2nd edition, 2002.

[53] S. Griffiths-Jones, H. Saini, S. van Dongen, E. A.J., "miRBase: tools for microRNA genomics", Nucleic Acids Res., 36(Database issue), D154–D158, 2008.

[54] J. Jurka, V.V. Kapitonov, A. Pavlicek, P. Klonowski, O. Kohany, J. Walichiewicz, "Repbase Update, a database of eukaryotic repetitive elements", Cytogenetic Genome Res., 110(1-4), 462–467, 2005.

[55] G. Wu, E.Y. Chang, "Class-boundary alignment for imbalanced dataset learning", in Proc. Workshop Learn. Imbalanced Data Sets, 49–56, 2003.

[56] Y. Freund, R.E. Schapire, "A decision-theoretic generalization of on-line learning and an application to boosting", in Proc. Second Eur. Conf. Comput. Learn. Theory, 23–37, 1995.

[57] J. Wickramaratna, S. Holden, B. Buxton, "Performance Degradation in Boosting", in J. Kittler, F. Roli, (Editors), "Mult. Classifier Syst.", Lect. Notes Comput. Sci., 2096, 11–21, Springer, Berlin / Heidelberg, 2001.

[58] X. Li, L. Wang, E. Sung, "AdaBoost with SVM-based component classifiers",

Eng. Appl. Artif. Intell., 21(5), 785–795, 2008.

[59] P. Rangel, F. Lozano, E. Garcia, "Boosting of Support Vector Machines with Application to Editing", in Proc. Fourth Int. Conf. Mach. Learn. Appl., 374–382, 2005.

[60] K. Ting, L. Zhu, "Boosting Support Vector Machines Successfully", in J. Benediktsson, J. Kittler, F. Roli, (Editors), "Mult. Classifier Syst.", Lect. Notes Comput. Sci., 5519, 509–518, Springer, Berlin / Heidelberg, 2009.

[61] B. Wang, N. Japkowicz, "Boosting support vector machines for imbalanced data sets", Knowl. Info. Syst., 25(1), 1–20, 2010.

[62] C.C. Chang, C.J. Lin, "LIBSVM: A library for support vector machines", ACM Trans. Intell. Syst. Technol., 2(3), 1–27, 2011.

[63] M. Hall, E. Frank, G. Holmes, B. Pfahringer, P. Reutemann, I.H. Witten, "The WEKA data mining software: an update", SIGKDD Explor. Newsl., 11(1), 10–18, 2009.

[64] S. Tyagi, C. Vaz, V. Gupta, R. Bhatia, S. Maheshwari, A. Srinivasan, A. Bhattacharya, "CID-miRNA: A web server for prediction of novel miRNA precursors in human genome", Biochem. Biophys. Res. Comm., 372(4), 831–834, 2008.

[65] Y. Wu, B. Wei, H. Liu, T. Li, S. Rayner, "MiRPara: a SVM-based software tool for prediction of most probable microRNA coding regions in genome scale sequences", BMC Bioinf., 12, 107, 2011.

[66] A. Grundhoff, C. Sullivan, D. Ganem, "A combined computational and microarray-based approach identifies novel microRNAs encoded by human gamma-herpesviruses", RNA, 12(5), 733–750, 2006.

[67] F. Sanger, G. Air, G. Barrell, N. Brown, A. Coulson, C. Fiddes, C. Hutchison, P. Slocombe, M. Smith, "Nucleotide sequence of bacteriophage φX174 DNA", Nat., 265, 687–695, 1977.

[68] R.D. Fleischmann, M.D. Adams, O. White, R.A. Clayton, E.F. Kirkness, A.R. Kerlavage, C.J. Bult, J.F. Tomb, B.A. Dougherty, J.M. Merrick, "Whole-genome random sequencing and assembly of Haemophilus influenzae Rd", Sci., 269(5223), 496–512, 1995.

[69] K. Liolios, N. Tavernarakis, P. Hugenholtz, N. Kyrpides, "The Genomes On Line Database (GOLD) v.2: a monitor of genome projects worldwide", Nucleic Acids Res., 34(Database issue), D332–D334, 2006.

[70] P. Klus, S. Lam, D. Lyberg, M. Cheung, G. Pullan, I. McFarlane, G. Yeo, B. Lami, "BarraCUDA - a fast short read sequence aligner using graphics processing units", BMC Res. Notes, 5, 27, 2012.

[71] M. Metzker, "Sequencing technologies - the next generation", Nat. Rev. Genet., 11, 31–46, 2010.

[72] H. Li, J. Ruan, R. Durbin, "Mapping short DNA sequencing reads and calling variants using mapping quality scores", Genome Res., 18(11), 1851–1858, 2008.

[73] A. Smith, W. Chung, E. Hodges, J. Kendall, G. Hannon, J. Hicks, Z. Xuan, M. Zhang, "Updates to the RMAP short-read mapping software", Bioinf., 25(21), 2841–2842, 2009.

[74] R. Li, Y. Li, K. Kristiansen, J. Wang, "SOAP: short oligonucleotide alignment

program", Bioinf., 24(5), 713–714, 2008.

[75] R. Li, C. Yu, Y. Li, T.W. Lam, S.M. Yiu, K. Kristiansen, J. Wang, "SOAP2: an improved ultrafast tool for short read alignment", Bioinf., 25(15), 1966–1967, 2009.

[76] A.M. Aji, L. Zhang, W. chun Feng, "GPU-RMAP: Accelerating Short-Read Mapping on Graphics Processors", in Proc. IEEE Int. Conf. Comput. Sci. Engin., 168–175, 2010.

[77] C.M. Liu, T. Wong, E. Wu, R. Luo, S.M. Yiu, Y. Li, B. Wang, C. Yu, X. Chu, K. Zhao, R. Li, T.W. Lam, "SOAP3: Ultra-fast GPU-based parallel alignment tool for short reads", Bioinf., 2012.

[78] J. Blom, T. Jakobi, D. Doppmeier, S. Jaenicke, J. Kalinowski, J. Stoye, A. Goesmann, "Exact and complete short-read alignment to microbial genomes using Graphics Processing Unit programming", Bioinf., 27(10), 1351–1358, 2011.

[79] K. Paszkiewicz, D.J. Studholme, "De novo assembly of short sequence reads", Briefings Bioinf., 11(5), 457–472, 2010.

[80] W.R. Jeck, J.A. Reinhardt, D.A. Baltrus, M.T. Hickenbotham, V. Magrini, E.R. Mardis, J.L. Dangl, C.D. Jones, "Extending assembly of short DNA sequences to handle error", Bioinf., 23(21), 2942–2944, 2007.

[81] P.A. Pevzner, H. Tang, M.S. Waterman, "An Eulerian path approach to DNA fragment assembly", PNAS, 98(17), 9748–9753, 2001.

[82] D. Sommer, A. Delcher, S. Salzberg, M. Pop, "Minimus: a fast, lightweight genome assembler", BMC Bioinf., 8(1), 64, 2007.

[83] D.R. Zerbino, E. Birney, "Velvet: algorithms for de novo short read assembly using de Bruijn graphs", Genome Res., 18(5), 821–829, 2008.

[84] Y. Liu, B. Schmidt, D.L. Maskell, "Parallelized short read assembly of large genomes using de Bruijn graphs", BMC Bioinf., 12, 354, 2011.

[85] S.F. Mahmood, H. Rangwala, "GPU-Euler: Sequence Assembly Using GPGPU", in Proc. 2011 IEEE Int. Conf. High Perform. Comput. Commun., 153–160, 2011.

[86] T. Smith, M. Waterman, "Identification of Common Molecular Subsequences", J. Mol. Biol., 147(1), 195–197, 1981.

[87] S. Altschul, T. Madden, A. Schaffer, J. Zhang, Z. Zhang, W. Miller, D. Lipman, "Gapped BLAST and PSI-BLAST: a new generation of protein database search programs", Nucleic Acids Res., 25(17), 3389–3402, 1997.

[88] M. Schatz, C. Trapnell, A. Delcher, A. Varshney, "High-throughput sequence alignment using Graphics Processing Units", BMC Bioinf., 8, 474, 2007.

[89] C. Trapnell, M. Schatz, "Optimizing data intensive GPGPU computations for DNA sequence alignment", Parallel Comput., 35(8), 429–440, 2009.

[90] S. Manavski, G. Valle, "CUDA compatible GPU cards as efficient hardware accelerators for Smith-Waterman sequence alignment", BMC Bioinf., 9, S10, 2008.

[91] L. Ligowski, W. Rudnicki, "An efficient implementation of Smith-Waterman algorithm on GPU using CUDA, for massively parallel scanning of sequence databases", in Proc. 2009 IEEE Int. Symp. Parallel Distrib. Process., 1–8, 2009.

[92] P. Vouzis, N. Sahinidis, "GPU-BLAST: using graphics processors to accelerate protein sequence alignment", Bioinf., 27(2), 182–188, 2011.

[93] Y. Liu, D. Maskell, B. Schmidt, "CUDASW++: optimizing Smith-Waterman sequence database searches for CUDA-enabled graphics processing units", BMC Res. Notes, 2, 73, 2009.

[94] Y. Liu, B. Schmidt, D. Maskell, "CUDASW+2.0: enhanced Smith-Waterman protein database search on CUDA-enabled GPUs based on SIMT and virtualized SIMD abstractions", BMC Res. Notes, 3, 93, 2010.

[95] G. Lei, Y. Dou, W. Wan, F. Xia, R. Li, M. Ma, D. Zou, "CPU-GPU hybrid accelerating the Zuker algorithm for RNA secondary structure prediction applications", BMC Genomics, 13, S14, 2012.

[96] G. Rizk, D. Lavenier, "GPU Accelerated RNA Folding Algorithm", in Proc. 9th Int. Conf. Comput. Sci.: Part I, 1004–1013, 2009.

[97] N. Markham, M. Zuker, "DINAMclt web server for nucleic acid melting prediction", Nucleic Acids Res., 33(Web Server issue), W577–W581, 2005.

©Saxe-Coburg Publications, 2014.
F. Magoulès, (Editor),
Patterns for Parallel Programming on GPUs
Saxe-Coburg Publications, Stirlingshire, Scotland, 281-310.

Chapter 12

Migrating a Big-Data Grade Application to Large GPU Clusters

**D. Tello[1], V. Ducrot[1], J.-M. Batto[2], S. Monot[1]
F. Boumezbeur[2], V. Arslan[1] and T. Saidani[1]**

[1]*Alliance Services Plus, Groupe EOLEN, Malakoff, France*
[2]*Unité MICALIS, INRA, Jouy-en-Josas, France*

Abstract

This chapter relates a typical example of porting a legacy application to GPU archi-tectures. The application named MetaProf aims to provide correlation patterns in meta-genomic catalogues and to help in identifying new species. Specificity of the application lies in the high volumetry of data and calculation handled in the process *i.e.* a matrix of 8 million genes by 800 samples as input data, the complexity of the calculation being quadratic. The time required to process such data with a sequen-tial single-core implementation exceeds one month on a commodity server. In this chapter, we describe first a parallel version of the algorithm for multi-core architec-ture based on hybrid MPI-OpenMP. Then we demonstrate how emerging GPU archi-tectures turned out to be an interesting alternative to these early implementations in terms of pure performance, scalability and power efficiency. Different programming models such as Cuda, OpenCL and HMPP are evaluated and compared. Our imple-mentations were tested on both high-scale GPU clusters such as TGCC Titane and Curie and GPU-based workstations. The conclusion of our work confirmed that Cuda implementations are the fastest on Nvidia GPU, whereas their OpenCL or HMPP show slightly less performance but are valuable in terms of portability and perenity. As far as the initial use case is concerned a GPU cluster such as Curie gave us the opportunity to bring the processing time of a 3 M matrix down to a few minutes.

Keywords: GPU, Cuda, OpenCL, OpenMP, MPI, HMPP, Curie, big data.

12.1 Introduction

12.1.1 Metagenomics Data Flood

MetaProf (Metagenomic Profiles) takes place in the sequencing and metagenomic analysis pipeline Meteor, itself used within INRA during the European project MetaHIT. Studied genes are part of the MetaHIT catalog and belong to bacteriological species populating the human tractus [15]. These species are subject to intensive studies since links have been established between them and specific pathologies.

Meteor can be seen as a sequencing data processing pipeline consisting of different components such as:

- assembling software for regenerating a new genome from DNA elementary sequences (reads).

- profilers and mappers aimed to map a DNA sequence in a genome.

- statistical tools allowing one to perform either a quality survey on sequencing data or to derive new information from a whole genome.

Metaprof is of the latter type, its purpose is to compute all correlation and anti-correlation coefs of N (number of genes) vectors of P samples.

Thanks to the OpenGPU project, AS+ and INRA had the opportunity to jointly study how part of the toolchain could be ported to massively parallel architectures such as GPU. The main goal was to prepare Meteor for the exponential growth of sequencing data which outpaces performance gains that could be expected from the classic processors power increase trend (Moore's Law) as shown in Figure 12.1.

12.1.2 Selection of Candidate Codes

Among all the Meteor candidate components studied, Metaprof has turned out to be a suitable target for GPU architectures, sharing the following characteristics with other codes:

- Calculation over total time ratio near 1.

- No dependancy between input data

- Few branching inside loops

Other codes studied during the project such as [2] and [16] mappers or assemblers such as [21] were left aside because they rely too heavily on heuristics, hence branching, or all to all communications.

Metaprof behavior is defined by a few input parameters

- path of the input (genes, samples) matrix to be processed

- correlation mode: Pearson or Spearman model

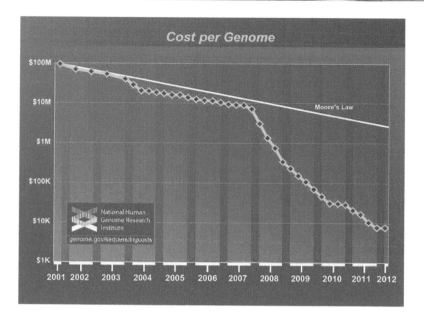

Figure 12.1: Sequencing costs trend *vs.* Moore's law

- threshold level applied to the output matrix

- (optional) number of OpenMP threads to be used per process, only relevant for OpenMP implementation

The current matrix consists of 3.3×10^6 vectors of 800 samples. Each vector stands for a gene inventoried in the MetaHIT catalog and each sample to a specific individual. Hence the whole matrix encompasses the genetic composition of the bacteria population of these 800 individuals. MetaProf computes the correlation and anti-correlation factors of each pair of genes: that is 5500 billion values for the above-mentioned matrix. Coefficients are given by Equation (12.1):

$$r_p = \frac{\sum_{i=1}^{N}(x_i - \bar{x})(y_i - \bar{y})}{\sqrt{\sum_{i=1}^{N}(x_i - \bar{x})}\sqrt{\sum_{i=1}^{N}(y_i - \bar{y})}} \tag{12.1}$$

12.2 Porting Metaprof to Multi-Core Architectures

The correlation matrix being symmetric, output data may be reduced to the upper part of the matrix. Further on, only the values above the threshold parameter if specified are kept. One file is generated for each MPI process.

The code structure is rather simple and consists of four main parts.

- Read input genes vs samples matrix

- Values normalization

- Calculation of the correlations values (double loop on the genes)

- Output of values above threshold in output files

12.2.1   First Optimizations

At first, a few optimizations were brought to the initial code (separate I/O and calculations, binary output) in order to get a ratio calculation over total time above 0.5. A
major constraint of Metaprof resides in the amount of data handled: the computation
complexity being quadratic, a factor 10 on the number of genes results in a factor 100
on the amount of data to be computed and stored. Eventually values are read and written in simple precision but all calculations are performed in double precision, in order
to limit the error propagation inherent in the floating point approximation.

12.2.2   Profiling

Computation time of the serial version being especially lengthy, benchmarks were
performed with a size-limited input matrix, namely 10,000 and 100,000 genes. Since
MetaProf complexity is quadratic it is then easy to derive from these results the computation time required for bigger matrixes such as the targeted 3.3 million genes. Further benchmarks were performed with the following parameters

- Pearson correlation mode

- Output value threshold: 0.6

- Number of samples per genes: 800

Number of genes	10,000	100,000
Read (s)	2.29	21.73
Normalization(s)	0.34	6.3
Correlation(s)	30.21	3057.5
Total time (s)	32.85	3085.67

Table 12.1: Profiling of Metaprof main subtasks

12.2.2.1   Hotspots

Profiling of the code by means of tools such as the Intel Amplifier XE confirms what
was to be expected from the previous benchmark: the main hotspot consists of the
functions computing the correlation and writing the ouput data.

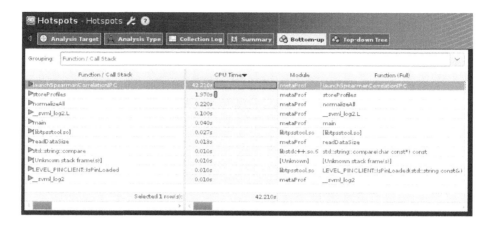

Figure 12.2: Hotspots profiling of MetaProf (serial) for 10,000 genes

Writes are performed as soon as the coefficients are computed and so dispatched during the whole processing timeline. Monitoring of the required bandwidth shows that writes don't exceed a few Mbytes per second and that the code is bound by the calculations and not by I/O disk access.

12.2.3 Porting to Multi-Core Based Clusters

Two approaches have been cumulated:

- OpenMP [14] for intra-node parallelism: for 100,000 genes, compute and write functions stand for 99 % off the total execution time. Therefore, specific care has been brought to parallelization of loops and regions of the encompassing code sections.

- MPI for inter-node parallelism: several MPI processes share the work as follows: each reads the whole input data, performs normalization and computes the assigned correlations using multiple OpenMP threads, then writes the values above threshold in a file dedicated to that process. Consequently there is one ouput file per process called, in order to get parallelized I/O if the underlying filesystem allows it.

A big advantage of the the correlations lies in the fact that they involve no communication between processes. Hence load balancing of the calculations between processes can be designed statically: each process calculates "number of genes / number of processes" correlations values. Work is dispatched according to the following pattern:

In order to ensure a correct load balancing between the MPI processes, the upper triangular matrix is scanned simultaneously according to top-to-middle and bottom-to-middle directions as shown in Figure 12.3.

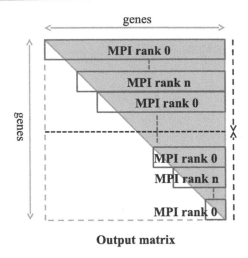

Output matrix

Figure 12.3: Metaprof initial load balancing strategy

First implementations, either full-MPI or hybrid MPI-OpenMP, based on this load balancing scheme have shown a correct scalability between nodes, but worsening when more cores were used per node. As confirmed by profiling, this decreasing efficiency resulted from the memory-bound nature of the code. Additional optimization allowed us to achieve almost optimal intra-node scalibility.

12.2.4   Single Node Benchmarks

12.2.4.1   Scalability

Table 12.2 displays times measured with the multi-core implementation of Metaprof on a single node.

Nb of genes	10,000			100,000		
Nb of threads	1	6	12	1	6	12
Read (s)	2.29	1.97	1.94	21.73	21.55	21.32
Normalization (s)	0.34	0.34	0.34	6.3	6.32	6.26
Correlation (s)	30.21	14.02	6.36	3057.5	1171.38	674.85
Total time (s)	32.85	16.34	8.65	3085.67	1199.39	702.58
Speed up	1	2.15	3.8	1	2.57	4.39
Efficiency (%)	100	33.5	31.6	100	29	36.6
Nb of operations	9.575E+10			8.23781E+12		
Mop/s	2914.8	5859.9	11069.4	2669.7	6868.3	11725.1

Table 12.2: Performance of Metaprof OpenMP for 10,000 and 100,000 genes

Figure 12.4 displays the related scalability plot.

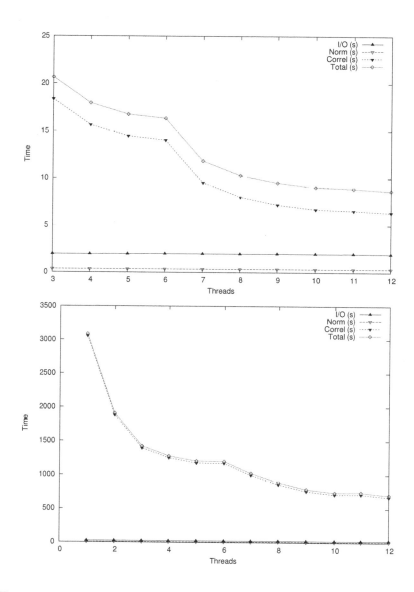

Figure 12.4: Scalability of MetaProf (OpenMP) for 10,000 and 100,000 genes

The plots above show evidence of the behaviour of the code in respect of the number of OpenMP threads. Note that OpenMP processes have been pinned in order to avoid the use of hyperthreading: each is assigned first on cores of the first socket then on cores of the second socket and so on. A saturation of the processors buses and/or caches is observed between 5 and 6 cores and then between 11 and 12 cores, resulting in almost no performance gain between these plots.

12.2.4.2   About Bindings

In order to better determine the impact of the placement of OpenMP processes on cores, we tested a different binding according to a cyclic pattern: on a two-socket node, even threads are assigned to the first socket whereas odd threads are assigned to the second. This allows us to get rid of observed memory bottlenecks when all cores are not used.

Though a saturation artifact remains when more than two threads per core are used, this new binding turned out to be more efficient when all cores of a node are only partially occupied. It is then possible to reach nearly optimal performances with 8 threads and achieve a better energy efficiency of each node when used in MPI/OpenMP configuration.

Derivation of the results for 100,000 genes let us expect 39 days total duration to handle the whole 3.3 M catalog on a single Westmere processor.

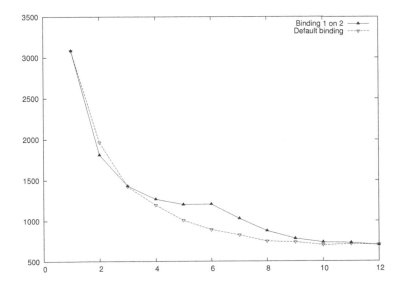

Figure 12.5: Impact of binding

12.2.4.3   Occupancy

As shown in Figure 12.6, another profiling session confirms that the MPI/OpenMP implementation is efficient in terms of core-occupancy.

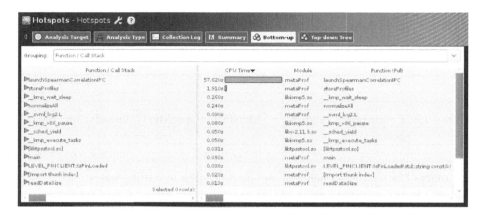

Figure 12.6: Hotspots profiling of MetaProf (OpenMP/8 threads) for 10,000 genes

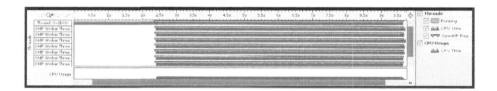

Figure 12.7: Execution timeline of MetaProf (OpenMP/8 threads) for 10,000 genes

12.2.4.4   Concurrency

A concurrency profiling also shows that the code is multi-threaded during almost all the execution time: time spent on a single thread encompasses read and normalization steps.

Please note that the profiler qualifies the number of processors used as poor, because it detects that the node is able to use 24 threads in parallel in hyperthreading mode, though hyperthreading is not advised for configurations showing a good concurrency. Hence only 12 threads were kept.

12.2.4.5   Locks and Waits

A good thread concurrency is required but not sufficient to ensure application performance: it is also relevant to check that these threads do not spend time waiting for

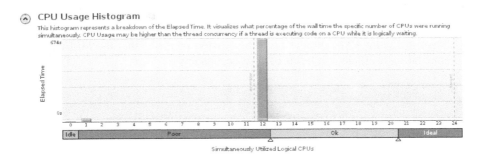

Figure 12.8: Concurrency profiling of MetaProf (OpenMP/12 threads) for 100,000 genes

each other. The screenshot below shows up time spent in waiting states: only 11 seconds are "spoilt" over the 8,000 s of CPU time that is around 0.1 % of total execution time.

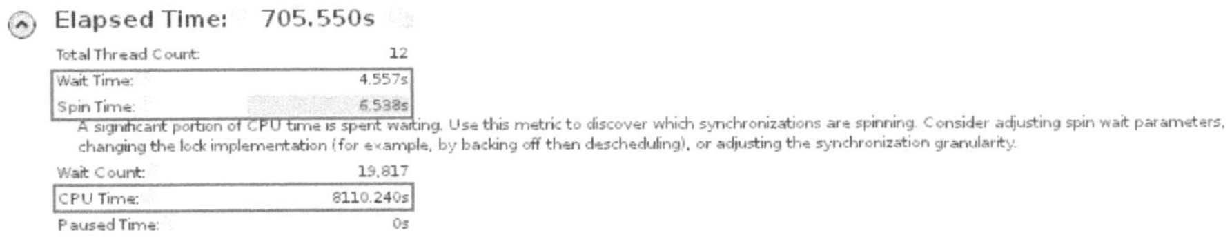

Figure 12.9: Locks and waits profiling of MetaProf (OpenMP/12 threads) for 100,000 genes

After validation of the intra-node behaviour, tests were performed to evaluate the code scalability on multi-node cluster platforms. These tests were performed on the standard partition of the Curie supercomputer hosted by the TGCC at Bruyères le Châtel and have proved that Metaprof is well suited for such architectures.

In these tests each MPI process distributes the calculations on eight OpenMP threads and each node hosts two MPI processes (one per socket). Reported measurements are those of the slowest MPI process. As expected, scalability restrained to computation time is excellent whereas global scalability is worsening as the number of MPI processes gets bigger. This results from the input-matrix loading steps which are incompressible and which get longer than the calculation steps when 16 MPI processes are used. Though this indeed impairs small test cases such as the ones above, the impact is lessened by the amount of calculation when a real-size matrix is processed. Access to the Curie Supercompter gave us the opportunity to set up a second benchmark campaign based on bigger matrixes such as 1M genes. The results displayed in Table 12.3 and Figure 12.10 once more showed good scalability (still with eight threads per process).

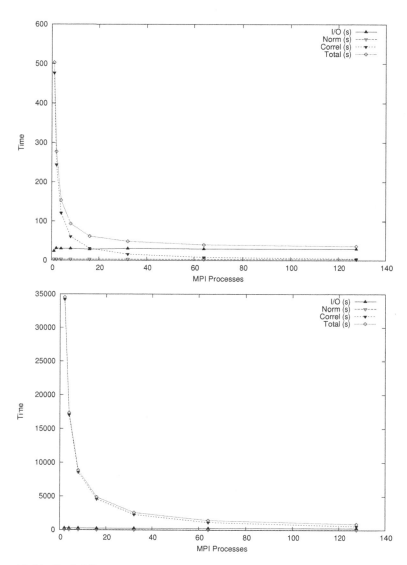

Figure 12.10: Scalability of Metaprof MPI-OpenMP for 100,000 and 1,000,000 genes

Number of genes	100,000					
Number of MPI processes	1	2	4	8	16	128
Correlation (s)	476.57	243.93	120.67	60.6	30.58	4.01
Total time (s)	502.82	277.53	153.3	93.43	61.48	36.01
Speed up	1	1.95	3.95	7.86	15.58	118.85
Efficiency (%)	100	97.7	98.7	98.3	97.4	92.8
Number of genes	1,000,000					
Number of MPI processes	1	2	4	8	16	128
Correlation (s)	66879	34232	17037	8546	4588	575
Total time (s)	n/a	34547	17340	8842	4875	890
Speed up	1	1.95	3.93	7.83	14.58	116.26
Efficiency (%)	100	97.7	98.1	97.8	91.1	90.8

Table 12.3: Performance of Metaprof MPI-OpenMP for 100,000 and 1,000,000 genes

12.3   Porting Metaprof to GPU

12.3.1   Cuda-MPI v0 Implementation (Shared Memory)

Considering the initial profiling of Metaprof, only the part dealing with the calculation of the correlation values was indeed ported to the GPU. Our first GPU implementation was based on Cuda API [13], tests performed a that time with OpenCL [7] having shown poorer performance. Later in our work, OpenCL-based implementations were built up, taking advantage of the improvements brought about by the latest OpenCL SDK.

In order to make the implementation deployable on a GPU-based cluster or workstations, that earliest MPI-Cuda implementation was derived from the MPI-OpenMP version of MetaProf. Cuda implementation itself consisted of a single kernel based on Equation (12.1) carrying out several operations successively (means, variances and correlations) some of them occupying fewer threads than others.

12.3.1.1   MPI Load Balancing

Figure 12.11 depicts the workflow of that implementation, restrained to process 0 for readability's sake. The work breakdown follows the same scheme as the MPI-OpenMP version.

12.3.1.2   Results

Thanks to the OpenGPU project we had the opportunity to test our first Cuda implementation as well as the optimized version on TGCC Titane and Curie hybrid clusters. Hereafter in Figure 12.12 the results for version v0 and an input matrix shrunk to 1 M genes are shown.

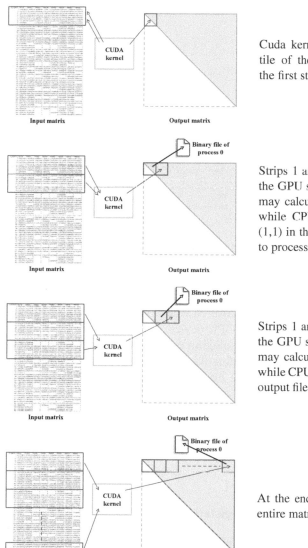

Cuda kernel calculates the first tile of the output matrix using the first strip twice.

Strips 1 and 2 are transferred to the GPU so that the cuda kernel may calculate tile (1,2). Meanwhile CPU writes the first tile (1,1) in the output file dedicated to process 0.

Strips 1 and 3 are transferred to the GPU so that the cuda kernel may calculate tile (1,3). Meanwhile CPU writes tile (1,2) in the output file dedicated to process 0

At the end of the first strip the entire matrix has been loaded

Figure 12.11: Metaprof MPI-Cuda v0 workflow

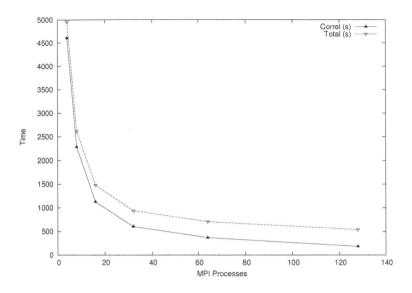

Figure 12.12: Scalability of Metaprof MPI-Cuda v0 for 1M genes (Curie)

12.3.1.3   Limitations

Nonetheless a few limitations were discovered which induced algorithmic changes in order to make it more suitable for the GPU device: for instance, direct transcription of the correlations loop in Cuda has resulted in register-greedy kernels which impair their parallel execution on the GPU. Moreover, following the usual guidelines [12], these early kernels made extensive use of the shared memory which in turn led to non-coalescent memory accesses.

That version is indeed not able to handle the full-sized 3 M genes with 2 MPI processes per node (that is one per GPU) because loading twice the input exceeds the 24 GB RAM available on each node.

12.3.2   MetaProf Cuda-MPI v1

12.3.2.1   Limiting the Number of Registers

Taking into account the drawbacks of that first version, a new implementation was set up based on a different formulation of the correlation factors:

$$r_{xy} = \frac{n \sum x_i y_i - \sum x_i \sum y_i}{\sqrt{n \sum x_i^2 - (\sum x_i)^2}\sqrt{n \sum y_i^2 - (\sum y_i)^2}} \quad (12.2)$$

This formula allows us to split the calculation into two distinct kernels and so limits the number of registers required for each and consequently favors the execution parallelism.

12.3.2.2   Getting Rid of Memory Constraints

The first Cuda version inherited a major drawback of the legacy Metaprof code: each MPI process, in charge of calculating two strips of the output matrix, had to load the entire matrix. On a multi-GPU machine where one MPI process is executed per GPU and because the amount of both input and output data is huge, memory bottlenecks may hinder a correct execution.

Therefore, a new MPI workflow has been proposed where input data is restricted to information required for calculation of a part of the ouput matrix, and are in turn tiled before being sent to the GPU, as shown in Figure 12.13. After the correlations values are computed, the related part of the output matrix is transferred from the GPU to the host.

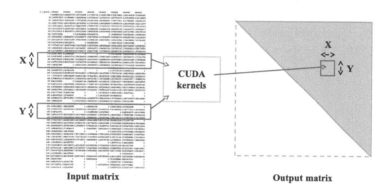

Figure 12.13: MPI workflow for MPI-Cuda implementation

The amount of work dispatched to each node is defined at runtime. MPI processes only load the strips of the input matrix required for the calculation of the correlation values located in the output matrix dedicated to them. Both zones are tiled and transferred to the GPU which calculate correlations values. This workflow ensures that at the end, each MPI process has loaded the entire input matrix at some step to feed the Cuda kernel.

12.3.2.3   Load Balancing

Figure 12.14 details how the load balancing is achieved with respect to the number of MPI processes.

12.3.2.4   Transfer/Calculation Overlapping

Task parallelism is also introduced by means of the Cuda streams features so that the CPU resource is not wasted and the GPU is continously fed during the process: CPU threads are in charge of writing the output data to the storage system.

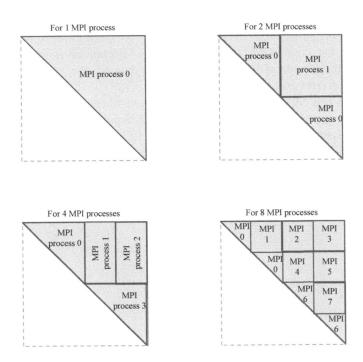

Figure 12.14: Metaprof MPI-Cuda v1 workflow

12.3.2.5   Improving Memory Access: Shared Memory vs Texture

Getting efficient memory accesses is a recurrent obstacle on the path to peak performance one would expect from GPU devices. Since all input data are only read for transposition we propose to store them in texture memory rather than shared memory, in order to maximize memory accesses. Texture memory can be considered as a read-only two-dimensional cache which offers quick transposition operations while maintaining data locality.

12.3.2.6   Results

Figure 12.15 displays results yielded by the optimized version including a more precise timing of the different steps.

That new version was able to handle the 3M genes matrix. Benchmarks with this size show that the load and normalization time are negligeable respect to the correlation calculations. As a matter of fact partial load of the data improves the ratio between calculation and total execution time. Thanks to these optimizations the application benefits from a near perfect scalability and an improved execution time: on

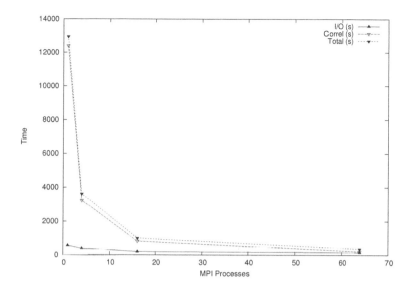

Figure 12.15: Scalability of Metaprof MPI-Cuda v1 for 1M genes

64 nodes equipped with only two GPUs, 40 minutes are required to process the 3M genes matrix.

Hereafter in Table 12.4 a comparison chart summarizing the speedups obtained with the different implementations of Metaprof.

Number of genes	100,000				
Implementation	Serial C(03 AVX)	OpenMP x8	Cuda	OpenCL	HMPP(Cuda)
Correlation (s)	2979.65	476.57	233.66	138.84	148.92
Total time (s)	3006.03	502.82	300.77	174.63	184.7
Speed up	1	6.3	12.8	21.5	20

Table 12.4: Metaprof MPI-Cuda v1 vs other CPU and GPU implementations

12.3.3 MPI-OpenCL Implementation

The OpenCL implementation keeps the same basics as the Cuda one with two notable exceptions: the overlap of GPU calculations and writes on disk and the type of GPU memory used. OpenCL does not include streams as Cuda does, however events available in OpenCL allow kernels and transfer-overlapping . Eventually the write function is activated by a callback in order to implement the asynchronism between calculations and writes as in Cuda code.

Figure 12.16 depicts the events workflow between the different kernels (in call order) with the callback.

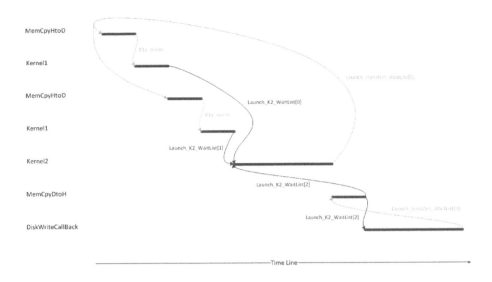

Figure 12.16: Event workflow of Metaprof MPI-OpenCL

In order to ensure data locality on the GPU and consequently efficient memory accesses, transpositions performed in texture memory in Cuda had to be re-implemented with the OpenCL SDK which does not support texture memory. An efficient solution was to carry them out on the CPU rather than on the GPU. The cost of this additional processing is balanced by the bandwidth and memory access gains when executing the kernels.

Against all odds, the Cuda version shows poorer performance than the other GPU implementations, which originates from the development platform used for the first implementations. That platform was based on a NVidia Tesla 1060 (GT200 architecture) which favored GPU texture memory over global memory. The latter benchmarks were performed on GPU based Fermi architecture and confirm that the trend is inversed: implementations based on global memory (such as HMPP) becomes more interesting than the version based on texture memory. Following that statement, a new Cuda (referred to as v2) version was developped according to the same workflow as the OpenCL version: transposition on CPU and global memory, except for a few data transfers which are performed on shared memory. Hereafter are the results of the benchmarks performed with that version.

Results with this new implementation confirm the previous assumption on the benefits to be expected from that approach on Fermi. Version v2 reveals itself more efficient than its OpenCL counterpart.

On the full matrix, version v2 now requires 54 minutes only on 64 GPUs whereas the v2 was performed in one hour 20 minutes on the same configuration.

Number of genes	100,000					
Implementation	Serial C (03 AVX)	OpenMP x8	Cuda v1	OpenCL	HMPP (Cuda)	Cuda v2
Correlation (s)	2979.65	476.57	233.66	138.84	148.92	128.1
Total time (s)	3006.03	502.82	300.77	174.63	184.7	164.61
Speed up	1	6.3	12.8	21.5	20	23.3

Table 12.5: Metaprof MPI-Cuda v2 vs other CPU and GPU implementations

12.3.4 Further Optimizations

12.3.4.1 Input File Format

A limitation common to all versions of Metaprof lies in the ASCII file format which results in harnessing read and parse operations to obtain the relevant information. Therefore, an alternative solution based on a binary file format has been proposed and implemented, which soon should be integrated into the Meteor platform. Figure 12.17 illustrates the data structure of file format.

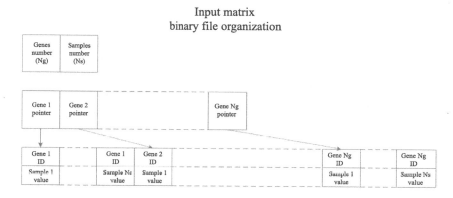

Figure 12.17: Metaprof binary file format

Table 12.6 lists the gains resulting from the use of a binary file format on Cuda version v1. Though the result presented shows an interesting factor 10, we must not lose sight of the fact that the more processes that are used, the higher the global gain will be: the time devoted to reading the input matrix is indeed almost fixed whereas the calculation itself is inverse linear with respect to the number of processes. Hence the test presented on 128 processes is especially valuable as it reflects the real use case of the application.

Moreover a new 8M genes matrix has been published by the BGI (Beijing Genomics Institute, China) at the very moment that implementation was finalized. This gave us the opportunity to test it on that new matrix. Results presented in Table 12.7 show that despite the massive increase in the calculations (as Metaprof is quadratic) the reading

Input file type	ASCII	Binary
Read (s)	148.6	12.73
Read speedup	1	11.7
Total time (s)	353.22	224.14
Global speed up	1	1.6

Table 12.6: MetaProf Cuda-MPI (v1) 1,000,000 genes × 800 samples, 128 MPI processes on Curie

time is now negligible with respect to the global execution time which still remains acceptable, at around 3 hours 30 minutes.

Read (s)	30.39
Normalisation (s)	281.76
Correlation (s)	12477.17
Total time (s)	12785.82 (*i.e.* 3h 33min)

Table 12.7: MetaProf Cuda-MPI (v1) 8,096,991 genes × 761 samples on Curie

12.3.4.2 Further Cuda Optimisations

Version Cuda-MPI v2 is further optimized in a new Cuda-MPI 2.5 version by factorizing

- Part of the calculations,

- Memory copies: to that end rolling buffers used to send data to the GPU were modified to send data in larger chunks at a lower frequency.

Table 12.8 which details the comparison between the different Cuda-MPI implementations shows a 5% gain with the latest version. Profiling of that version with Cuda Nsight on a Tesla 2075 GPU allows us to extract a few interesting values: the most resource-greedy kernel climbs up to 738 Gops. A quarter of these operations are performed in double precision and the other three querters in simple precision (index calculations notably). According to that ratio and to the theoretical peak throughput of a Tesla 2075 (1030 GFlops in simple precision 515 GFlops double-precision), the maximum throughput that could be obtained would be 901 Gops. As a conclusion our implementation reaches 80 % of the peak.

Note that this is allowed by the compute-bound behaviour of the v2 and v2.5 versions unlike version v1 which is memory bound.

Number of nodes	32		
Number of MPI processes	64		
Implementation version	Cuda v1	Cuda v2	Cuda v2.5
Correlation (s)	4336.21	1926.73	1831.65
Speed up	1	2.25	2.37

Table 12.8: MetaProf Cuda-MPI 3,300,000 genes × 800 samples, 128 MPI processes on Curie

12.3.4.3 MPI Processes Interleaving

Additional tests were conducted to test distribution patterns based on more than one MPI process per GPU in order to maximize the GPU occupancy.

Number of nodes	32	32	64
Number of MPI processes	64 (1 per GPU)	256 (4 par GPU)	256 (2 par GPU)
Correlation (s)	1831.65	1161,05	641,62
Speed up	1	1.58	2.85

Table 12.9: MetaProf Cuda-MPI (v2.5) 3,300,000 genes × 800 samples, 128 MPI processes on Curie

Table 12.9 shows that increasing the number of MPI processes per GPU allows us to increase the speed of the execution further. For the same number of processes, doubling the number of nodes remains the most efficient solution but using more than one process per node is recommended with Metaprof, *e.g.* going from 32 to 64 nodes with one process per node yields a speedup around 2, if two processes are used per GPU the speedup is near 3.

12.3.5 Parallelization Assistance Tools

12.3.5.1 Approach

As shown in the previous sections, the GPU implementations of MetaProf allow us to divide the computation time by at least 20 compared to a sequential version and by more than 3 compared to an 8-cores parallel version. In order to cover all the different GPU programming models, an HMPP [3] implementation has been made with CAPS' help. A first try has been given starting from the CPU sequential implementation. The speedups obtained were below what was expected . The OpenCL version, whose architecture and data model have been reorganized specifically for a GPU, has been converted to C code. The HMPP implementation shown below has been built over this code.

12.3.5.2   Results

With an initial code adapted to GPU architecture, the HMPP performance is worthy of interest and even equivalent to what is obtained with the other GPU implementations. Indeed, as shown in the benchmarks, the HMPP implementation reaches 84% of the performance of the "manual" Cuda code. With the new MetaProf CPU code stemming from the OpenCL version, the performance is equivalent to the initial C code but behaves better with OpenMP.

Implementation	Serial C (O3 AVX)	OpenMP x8threads	Cuda	OpenCL	HMPP (Cuda)
Correlation (s)	2979.65	476.57	128.1	138.84	148.92
Total time (s)	3006.03	502.82	164.61	174.63	184.7
Speed up	1	6.3	23.3	21.5	20

Table 12.10: Performance of Metaprof HMPP implementation for 100,000 genes

Notice that the tests were carried out with HMPP 3.1. This version automatically converts the computation loops into Cuda GPU kernels (OpenCL backend is not available in the latest HMPP versions). The performances of different CPU and GPU implementations have been measured on a single Curie TGCC/CCRT supercomputer node.

12.3.5.3   Conclusion

The HMPP automatic parallelization tool is thus interesting but reveals all its potential with reshaped codes. In order to get maximal performances, it is indeed essential to submit convenient data organization to the GPU, and to set up the computation loops in order to maximize GPU occupancy of generated kernels. Our vision of the product has therefore evolved during the project. We were initially thinking about using HMPP to predict what performance gain could be obtained when porting a code on GPU and then being able to commit on speedups. From our experience, using HMPP on legacy codes without reshape, does not allow significant speedups. On the other hand, the tool has the advantage of dissociating the code from the target programming model (Cuda, OpenCL) and then keeping an easy maintainability of the code even for a developer who is not familiar with GPU development.

12.3.6   Summary

Table 12.11 sums up the different parallelism options.

12.3.7   Power Efficiency

Through a partnership with Bull, AS+ had the opportunity to compare both CPU and GPU implementations in terms of energy consumption. Two blades have been pro-

Version	Cuda v0	Cuda v1	OpenCL	HMPP
Number of kernels	1	2	2	2
Memory used	Global + Shared	Global + Texture	Global	Global
Parallelism CPU/GPU	Streams	Streams	Events + Callback	n/a
Amount of data loaded per process	Total	Partial	Partial	Partial

Table 12.11: Speedup comparison for different GPU implementations

vided:

- Bull B500 with 2 × Sandy Bridge E5-2680

- Bull B505 with 2 × Nehalem E5649 and 2 × Tesla M2090 (ECC on)

12.3.7.1 OpenMP Implementation Power Efficiency

To start with, a few OpenMP runs were done on B500 displayed in Table 12.12:

Total number of OpenMP threads	1	2	4	8	16	32
Number of MPI processes	1	1	1	1	1	1
Correlation time (s)	4216	2122.52	1138.73	602.69	363.31	230.38
Total time (s)	4234	2139.73	1155.97	619.92	380.57	247.62
Consumption of the blade (J)	549009	362526	217019	149126	122475	86961

Table 12.12: Power consumption of Metaprof OpenMP implementation for 100,000 genes

Note that Hyperthreading has been used to reach 32 threads on this specific run. In the most favourable case, 86961 J or 24Wh were necessary to process a 100,000 genes matrix. In these conditions, the execution requires $8.23781E+12$ operations, which represents an average throughput of 33.3 Gops on 32 threads and an energy ratio of 383 Kops/J or 1.39 Gops/Wh.

12.3.7.2 MPI+OpenMP Implementation Power Efficiency

A second benchmark session was launched to check how the application behaves during MPI+OpenMP runs, results of which are displayed in Table 12.13.

OpenMP processes were equitably spread on both MPI processes. With MetaProf, mixing both programming models is less efficient than OpenMP alone on a low number of cores. On 8 cores, 149126 J (41 Wh) is needed with OpenMP compared to 163840 J (45.5 Wh) with MPI+OpenMP.

Total number of OpenMP threads	4	8	16
Number of MPI processes	2	2	2
Correlation time (s)	1341.22	812.01	652.28
Total time (s)	1359.04	829.88	670.78
Consumption of the blade (J)	235735	163840	165082

Table 12.13: Power consumption of Metaprof OpenMP implementation for 100,000 genes

12.3.7.3 GPU Implementation Power Efficiency

Some tests have also been done on Bull's Fermi GPU blade:

Number of MPI processes	1	2
Correlation time (s)	231	117.79
Total time (s)	302	173.16
Consumption of the blade (J)	57381	34565

Table 12.14: Power consumption of Metaprof Cuda implementation for 100,000 genes

Notice that in the GPU implementation, only one CPU core is used per MPI process. Using a GPU let us divide the energy consumption by 9,5 compared to a sequential CPU implementation. When both GPUs are requested on the Bull B505 and all the CPU cores on the B500, the Cuda implementation remains twice as fast on 100,000 genes. In terms of energy consumption, the CPU version needs 2.5 times more electrical resources.

12.3.7.4 Conclusion

Despite the general consumption increase due to the addition of two GPUs, the performance gain of the Cuda implementation and the lower request for CPU power allows us to drastically reduce the power needed to process the matrix. The energy efficiency of the hybrid setup could be even higher with two extra GPUs in order to split the computation on four MPI processes.

12.3.8 What about Workstations

Early in 2012, contacts with HP led to numerous tests of a Cuda v1 implementation on two server setups: HP SL390 2U (4 nodes) and 4U (1 node). Therefore, the influence of different parameters were quantified. Here is a set of the aspects reviewed:

12.3.8.1   Scalability

The benchmarks highlight that the execution time remains the same between a one-node (setup 1) and a multi-node (setup 2) MPI distribution.

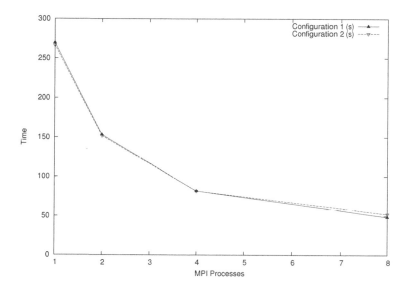

Figure 12.18: Scalability of Metaprof MPI-Cuda v1 for 100,000 genes × 800 samples

Gathering 8 GPU on the HP GPU setup 2 involves a reduction of the PCI-Express bandwidth for each. 8 lanes feed the GPU instead of 16. Despite this side effect, the performances do not decrease compared to a more "regular" setup provided with three 16-lane GPUs. Obviously, MetaProf does not saturate the PCI-Express bandwidth.

12.3.8.2   GPU Occupancy Rate

The screenshot below is from the HP Cluster Management Utility [5]. This software allows one to monitor real-time CPU, RAM and GPU occupancy of the 4 nodes (HP GPU computing setup 1) on which the code has been executed.

During the calculation phase, all 3 GPU sets of each node are under a 100% load.

Note that to ensure that every time frame on the GPU is filled, 32 MPI processes were launched on the 12 GPU setup, which means eight processes per node.

12.3.8.3   System Global Monitoring

Below in Figures 12.20 and 12.21, is an overview of the curves CMU provides while monitoring the system. Each line matches with the activity of a node of HP GPU computing setup 1. The following curves represent the reading step of the input matrix. The Lustre file system (right curve) is under load at the beginning, then as soon as the

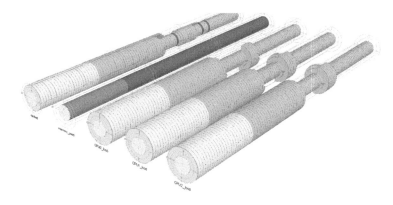

Figure 12.19: Real time occupancy from HP CMU

application has some data at its disposal, the CPUs (left curves) start the ASCII data acquisition step.

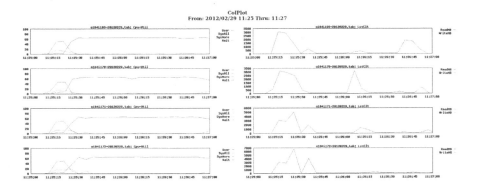

Figure 12.20: Metaprof I/O reading phase

The next curves relate the coefficients calculation. The CPU load decreases while the GPU load increases. During this step, coefficients higher than the threshold are written on the Lustre as soon as they are computed by the GPUs.

12.3.8.4   Out of Memory Issue

A memory overflow has been detected when running MetaProf on the HP GPU computing 2 setup. Indeed, the actual version of MetaProf uses considerable memory resources while reading input data. Consequently, before launching a high number of MPI processes on a node, it is recommended to check that enough memory is avail-

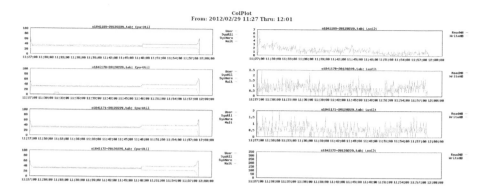

Figure 12.21: Metaprof GPU vs CPU load

able. Formula 12.3 gives an approximation of the amount of memory required:

$$mem_{required} = \frac{8.N_{genes}.N_{samples}.N_{MPIprocesses}}{N_{nodes}.\sqrt{N_{MPIprocesses}}} \qquad (12.3)$$

As an example, to process a 3,300,000 genes matrix with 8 MPI processes on a single node, around 60 GB of RAM are required.

Note that some optimizations such as rolling buffers or shared memory segments could be implemented in order to decrease down to 10 GB (3.3M genes and 800 samples on an 8 GPU node) the amount of memory needed.

12.3.8.5 Influence of Other Parameters

Benchmarks performed on HP workstations gave us the opportunity to test the influence of various parameters such as compiler, power capping and the disk system illustrated in Figure 12.22.

Impact of Disk System In order to evaluate the impact of the I/O system, some tests were done with a Raid0 system built with 4 SAS disks. The application needs a high throughput when loading the input matrix. Then, output data are written during execution at an average rate of 2 MB/s. The results exposed next show little difference between Lustre and local disks with MetaProf. To process 1,000,000 genes with 32 MPI processes, the Lustre is only 3% faster than the local Raid system.

The initialisation step during which the input matrix is read takes two minutes on Lustre and three minutes on the Raid0 system. The tested Lustre file system can reach 7 GB/s. Data are loaded within 15 seconds and are then stored in cache and processes by the code. The SAS system provides an average of 140 MB/s in a two minute period. Data are processed as soon as they are retrieved by the I/O system, partially hiding the higher reading time. The I/O system is not dominant in order to maintain a high level of performance with this code.

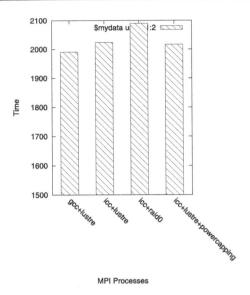

Figure 12.22: Influence of disk system, power-capping and compiler on performance

GPU Power Capping Impact Global performance remains the same when power capping functionality is enabled on GPUs.

Compiler Impact The compiler choice (GCC / ICC) has very little impact on performances. Nothing is surprising here as most of the computation is done by the GPUs, The compilers do not seem to distinguish between each other on optimizations applied to the CPU part though.

12.4 Conclusion

A state-of-the-art parallelisation solution on multi-nodes/multi-cores architectures, based on MPI and OpenMP gave us the opportunity to bring down the execution time of MetaProf *e.g.* with a speedup of 12.4 on a 16 cores Sandybridge node. Porting the application to GPU architectures has futher lowered the execution time with speedups of 23 with respect to the optimized serial CPU version.

The multi-GPU version of the application has even led to changes in the user experience, since the reduced execution time allowed us to ensure a minimal interactivity to the user: several simulations can now be performed in one day vs several weeks for a single one on the sequential version. For example when cumulating all improvements brought to the code (most efficient Cuda implementation + input binary file) only 13 minutes are required to process a 3.3 M genes matrix on 64 bi-GPU nodes. To achieve this result, several GPU API and various implementations have been tested. Our conclusion is that the manual Cuda port still remains the most efficient solution.

The OpenCL API also yields good results but suffers from a few missing features with respect to the Cuda API (memory types, events). Automatization tools such as HMPP may also give good results assuming that the initial CPU code has been re-designed according to the GPU constraints and that the data structure are adapted. The main interest then lies in the decoupling between the C code and the GPU implementation. Changes brought to the memory print (partial load of the input matrix) with the GPU version ensure a better durability for Metaprof, allowing it to keep the pace of the increasing data size (more 10 M genes in a near future) Right now, the amount of data produced by Metaprof lies between hundreds of GB and tens of GB. Hence, the next step would be to parallelize and optimize the post-processing applied within Meteor after Metaprof, notably the clustering algorithms used at this stage possibly based on works such as [4] and [9].

References

[1] A.K.C. Ahamed, F. Magoules, "Fast Sparse Matrix-Vector Multiplication on Graphics Processing Unit for Finite Element Analysis", in IEEE 14th International Conference on High Performance Computing and Communication 2012, IEEE 9th International Conference on Embedded Software and Systems (HPCC-ICESS), 1307–1314, June 2012.

[2] S.F. Altschul, W. Gish, W. Miller, E.W. Myers, D.J. Lipman, "Basic local alignment search tool", Journal of molecular biology, Oct. 1990. doi:10.1006/jmbi.1990.9999

[3] CAPS Entreprise, "HMPP Workbench 3.0", HMPP Directives Reference Manual, 2.4 edition, January 2012.

[4] V. Garcia, E. Debreuve, M. Barlaud, "Fast k nearest neighbor search using GPU", in 2008 IEEE Computer Society Conference on Computer Vision and Pattern Recognition Workshops, IEEE, 2008. doi:10.1109/CVPRW.2008.4563100

[5] Hewlett-Packard Development Company, "HP Cluster Management Utility V4.2, User Guide", March 2010.

[6] K. Karimi, N. Dickson, F. Hamze, "A performance comparison of CUDA and OpenCL", arXiv preprint arXiv:1005.2581, 2010.

[7] Khronos OpenCL Working Group, "The OpenCL Specification", KHRONOS Group, 1.2 edition, November 2011. www.khronos.org/registry/cl/specs/opencl-1.1.pdf

[8] D.B. Kirk, W.m.W. Hwu, "Programming Massively Parallel Processors: A Hands-on Approach", Morgan Kaufmann Publishers Inc., San Francisco, CA, USA, 1st edition, 2010.

[9] Y. Liu, B. Schmidt, D. Maskell, "DecGPU: distributed error correction on massively parallel graphics processing units using CUDA and MPI", BMC Bioinformatics, 12(1), 2011. doi:10.1186/1471-2105-12-85

[10] S. Manavski, G. Valle, "CUDA compatible GPU cards as efficient hardware accelerators for Smith-Waterman sequence alignment", BMC bioinformatics, 9(Suppl 2), S10, 2008.

[11] J. Marzat, Y. Dumortier, A. Ducrot, *et al.*, "Real-time dense and accurate parallel optical flow using CUDA", in 7th International Conference WSCG, 2009.

[12] NVIDIA Corporation, "CUDA C Best Practices Guide", 4.0 edition, 2011. http://developer.download.nvidia.com/compute/DevZone/docs/html/C/doc/CUDA_C_Best_Practices_Guide.pdf

[13] NVIDIA Corporation, "CUDA Programming Guide", 4.1 edition, 2012. http://developer.download.nvidia.com/compute/DevZone/docs/html/C/doc/CUDA_C_Programming_Guide.pdf

[14] OpenMP Architecture Review Board, "OpenMP API, Version 3.1", July 2011. http://www.openmp.org/mp-documents/OpenMP3.1.pdf

[15] J. Qin, R. Li, J. Raes, M. Arumugam, K.S. Burgdorf, C. Manichanh, T. Nielsen, N. Pons, F. Levenez, T. Yamada, D.R. Mende, J. Li, J. Xu, S. Li, D. Li, J. Cao, B. Wang, H. Liang, H. Zheng, Y. Xie, J. Tap, P. Lepage, M. Bertalan, J.M. Batto, T. Hansen, D. Le Paslier, A. Linneberg, H.B. Nielsen, E. Pelletier, P. Renault, T. Sicheritz-Ponten, K. Turner, H. Zhu, C. Yu, S. Li, M. Jian, Y. Zhou, Y. Li, X. Zhang, S. Li, N. Qin, H. Yang, J. Wang, S. Brunak, J. Dore, F. Guarner, K. Kristiansen, O. Pedersen, J. Parkhill, J. Weissenbach, P. Bork, S.D. Ehrlich, J. Wang, "A human gut microbial gene catalogue established by metagenomic sequencing", Nature, 464, 59-65, 2010. doi:10.1038/nature08821

[16] S.M. Rumble, P. Lacroute, A.V. Dalca, M. Fiume, A. Sidow, M. Brudno, "SHRiMP: Accurate Mapping of Short Color-space Reads", PLoS Comput Biol, 5(5), e1000386, 2009. doi:10.1371/journal.pcbi.1000386

[17] S. Ryoo, C. Rodrigues, S. Baghsorkhi, S. Stone, D. Kirk, W. Hwu, "Optimization principles and application performance evaluation of a multithreaded GPU using CUDA", in Proceedings of the 13th ACM SIGPLAN Symposium on Principles and practice of parallel programming, 73–82, ACM, 2008.

[18] J. Sanders, E. Kandrot, "CUDA by example: an introduction to general-purpose GPU programming", Addison-Wesley Professional, 2010.

[19] J. Stratton, S. Stone, W. Hwu, "MCUDA: An efficient implementation of CUDA kernels for multi-core CPUs", Languages and Compilers for Parallel Computing, 16–30, 2008.

[20] V. Volkov, "Better performance at lower occupancy", in GPU Technology Conference 2010, GTC '10, 2010.

[21] D.R. Zerbino, E. Birney, "Velvet: Algorithms for de novo short read assembly using de Bruijn graphs", Genome Research, May 2008.

©Saxe-Coburg Publications, 2014.
F. Magoulès, (Editor),
Patterns for Parallel Programming on GPUs
Saxe-Coburg Publications, Stirlingshire, Scotland, 311-326.

Chapter 13

Testing Random Numbers: When OpenCL is the Right Choice

J.M. Chauvet and E. Mahé

MassiveRand Corporation, Boulogne, France

Abstract

Testing random numbers relies on a heavy battery of statistical tests that can take hours of computing for small samplings of numbers. Our main goal is to demystify this slow checking process by showing the parallel nature of two representative tests and how to port them on OpenCL capable architectures. Concepts will be illustrated with two examples of test codes translated from C to OpenCL. Portability across the latest version of commercial processors exposing radically different model of parallelism is achieved. Benchmarks will be provided to compare CPU and GPU, the influence of the number of threads in blocks and CUDA vs OpenCL performances. This work, taken in the context of testing the quality of the true random number generator (TRNG) invented and patented by MassiveRand, is related to an OpenCL port of the complete NIST test suite on GPU and CPU and provides a totally new and safe way of dealing with RNG.

Keywords: hardware accelerators, portability, parallel programming, random number test.

13.1 Introduction

Computerized random numbers are based on a paradoxical fact: they are not random at all but rely on algebraic formulas (congruence, quadratic residues, *etc.*) which make them totally predictable. If this defect is not an issue for scientific applications like simulation, for cryptography, it is as a hell. Many security attacks are driven through the statistical bias or too short periods of the pseudo random number generator

(PRNG). The famous Mersenne-Twister, which seems to have all the required qualities for a Monte-Carlo simulation, is highly discouraged for public key infrastructure or password generation.

In order to solve this issue, the National Institute of Standards and Technology (NIST) publishes a regularly updated statistical test suite to help random number generator (RNG) designers "in detecting deviations of a binary sequence from randomness". This suite is today a mandatory step that every RNG has to go through to be used in any cryptographic application.

However, the biggest problem in applying the NIST test suite is time. A 128 Mbits file can take up to five hours to run all tests on a modern computer which prevents any real-time proof being achieved in a reasonable time.

Basic modern processors (CPU) have at least two cores and can execute four threads efficiently, an amount of calculation power that can be doubled for high end processors which include larger cache and higher bandwidth memory. In order to use this computing capability, programs have to be parallelized, a tricky process for programs which were not developed to run on a many-core architecture. This issue can be even worse if targeting the fine grain of graphical processing unit (GPU) parallelism is the goal. Intel, Nvidia or ATI have achieved great work in setting up standards (OpenCL) and framework (CUDA) that help the developers to build, debug and tune their codes on such new powerful processors. Testing random numbers is an embarrassingly parallel process because each test can be executed independently on different number sequences. Some of them are easy to parallelize while others rely on more complex algorithms that require deeper analysis. For this work, we decided to present only two tests (MonoBit and Poker) to illustrate the power of parallelism and how to conduct best choices between different approaches: CPU vs GPU, optimized sizes of thread grids and CUDA versus OpenCL.

This work is divided into two parts: the first one shows how to transform a sequential algorithm to a parallel program; the second one presents benchmarks comparing speed up improvements by using different hardware and how to optimize without breaking portability.

13.2   Related Works

An initial battery of statistical tests for uniform RNGs was offered by the 1969 first edition of Knuth [1]. Marsaglia [2] published in 1968 an article about random number generator defects for Monte Carlo simulations based on multiplicative congruential. He then developed a set of statistical tests for measuring the quality of a random number generator famously known as "Diehard Tests" [3] setting up much research in this domain. Among different works, two of them remain the official references: the NIST test suite [4] published in 1997 and regularly updated (August 11, 2010 for the latest version) and TestU01 introduced by L'Ecuyer [5] in 2000. Using parallel architectures for this purpose is a relatively new trend involving FPGA [6] or GPU [7] and finally CUDA [8]. Benchmarking CUDA vs OpenCL is described in [9] which relies on standard algorithms (matrix multiplication) rather than on real cases.

13.3   Porting MonoBit and Poker Tests to OpenCL and CUDA

Two priorities guided the choice of the MonoBit and Poker tests:

- No other test can be conducted if any one of the two tests fails

- They are simple to understand and can efficiently help to figure out parallelism

Random numbers tested for this work are generated by the MassiveRand TRNG (MR-TRNG). Testing a TRNG is more crucial than testing a PRNG because of the non-deterministic dimension of this kind of generator. Statistical qualities of such generators have to be measured to prevent any bias forged by some physical deviations (temperature, noise source, acquisition). The German standard organization, since 2001, classified as mandatory this type of statistical tests for a TRNG to be certified (AIS 31 recommendations).

Highlighting potential benefits by using the computing power of multi-core processors or massively parallel GPUs was the first priority of this work. We focused on portability without optimizing one version for a particular platform to enabling fair and reliable benchmarks. OpenCL compilers are included in specific drivers for each hardware and provided by Intel (CPU and IGP), AMD / ATI (GPU) and Nvidia (GPU). For both CUDA and OpenCL executions, we did not use any specific compiler options.

The random numbers tested in this work are generated directly on each device by invoking the MR-TRNG kernel. In this way we avoid the painful memory transfer process between devices.

We do not provide any description of CUDA or OpenCL computing models. Many references can be found in [10–12].

13.3.1   The MonoBit Test

The focus of the test is the proportion of zeroes and ones for the entire sequence. The purpose of this test is to determine whether the number of ones and zeros in a sequence are approximately the same as would be expected for a truly random sequence. The test assesses the closeness of the fraction of ones to $1/2$, that is, the number of ones and zeroes in a sequence should be about the same. All subsequent tests depend on the passing of this test.

13.3.1.1   Choice of the Right Data Format

The NIST Test Suite works on a sequence of [0,1] packed into an unsigned char array. This format is far from being optimal on a 32 bits GPU. Instead of expanding the unsigned int stream delivered by the MassiveRand TRNG into a 32 * n bit array, we choose to write the _popc (population count, number of one bits) function. The _popc (_popcount or _popcnt) binary instruction is not available in all OpenCL compilers and will be not used in order to achieve fair benchmarks for all tested architectures.

13.3.1.2 Working with Fixed Size

As recommended in the FIPS-140 specifications [13], we decided to implement the Monobit calculation for a set of 20000 bits, removing the erfc() function for this test. This choice does not affect the quality of the test and eases considerably the implementation while improving the speed of calculation. From [13], the C implementation to parallelize is described in Algorithm 13.1.

Algorithm 13.1: Serial version of MonoBit code

Input: $random$: array of random numbers to test, $size$: size of $random$
Output: $errors$: number of errors
begin
    $block = size\ /\ 625$
    $errors = 0$
    $monobit = 0$
    $MINONES = 9725$
    $MAXONES = 10275$
    for $i = 0$ **to** $block - 1$ **do**
        for $j = 0$ **to** 4 **do**
            $val = random[(625 * i) + j]$
            $monobit$ += popc(val)
        end
        $errors$ += $(MonoBit <= MINONES\ ||\ MonoBit >=$
        $MAXONES)$
    end
    return $errors$
end

MINONES and MAXONES constants define the minimum and the maximum value ones (1s) that a set of 20000 bits cannot exceed. 625 is the number of 32 bits unsigned integers to test to reach the 20000 bits (625 * 32 = 20000). The MonoBit function computes the sum of failures stored in errors of an array of size random numbers. This code is used to benchmark the serial version of the Monobit Test.

13.3.1.3 OpenCL Implementation

To implement the Monobit test in OpenCL, we followed these requirements:

Algorithm 13.2: OpenCL implementation of MonoBit test

Input: *random*: array of random numbers to test
Output: *gpuMonobits*: number of errors
begin

> *tid*: work-item id
> *bid*: work-group id
> *Freq*[128]: local memory array
> $MINONES \leftarrow 9725$
> $MAXONES \leftarrow 10275$
> *Freq*[*tid*]$\leftarrow 0$
> // compute 125 * 5 integers
> **if** *tid* < 125 **then**
> > **for** $k \leftarrow 0$ **to** 5 **do**
> > > *val* $\leftarrow$ *random*[(*tid* * 5)+k + (*bid* * 625)]
> > > *Freq*[*tid*] += popc(*val*)
> >
> > **end**
>
> **end**
> // sync local memory
> barrier(CLK_LOCAL_MEM_FENCE)
> // reduction in local memory
> **if** *tid* < 64 **then**
> > *Freq*[*tid*] $+ = Freq$[*tid*+64]
> > barrier(CLK_LOCAL_MEM_FENCE)
>
> **end**
> ...
> Repeat for *tid* $< 32,16,8,4,2$
> ...
> // reduction in global memory
> **if** *tid* $= 0$ **then**
> > *Freq*[*tid*] $+ = Freq$[*tid*+1]
> > atomic_add(*gpuMonobits*,(*Freq*[0] $<= MINONES$|| *Freq*[0] $>=$
> > $MAXONES$))
>
> **end**

end

- 20000 bits (625 unsigned integers) are processed by one work-group. A sequence of N random numbers is split into N / 625 work-groups. This the first level of parallelism.

- Inside each work-group, a set of T threads computes 625 random numbers. This is the second level of parallelism.

- The maximum number of work-items per work-group is architecture dependent.

In order to save portability, the minimum number of integers processed by each work-item is set to 5. Later we will test the best value for each architecture.

- For each work-group, parallel reduction is processed in local memory.

- Finally, each work-group computes the reduction in global memory by invoking the atomic_add function available for all tested architectures.

The code of Algorithm 13.2 shows how to implement the previous requirements. We first create the Freq array in local memory that will be used by all the work-items to store the bit count results. All the work-items will set this array to zero. We then test if the tid (work-items id) is less than 125, in order to exactly compute 125 * 5 unsigned integer bit counts (or 625 integers or 20000 bits) per work-group. A synchronization barrier is required before the reduction step to insure all work-items fill the Freq array. Because the number of work-items is 128, we can now compute the reduction step by summing every Freq value, thanks to the addition associative property. At tid == 0, we finally use the atomic_add function to safely store the result of each block into the global memory variable gpuMonobits. If for instance the size of the random array is 16777216, to invoke the MonoBit kernel, (4096 * 4096) / 625 = 26843 work-groups of 128 work-items are needed, which is a reasonable amount of computation. This invocation looks like:

```
clEnqueueNDRangeKernel(queue,Monobits,1,NULL,
      globalThreads,localThreads,0,NULL,&ndrEvt2);
```

CPUs do not implement a set of threads running simultaneously in a warp. In order to perform portability, a synchronization barrier must be set after each reduction step to enable data coherency. Because of OpenCL's verbosity, we do not provide all the required code to invoke the MonoBit kernel.

Based on [14] recommendations, the popc() function is implemented as follows:

```
int popc(unsigned int a)
{
  a = a - ((a >> 1) & 0x55555555);
  a = (a & 0x33333333) + ((a >> 2) & 0x33333333);
  return
    ((a + (a >> 4) & 0xF0F0F0F) * 0x10101010) >> 24;
}
```

13.3.2   The Poker Test

The Poker test was first described by Knuth [1] and aims at dividing the 20000 bits stream into 5000 non-overlapping consecutive 4 bits segments. Every segment is counted in the [0,15] interval (24) and a chi-squared test on X with 15 degrees of freedom is performed. The acceptance region is $2.16 < X < 46.17$. The Poker Test is derived from the Serial Test with a fixed length of 16 values. This test includes floating operations and will help to benchmark float precision performances. The sequential implementation is described in Algorithm 13.3. Like the MonoBit Test, this test follows the same 625 integers (20000 bits) principle but adds a 4 bytes sum operation on the Poker array. For each block, a chi-squared is then computed on X whose result is tested between the MINPOKE and MAXPOKE values. This code is used to benchmark the serial version of the Poker Test.

Algorithm 13.3: Serial version of Poker test

Input: *random*: array of random numbers to test, *size*: size of *random*
Output: *errors*: number of errors
begin

$block \leftarrow size / 625$
$errors \leftarrow 0$
$monobit \leftarrow 0$
$MINPOKER \leftarrow 2.16$
$MAXPOKER \leftarrow 46.17$
for $i \leftarrow 0$ **to** 15 **do**
$\quad Poker[i] = 0$
end
$X \leftarrow 0.0$
for $i \leftarrow 0$ **to** $block-1$ **do**
$\quad$ **for** $j \leftarrow 0$ **to** 4 **do**
$\quad\quad$ **for** $k \leftarrow 0$ **to** 3 **do**
$\quad\quad\quad val \leftarrow random[(625 * i) + j]$
$\quad\quad\quad ++Poker[val \& 0xF]$
$\quad\quad\quad ++Poker[(val \gg 4) \& 0xF]$
$\quad\quad\quad val \gg= 8$
$\quad\quad$ **end**
$\quad$ **end**
end
for $i \leftarrow 0$ **to** 15 **do**
$\quad X+ = Poker[i] * Poker[i]$
end
$X = (16.0 * X \div 5000.0) - 5000.0$
$errors+ = (X <= MINPOKER \parallel X >= MAXPOKER)$
return *errors*

end

13.3.2.1 OpenCL Implementation

Algorithm 13.4 shows the implementation of the Poker test which presents many similarities with the MonoBit OpenCL code. The main differences between MonoBit and

Algorithm 13.4: OpenCL implementation of Poker test

Input: *random*: array of random numbers to test
Output: *gpuPoker*: number of errors
begin
    tid: work-item id
    bid: work-group id
    Poker[128][16]: local memory array
    $MINPOKER \leftarrow 2.16$
    $MAXPOKER \leftarrow 46.17$
    for $i \leftarrow 0$ **to** 15 **do**
        | $Poker[tid][i] \leftarrow 0$
    end
    `// compute 125 * 5 integers`
    if $tid < 125$ **then**
        for $k \leftarrow 0$ **to** 4 **do**
            $val \leftarrow random[(tid * 5) + k + (bid * 625)]$
            for $k \leftarrow 0$ **to** 3 **do**
                $+ + Poker[tid][val \mathbin{\&} 0xF]$
                $+ + Poker[tid][(val \gg 4) \mathbin{\&} 0xF]$
                $val \gg= 8$
            end
        end
    end
    `// sync local memory`
    barrier(CLK_LOCAL_MEM_FENCE)
    `// reduction in local memory`
    if $tid < 64$ **then**
        for $i \leftarrow 0$ **to** 15 **do**
        | $Poker[tid][i] \mathrel{+}= Poker[tid + 64][i]$
        end
        barrier(CLK_LOCAL_MEM_FENCE)
    end
    ...
    Repeat for $tid < 32,16,8,4,2$
    ...
    `// reduction in global memory`
    if $tid = 0$ **then**
        $X \leftarrow 0$
        for $i \leftarrow 0$ **to** 15 **do**
            $Poker[tid][i] \mathrel{+}= Poker[tid + 1][i]$
            $X \mathrel{+}= Poker[0][i] * Poker[0][i]$
        end
        $X = (16.0 * X \div 5000.0) - 5000.0$
        atomic_add($gpuPoker$,($X <= MINPOKER \| X >= MAXPOKER$))
    end
end

Poker tests are the memory operations in the Poker array and the floating point operations at the end of the Poker kernel. The Poker test is memory bounded and requires many more local memory accesses than the MonoBit test. This OpenCL implementation will demonstrate how each device manages bank conflicts or non coalescent accesses. The chi-squared test requires floating point operations and will help to test this computing capability of each device.

13.4 Results

For the purpose of this work, we decided to benchmark the MonoBit and Poker test on different hardware architectures. The portability of the MonoBit and Poker tests enables us to proceed with five types of benchmarking:

- Serial vs parallel code

- Scalability

- Work-group size

- IGP vs CPU

- OpenCL vs CUDA

13.4.1 Hardware Configuration

On the same platform, we installed two different desktop GPUs: an AMD Radeon 7970 and a Nvidia GTX 580. We did not use the latest Nvidia Kepler GXT 680 which is less powerful for computing than the previous Fermi generation. For the CPU, we used an Ivy Bridge 3770K with and an HD 4000 IGP (integrated graphics processor). The latest Intel OpenCL SDK (1.5) allows one to run OpenCL kernels on both hardware. Table 13.1 describes this hardware.

	Clock (MHz)	Memory Type	Memory Clock (MHz)	Number of Cores
GeForce GTX 580	772	GDDR5	1002	512
AMD 7970	925	GDDR5	1375	2048
i7-3770K	4200	DDR3	800	8
HD 4000	1250	DDR3	800	16
Operating System	Windows 7 64 bits			
OpenCL drivers	Nvidia: 301.32, AMD: 8.980, Intel: 8.15.10			
Compiler	Visual Studio 2008 with Full Optimisation options			

Table 13.1: Hardware and software configurations

13.4.2   Serial versus Parallel Code

The main goal to achieve when moving serial code to parallelism is speedup. Results
are shown in Figure 13.1. The Radeon HD 7970 provides an impressive 37 speedup,
almost double that of the GTX 580 (19). We will check later if CUDA can change
this situation. The 3770K processor significantly improves the random testing time by
almost 5. This hardware is the only one able to accelerate the Poker test better than
the MonoBit test. The following lines of code may explain this:

```
++Poker[tid][(unsigned char)val & 0xF];
++Poker[tid][((unsigned char)val >> 4) & 0xF];
```

By randomly indexing the Poker array value, many shared memory bank conflicts
are generated on GPU which is not the case for the CPU cache model. This could be
improved by following the [15] recommendations.

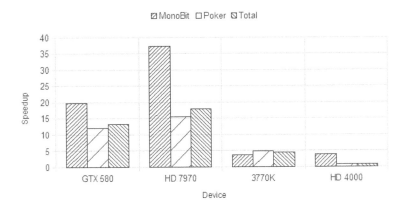

Figure 13.1: Device speedups by device

13.4.3   Scalability

Multi-core architectures expose the ability to better handle a large set of data then
mono-core. For this work, we applied both kernels on different sizes of random number samples (Table 13.2). For unknown reasons, it was not possible to allocate more
than 268 mega bytes (8192) for the HD 4000 device.

13.4.3.1   Monobit Scalability

Figure 13.2 shows the scalability results for different sample sizes. The Y axis (in
logarithmic ruler) shows run time in seconds. We can distinguish three groups of
scalability: the Radeon HD 7970 and the GTX 580 with a very good scaling capability;

Dimension	Sample Size
2048	17 Mega bytes
4096	67 Mega bytes
6144	151 Mega bytes
8192	268 Mega bytes
10240	419 Mega bytes

Table 13.2: Size of tested random numbers by dimension

the 3770K and HD 4000 expose the same scalability. The serial C code, as expected, is the last one.

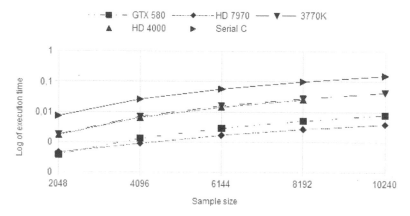

Figure 13.2: Scalability of MonoBit test

13.4.3.2 Poker Scalability

In Figure 13.3, we can see that Radeon HD 7970 and GTX 580 scale closely. The HD 4000, for this test, is far behind the first group and scales as badly as the serial version. The OpenCL parallelism model enables, even for very different hardware, a large capacity for scalability. Each OpenCL compiler attached to a dedicated device achieves great work in optimizing one single kernel source for a specific platform. The two GPUs have good potential in processing a larger set of data (high end graphic cards will soon have more than 4 giga bytes of memory). The 3770K CPU has a surprisingly good scalability capacity. Intel seems to do an efficient work in optimizing the Ivy Bridge architecture and its OpenCL compiler. The difference between HD 4000 and 3770K for the Poker test can be explained by the floating capabilities of the CPU that an IGP, not designed for this purpose, may not have.

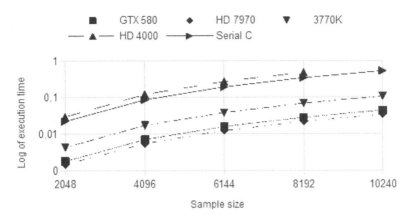

Figure 13.3: Scalability of Poker test

13.4.4   Choosing the Right Work-Group Size

The only way to optimize kernels for a specific hardware without breaking the portability is to determine the most accurate work-group size for each device. The reduction part of each kernel allows only power to two sets of work-items. The numbers that fit this mandatory requirement are 1, 8, 32 and 128 to compute exactly 625 integers or 20000 bits by work-group (Table 13.3).

Number of work-item by work-group	Number of integer by thread	Number of active work-items by work-group
1	625	1
8	125	5
32	25	25
128	5	125

Table 13.3: Number of work-items by work-group

Both kernels were written to fit algorithmically each work-group size in order to remove unnecessary tests and synchronization barriers. The four new kernels tested were benchmarked for each random number sample.

13.4.4.1   GPU Work-Group Size

For the three GPUs, the best work-group size is 128 work-items per work-group. Figure 13.4 shows the resulting execution times by size for the Radeon HD 7970. When the number of integers processed by one work-item increases (from 5 to 625), the execution time grows in the same way. According to Brent's Theorem [16], there is a balance between the number of cores of a parallel random access machine (PRAM)

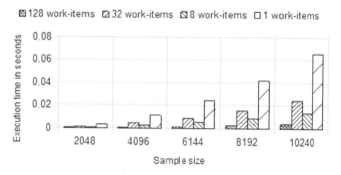

Figure 13.4: Radeon HD 7970 performances by work-group size (MonoBit)

and the sequential work to be done per core. For all types of GPU, it seems that 128 work-items is the right amount of workload to assign to each work-group.

13.4.4.2 CPU Work-Group Size

The 3770K has a radically different architecture and is the only CPU studied in this work. The best results are obtained by assigning only one work-item per work-group. Figure 13.5 shows the execution times for this device.

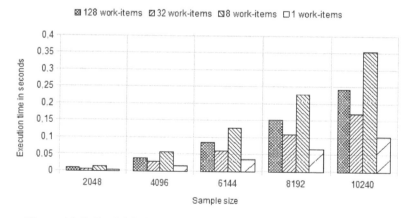

Figure 13.5: Intel 3770K performances by work-group size (Poker)

This is not surprising. According to [17]: "...the OpenCL CPU runtime executes a work-group within a single operating system thread ...there is no parallelism between multiple work-items within a work-group." Only height system threads were created when checking the kernel execution on Windows 7, two per core able to run two simultaneous threads. Increasing the number of work-items per work-group adds complexity (divergence, cache misses, synchronization) to the scheduling process on the CPU. If programers want to get the best performances without breaking portability across different devices, the size of work-group is a critical parameter.

13.4.5 IGP vs CPU

The actual hardware trend is to include within each CPU a GPU (IGP) to provide basic display and accelerated functions like video decompression. The latest version of the Intel OpenCL SDK enables a kernel execution on both processors (CPU and IGP). Figure 13.6 shows the speedup results of the HD 4000 IGP and the 3770K CPU based on the serial C version. For the MonoBit test, the IGP performs as well as the 4 cores / 8 threads CPU. The poor performances of the IGP for the Poker test are due to the lack of high speed floating point operations. However, IGPs can be used as a second resource if the type of calculation is adapted and tuned for this type of GPU.

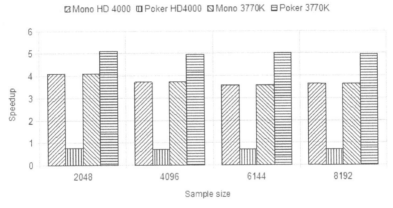

Figure 13.6: Performances of MonoBit and Poker tests for HD 4000 and 3770K devices

13.4.6 CUDA vs OpenCL

To bench OpenCL vs CUDA performances, we used the possibilities offered by Nvidia to run both types of kernel on the GeForce GTX 580. As previously tuned, only CUDA MonoBit and Poker kernels with a block of 128 threads were run. Table 13.4 shows the speedups OpenCL vs CUDA. For the MonoBit test, CUDA performs 50% better than OpenCL. For the Poker test, 12% are the average results.

While with the previous OpenCL drivers vs run-time CUDA was faster up to 2x, a lot of work has been achieved by Intel, AMD and Nvidia in optimizing the integrated OpenCL compilers and performances are now almost on a par. We can expect this trend to be supported in the coming years that will position OpenCL as a competitive choice for HPC with portability as a great advantage. Figure 13.7 shows the comparison between the Radeon HD 7970 results and the CUDA/OpenCL version run on

OpenCL vs CUDA	Speed up MonoBit	Speed up Poker
2048	1.53	0.84
4096	1.47	1.07
6144	1.46	1.12
8192	1.46	1.14
10240	1.46	1.15

Table 13.4: CUDA speedup versus OpenCL on GeForce GTX 580

the GeForce GTX 580. The Radeon still performs better than the CUDA GeForce but differences are minimal.

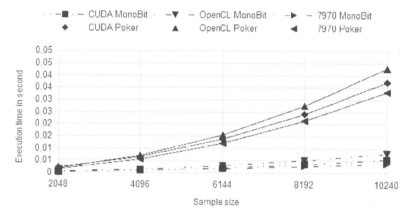

Figure 13.7: Performances of CUDA / OpenCL on GeForce GTX 580 and Radeon HD 7970 (Poker and Monobit)

13.5   Conclusion and Future Work

Testing random numbers can achieve large benefits in terms of performance by using OpenCL on any type of multi-core architecture. The OpenCL portability offers new perspectives in providing programers with multiple hardware targets. For instance, some tests are not embarrassingly parallel. The Longest test counts the number of consecutive 1s and 0s in a sample of 20000 bits. On the GPU, this test needs inter thread and block communications which are not easy to implement. Our last OpenCL benchmarks show that this test is faster to run on CPU than on GPU. The OpenCL standard provides the flexibility to choose the best platform and eases the complex optimization process.

References

[1] D.E. Knuth, "Seminumerical algorithms", The Art of Computer Programming, 2, Addison-Wesley, Third Edition, 1997.

[2] G. Marsaglia, "Random numbers fall mainly in the planes", Proc. Natl. Acad. Sci., 61(1), 25-28, 1968.

[3] G. Marsaglia, "The Marsaglia Random Number", CDROM, 1995. http://www.stat.fsu.edu/pub/diehard/

[4] National Institute of Standards and Technology (NIST), "Random Number Generation", 2010. http://csrc.nist.gov/groups/ST/toolkit/rng/index.html

[5] P. L'Ecuyer, R. Simard, "TestU01: A C Library for Empirical Testing of Random Number Generators", 2007. http://www.iro.umontreal.ca/~simardr/testu01/tu01.html

[6] R. Santoro, O. Sentieys, S. Roy, "On-the fly evaluation of FPGA-based True Random Number Generator", IEEE Computer Society Annual Symposium, 2009.

[7] A. Suciu, L. Zegreanu, C.T. Zima, "Statistical Testing of Random Number Sequences Using Graphics Processing Units", Fourth Balkan Conference in Informatic, 2009.

[8] A. Suciu, L. Zegreanu, C.T. Zima, "Statistical testing of random number sequences using CUDA", Proceedings of the 2010 IEEE 6th International Conference on Intelligent Computer Communication and Processing, 2010.

[9] K. Komatsu, K. Sato, Y. Arai, K. Koyama, H. Takizawa, H. Kobayashi, "Evaluating Performance and Portability of OpenCL Programs", Fifth International Workshop on Automatic Performance Tuning, 2010.

[10] Nvidia Developer Zone, "OpenCL developer resources", 2012. http://developer.nvidia.com/opencl

[11] AMD Developer Central, "Heterogeneous Computing", 2012. http://developer.amd.com/zones/OpenCLZone/Pages/default.aspx

[12] Intel Software, "Visual Programming Source", 2012. http://software.intel.com/en-us/articles/vcsource-tools-opencl-sdk/

[13] National Institute of Standards and Technology (NIST), "Security Requirements for Cryptographic Modules", 2001. http://csrc.nist.gov/publications/fips/fips140-2/fips1402.pdf

[14] H.G. Dietz, "The Aggregate Magic Algorithms", University of Kentucky, 2012. http://aggregate.org/MAGIC/

[15] V.Podlozhnyuk, "Histogram calculation in CUDA", Nvidia, 2007. http://www.naic.edu/~phil/hardware/nvidia/doc/src/histogram/doc/histogram.pdf

[16] Everything 2, "Brent's theorem", 2003. http://everything2.com/title/Brent\%2527s+theorem

[17] B.R. Gaster, L. Howes, D.R. Kaeli, P. Mistry, D. Schaa, "Heterogeneous Computing with OpenCL", Morgan Kaufman, 2012.

Index

SAXE-COBURG
PUBLICATIONS
mmxiv